MW00783471

Architectural Element 2

STAIRS

지은이	담디 편집부 엮음
펴낸이	서경원
편집	나진연
디자인	이철주
펴낸곳	도서출판 담디
등록일	2002년 9월 16일
등록번호	제 9-00102호
주소	서울시 강북구 삼각산로 79, 2층
전화	02-900-0652
팩스	02-900-0657
이메일	damdi_book@naver.com
홈페이지	www.damdi.co.kr

Compiler	DAMDI Publishing House
Publisher	Kyongwon Suh
Editor	Jinyoun Na
Art Director	Cheolju Lee
Publishing	DAMDI Publishing House
Office Address	2F, 79, Samgaksan-ro, Gangbuk-gu, Seoul, 01036, Korea
Tel	+82-2-900-0652
Fax	+82-2-900-0657
E-mail	damdi_book@naver.com
Homepage	www.damdi.co.kr

정가 88,000원
Printed in Korea
ISBN 978-89-6801-075-0 (94540)
978-89-6801-073-6 (set)

이 도서의 국립중앙도서관 출판예정도서목록(CIP)은 서지정보유통지원시스템 홈페이지(http://seoji.nl.go.kr)와 국가자료공동목록시스템(http://www.nl.go.kr/kolisnet)에서 이용하실 수 있습니다.(CIP제어번호: CIP2018003391)

Architectural Element 2
STAIRS

담디 DAMDI

Contents

Interview with Architects

What is the Stairs?

Q1

What is
the favourite stairs
you've designed and why?

b4architects

"It was an exciting experience for us to insert a modern customized element in a great historical context also for the very accurate realization made by expert artisans that followed with great attention our drawings.

위대한 역사적 문맥안에 현대적인 맞춤 요소를 삽입하는 것과, 숙련된 장인들이 심혈을 기울여 **우리의 드로잉을 매우 정교하게 실현시키는 것** 또한 흥미로운 경험이었다."

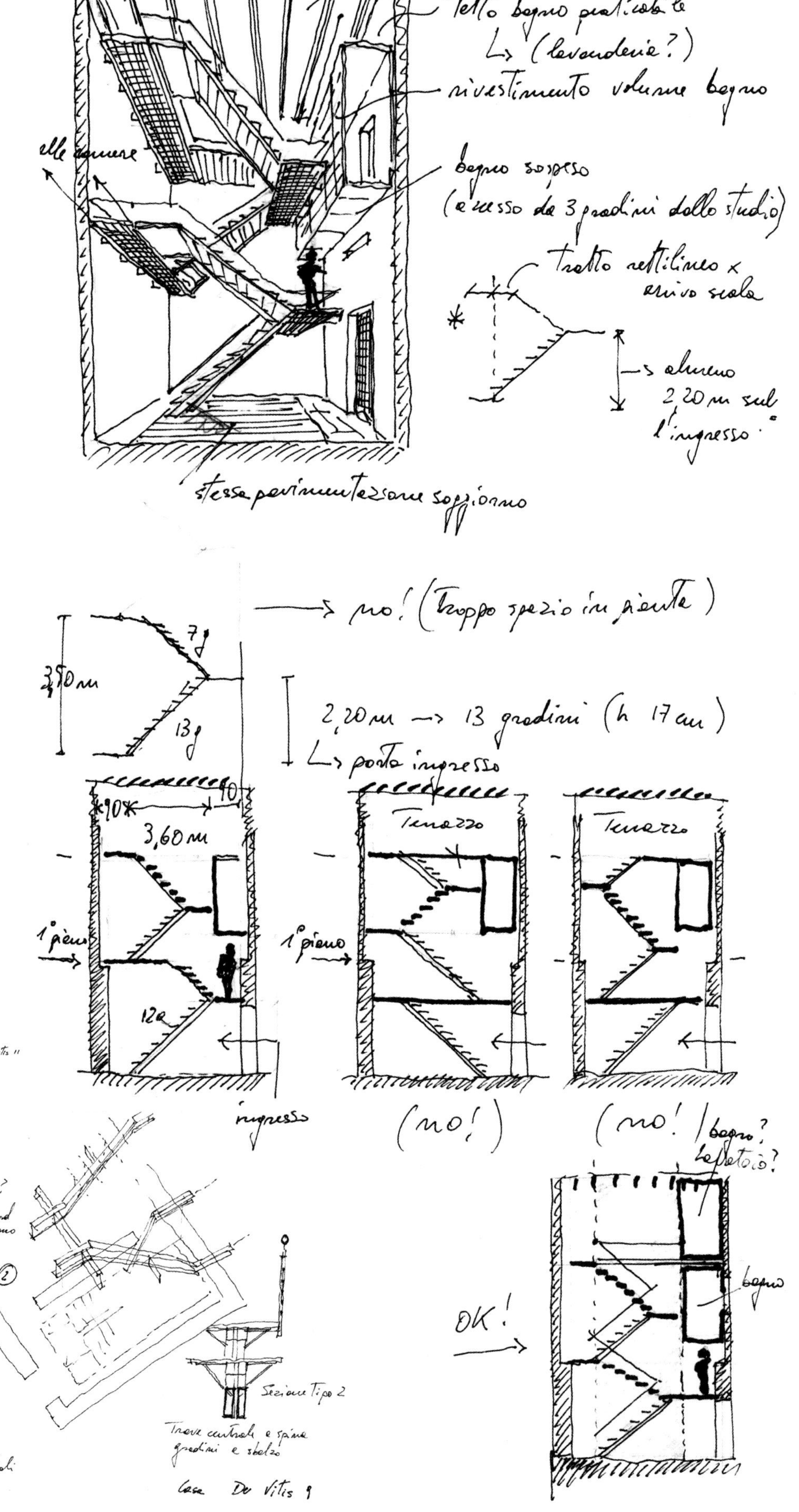

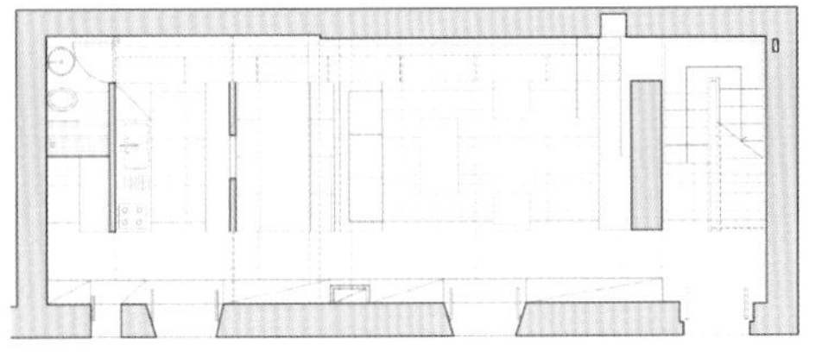

Ground Floor

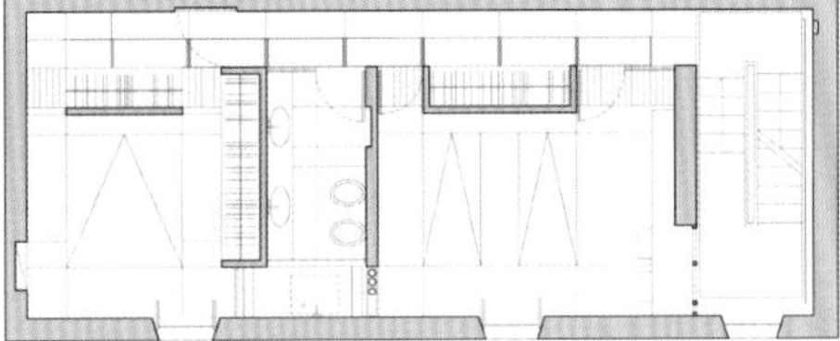

First Floor

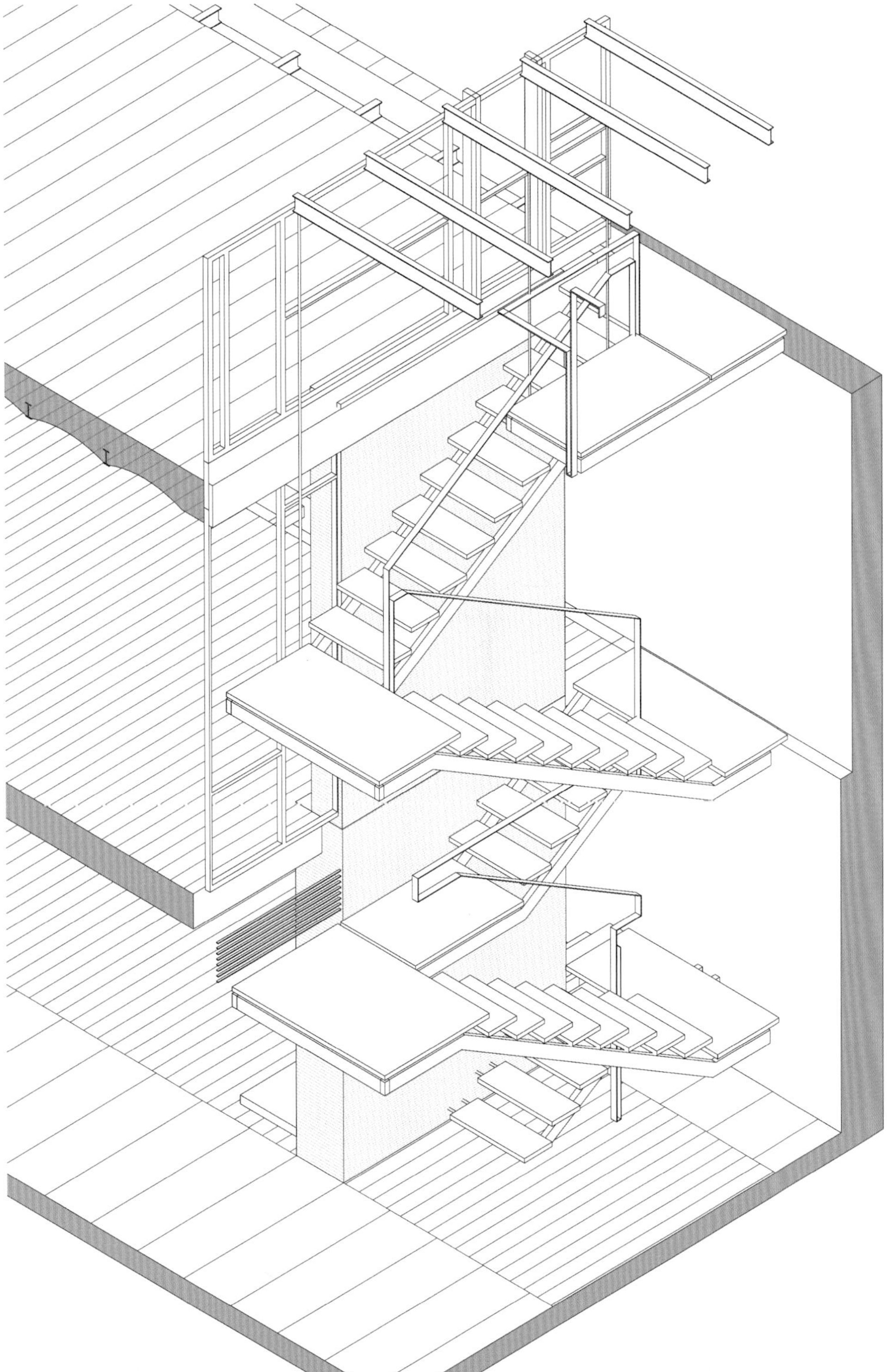

Long Answer

Some years ago we worked on the renewal of an apartment located in the heart of the historical centre of Rome, close to the Pantheon and P.za Navona organized on two levels and a roof terrace with a spectacular view on the main monuments and domes of Rome all around. The client gave us free rein for the design, so we proposed a light steel stairs ensuring the connection between the various levels and one of the entrance that was on an intermediate height, memory of the preexistent spatial situation. The stairs was equipped also with a special lighting system.
It was an exciting experience for us to insert a modern customized element in a great historical context also for the very accurate realization made by expert artisans that followed with great attention our drawings.

BOARD

“ which we called the “public section”.

우리는 그 계단을 “**대중을 위한 단면**”이라고 부른다. ”

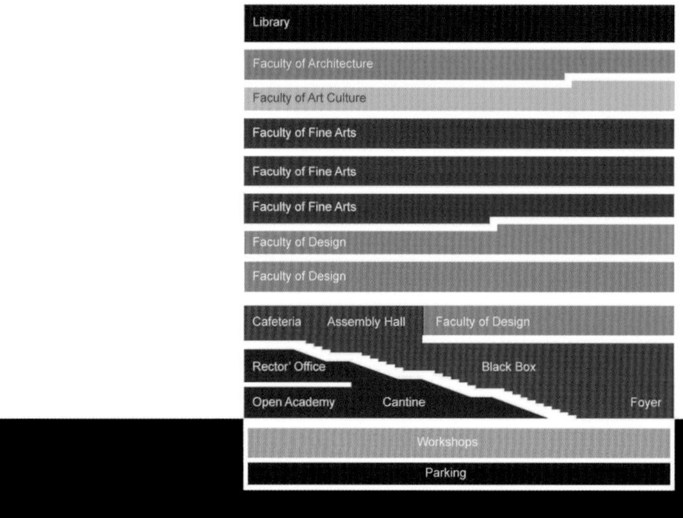

Long Answer

One of my favourite stairs we designed was for the New Building for the Estonian Academy of Arts in the city of Tallinn. There, we clustered the entire public programme of the building that contained all the auditoriums and galleries of the academy and created a huge stair out of it, which we called the “public section”. It cuts through the entire building but, thanks to acoustic curtains that separate the different units, remains functional even during lectures, performances, or events. Without any event going on, the stair functions as an extension of the foyer of the academy located on the ground floor.

New Building for the Estonian Academy of Arts

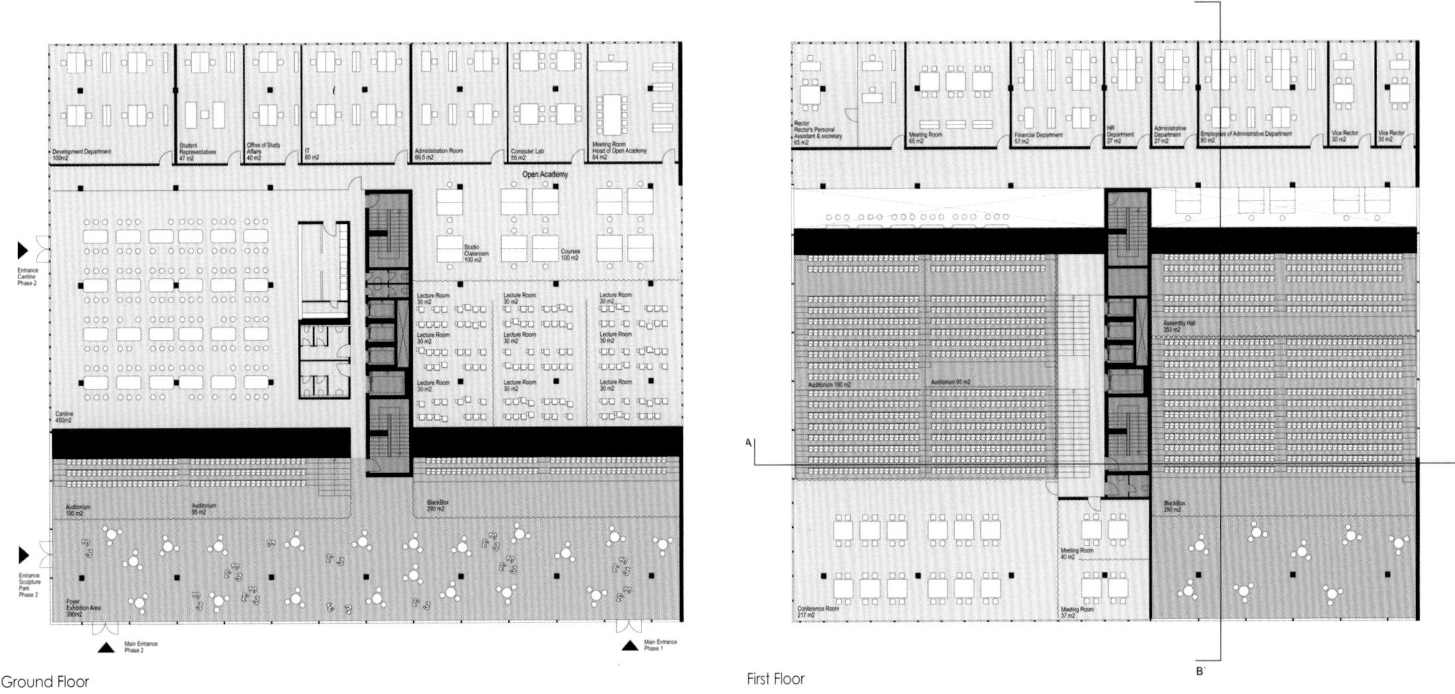

Ground Floor

First Floor

ELA - Edu Lopez Architects

" The stairs, as we all know, is a vertical connecting element that relates different spaces in height.

우리 모두가 알고 있듯 계단은 서로 다른 높이의 **공간들을 수직으로 연결하는 요소**이다. "

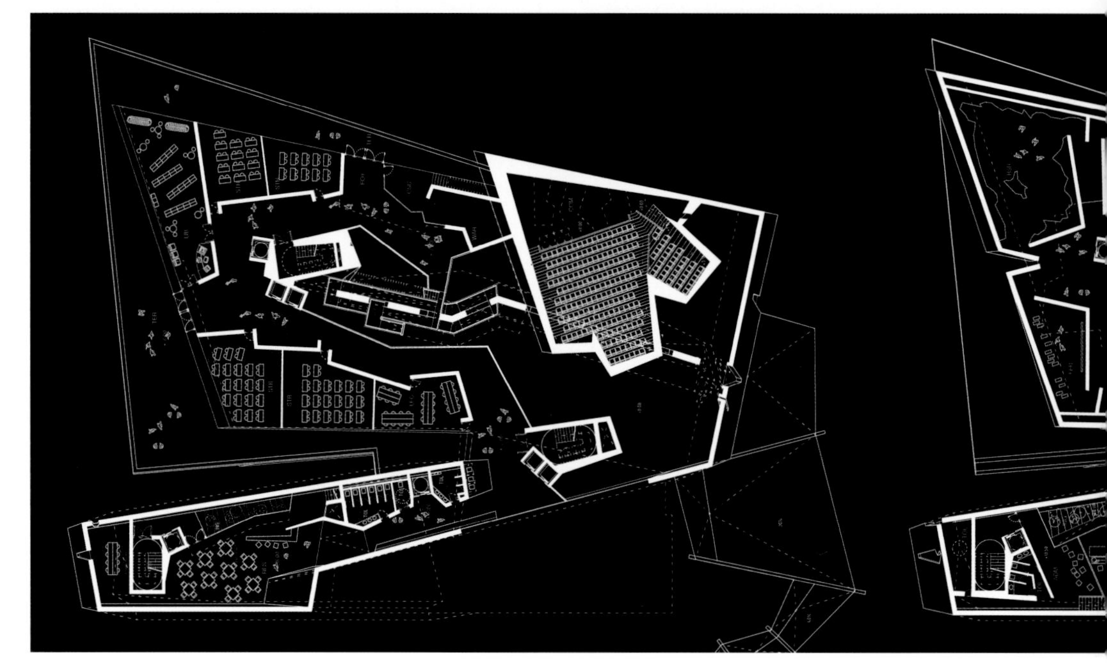

Long Answer

The stairs, as we all know, is a vertical connecting element that relates different spaces in height. Particularly I have always been in favor of creating a kinder element and with more possibilities whenever you can as is the ramp. The ramp as a vertical connection makes it possible to see better spatial relationships in the building and leads to a more competitive aspect of space. In our case we are going to talk about a ramp that was designed for the project of the risk prevention center in Istanbul. This ramp is placed in the center of the building and is visible from all points of the building. Its main characteristic is that it is structurally anchored to a large wall that runs through the entire height of the building, which is broken and opened to create visuals from different points on the ramp. This creates a close relationship between the inner space of the center and the user. In the following sketches you can see how it is made the ramp along with the wall. As you can see it is not possible to speak of two individual elements, but unitary ones, as the ramps' landings are linked together with the openings of the wall. The ramp is a simple slab of concrete anchored to the wall with a 3 + 3 glass railing with transparent butyral, which is lined with alabaster to be able to illuminate it in certain parts.

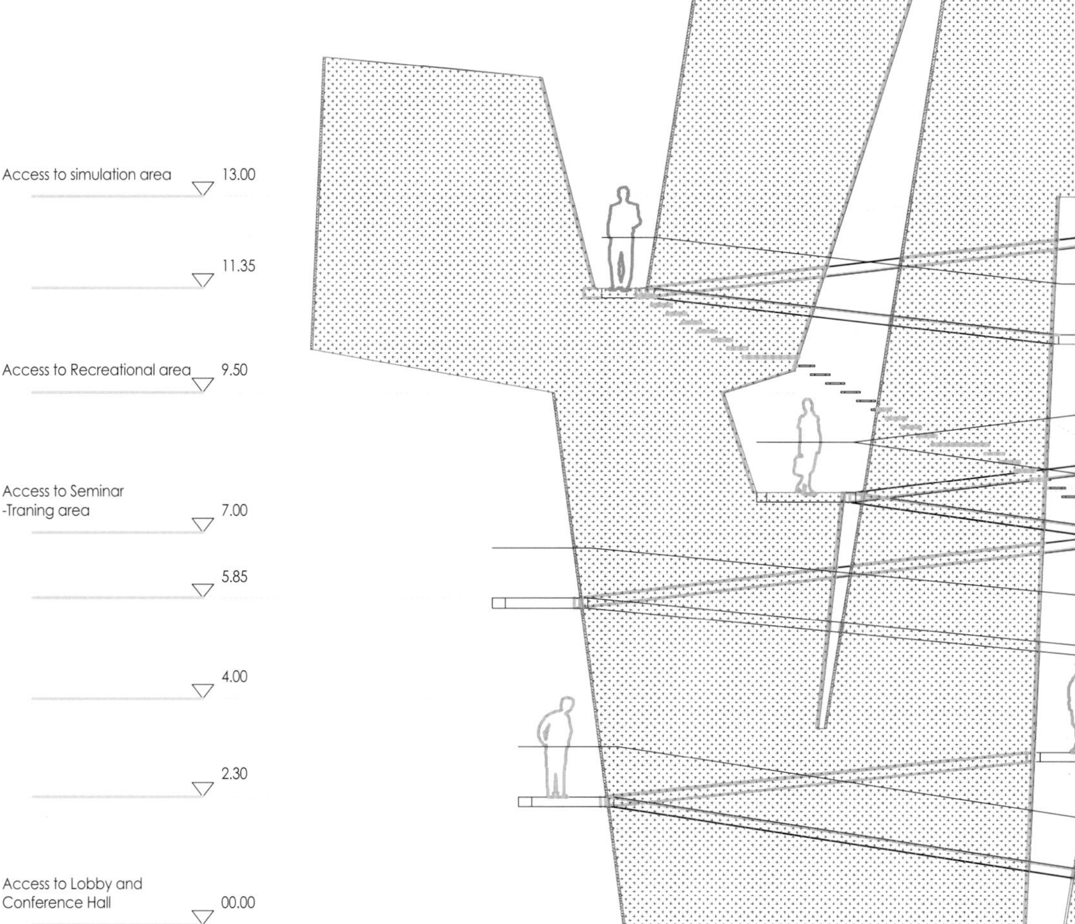

Floor plan of the building

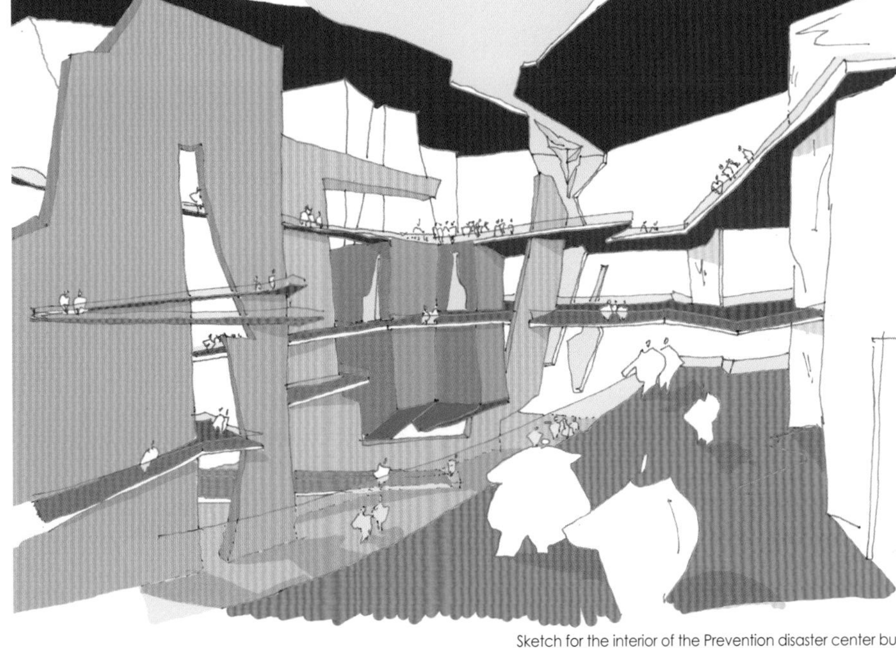

Sketch for the interior of the Prevention disaster center building

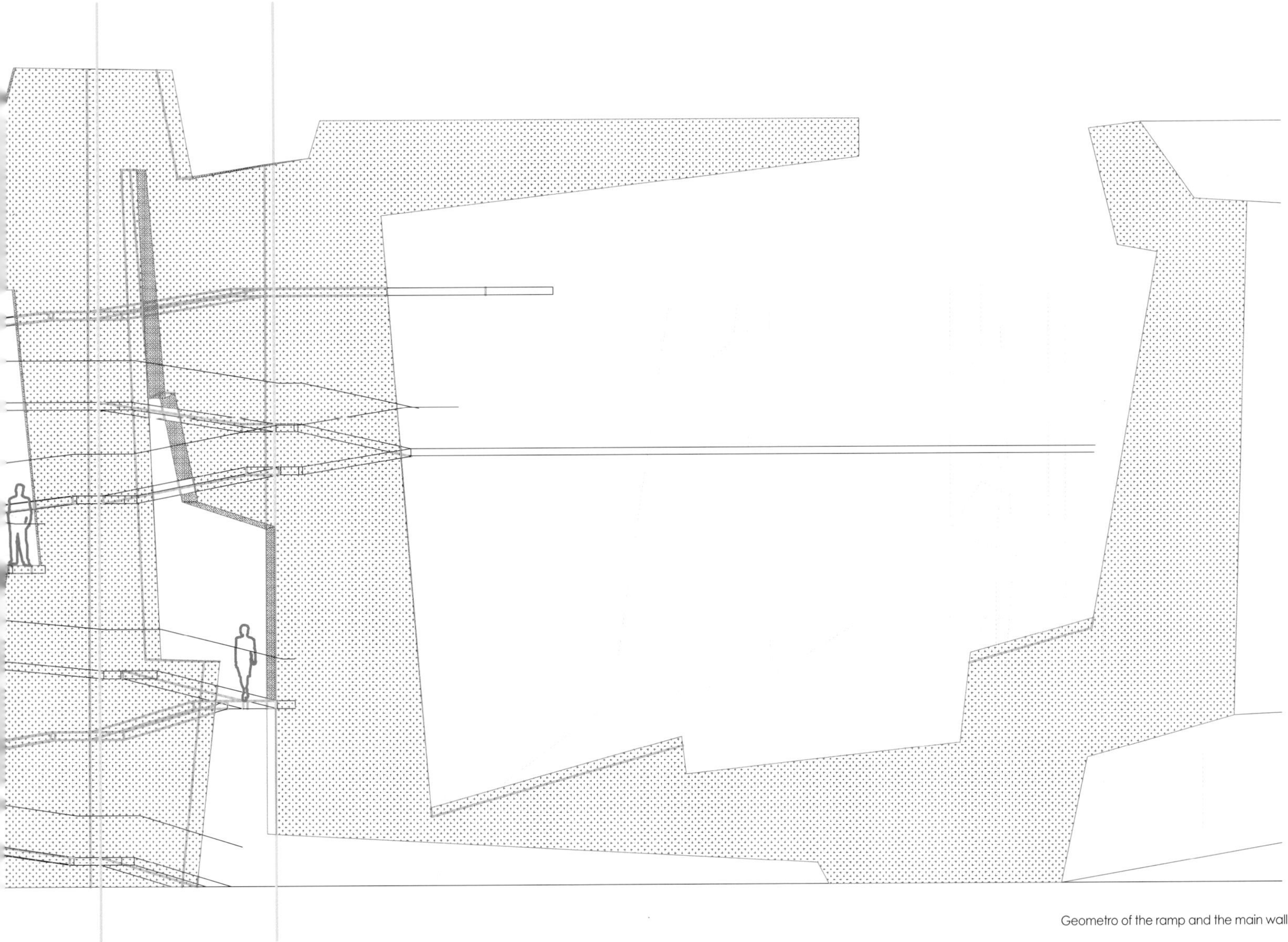

Geometro of the ramp and the main wall

The risk prevention center

Ezequiel Farca + Cristina Grappin

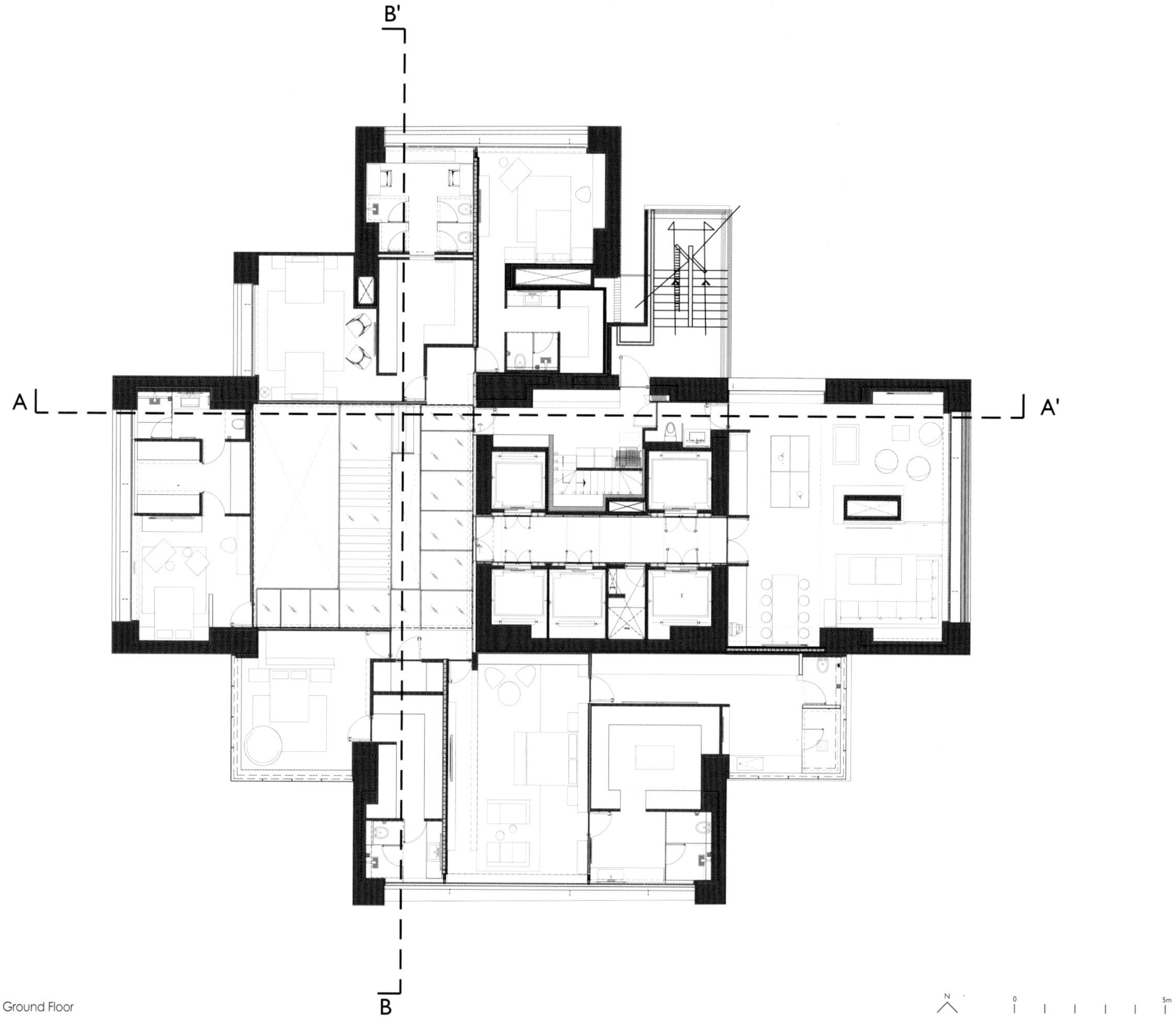

B'

A

A'

B

Ground Floor

N

0 5m

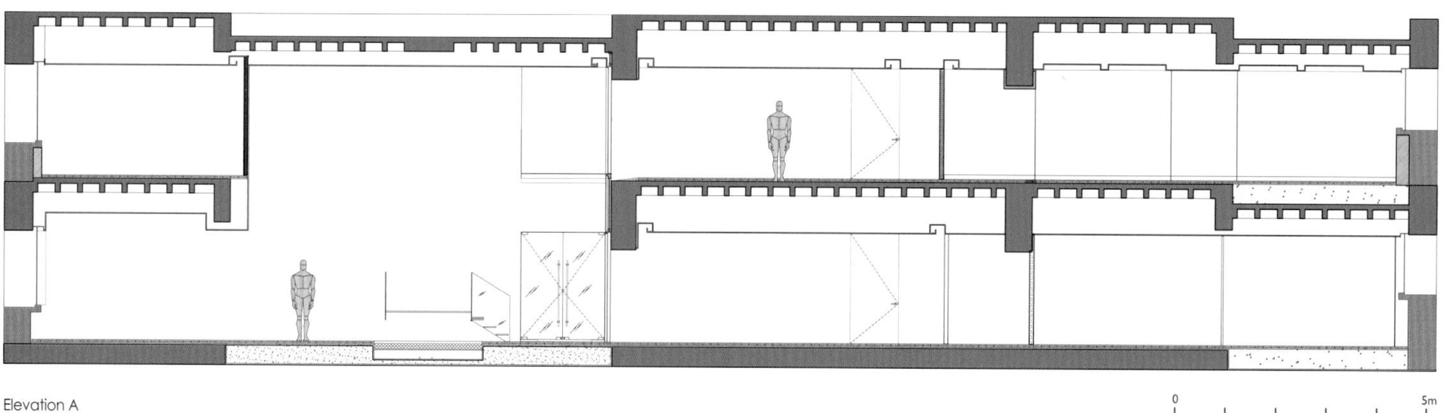

Elevation A

0 5m

Long Answer

A few years ago, we designed an apartment in Mexico City for an art collector. The client's collection was colorful, specifically pop art, so we focused on designing a space that could integrate and to compliment with the art pieces. For the design of the stairs we wanted them to function as an observation point, apply glass (client request) with green shades and translucent handrails allowing the view to be clean. In front of the last step we placed an important part of the collection in the whole wall, this being the first view of the division of the private program.

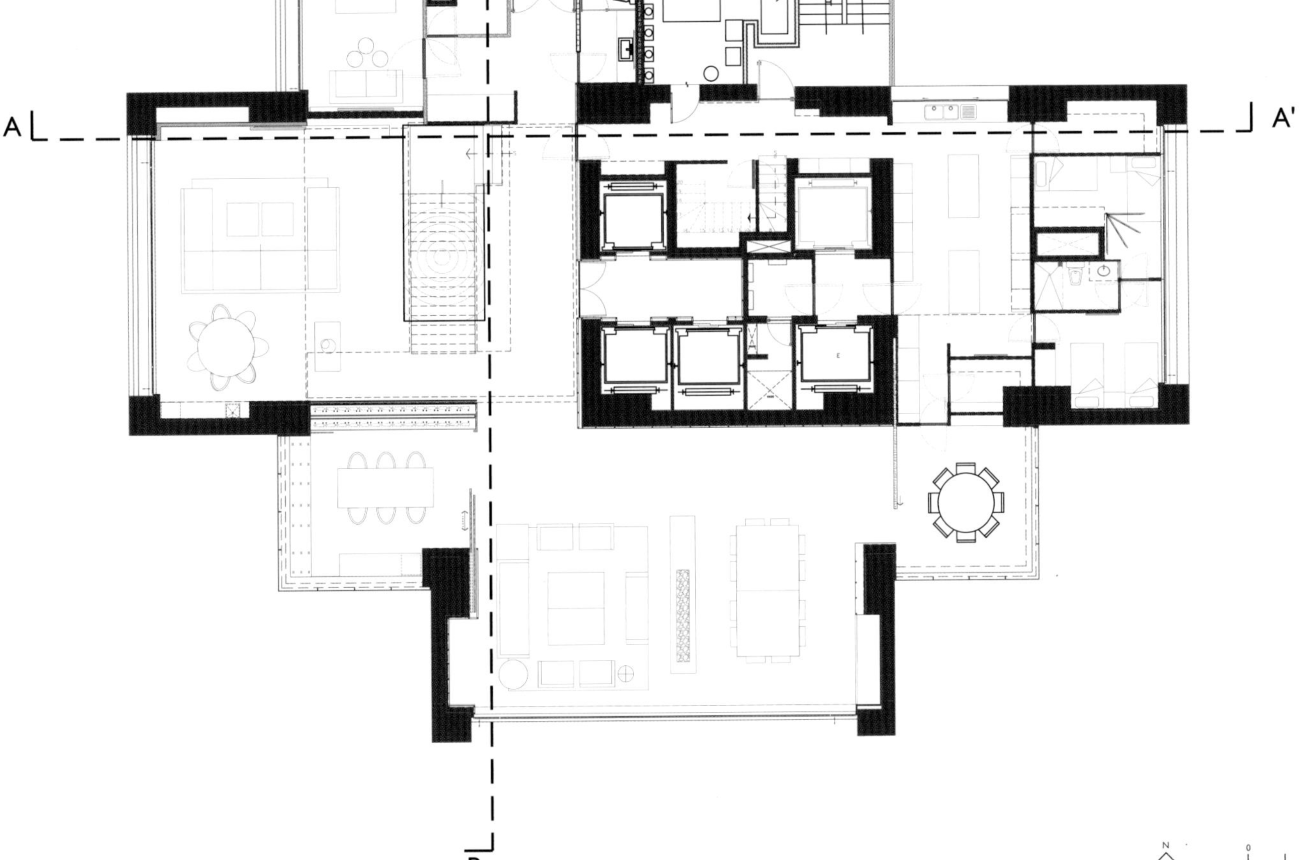

First Floor

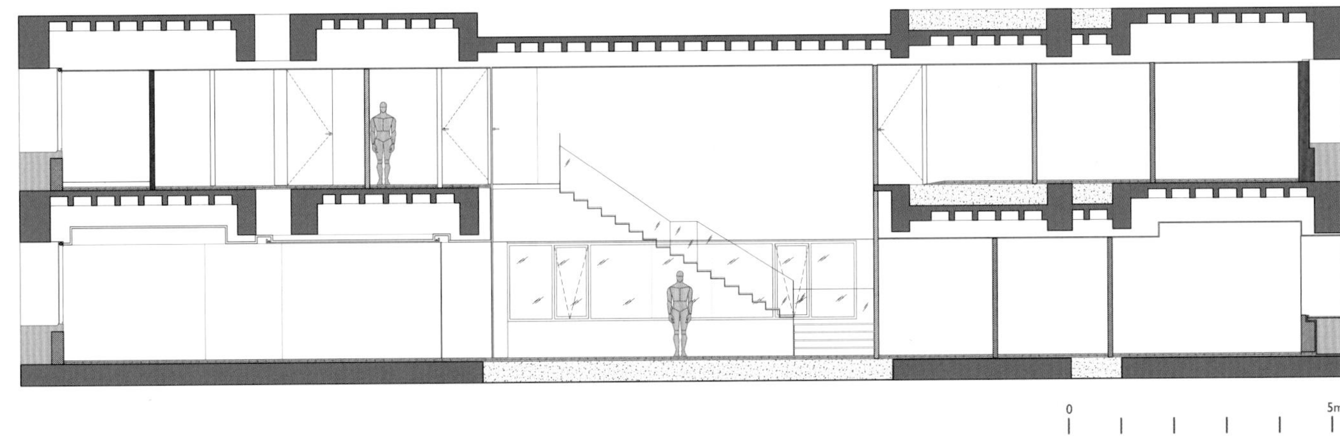

Elevation B

"We focused on designing a space that could integrate and to compliment with the art pieces.

우리는 예술 작품들과 융합되고 시너지효과를 내는 공간을 설계하는데 초점을 맞췄다. "

© Jaime Navarro

Katsuhiro Miyamoto & Associates

" The staircase in the residential project, KURAKUEN is one of my favourite due to its organic form and finish.

쿠라쿠엔(KURAKUEN) 주택 프로젝트 계단의 유기적 형태와 마감효과를 가장 좋아한다. "

Long Answer

The staircase in the residential project, KURAKUEN is one of my favourite due to its organic form and finish. It is finished in terrazzo to create a uniform seamless finish with the wall and floor.

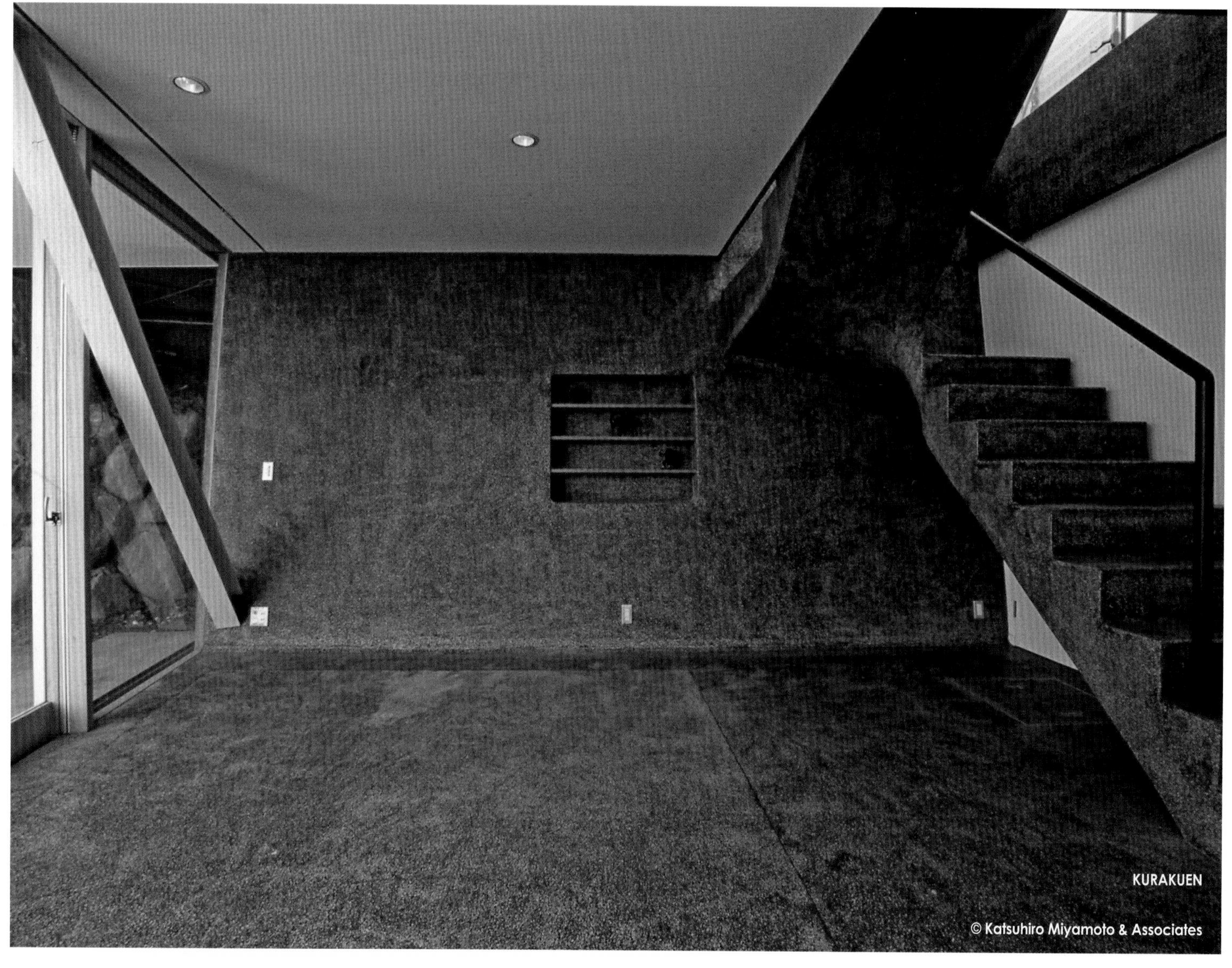

KURAKUEN

© Katsuhiro Miyamoto & Associates

LGSMA

Long Answer

Among the stairs that I designed, the one I consider the most succesful is the main staircase connecting the two floors in the Hall of Ospedale del mare in Naples, Italy.

The Hall is a two-storey cilinder, enclosed with panels in glass and fibre-reinforced concrete in different colours, changing from blue to green. The panels have different inclinations and give movement to the facade, hence felt fragmented in the horizontal direction.

The slabs present big circular holes, allowing the interiors to be enlighted from the skylights on the roof.

The glass covers the walls and encloses an inner garden, reflecting the light in different ways and creating wide bright areas.

The circular cuts have the power to create a tribute to Piranesi, visually linking the two floors. They also reselble the cuts that Gordon Matta Clark made at Marais in Paris, a building that was demolished to raise the Beaubourg. The feeling is to be in a very bright and open space where horizontal and vertical floors become a single plane that transforms along the way. In order to enphasize such deformation of space, the circular cuts in the slabs are slightly disaligned on the vertical axis, creating an imperceptible blur that has the strenght to destabilize the perception of the place. The stairs create a direct connection between the floors following the light that passes throught them. It is a simple staircase, a straight line that defines visive continuity between the two floors.

© Ian+

2|H

“The stairs create a direct connection between the floors following the light that passes throught them. It is a simple staircase, a straight line that defines visive continuity between the two floors.

계단은 직선 모양의 단순한 계단으로 원형 창들 사이로 들어오는 빛을 따라서 적극적으로 층 사이를 연결하고 그 연결성이 뚜렷이 보인다.”

Ospedale de mare

Miha Volgemut architect

“They create a rather dramatic effect together with the concrete wall in the background, and the impression is like a crane from the construction site has fallen into the house.

이 계단은 콘크리트 벽을 배경으로 꽤 역동적인 효과를 내며, 마치 학 한 마리가 건설현장에서 날아와 집안으로 들어온 것 같은 느낌이다.”

Long Answer

It is the stairs for a private house, that I designed as a piece of installation going through the space. They create a rather dramatic effect together with the concrete wall in the background, and the impression is like a crane from the construction site has fallen into the house. They create interesting harmony between rawness and elegance.

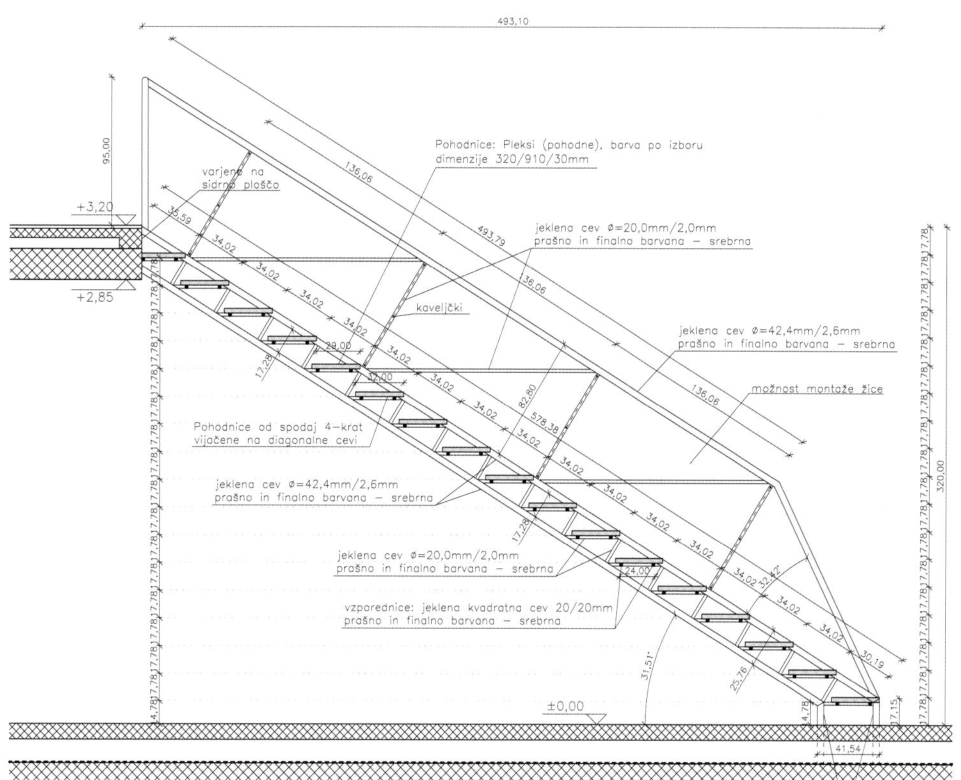

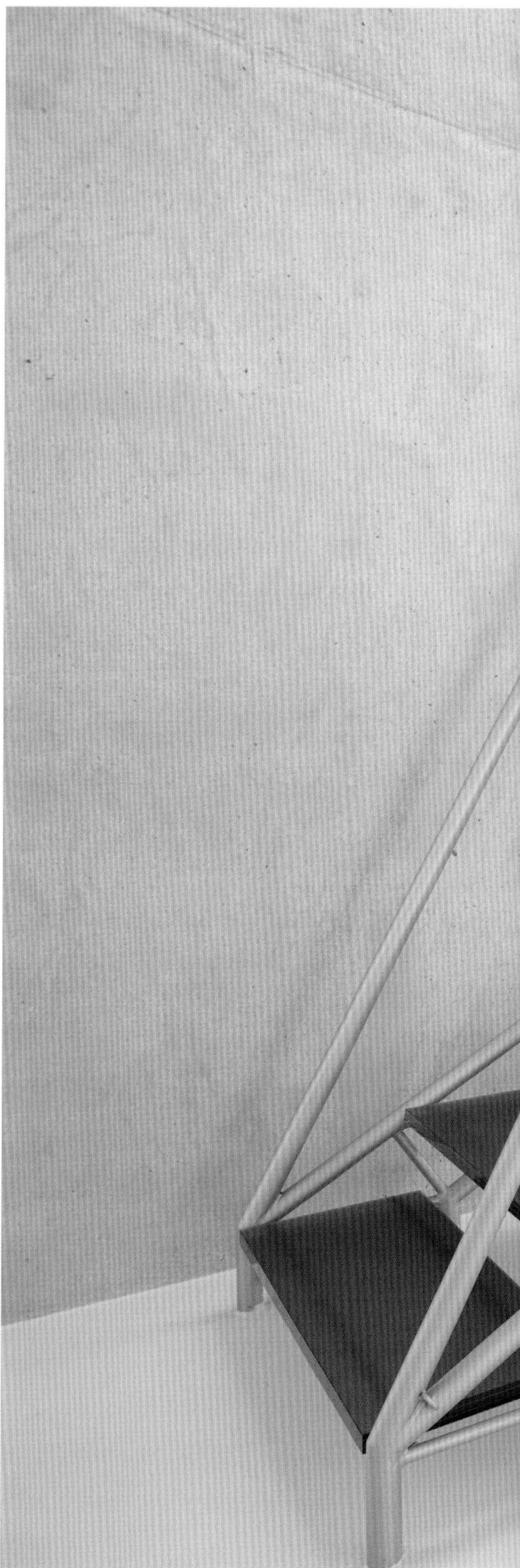

© Grega Eržen

Moussafir Architectes

" As for a staircase, this house is a kind of vertical loft made of one single open space.

계단에 있는 한, 이 집은 한개의 탁트인 공간으로 만들어진 일종의 수직적인 공간이다. "

Long Answer

My favourite design is the "Maison Escalier" ("Stair House") which is composed of spiraling floors cantilevered around a central core containing servant spaces. The house concept turns out to be an inhabited staircase with landings that become open living spaces connected at different levels to water supply facilities (bathrooms, kitchen, wc) located in the core. As for a staircase, this house is a kind of vertical loft made of one single open space. On top of the spatiality it generates, what I like in this project is that it raises the question of the sedentary and the nomadic which are 2 major components of human living.

©MA

Maison Escalier

NL Architects

> " The Rotating Spiral Stair was pretty amazing.
>
> Rotating Spiral Stairs는 꽤 대단했다. "

Long Answer

The Rotating Spiral Stair was pretty amazing. It was the center piece of a shop for Mandarina-Duck in Paris that we designed around the year 2000 and that was already destroyed only 2 years later.

It was a large and comfortable helicoidal stair with the bizarre capacity that it could turn. The stair was placed on a slowly spinning plateau, the movement inviting shoppers to enter the next level.

Shop for Mandarina-Duck

Rotating Spiral Stairs

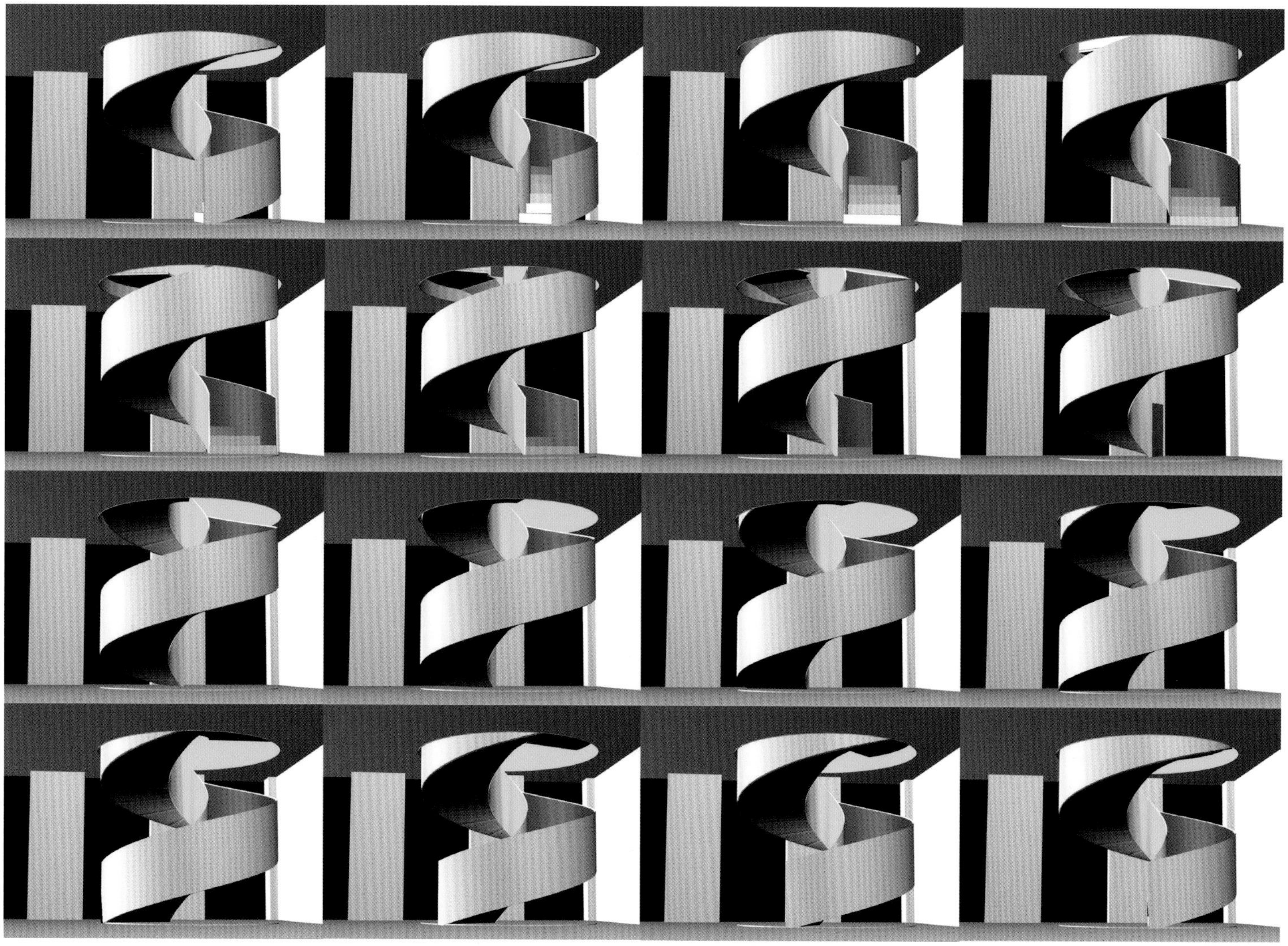

object-e architecture

“Stairs have always had a special place in architecture.

건축에서 계단은 늘 특별한 곳에 위치한다.”

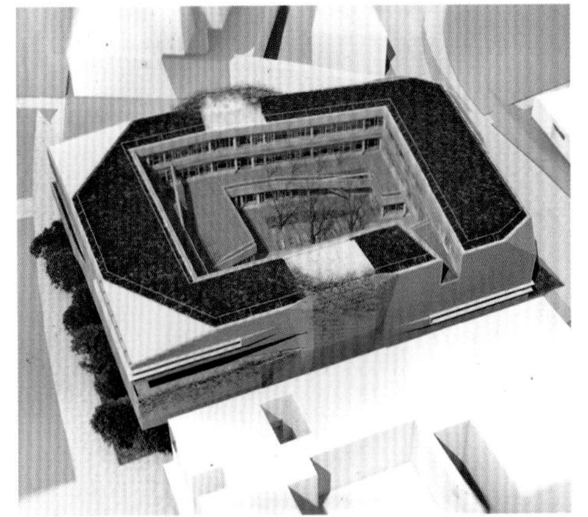

Long Answer

Stairs have always had a special place in architecture. First, on a symbolic level: they represent a journey, an ascent to something else. They also help create a climax. Therefore it is not a surprise that we often find staircases playing an important (symbolic) role in religious buildings, or buildings hosting governmental or any other form of institutional power: You have to ascent - to go above yourself - to reach an altar or a place where power is exercised. In those cases of course, their design is extremely important.

However, apart from the symbolic level, that can take different forms in different cultures or contexts, stairs also constitute an important tectonic element. In other words, stairs can define and organize space independently from their symbolic value. That happens because they fall between the main tectonic elements of a building. For example, Gottfried Semper in his "Four Elements of Architecture" specifies, as his book's title suggests, four main tectonic elements: hearth, roof, enclosure and mound. The staircase is not among them, making it on a first level a less important element, but at the same time one the can bridge the other four. A staircase, when existent, can become the binding element between the rest. It is also a tectonic element that offers the most in terms of detail in a design. Because of its relative complexity as a structure, its design can alter significantly the character of building. Or, if we go back to Semper, it can be the element that assigns a certain style to the design. That complexity of the staircase, in contrast to other important tectonic elements, like the wall, the openings etc, is also very evident if the way that it is used in other art forms: In cinema for example staircases are used quite often in order to add complexity and depth to important scenes. Alfred Hitchcock for instance, uses staircases regularly in

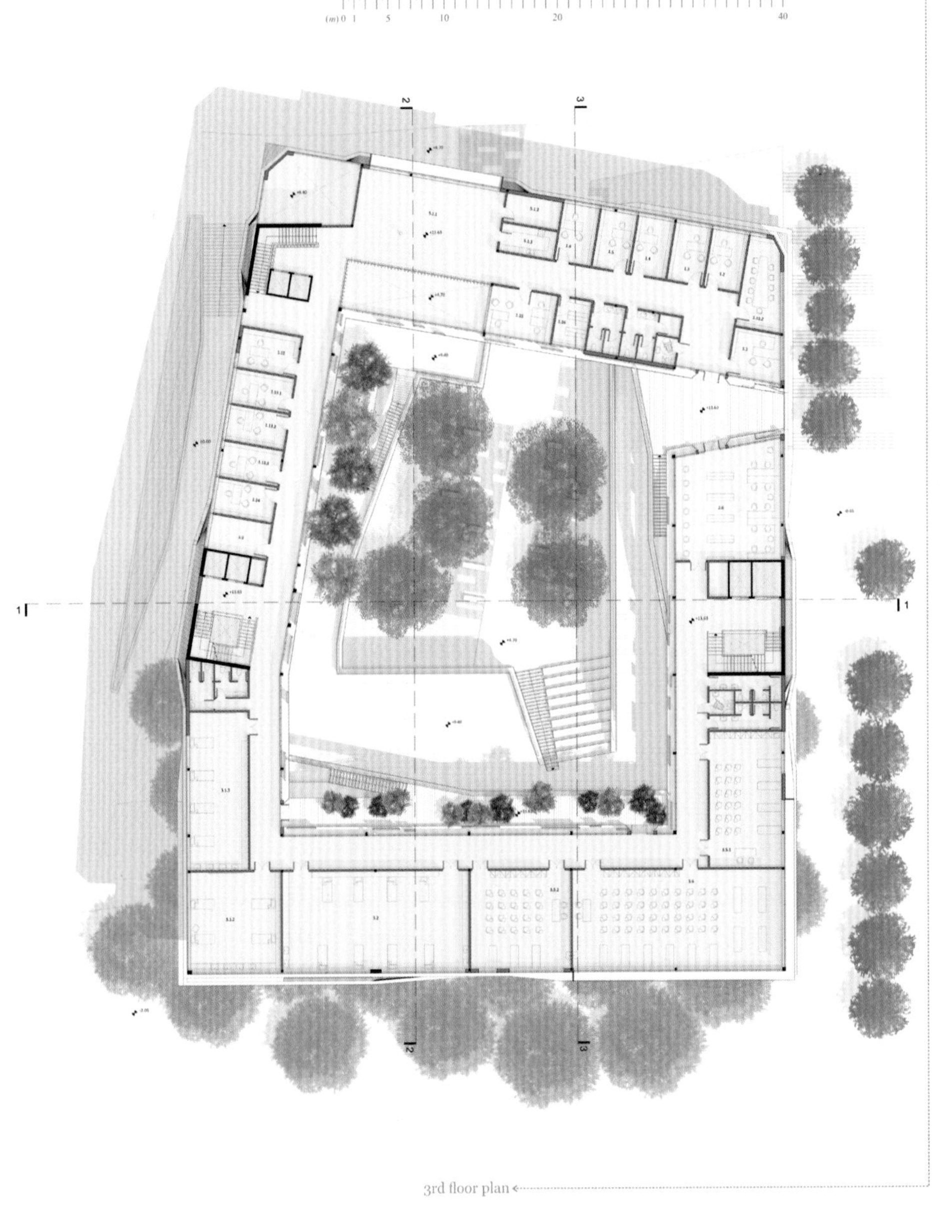

3rd floor plan

many of his films for that effect - for example in 'Vertigo' in order to build tension.

For all of the above reasons, the design of the staircases plays always an important role in our projects. Especially for proposals, like competition entries, where a sense of detail and refinement has to be present even when not every aspect of a building has be resolved. In those cases the design of the staircase can greatly enhance the proposal.

In the next two examples the design of the staircase(s) is in the center of the proposal. The first example is a competition entry for the new Medical School at the university campus of Nicosia. The building has a typical cloister organization. It is relatively closed on the outside but at its center has an open courtyard, invisible from the outside, that becomes its heart. In fact, the courtyard itself is treated as a large staircase. Each floor of the building steps back from the atrium creating this way a stepped open space to be occupied by the students and faculty of the school. Consequently the connections between those 'floor steps', the actual staircases become important: They are the only elements that derive from the main direction of the building, meeting it in a slight angle and emphasizing this way their presence. The occupants of the building are encourages through the design of the stairs to change levels and come in contact with the different levels of the school, which on the main volume are hosting different function that in most cases work independently. In other words, the series of staircases, including a small amphitheatric structure, have the purpose of bringing together the people that work or study in different parts of the school; to become the binding element in the social life of students and faculty.

"The series of staircases: to become the binding element in the social life of students and faculty.

계단의 연속성: 학생들과 교직원들이 결속되는 사교의 장소이다."

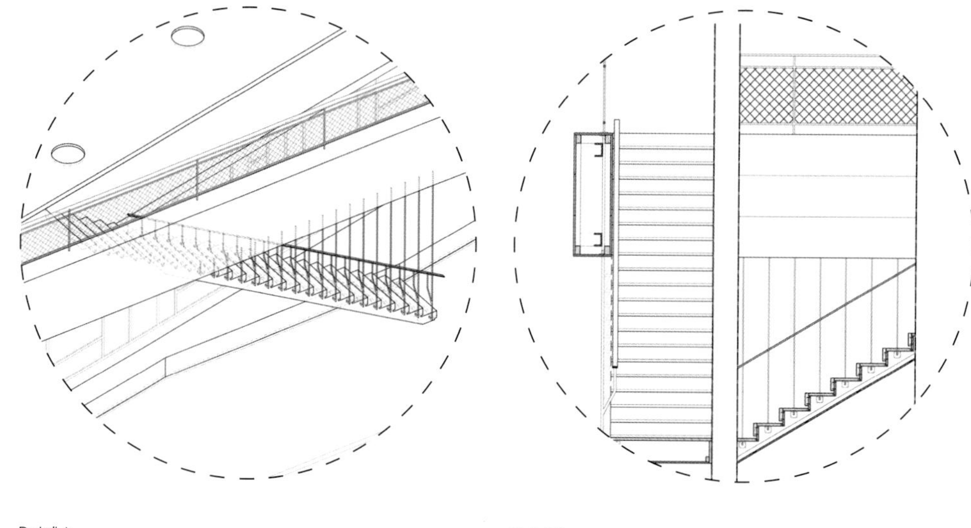

Detail A

Detail B

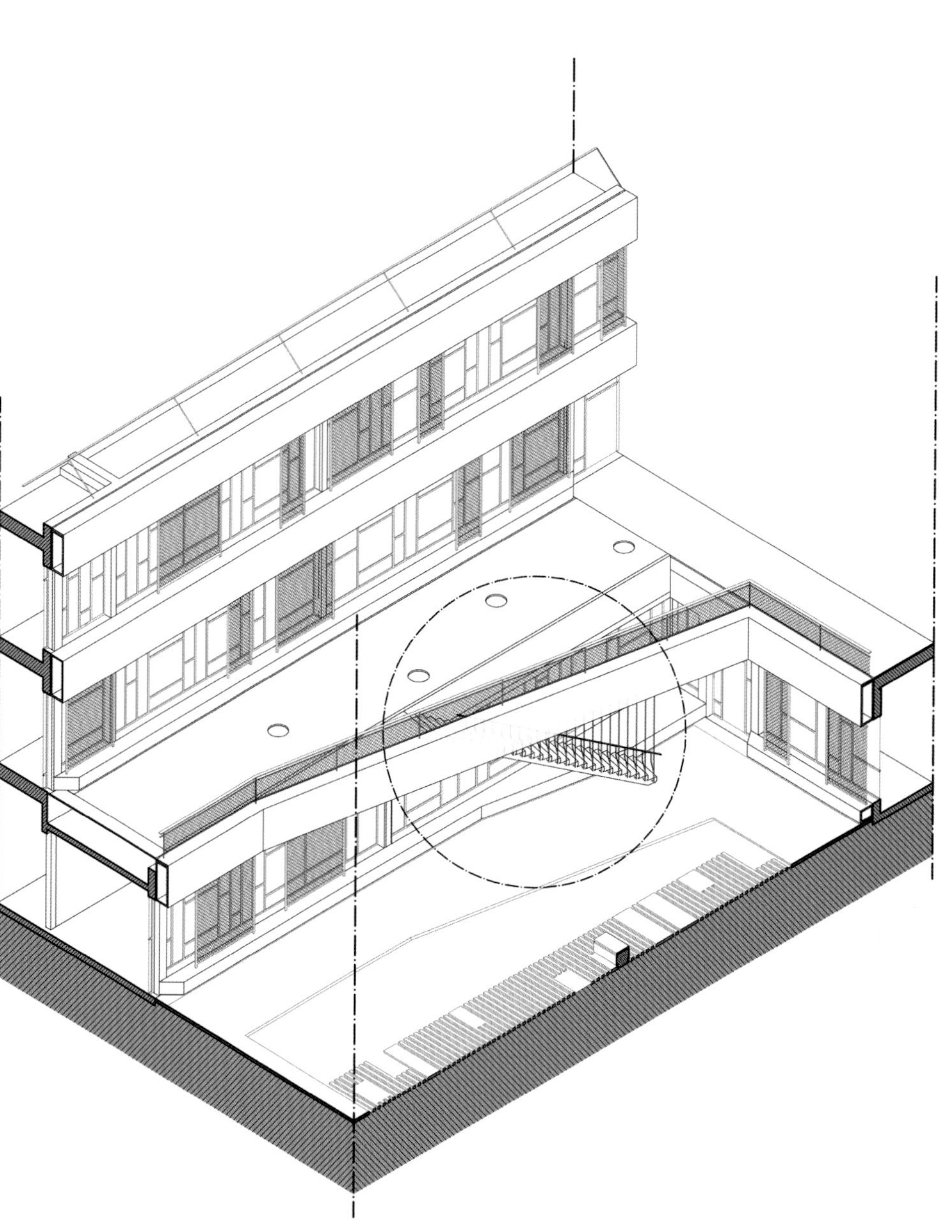

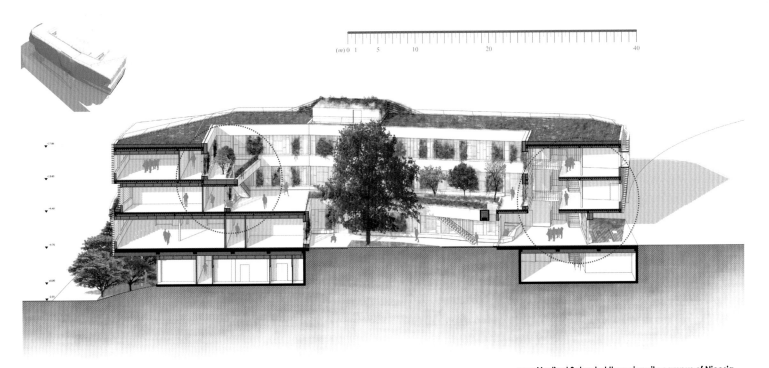

Section 1-1

(m) 0 1 5 10 20 40

new Medical School at the university campus of Nicosia

Section 2-2

In the second example, a 200m2 summer resident on the island of Paros, Greece, the staircase holds a similar binding role, but in a different way: it is the connecting element between the four volumes that constitute the house: It distributes movement between private and more public spaces, between the upper and the lower level, between enclosed and open space. It also constitutes the dividing line between the two small activity pots that can be found in the house: a small pool on the one side, and a private garden in the other. As a result the staircase becomes a place where most of the life in the house will take place.

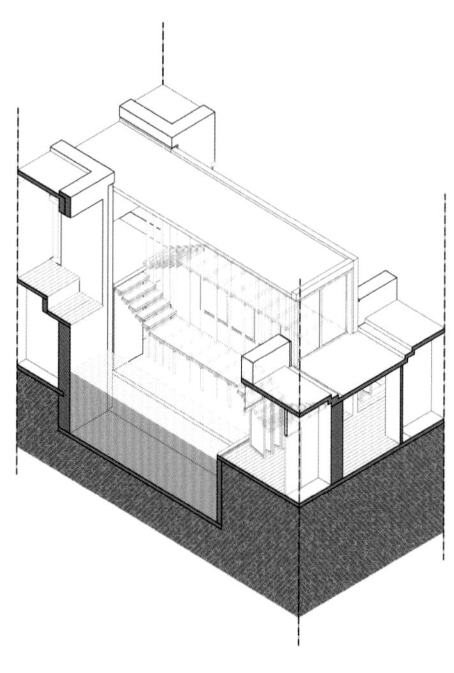

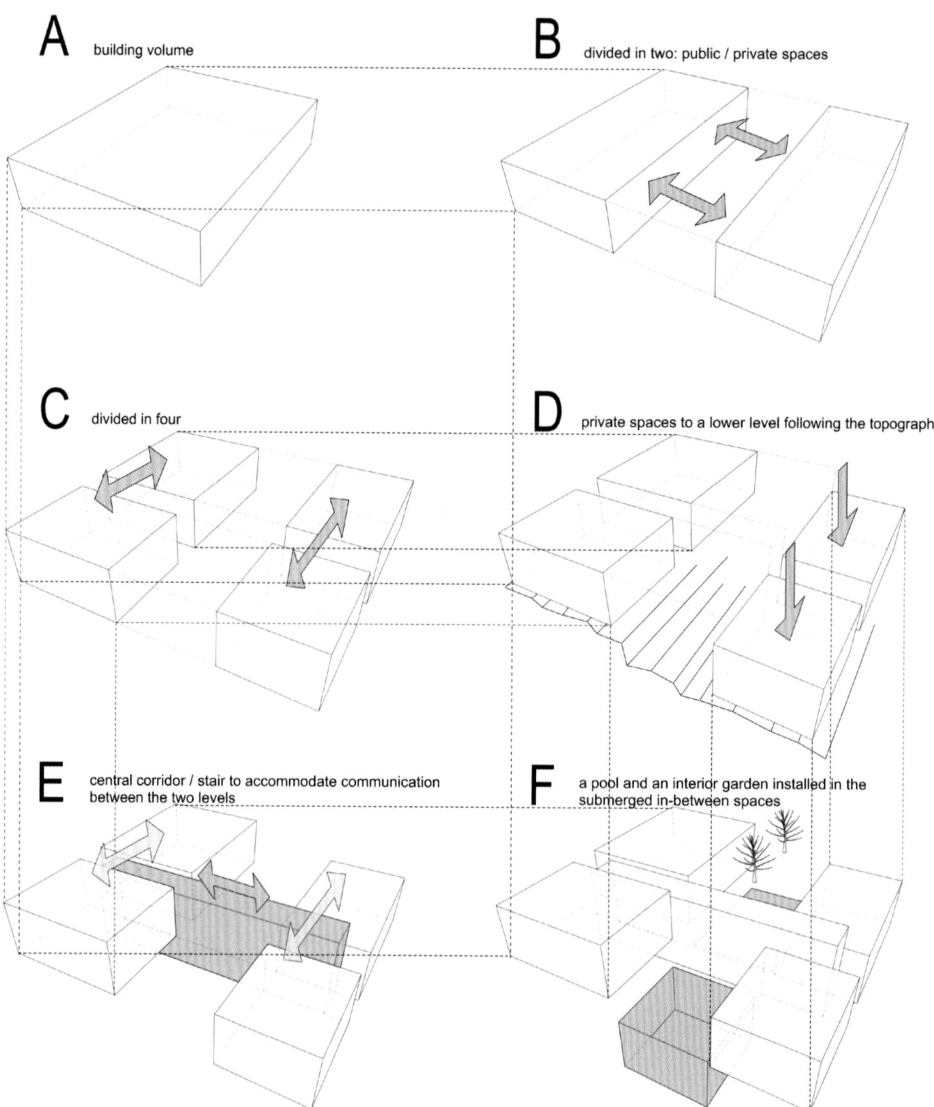
A building volume
B divided in two: public / private spaces
C divided in four
D private spaces to a lower level following the topography
E central corridor / stair to accommodate communication between the two levels
F a pool and an interior garden installed in the submerged in-between spaces

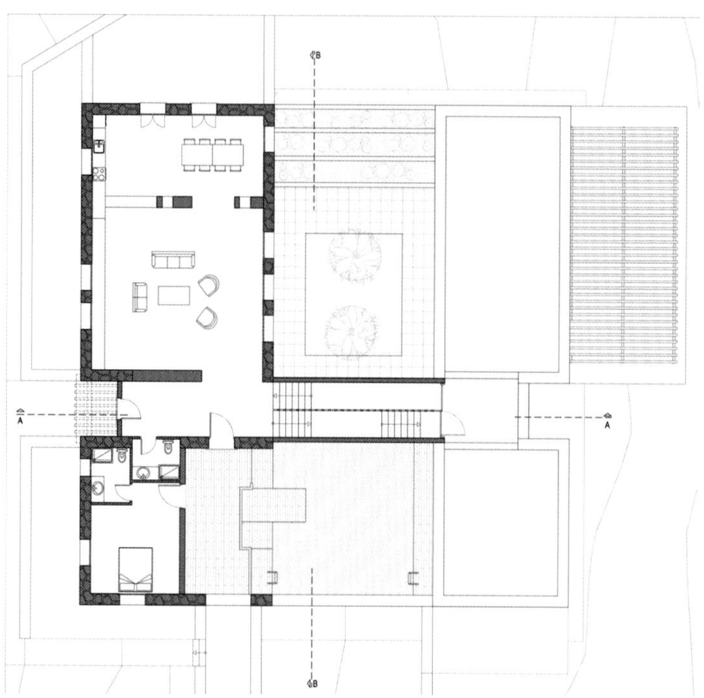

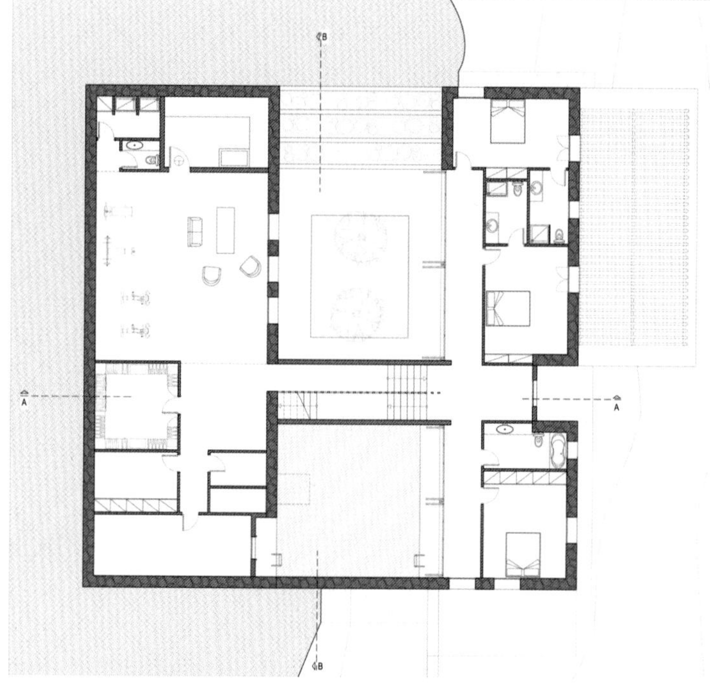

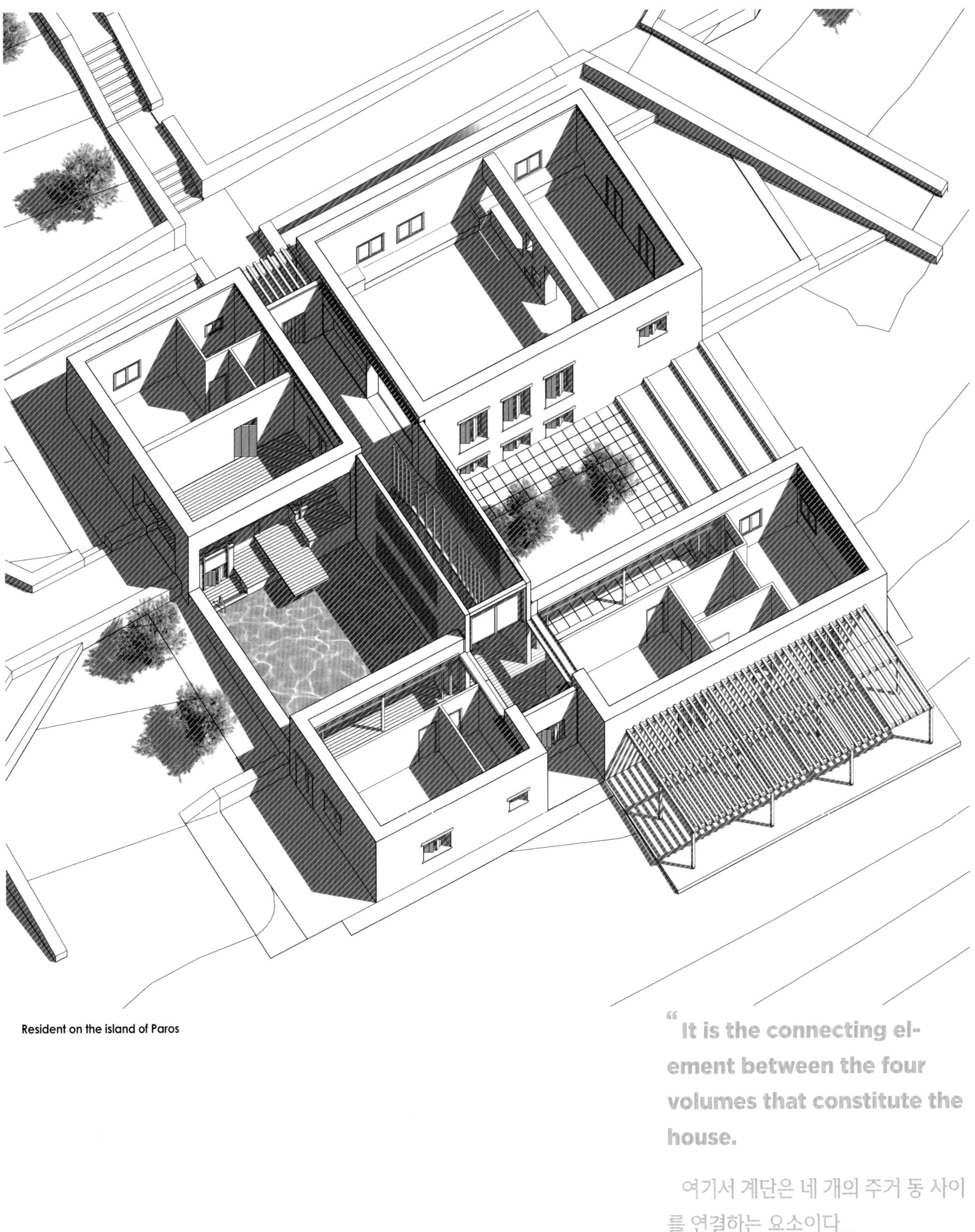

Resident on the island of Paros

"It is the connecting element between the four volumes that constitute the house.

여기서 계단은 네 개의 주거 동 사이를 연결하는 요소이다."

OPA

"The blue stair in the Hidden House, because it is a wonderfully psychological space. As a result, the immersive color zone is surprisingly unstable over time.

Hidden House의 푸른색 계단으로, 굉장히 심리적인 공간이다. 그 결과, 색이 집중된 이 영역은 끊임없이 급변한다."

Long Answer

The blue stair in the Hidden House, because it is a wonderfully psychological space. The house has a split personality, compose of two sides with radically different characters: one side is drenched in pastel blue paint; the other side is restricted exclusively to raw materials. The four-story stair is angled in plan and topped by a skylight, so its blue planes are differentiated from each other in tone, changing colors throughout the day depending on the specific mix of natural and electrical light. As a result, the immersive color zone is surprisingly unstable over time.

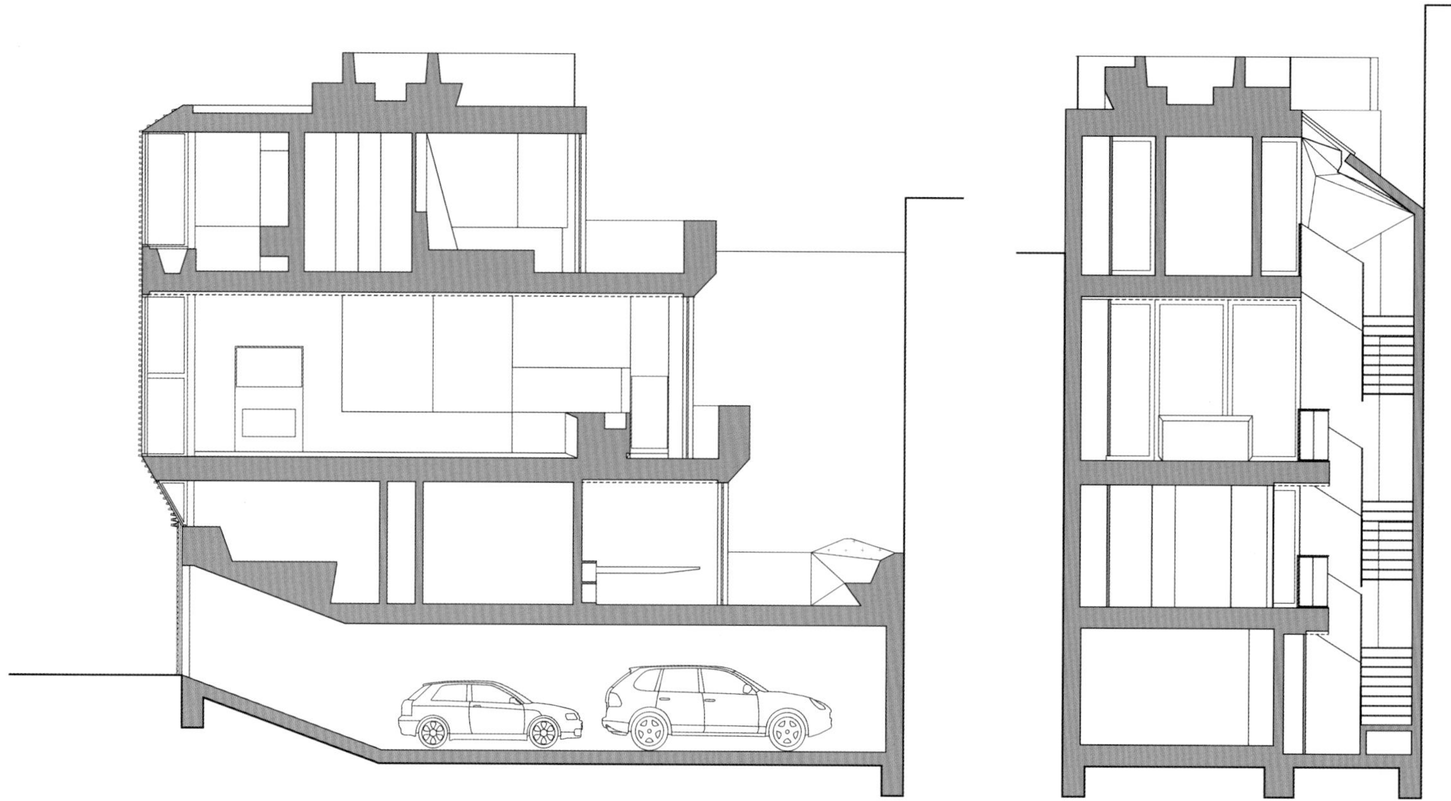

Hidden House

SLOT STUDIO

“The stairway is much more than a circulation device and has become an activator of space and promoter of the interaction of students with the environs.

계단은 통로적 장치이기 보다는 공간을 활성화 시키고 학생과 환경 간의 소통을 촉진시키는 매개체가 된다. ”

Long Answer

Our favorite stairway is one we designed for the Faculty of Architecture of Delft, a contest we participated in 2008. Beyond the formal expression of the stairway and its basic circulation function, it is a fundamental structure of the building itself. In fact, 23 flights of stairs serve to undergird the entire height of the building, creating a large scale public space at street level.

In this way, the stairway is much more than a circulation device and has become an activator of space and promoter of the interaction of students with the environs.

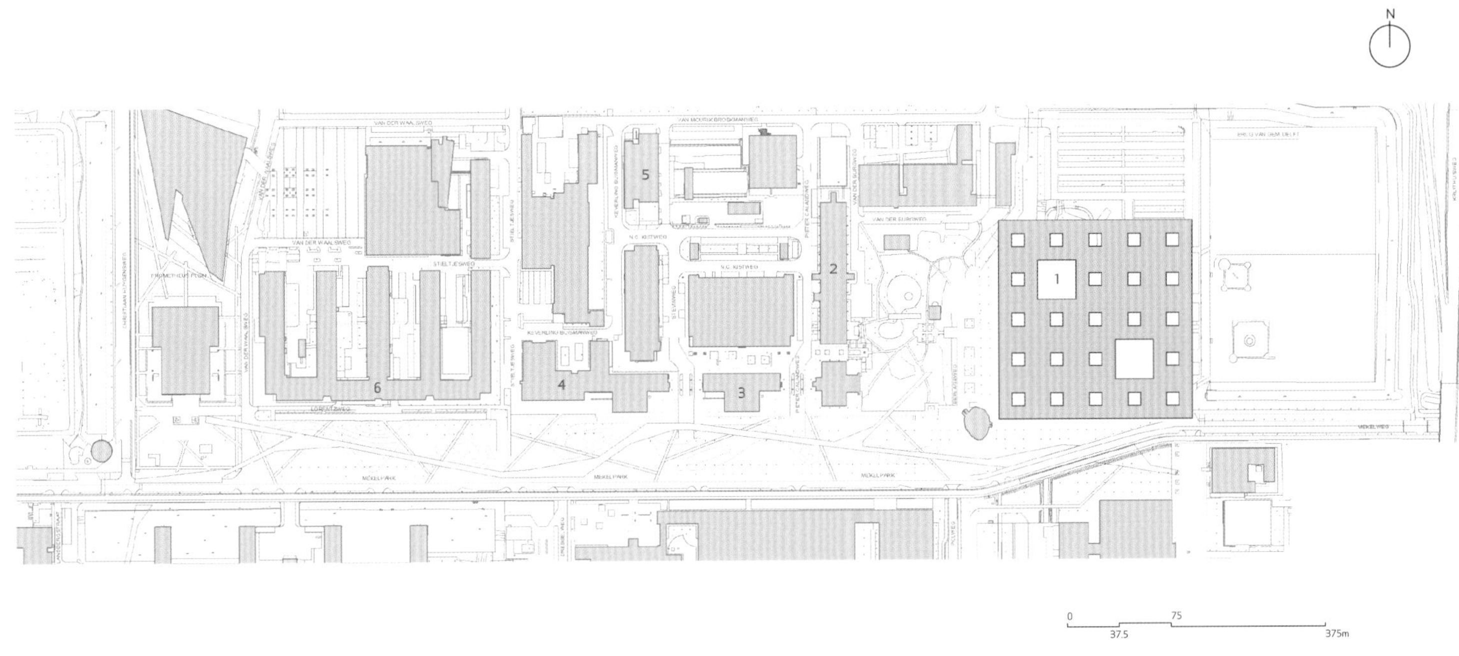

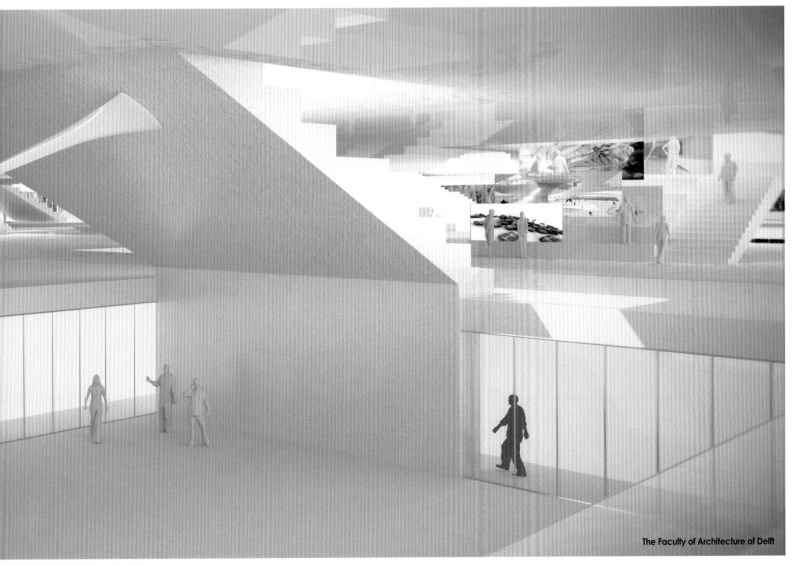

The Faculty of Architecture of Delft

Stefano Corbo Studio

" The most significant staircase I've designed in my career is not a real staircase: it's an urban promenade for a new Headquarters building, in Taiwan.

내 경력에서 가장 의미심장한 계단은 실제로는 계단이 아니다; 대만의 신축 오피스 빌딩에 조성된 도심 산책로이다. "

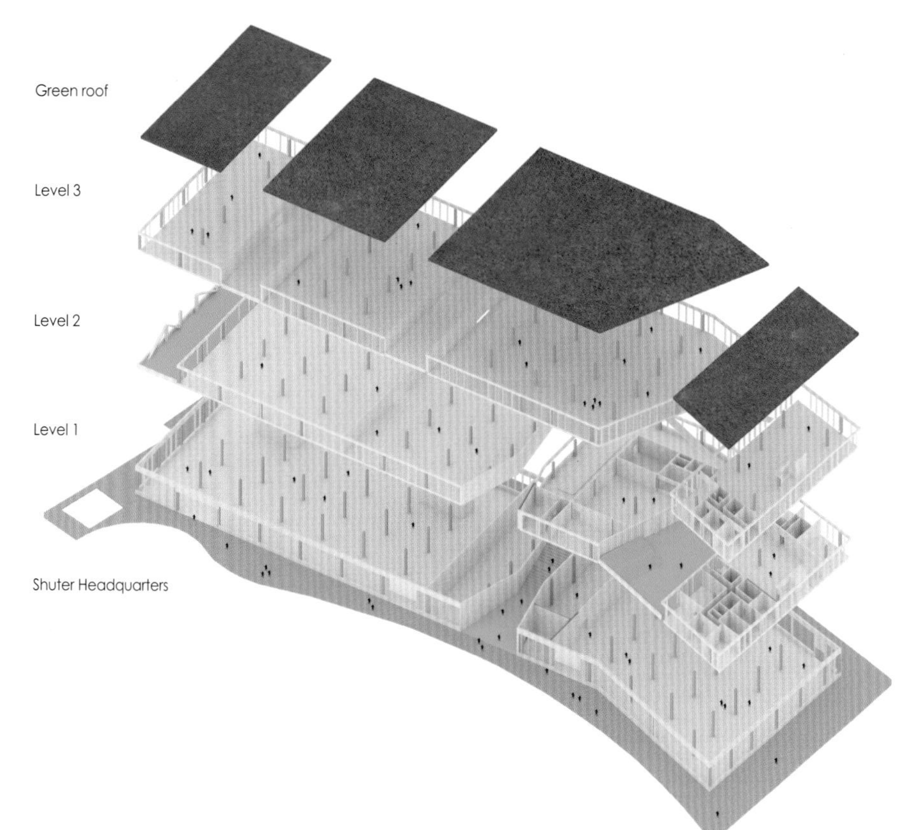

Long Answer

The most significant staircase I've designed in my career is not a real staircase: it's an urban promenade for a new Headquarters building, in Taiwan.

The project, called "Vertical Garden", was conceived as a sort of continuous axis that from the city guides the visitor up to the rooftop of the building. Within this sequence of different spaces, the staircase works as a main filter between the exterior and the interior of the project.

New Headquarters building, in Taiwan

TOUCH Architect

"NJ Villa which is not focusing on shape or material of the staircase, but focusing on using the stairs hall to block the sun heat from the South, which is acts as a vacuum insulation.

NJ Villa의 계단으로 형태와 재료에 초점을 맞추기 보다는, 남쪽에서 들어오는 햇빛의 열기를 차단하기 위한 진공절연 기능에 초점을 두었다. "

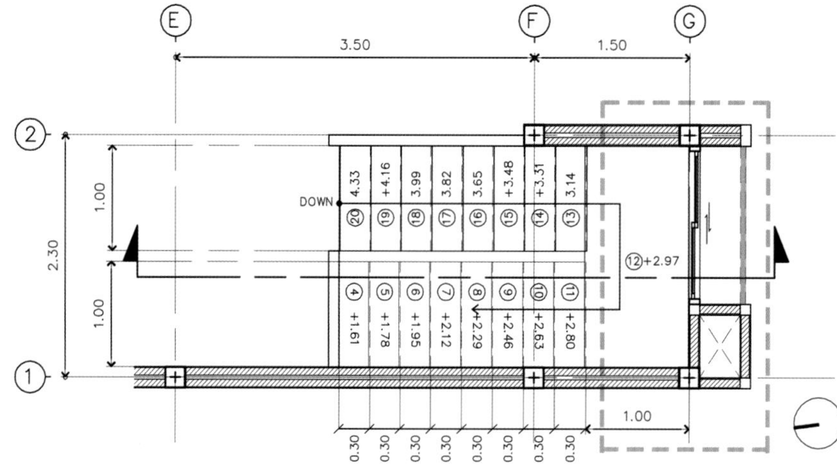

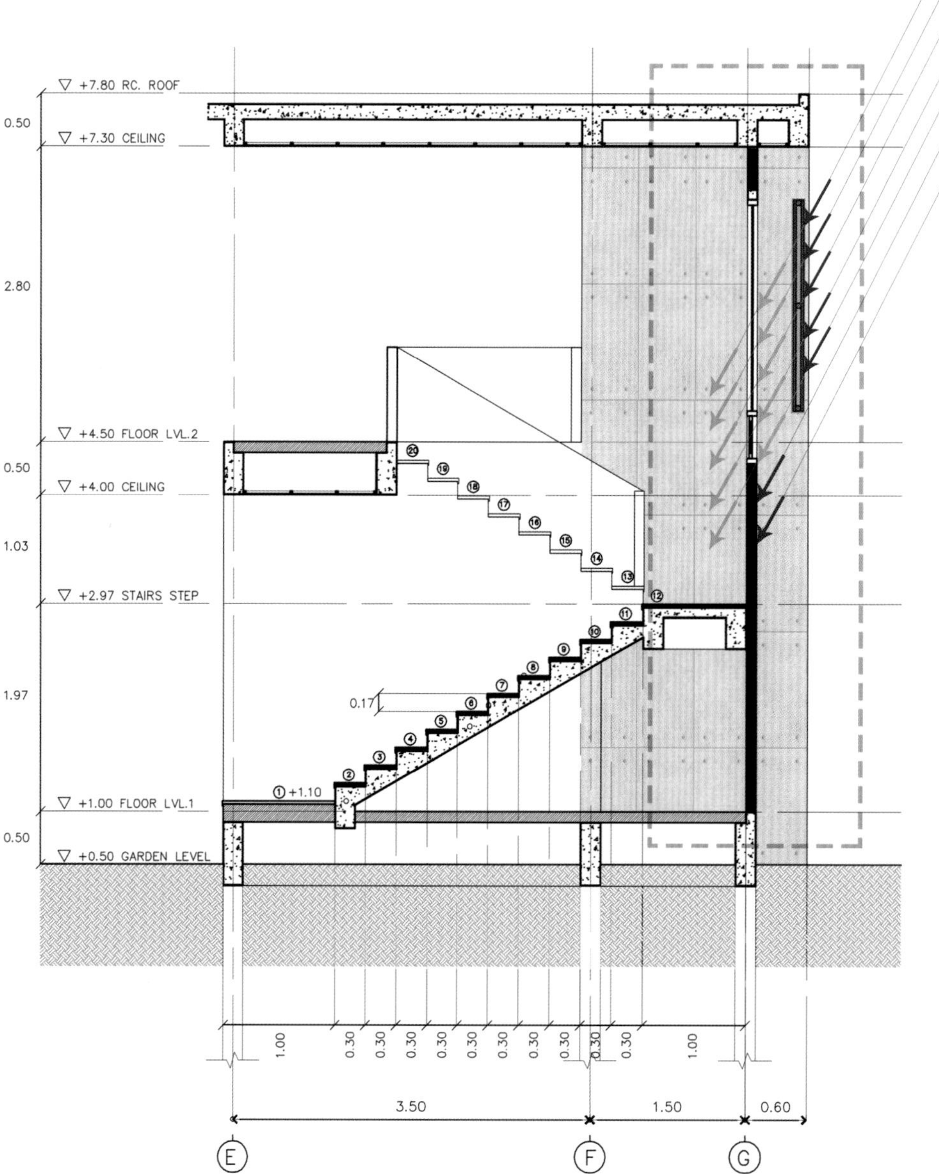

Long Answer

The most favourable stairs design of us is the stairs hall is NJ Villa which is not focusing on shape or material of the staircase, but focusing on using the stairs hall to block the sun heat from the South, which is acts as a vacuum insulation. Moreover, there are three vertical fins and wooden panels which act as a shading device for this stairs hall either. The wooden panel was placed in shifted line to create indirect light from outside instead of using electrical lighting inside while avoiding heat.

NJ Villa

© Chalermwat Wongchompoo

TROPICAL SPACE

"The stair could be a small family library or small inner garden, where grandparent can put their own tree pots and read fairy tales for their kids.

그 계단은 작은 가족 도서관이나 작은 내면 정원이 될 수도 있고, 할아버지가 자신만의 나무 항아리를 집어 넣고 동화를 읽을 수 있는 작은 집이 될 수도 있다. "

Long Answer

My favorite design is the Stair for Wasp House. It is not only use for circulation but also for family community space.

In the density city like Saigon, we don't have enough space to create the traditional buffer zone spaces - space use for circulation, preventing heat and rain and the most important function is connecting people. We try to bring it 's spiritual to Wasp House - a house for modern city style family and hope that we can bring members in family more closer to each other

The stair could be a small family library or small inner garden, where grandparent can put their own tree pots and read fairy tales for their kids.

Wasp House

© QuangDam

본인의 설계안 중 가장 성공적인 계단 디자인은 무엇인가? 그 이유는?

P.008

몇 년 전에 우리는 로마 역사 중심부에 있는 한 아파트 리뉴얼 작업을 한 적이 있다. 2 개 층과 근처 판테온과 나보나 광장을 비롯한 로마 도처의 주요 건축물과 대성당들의 장관이 내려다보이는 루프테라스로 된 건물이었다. 건축주는 우리에게 디자인 자유권을 주었고, 우리는 기존 공간을 연상시키는 중간 높이의 출입구 중 하나와 여러 층들을 확실히 연결시키는 경량 철골 계단을 제안하였다. 계단에는 특수조명시스템도 갖추었다. 위대한 역사적 문맥안에 현대적인 맞춤 요소를 삽입하는 것은 흥미로운 경험이었으며, 숙련된 장인들이 심혈을 기울여 우리의 드로잉을 매우 정교하게 실현시키는 것 또한 흥미로운 경험이었다.

b4architects

P.010

우리가 디자인한 계단 중 탈린도시에 위치한 에스토니아 미술 대학 신축건물의 계단을 가장 좋아한다. 거기서 우리는 강당과 갤러리를 포함한 모든 대중 프로그램들을 한 곳에 모았고 그 곳에서 뻗어 나오는 커다란 계단을 만들었다. 우리는 그 계단을 "대중을 위한 단면"이라고 부른다. 이 계단은 건물 전체를 가로지르지만 여러 유닛들을 분리하는 흡음막들 덕분에 강의나 공연 또는 행사 중에도 계단을 사용할 수 있다. 아무런 행사가 없을 경우 계단은 1층 건물 로비의 확장공간이 된다.

BOARD

P.012

우리 모두가 알고 있듯 계단은 서로 다른 높이의 공간들을 수직으로 연결하는 요소이다. 특히 우리는 램프와 같은 친절한 계단을 설계하는데 더 많은 기회를 열어놓고 있다. 수직연결요소로서 램프는 공간적 유대감을 더 느끼게 해주며 공간을 보다 더 경쟁력 있는 곳으로 만든다. 우리는 한 사례로 이스탄불의 재난방지센터 프로젝트의 램프 디자인을 이야기하려 한다. 이 램프는 건물 중앙에 설치되어 건물 어디에서도 볼 수 있다. 건물 천장 높이의 거대한 벽 구조에 튼튼하게 고정되어 있어 램프 어디에 있느냐에 따라 벽이 갈라져 보이기도 하고 오픈되어 보이기도 한다. 이런 효과는 센터 내부공간과 이용자 사이의 밀접한 관계를 형성한다. 다음의 스케치를 보면 벽을 따라 램프가 어떻게 제작되었는지 알 수 있다. 스케치에서 볼 수 있듯 램프 경사로가 벽에 뚫린 틈과 연결되어 있기 때문에 벽과 램프를 하나가 아닌 별개의 두 요소로 보기는 불가능하다. 램프는 간단한 콘크리트 슬라브 구조로 벽에 고정되어 있으며, 난간은 3+3 유리 재질로 설화 석고 띠가 둘러져 부분 발광 되는 투명 부티랄 소재가 부착되어 있다.

ELA - Edu Lopez Architects

P.014

몇 년 전에 우리는 한 아트 콜렉터를 위해 멕시코 시티에 위치한 아파트 (인테리어) 설계를 한 적이 있다. 건축주의 소장품들은 다채로웠으며, 특히 팝 아트가 주를 이뤘다. 우리는 예술 작품들과 융합되고 시너지효과를 내는 공간을 설계하는데 초점을 맞췄다. 계단이 관찰자의 시점이 되기를 원했기 때문에 녹색 빛이 도는 유리와(건축주의 요구사항이었다) 투명 난간을 사용하여 시야를 투명하게 만들었다. 마지막 계단스텝 앞 벽 전면에는 콜렉션 중 매우 중요한 작품을 걸어 사적 공간으로 들어서자 마자 제일 처음 눈에 들어오게 계획하였다.

Ezequiel Farca + Cristina Grappin

P.018

쿠라쿠엔(KURAKUEN) 주택 프로젝트 계단의 유기적 형태와 마감효과를 가장 좋아한다. 벽, 바닥과 매끄럽게 균일한 효과를 내기 위해 계단을 테라초(대리석을 골재로 한 콘크리트)로 마감하였다.

Katsuhiro Miyamoto & Associates

P.019

가장 성공적으로 설계한 계단은 이탈리아 나폴리에 있는 Ospedale de mare홀의 두 개 층을 잇는 메인 계단이다.

이 홀은 2개층의 원통 모양으로 유리 판넬과 블루와 그린 계열 사이의 여러 톤을 가진 섬유강화 콘크리트로 마감되었다. 유리 판넬은 다양한 각도로 깎여 수평방향에서 보면 조각난 것처럼 보여 입면을 생동감 있게 만든다.

지붕 슬라브에는 커다란 원형 채광창들이 나 있어 실내를 비춘다.

벽을 감싸고 내부 정원을 에워싸고 있는 유리는 빛을 다양한 각도로 반사해 공간을 환하게 밝혀준다.

원형 창들은 피라네시를 향해 강한 숭배적인 빛을 비추고 이 빛은 두개의 층을 시각적으로 연결한다. 마치 층들의 수평적이고 수직적인 요소들이 한데 어우러져 길을 따라 형태가 변하는 하나의 면처럼 인식되어 굉장히 밝고 오픈 된 공간같이 느껴진다. 이런 공간적 변형을 강조하기 위해 슬라브에 뚫린 원형 창들은 수직 축에서 살짝 어긋나 있어 미미하게 시야를 흐려 공간의 명확한 인지를 방해한다. 계단은 직선 모양의 단순한 계단으로 원형 창들 사이로 들어오는 빛을 따라서 적극적으로 층 사이를 연결하고 그 연결성이 뚜렷이 보인다.

LGSMA_

P.022

한 개인 주택에서 설계한 공간을 가로지르는 설치작품과 같은 계단이다. 이 계단은 콘크리트 벽을 배경으로 꽤 역동적인 효과를 내며, 마치 학 한 마리가 건설현장에서 날아와 집안으로 들어온 것 같은 느낌이다. 집과 계단은 날것의 느낌과 우아함을 겸비한 흥미로운 조화를 이룬다.

Miha Volgemut architect

P.024

내가 제일 좋아하는 디자인은 가정부 공간이 있는 코어를 중심으로 켄틸레버 구조로 나선형으로 상승하는 바닥으로 구성된 "Maison Escalier" (Stair house)이다. 이 집은 사람이 이동하는 계단의 참이 개방된 거실이 되는 컨셉으로 거실은 각 층마다 집 코어의 급수시설(욕실과 부엌, 화장실 등)과 연결된다. 계단을 중심으로 본다면, 이 집은 하나의 열린 공간에 의해 만들어진 일종의 수직 상승 공간이다. 나선형 구조 외 내가 이 프로젝트에서 좋아하는 부분은 인간 생활에서 가장 중요한 2가지 구성요소인 정착과 유목에 대한 의문을 제기한다는 점이다.

Moussafir Architectes

P.026

Rotating Spiral Stairs는 꽤 대단했다. 2000년에 우리가 설계한 파리 만다리나덕 매장 중심에는 이 나선형 계단이 있었지만, 불과 2년만에 (매장이 문을 닫아) 없어졌다.

이것은 빙글빙글 돌아가는 독특한 기능을 가진 크고 편안한 나선형의 계단이었다. 계단은 천천히 회전하는 판위에 설치되어 고객이 다음층으로 이동할 수 있게 유도했다.

NL Architects

P.027

건축에서 계단은 늘 특별한 곳에 위치한다. 첫째, 상징적 단계: 계단은 다른 어딘가를 향해 올라가는 여행과 같으며, 클라이맥스를 조성한다. 이런 이유로, 종교 건축이나 정부청사, 그 외 다른 제도적 권력을 상징하는 건축물에서 영향력 있는 (상징적) 계단을 많이 볼 수 있는 건 놀라운 일이 아니다. 계단을 올라 -자기 분수를 넘어- 제단이나 권력이 행해지는 장소에 도달해야 한다. 이런 목적을 가진 계단은 디자인이 매우 중요하다.

그러나 상징적 단계에서 벗어나면 계단은 여러 문화나 문맥 안에서 다양한 형태를 취하기도 하고 중요한 구조적 요소가 될 수 있다. 다시 말해, 상징적 가치와는 무관하게 계단으로 공간을 특정 짓거나 체계화할 수 있다는 것이다. 이것이 가능한 이유는 계단이 건축물의 메인 구조에서 빗겨 나 있기 때문이다. 예를 들어, 고트프리드 젬퍼는 그의 저서 "건축의 네 가지 요소"에서 책 제목처럼 네 가지 구조적 요소들을 언급하였다. 난로, 지붕, 벽, 그리고 주축. 계단은 1순위에는 들지 않지만, 다른 네 가지 요소들을 동시에 연결하는 브릿지가 될 수 있다. 계단이 존재하면 그 외 요소들이 하나로 결속된다. 또한 계단은 가장 섬세하게 디자인되는 구조물이다. 상대적으로 복잡한 구조로 되어 있기 때문에 디자인에 따라 건물의 성격도 변할 수 있다. 다시 젬퍼로 돌아가면, 계단은 특정 스타일을 적용할 수 있는 대상이 된다. 벽이나 입구와 같은 다른 주요 구조적 요소와는 달리 계단이 다른 예술 매체에 활용될 경우 그 복잡성은 더 두드러진다. 영화에서 중요한 장면에 갈등의 깊이를 더해주기 위해 흔히 계단이 사용된다. 예를 들어, 알프레드 히치콕은 '현기증'이라는 영화에서 긴장감을 조성하기 위해 계단을 사용한 것처럼 그의 많은 영화에 자주 계단을 등장시켜 그러한 효과를 주었다.

위의 모든 이유로, 계단 디자인은 우리 프로젝트에서 매우 중요하다. 특히 공모전처럼 다른 모든 건축적 접근보다도 디테일적 감각과 세련된 표현이 더 중요할 경우, 우리는 계단 디자인으로 설계안의 가치를 높인다.

다음에 선보이는 두 사례에는 계단이 프로젝트의 정 중앙에 위치해 있다. 첫 번째 사례는 니코시아 대학의 의과대학 신축 공모전에 제안한 설계안이다. 건물은 전형적인 회랑 구조로 되어 있다. 회랑은 밖으로는 닫혀 있어 외부에서 보이지 않지만, 내부로는 건물의 중심이 되는 오픈 중정이 있다. 실제로 이 중정은 그 자체가 거대한 계단처럼 보인다. 건물의 층들은 계단처럼 아트리움으로부터 올라갈수록 후퇴되어 학생이나 교직원들이 사용할 수 있는 계단 형태의 테라스 공간을 형성한다. 여기서 중요한 것은 이러한 '층 계단'을 연결하는 실제 계단들이다. 이 계단들은 건물의 유일한 메인 통로로 계단의 존재를 부각시키기 위해 약간 기울어진 각도로 배치하였다. 층마다 다른 학년으로 나뉘어져 대부분 독립적으로 사용되지만, 계단을 따라가다 보면 자연스럽게 다른 학년과 만나게 된다. 즉, 작은 원형극장 같은 구조와 계단의 연속성은 학교 여러 곳에서 일하고 공부하는 사람들을 모으기 위한 목적을 달성한다: 학생들과 교직원들이 결속되는 사교의 장소이다.

두 번째 사례는 그리스 파로스섬에 위치한 200m² 별장으로, 똑같이 사람들을 결속시키는 계단이지만, 그 방법이 다르다. 여기서 계단은 네 개의 주거 동 사이를 연결하는 요소이다. 사적인 공간과 공적인 공간, 위층과 아래층, 그리고 닫힌 공간과 열린 공간 사이의 이동을 구분 짓는다. 또한, 집 내부의 두 곳의 작은 활동 공간을 구분 짓는 경계선이기도 하다. 한 쪽으로는 수영장, 다른 한 쪽으로는 개인 정원. 결론적으로 계단은 집에서의 거의 모든 생활이 행해질 장소가 될 것이다.

object-e architecture

P.032

Hidden House의 푸른색 계단으로, 굉장히 심리적인 공간이다. 이 주택은 전혀 다른 두 성향으로 나뉜다: 한 쪽은 파스텔 블루톤으로 도색 되었고, 다른 한 쪽은 철저히 자연 재료만으로 표현되었다. 계단 위로 내리비추는 햇빛은 인공조명과 섞이며, 그 섞이는 정도에 따라 온 종일 푸른 계단참의 톤이 각기 다르게 변화한다. 그 결과, 색이 집중된 이 영역은 끊임없이 급변한다.

OPA

P.034

우리가 가장 좋아하는 계단은 2008년에 참가했던 델프트 공대의 건축학과 설계공모전에서 디자인한 계단이다. 이 계단은 형식적인 형태와 통로의 기본 기능을 넘어서서 스스로가 건물의 기본 구조가 된다. 자세하게는 23개의 계단 참이 건물 전체 높이를 단단하게 지지하는 구조이며 1층에는 넓은 공공 공간이 설계되었다. 이런 면에서 계단은 통로적 장치이기 보다는 공간을 활성화 시키고 학생과 환경간의 소통을 촉진시키는 매개체가 된다.

SLOT STUDIO

P.036

내 경력에서 가장 의미심장한 계단은 실제로는 계단이 아니다; 대만의 신축 오피스 빌딩에 조성된 도심 산책로이다. "수직 정원"이라고 불리는 이 산책로는 사람들을 도심에서부터 빌딩 옥상까지 이끄는 연속된 축의 시작점으로 구상되었다. 산책로에서 빌딩 옥상까지 이어지는 다양한 공간의 일련속에서 계단은 빌딩외부와 내부사이의 중심 필터 역할을 한다.

Stefano Corbo Studio

P.038

우리 디자인 중 가장 마음에 드는 계단은 NJ Villa의 계단으로 형태와 재료에 초점을 맞추기 보다는, 남쪽에서 들어오는 햇빛의 열기를 차단하기 위한 진공절연 기능에 초점을 두었다. 게다가, 계단을 가리는 세 개의 우드 차양 버티컬 블라인드 시스템을 설치하였다. 블라인드의 우드 패널들은 비스듬히 기울어져 있어 바깥 직사광을 끌어들이기 때문에 열 차단이 되는 동안 실내 전기조명을 켤 필요가 없다.

TOUCH Architect

P.040

내가 가장 좋아하는 계단은 Wasp House의 계단이다.

이 계단은 이동을 위해 사용될 뿐만 아니라 가족 간의 소통 공간으로도 활용된다. 사이공(호치민)과 같이 복잡한 도시에는 전통적 완충 공간 -이동 공간이면서 열기와 비를 차단해 주며 가장 핵심적으로 사람들을 연결하는 공간 - 을 위한 공간이 여의치 않다. 우리는 이런 (완충 공간의) 정신을 Wasp House에 적용하려 하였다.- 현대적 도시형 가족을 위한 집이며 가족 구성원들이 서로 더 가깝게 지낼 수 있는 집이 되면 좋겠다.

계단은 조부모가 직접 화분을 가져다 놓기도 하며 손자 손녀들에게 동화책도 읽어 줄 수 있는 작은 실내 정원이나 작은 도서관이 될 수 있다.

TROPICAL SPACE

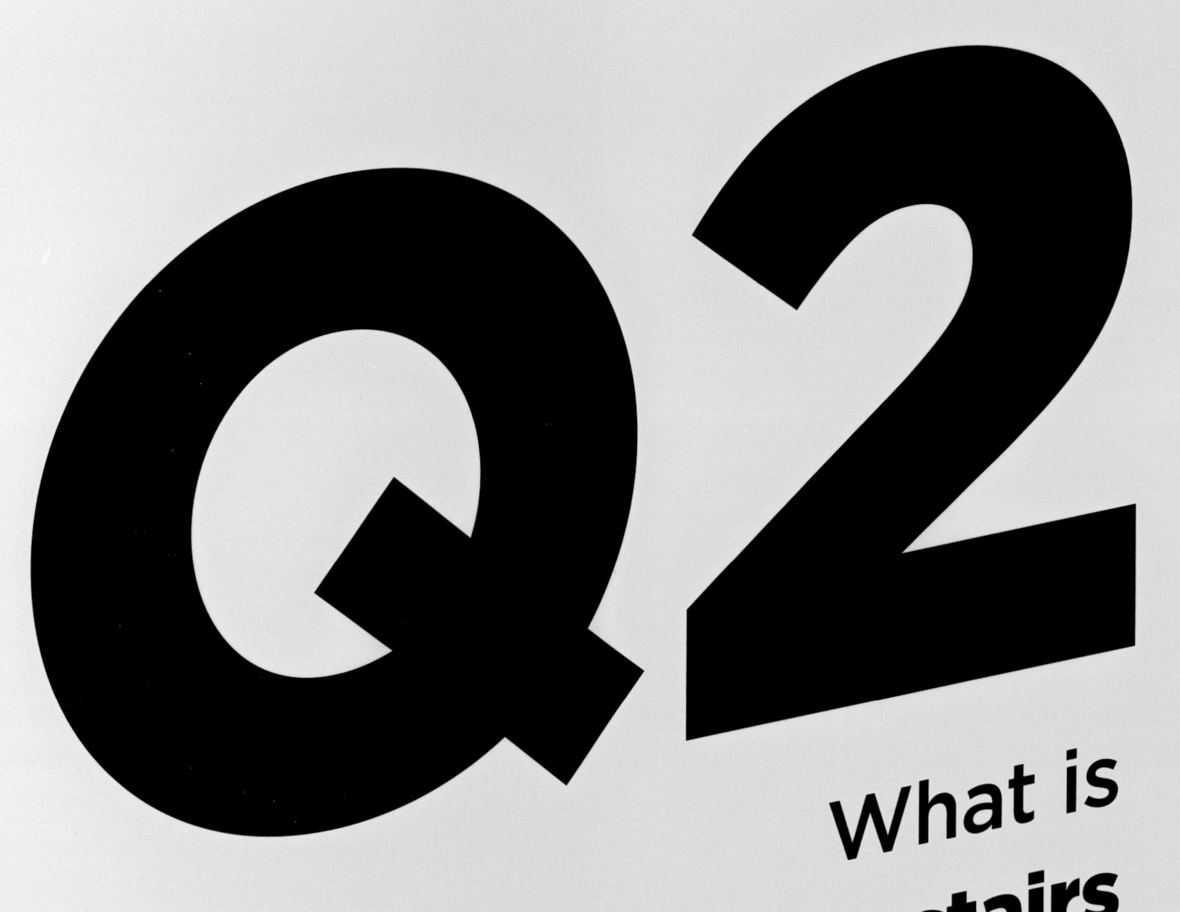

Q2

What is **the least favourite stairs** you've designed and why?

b4architects

> " The project came back with the revision of client's professionals but completely transformed in its sense, and the solution for the group of stairs lost all its lightness with the request of the insertion of a lot of pillars below. So we had to accept a compromise that didn't satisfy none.
>
> 프로젝트는 건축주의 전문가들에 의해 전혀 다른 느낌으로 변형 되어 돌아왔으며, 계단 아래에 많은 기둥들을 삽입하라는 요청으로 가벼움을 완전히 상실한 상태였다. 그렇게 하여 우리는 전혀 만족스럽지 못한 타협을 받아들여야만 했다"

© G. Evels

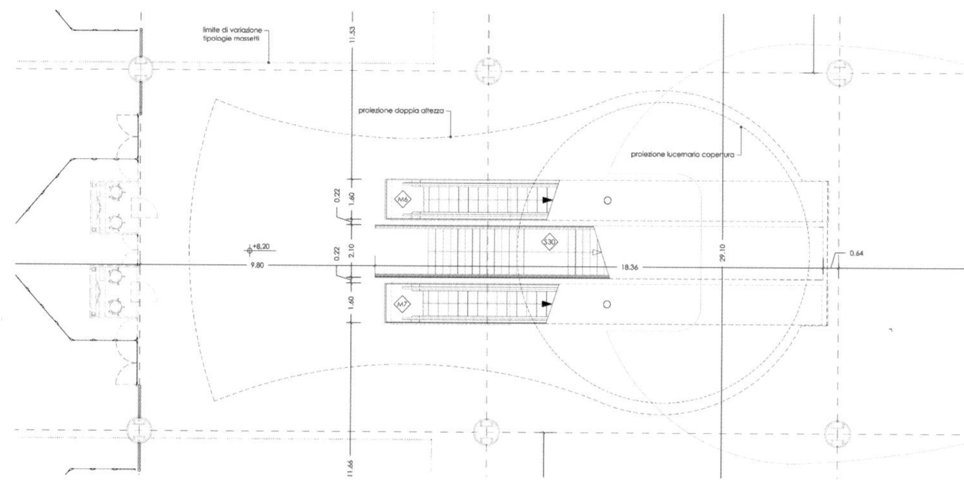

Ground Floor

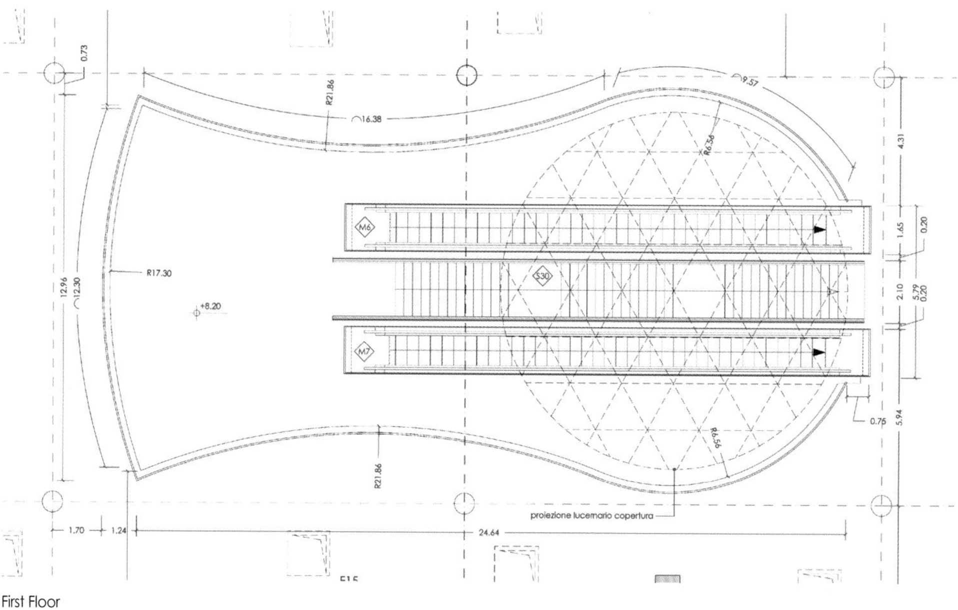

First Floor

Long Answer

Few years ago an engineering society asked us to join their team design for the architectural project and interior design of a part of the Rome Fiumicino Airport. We worked with great enthusiasm with all the staff. There was a moment that we were involved in a special custom design of a group of escalators together fixed stairs. We spent great energy to solve a complicated crossroad for passengers, but at the end we found an elegant solution that was sent to the client for a final review. The project came back with the revision of client's professionals but completely transformed in its sense, and the solution for the group of stairs lost all its lightness with the request of the insertion of a lot of pillars below. We demonstrated that was no necessary but for the timing scheduled for the project was too late to propose an alternative, so we had to accept a compromise that didn't satisfy none.

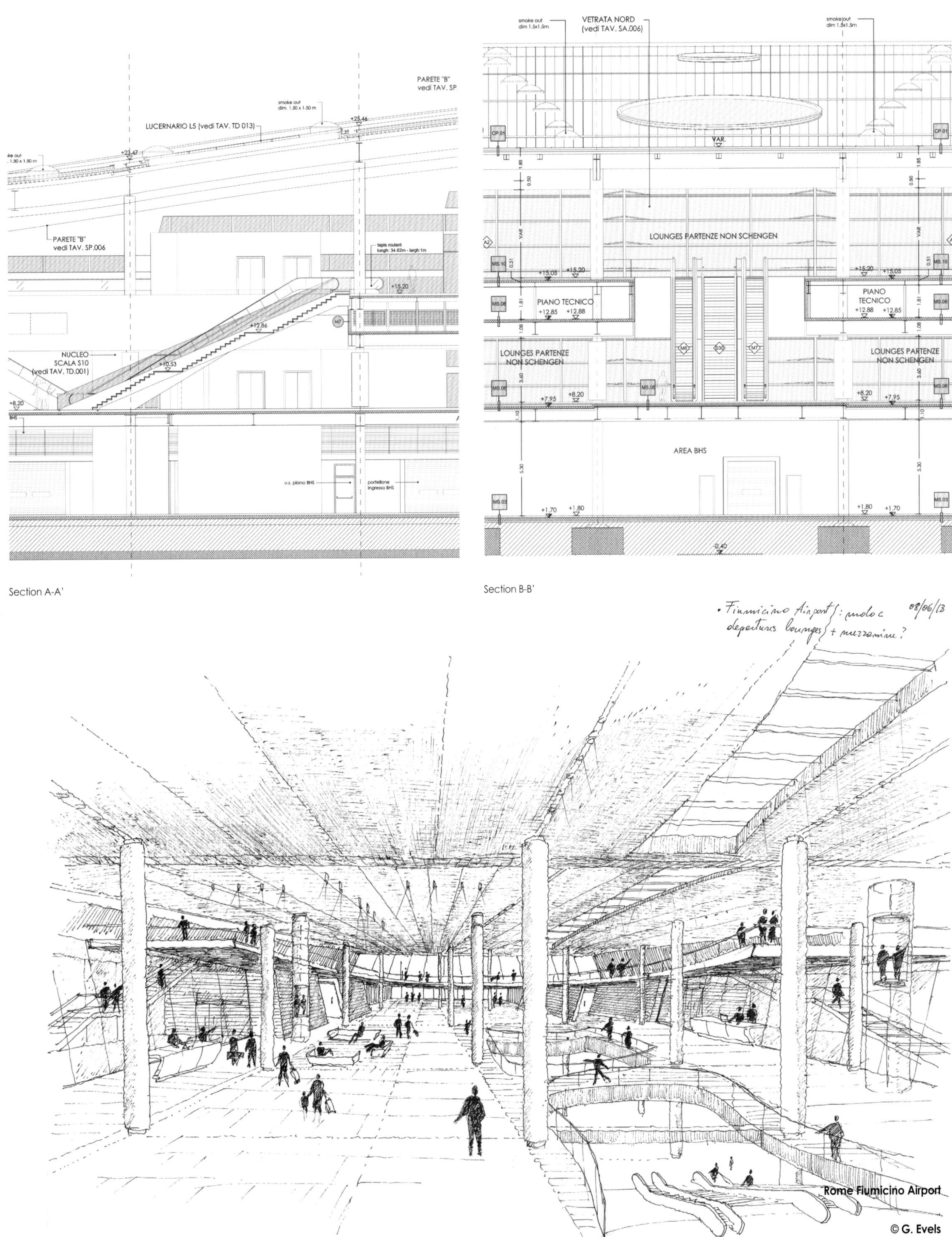

Section A-A'

Section B-B'

Rome Fiumicino Airport

© G. Evels

BOARD

" For the stairs in the building might have appeared a bit too provocative and controversial for a foundation with strong ties to Marxist philosophy and Marxist theory.

마르크주의 철학과 이론의 성향이 강한 재단의 건물에서 에스컬레이터를 계단처럼 사용하는 것은 어쩌면 너무 도발적이거나 논란의 여지가 있을 수 있었겠다. "

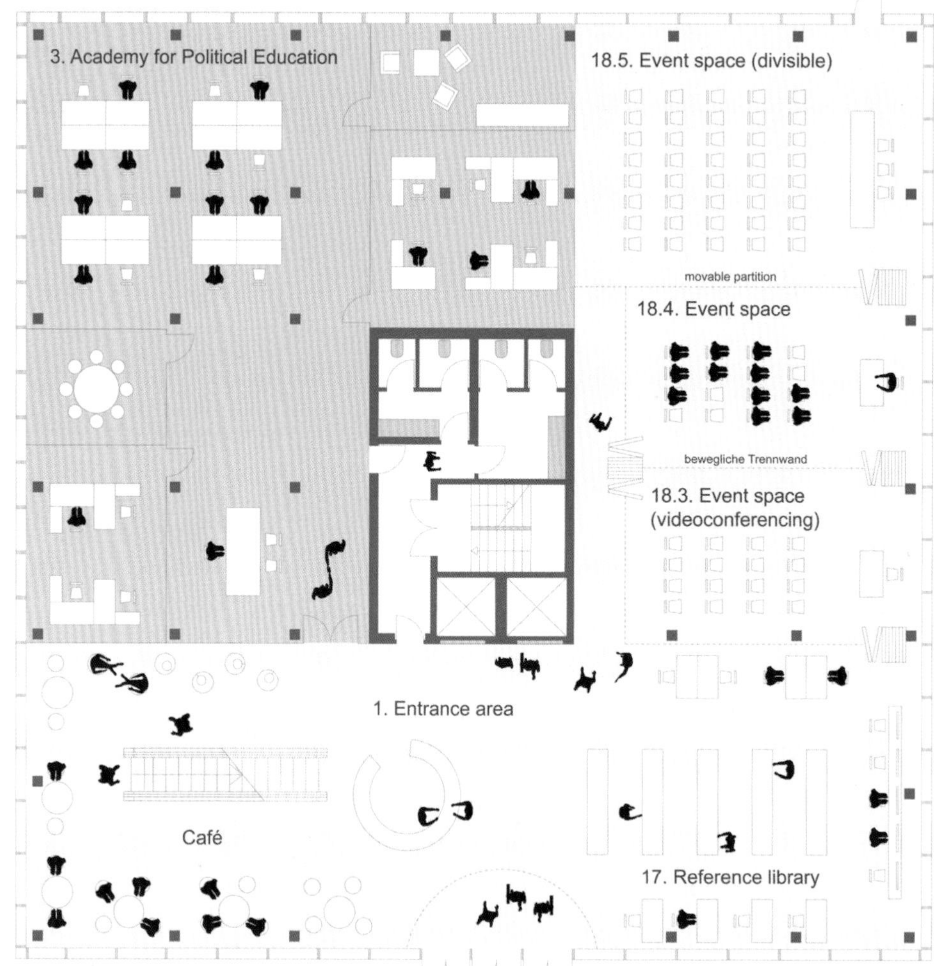

Ground Floor

Long Answer

When recently we worked on a design for a new office and administration building for the Rosa Luxemburg Foundation in Berlin, we proposed six large escalators that bring the visitors from the foyer to the top floor and a roof terrace that allows a view of the city and the TV tower on the Alexanderplatz. It is not that I disliked these escalators, I like them a lot. However, after our project was not selected during the competition in which we took part, I was wondering whether the use of escalators, to a certain extent the symbols of commercialization and capitalism, for the stairs in the building might have appeared a bit too provocative and controversial for a foundation with strong ties to Marxist philosophy and Marxist theory.

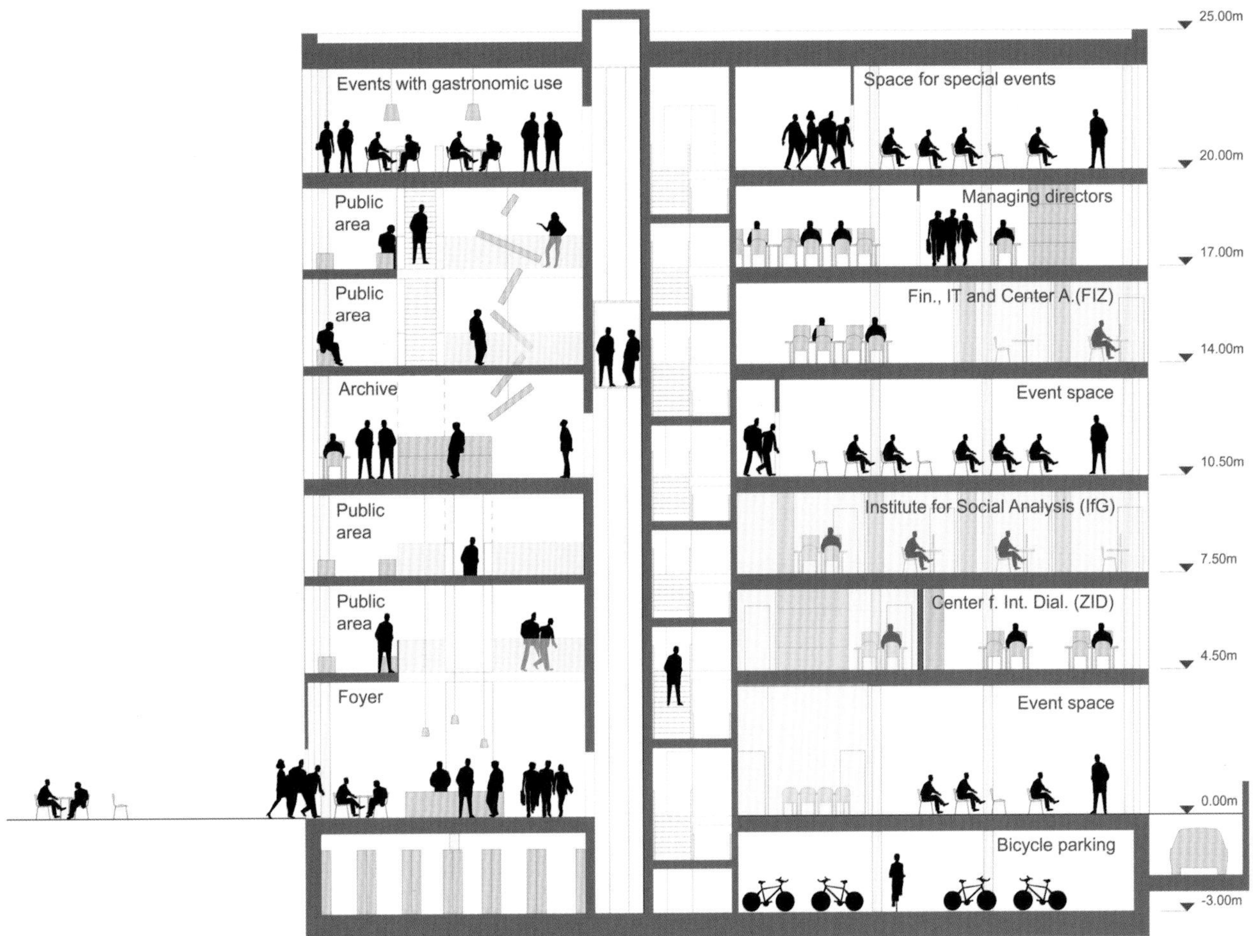

Section A-A'

The Rosa Luxemburg Foundation

ELA - Edu Lopez Architects

" Undoubtedly some of the stairs that, to my mind are the worst, are those that require a single function, such as evacuation and require a very strict regulation of size and position with respect to the building.

망설일 필요도 없이 우리가 생각하는 최악의 계단은 대피와 같은 단일 기능만이 요구되거나 건물 조건상 크기와 위치가 엄격히 규제되는 경우이다. "

Exterior perspective view

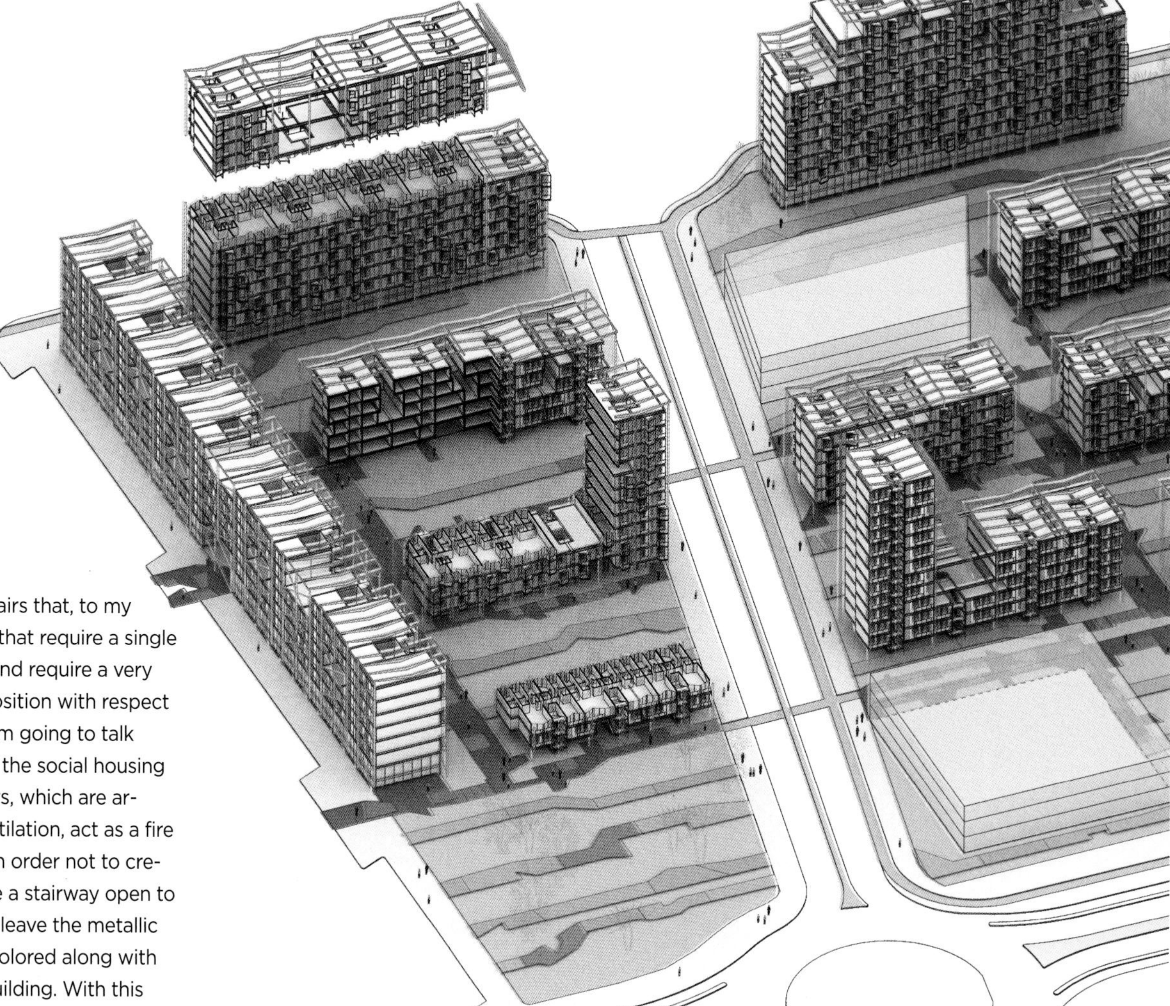

Axonometric view of the complex buildings

Long Answer

Undoubtedly some of the stairs that, to my mind are the worst, are those that require a single function, such as evacuation and require a very strict regulation of size and position with respect to the building. In this case I am going to talk about the evacuation stairs of the social housing of Malaga in Spain. These stairs, which are arranged in front for natural ventilation, act as a fire escape element. In this case, in order not to create a residual space, we create a stairway open to the outside by its landing and leave the metallic structure seen, which will be colored along with the general structure of the building. With this we create a staircase that gives unity and formal sense to the big residential buildings.

“Various egress stairs, because of a deadly combination of grim detailing and no daylight.

여러 대피 계단들이다. 빛이 들지 않는 음산한 디테일의 죽은 듯한 조합이다.”

NL Architects

Long Answer

Any stair that we build in housing projects in the Netherlands. They somehow dodge the design process; they are generated by the industry: cheap and efficient, but not very attractive. The paradox is that these stairs are the closest thing to robotization in our profession. This type of stair is fully optimized, with the least material used, incredible precision in manufacturing, scripting, computation, CNC milling. Very impressive. My father always told me that if form follows force this by definition leads to beauty. But the results are disappointing. Apparently this is a myth. These stairs are super intelligent but look stupid!

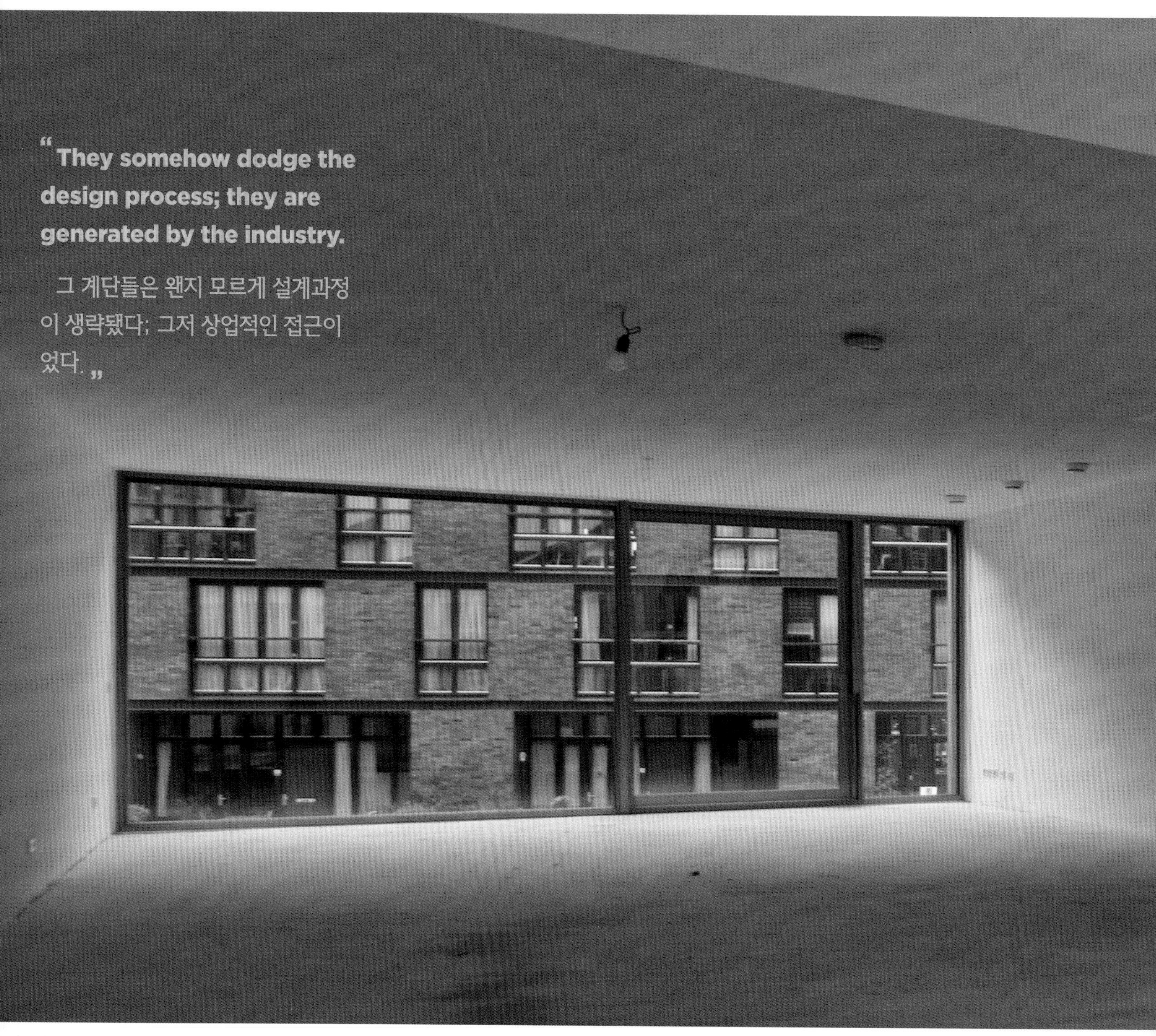

"They somehow dodge the design process; they are generated by the industry.

그 계단들은 왠지 모르게 설계과정이 생략됐다; 그저 상업적인 접근이었다."

Housing projects in the Netherlands.

SLOT STUDIO

Long Answer

Designing something as basic as a stairway is always a creative challenge, insofar as it entails questioning basic systems of composition where elemental precepts of form and function are closely linked. The ones that we don't like are those that do not challenge us, those that because of technical restrictions and building codes serve only as a linking resource.

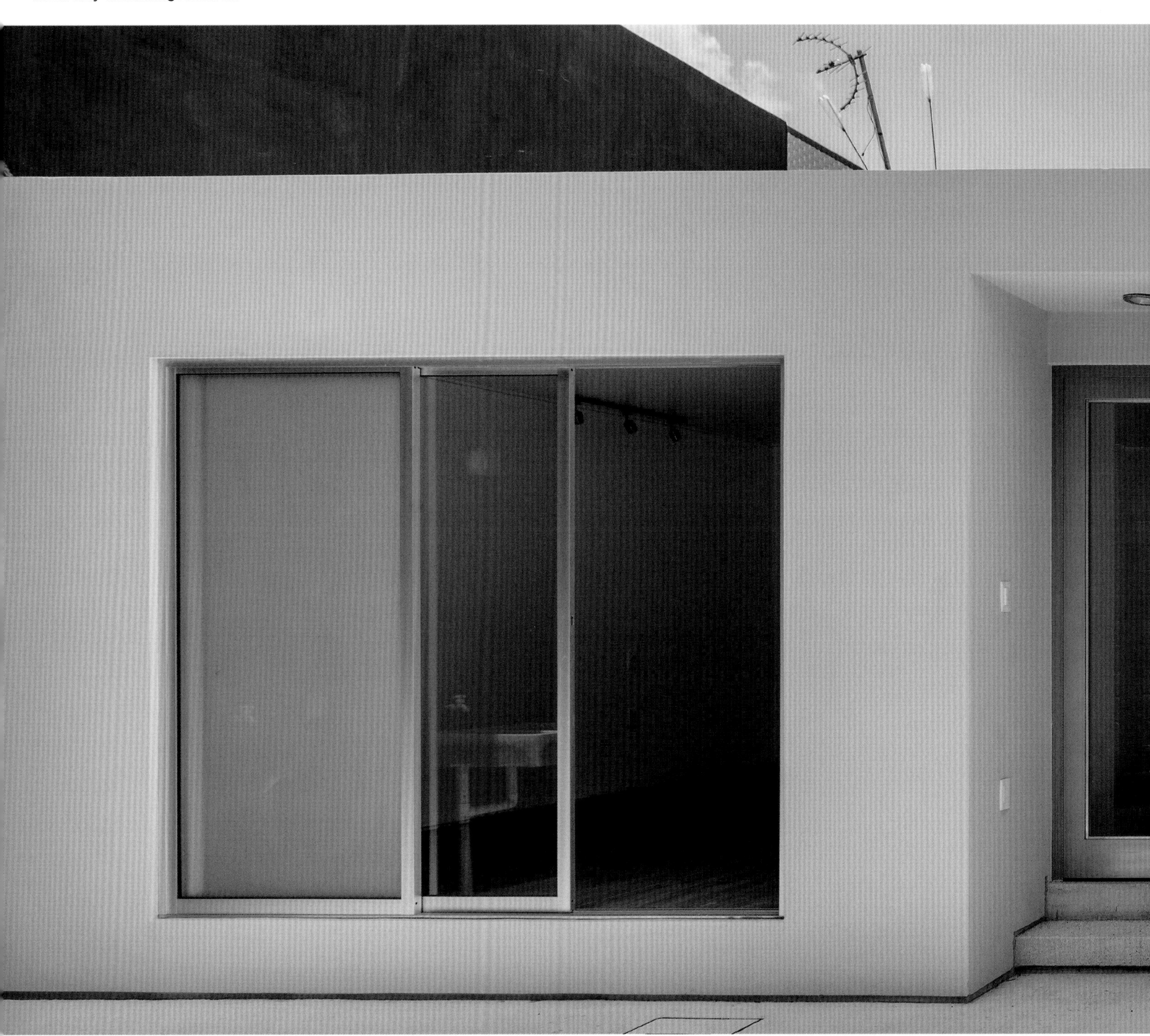

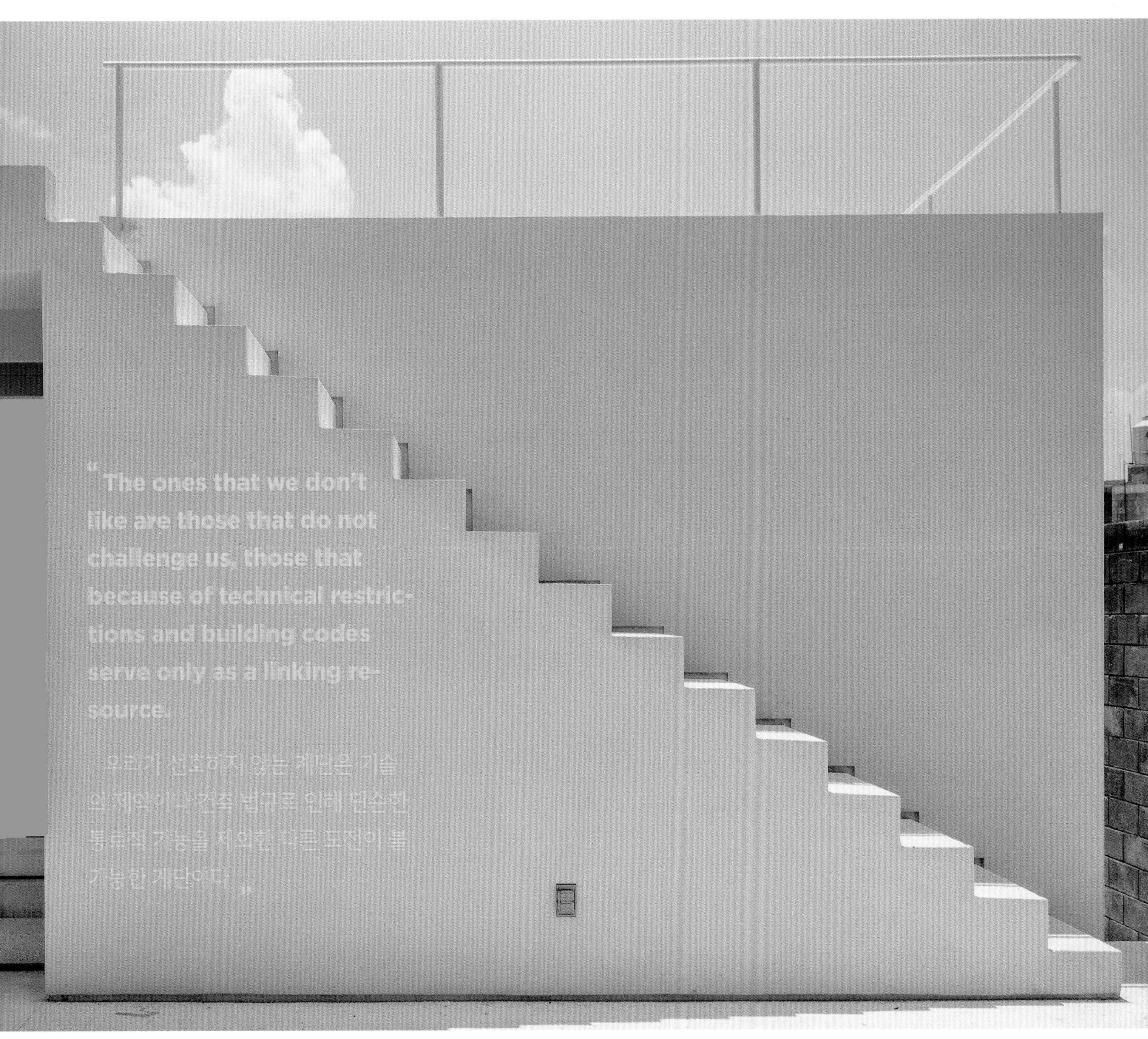

"The ones that we don't like are those that do not challenge us, those that because of technical restrictions and building codes serve only as a linking resource.

우리가 선호하지 않는 계단은 기술의 제약이나 건축 법규로 인해 단순한 통로적 기능을 제외한 다른 도전이 불가능한 계단이다."

TOUCH Architect

" It was very hard in construction since the extremely slope of the terrain caused a lot of obstacle during the construction.

경사가 급한 지형이라 여러 방해 요건들이 초래되어 시공하기에 매우 어려웠다. "

Long Answer

The stairs of TREE Sukkasem VILLA which is located on top of the hill. It was very hard in construction since the extremely slope of the terrain caused a lot of obstacle during the construction. Thus, it had been redesigned in order to follow the curve of the terrain.

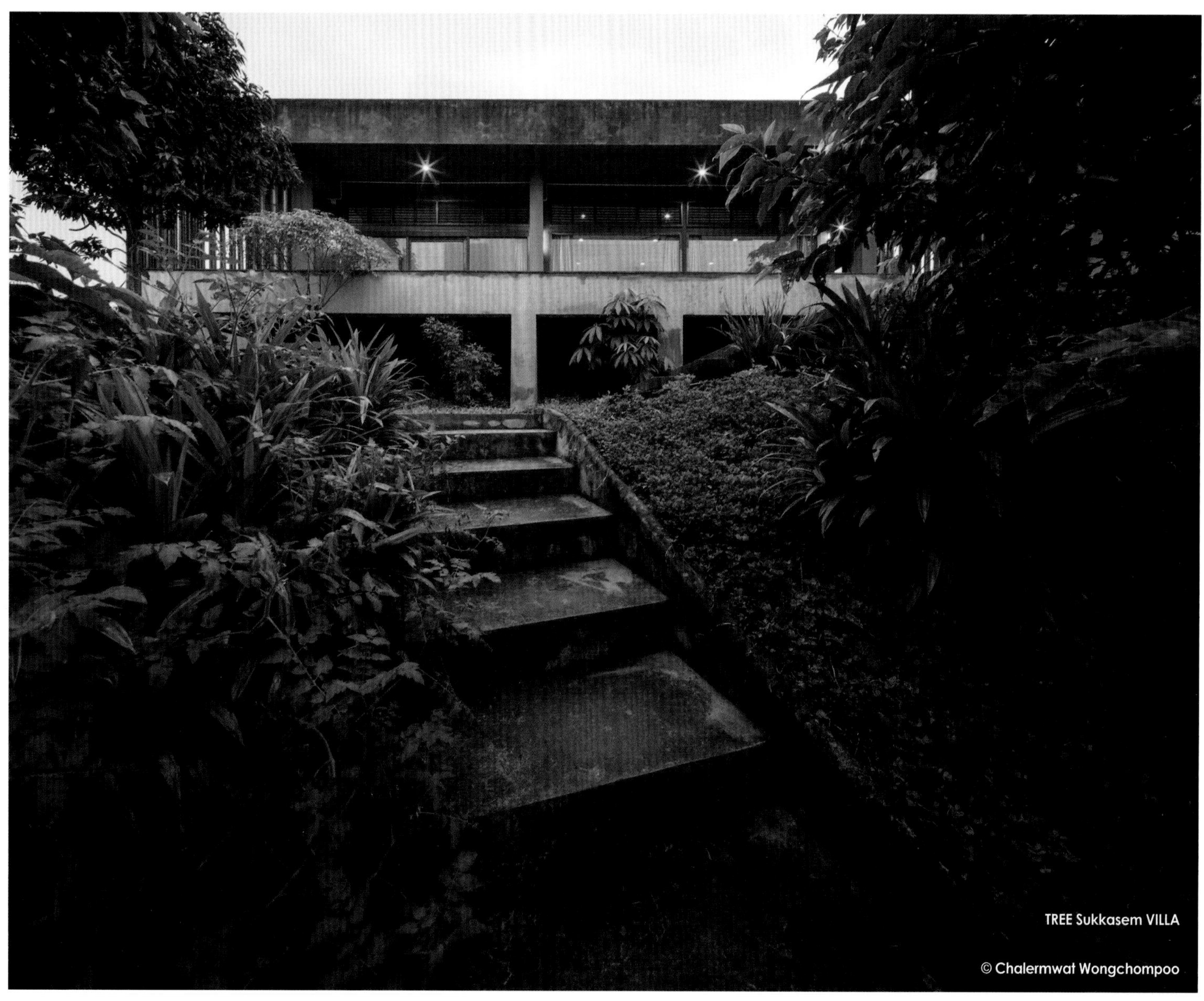

TREE Sukkasem VILLA

© Chalermwat Wongchompoo

자신이 설계한 계단 중 마음에 들지 않는 것은 무엇인가? 그 이유는?

Ezequiel Farca + Cristina Grappin

I don't have any. I think that every stair design has its own special purpose, they are a path of something new to discover in a place.

그런 계단은 없다. 모든 계단 디자인은 그 만의 특별한 목적이 있다고 생각한다. 계단은 어딘가로 향하는 새로운 모험의 길이다.

Stefano Corbo Studio

Normally all of those vertical connectors that only respond to functional requirements are aesthetically irrelevant: sometimes these elements are invisible or separated by the main circulation system of the building.
All of my projects are characterized by plenty of such staircases: these are necessary for the functioning of architecture.

기능적 요건만 충족시키는 수직 연결 통로는 거의 다 미적인 것 과는 거리가 멀다: 심미적인 요소들은 때론 감춰져 있거나 주된 순환체계 기능으로 인해 분산 되기도 한다.
모든 나의 프로젝트에는 이런 계단들이 많다: 이들은 건축 기능을 위해서 불가피하다.

Miha Volgemut architect

All stairs that serve pure function without any creative ambition are my least favourite, I surely designed couple of them. The stairs are always an opportunity to design something more, if not the shape or geometry, it can be lightning or materialization etc.

창의적인 도전 없이 그저 단순한 기능만을 가진 계단이 제일 별로이다. 나도 분명이 그런 계단을 몇 번 디자인한 적 있다. 계단은 언제나 무언가를 더 디자인 할 수 있는 기회이다. 형태나 모양으로 안된다면 조명이나 재료 등으로 할 수 있다.

TROPICAL SPACE

All staircase, which just only use for circulation

이동만이 목적인 모든 계단.

Moussafir Architectes

There are many: all stairs which are only functional, which deal with physical elevation with no concern for spiritual elevation.

많이 있다: 정신적 고양에 대한 고민없이 물리적인 상승만을 고려한 단지 기능적인 모든 계단이다.

P.046

최근 몇 년 전에 한 엔지니어링 단체가 우리에게 로마 피우미치노 공항 일부를 위한 건축 설계 및 인테리어 디자인 프로젝트에 디자인 팀으로 참여해 달라고 요청해왔다. 우리는 모든 직원들과 함께 엄청난 열정을 쏟으며 작업하였다. 그 과정에서 집결되어 있는 에스컬레이터들과 고정된 계단을 위한 특별 맞춤 디자인 작업에 참여하게 되었다. 사용자들의 편의를 위해 복잡한 교차공간을 해결하는데 많은 시간이 걸렸지만, 마침내 멋진 해결책을 찾아냈고, 최종 검토를 위해 클라이언트에게 전달하였다. 프로젝트는 건축주의 전문가들에 의해 전혀 다른 느낌으로 변형 되어 돌아왔으며, 계단 아래에 많은 기둥들을 삽입하라는 요청으로 가벼움을 완전히 상실한 상태였다. 우리는 그 기둥들이 필요 없다고 증명해 봤지만, 프로젝트 진행 스케줄 상 다른 대안을 제안하기에 너무 늦은 시기였다. 그렇게 하여 우리는 전혀 만족스럽지 못한 타협을 받아들여야만 했다.

b4architects

P.048

최근 우리는 베를린에 있는 로사 룩셈부르그 재단의 사무 및 행정 사옥 설계 공모전에서 로비에서부터 도시전경과 알렉산더 광장의 베를린TV 타워가 보이는 꼭대기 층 및 루프테라스까지 이어지는 여섯 개의 커다란 에스컬레이터를 제안하였다. 이 에스컬레이터들을 싫어한다는 게 아니다. 매우 좋아한다. 하지만, 공모전에서 우리 설계안이 채택되지 않은 뒤 나는 에스컬레이터의 사용이 다소 상업화와 자본주의를 상징한 게 아니었는가 하는 의문이 들었다. 마르크주의 철학과 이론의 성향이 강한 재단의 건물에서 에스컬레이터를 계단처럼 사용하는 것은 어쩌면 너무 도발적이거나 논란의 여지가 있을 수 있었겠다.

BOARD

P.050

망설일 필요도 없이 우리가 생각하는 최악의 계단은 대피와 같은 단일 기능만이 요구되거나 건물 조건상 크기와 위치가 엄격히 규제되는 경우이다. 그 예로 스페인 말라가의 공동주택의 피난 계단에 대해 이야기 하겠다. 이 계단은 자연 환기 시설 전면에 배치되어 화재 탈출구로 쓰인다. 잔여 공간이 생기지 않도록 계단 참을 바깥으로 빼어 열린 계단으로 디자인하였고 건물 구조 색과 어울리게 계단의 철골 구조를 그대로 노출시켰다. 이렇게 해서 우리는 그나마 커다란 주거 건물에 통일성과 양식의 개념을 부여하는 계단을 창조한 셈이다.

ELA - Edu Lopez Architects

P.051

여러 대피 계단들이다. 빛이 들지 않는 음산한 디테일의 죽은 듯한 조합이다.

OPA

P.052

모든 네덜란드 주택 프로젝트에서 설계한 계단이다. 그 계단들은 왠지 모르게 설계과정이 생략됐다; 그저 상업적인 접근이었다: 저렴하고 효율적이지만, 그다지 매력 없는. 역설적이게도 이 계단들은 우리 경력 중 가장 자동화에 가까운 것들이었다. 이런 유형은 최소한의 재료로 믿기 어려울 정도로 정확한 제조, 스크립팅, 산출, CNC milling 과정을 거친 최적화된 상태의 계단이다. 매우 인상적이다. 내 아버지는 늘 나에게 '힘에 의한 형태는 그 자체로도 아름답다.'라고 말씀하셨다. 하지만, 그 결과는 실망스럽다. 이 말은 근거 없는 믿음인 듯하다. 이 계단들은 무지 똑똑하지만, 못 생겼다!

NL Architects

P.054

계단처럼 가장 기본적인 무언가를 디자인하는 데에는 형태와 기능이 밀접한 관계에 놓인 기본구성시스템을 갖춰야하기 때문에 늘 창의적인 도전이 필요하다. 우리가 선호하지 않는 계단은 기술의 제약이나 건축 법규로 인해 단순한 통로적 기능을 제외한 다른 도전이 불가능한 계단이다.

SLOT STUDIO

P.056

태국 TREE Sukkasem VILLA의 계단으로 언덕 꼭대기에 설계된 주택이다. 경사가 급한 지형이라 여러 방해 요건들이 초래되어 시공하기에 매우 어려웠다. 결국, 지형 곡선에 따라 재 설계하였다.

TOUCH Architect

Q3

Are there any **memorable moments** about designing stairs?

b4architects

Long Answer

During an intense period in a complicated building site due to structural reasons in a renewal operation for an historical house on two levels in Rome, we demolished an old stair in masonry to replace it with a new one in steel and wood. The landing system of the new stair was inverted to best use the windows of the first floor that were located on one side only. During the construction the national regulation for seismic protection was changed in many aspects. The result on the work was that after the new rules all the new architectural part added or reconstructed in a building must be isolated and not connected with the preexisting bearing walls. So we forced a new solution and the stair was completely suspended on steel cables to the roof slab of the stairwell conveniently reinforced and the stair was connected to the walls with only thin spacer brackets. The final architectural effect was very interesting for us because at the end we obtained a very light stair not in direct contact with the perimetral walls inserted in an heavy structure made of masonry walls. This was exalted also by the choice to insert in the space between the steel beams and the walls a dedicated lighting system.

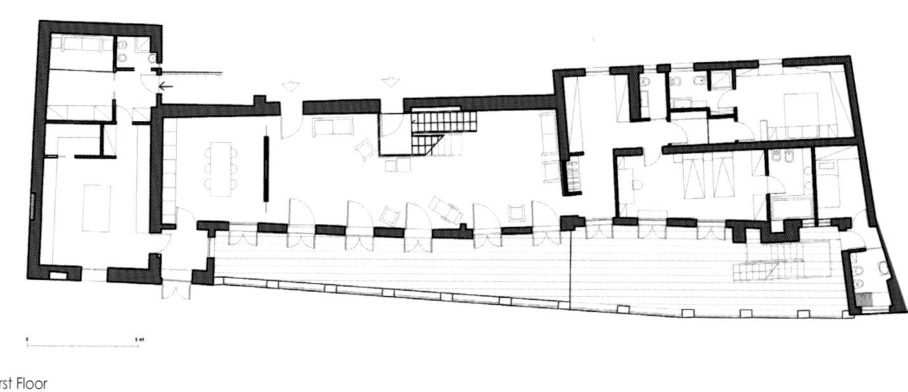

First Floor

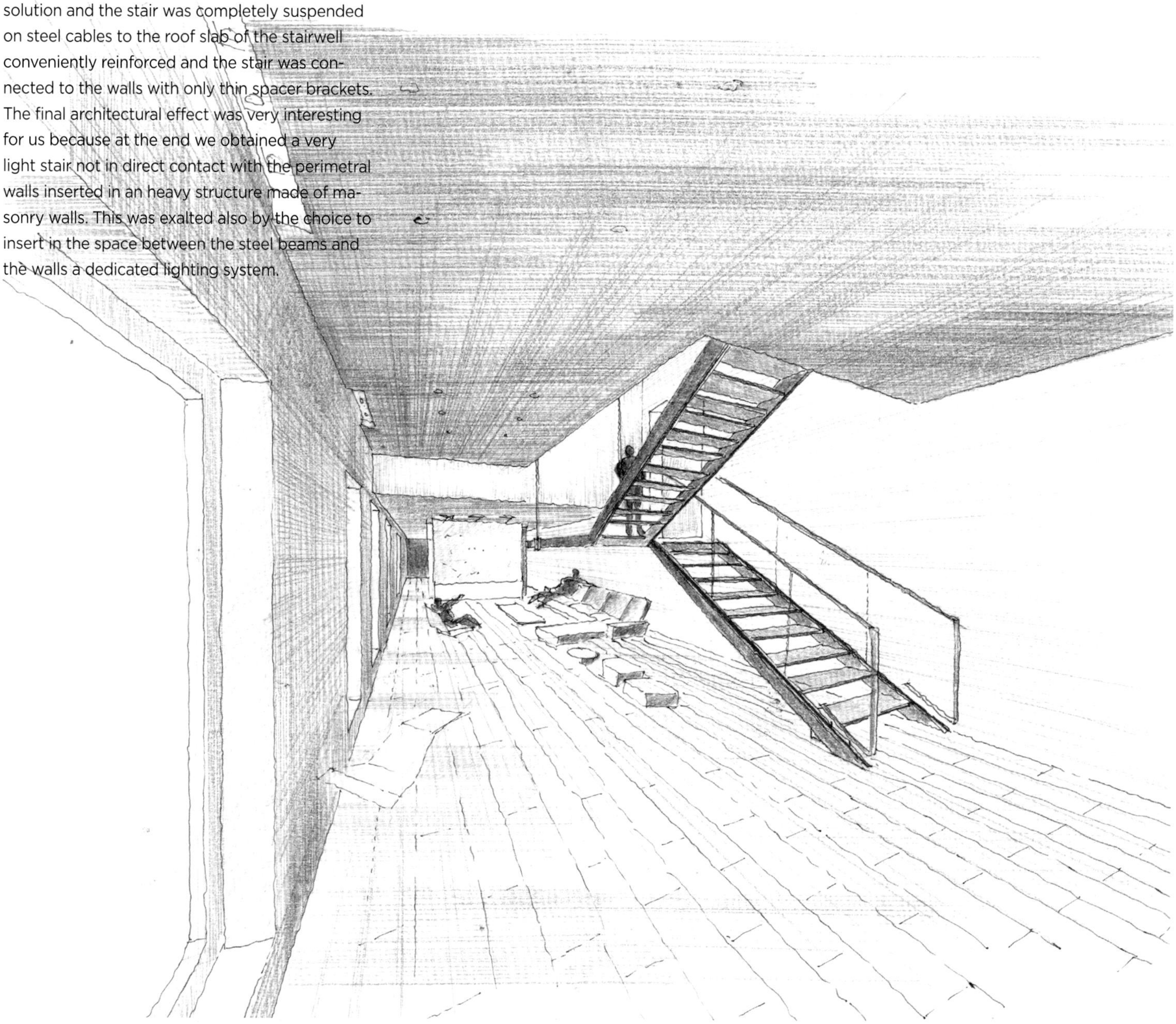

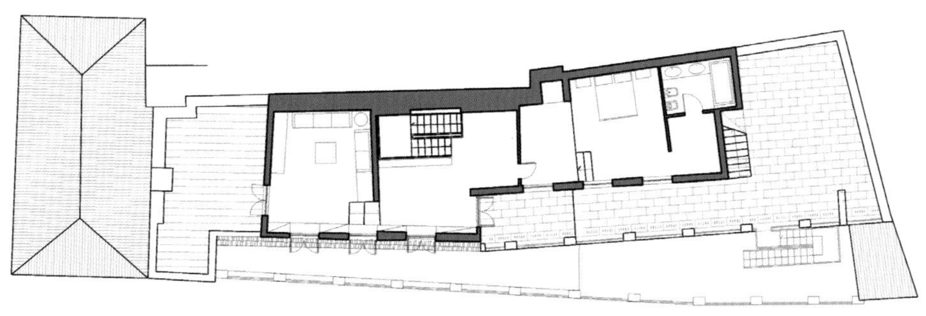

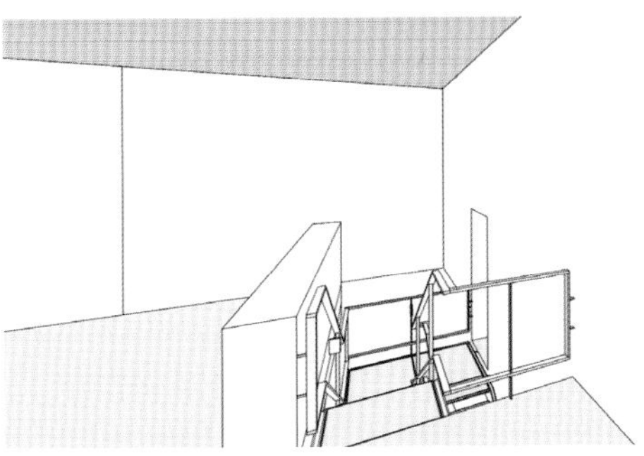

Second Floor

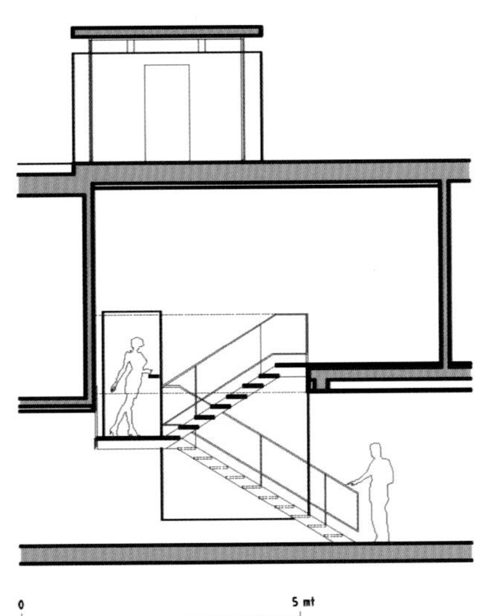

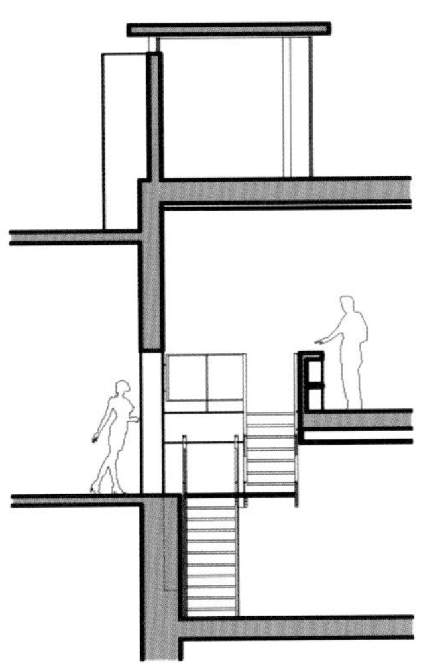

Section Detail on the Stairs

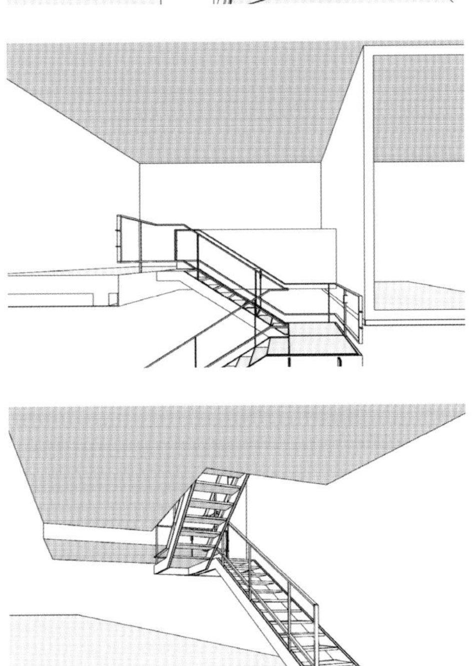

Perspective on the Stairs

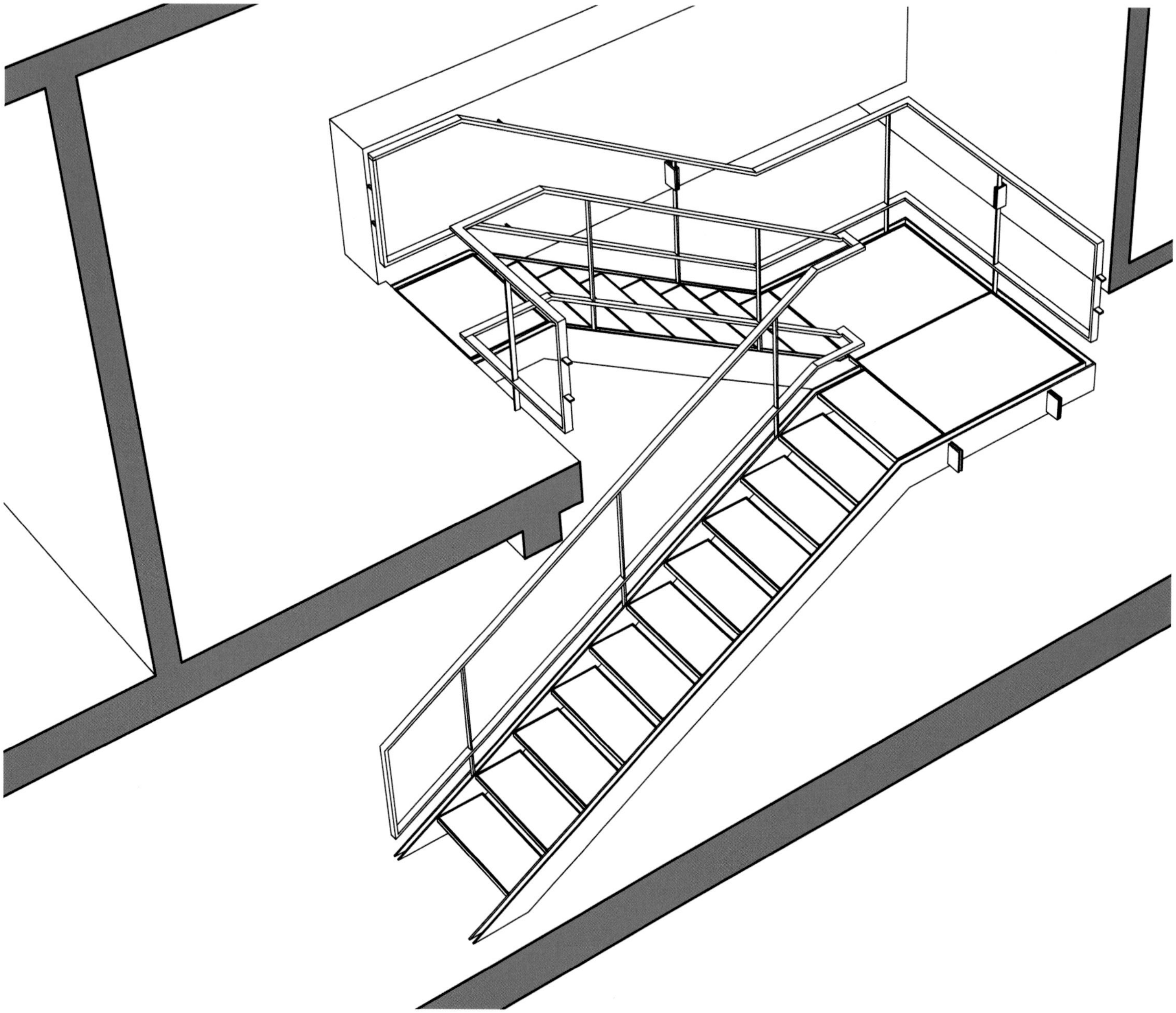

"The landing system of the new stair was inverted to best use the windows of the first floor that were located on one side only.

한쪽 벽면에만 위치한 일층 창문을 가장 용이하게 사용할 수 있도록 계단참 구조를 변형하였다."

e house

BOARD

“We had to improvise and designed a metal ladder-like stair that was heavy enough to bring you up safely but light enough to transport and hang inside of the toilet with the rain-shower.

우리는 즉흥적으로 안전하게 올라갈 수 있을 정도로 튼튼하면서 샤워실이 있는 화장실로 옮겨 걸어 둘 수 있을 정도로 가벼운 철제 사다리 계단을 디자인하였다.”

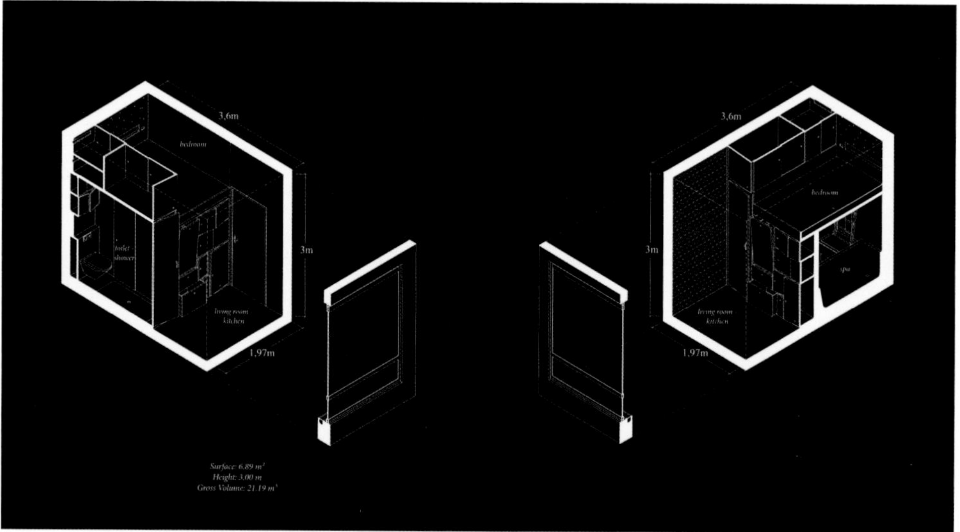

The four rooms

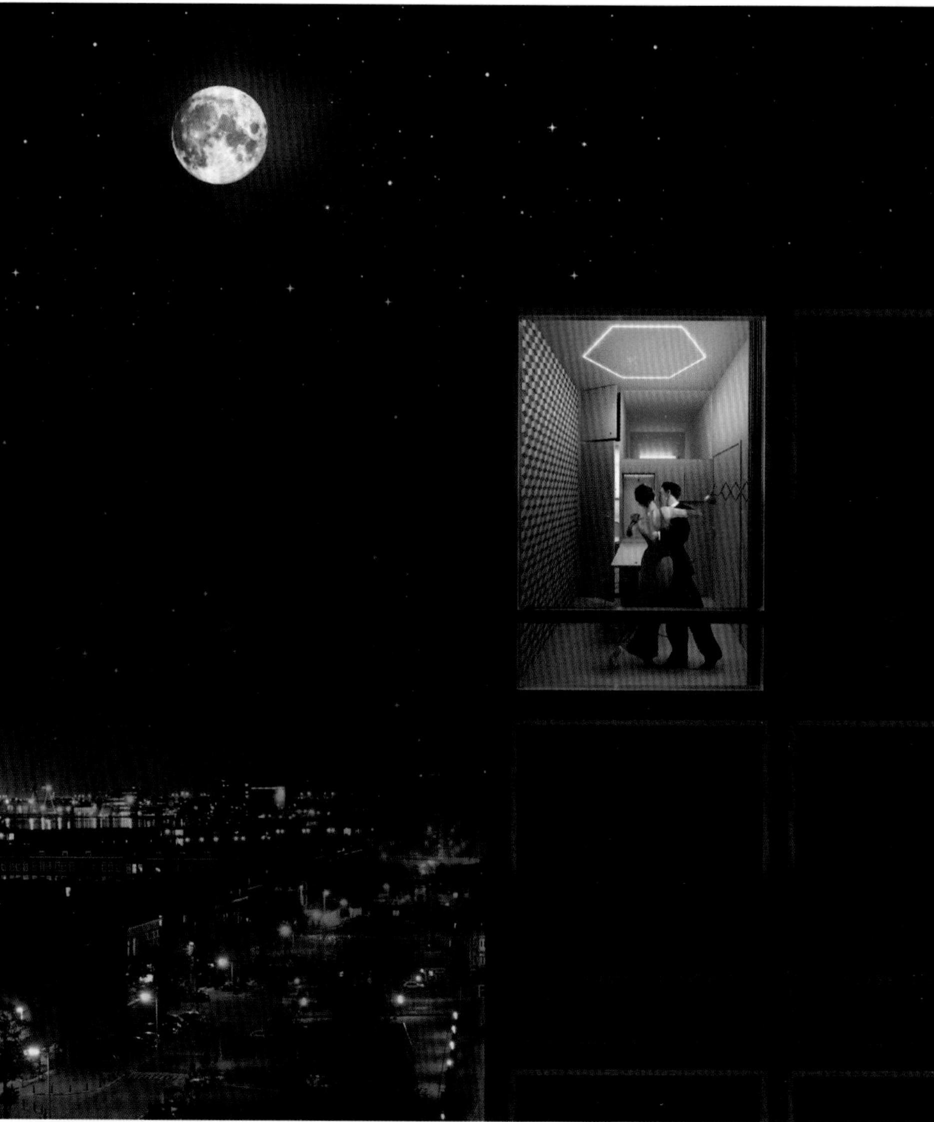

Long Answer

Together with the office STAR – strategies and architecture - we designed a very small living space in Rotterdam that is 3m high, 1,97m wide, and 3,6m long. We called it “The Cabanon” and believe that - with a size of 6,89m2 - it is most likely the smallest apartment in the world. It has four rooms: a living room with kitchen, a toilet with rain-shower, a bedroom with plenty of storage, and a spa. Once we finished the design, we realized that the apartment was so small that there was not sufficient space for a proper stair that would bring you up to the elevated bedroom. So, we had to improvise and designed a metal ladder-like stair that was heavy enough to bring you up safely but light enough to transport and hang inside of the toilet with the rain-shower.

© BOARD and STAR – strategies and architecture

The Cabanon

© BOARD and STAR – strategies and architecture

ELA - Edu Lopez Architects

" The visual relationships that are created between the two ramps are very patent and strong since everyone sees everyone but they really do not know at what point of the building they are.

두 램프 사이에서는 모두가 모두를 볼 수 있지만 자신이 정확히 어디에 있는지 알 수 없는 특이하면서도 강렬한 시각적 관계가 일어난다. "

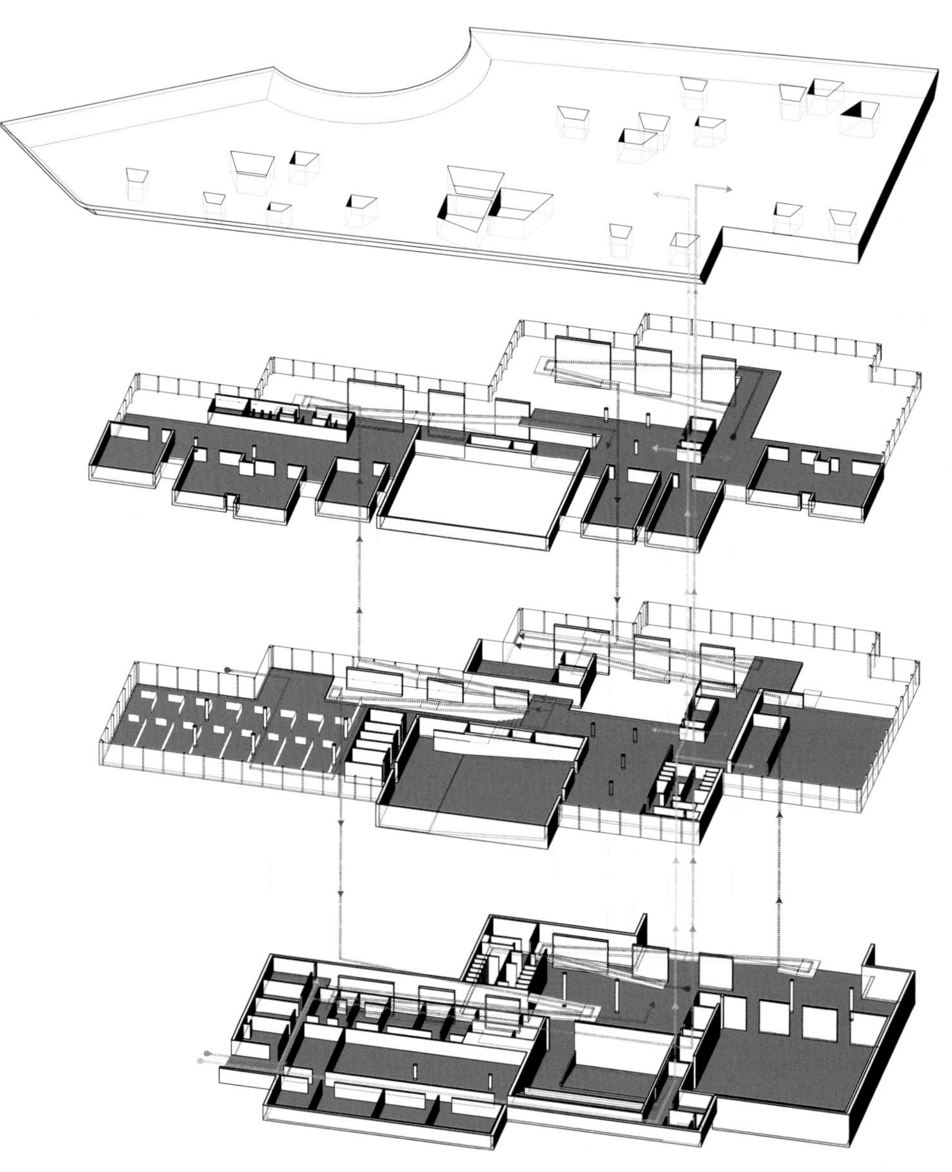

Circulation scheme of the visitor center for the Reichstag

Long Answer

For me to design any ladder or ramp is always a unique challenge, because they are usually a main object in all our projects. I usually create the interior spaces around an element that connects different spaces in height and that articulates the circulation. This is the precise case of the ramps that were created for the visitor center of the Reichstag in Berlin. The client needed a double circulation, one of entrance and another of exit, where the users could not be mixed by the own security of the building. For them the action I decided to do is to create a double filter through two ramps, The first of them gave access to the visitor center and served as a security mode and the second of them gave service to the exit of the own center after having visited the Reichstag. With this we were able to divide the building in two through the circulation, but at the same time creating the same space. The visual relationships that are created between the two ramps are very patent and strong since everyone sees everyone but they really do not know at what point of the building they are.

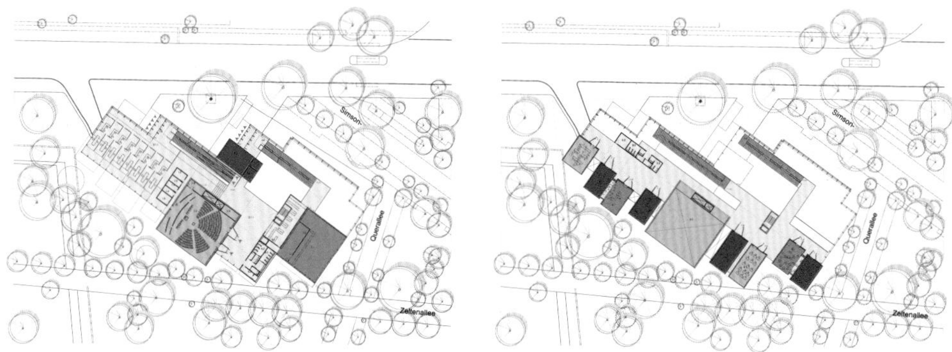

Floor plan of the building

Ezequiel Farca + Cristina Grappin

> " **But finally we learned about the resistance of the material and the aesthetics.**
>
> 결론적으로 우리는 재료와 미학은 별개라는 것을 깨달았다. "

Long Answer

The art collector, the one of the first question, asked us for the stairs to be made of glass, for us it was a challenge, we had never made similar ones, but finally we learned about the resistance of the material and the aesthetics. I was initially quite skeptical about the style.

© Jaime Navarro

Katsuhiro Miyamoto & Associates

> " The gradient of the staircase changes from the bottom (public) to the top (private), thus creating a rhythmic ascent.
>
> 계단 아래(공공공간)에서 위로(사적 공간)갈수록 경사도가 변하여 계단을 오르는 게 리드미컬하다. "

Long Answer

One memorable staircase design is from another project, SoHo functioning as a small office / home office. Designed as a one room space with split levels for various functions, there are 4 flights of staircase connecting each level. The gradient of the staircase changes from the bottom (public) to the top (private), thus creating a rhythmic ascent.

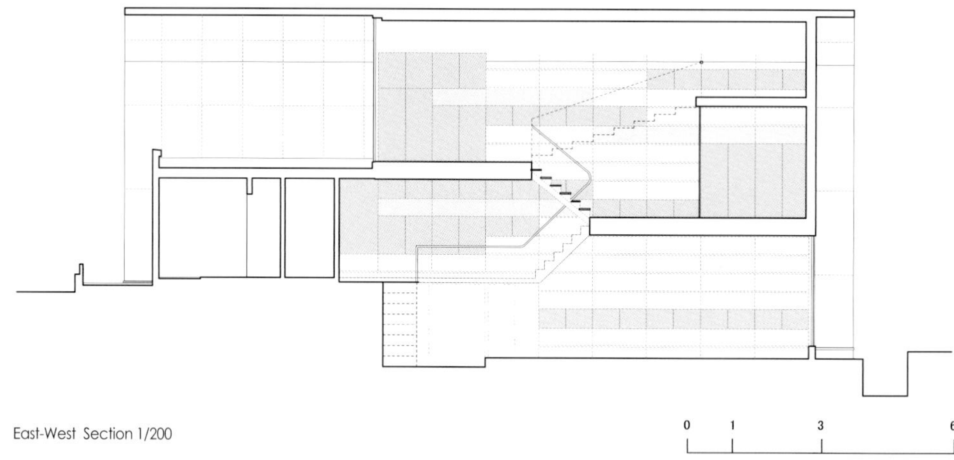

East-West Section 1/200

SoHo

Moussafir Architectes

"Apart from the fact that stairs are often tricky regarding geometry and construction, their design appears to me mostly related to their surroundings.

대개 계단은 형태적으로나 구조적으로 까다롭다는 사실 이외에 계단의 디자인은 주변 환경과 가장 큰 연관성이 있는 것 같다."

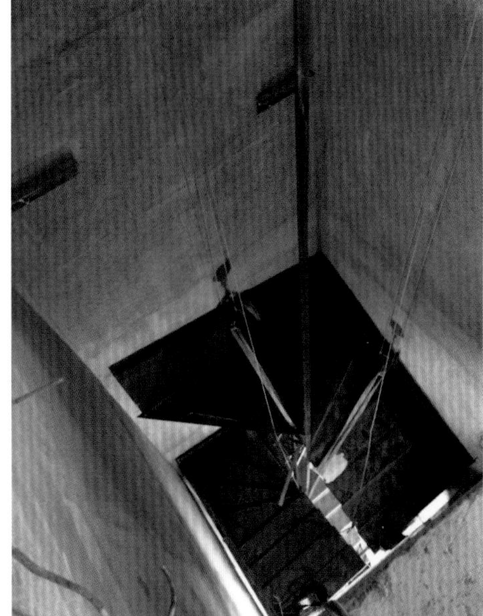

Long Answer

Apart from the fact that stairs are often tricky regarding geometry and construction, their design appears to me mostly related to their surroundings. A memorable moment I can think of, is when we were obliged to tear down a piece of concrete wall at the top of a staircase in order to enter prefabricated steel parts of the stairs which were suspended and had to be positioned starting from the bottom.

NL Architects

"In order to enlarge the joy of browsing through the building we hope to manipulate the direction of the flow .

이동의 방향을 조작함으로써 건물을 둘러보는 즐거움을 증대 시킬 수 있기를 기대한다."

Long Answer

We are currently building the Groninger Forum. This 'center for information and debate' is conceived around a large atrium with horizontal branches, squares in the air, that are connected with escalators. In order to enlarge the joy of browsing through the building we hope to manipulate the direction of the flow : a kind of deejay that decides if they move up or down.

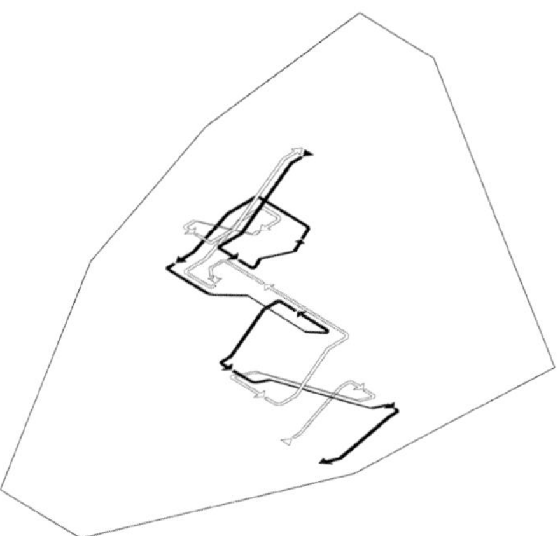

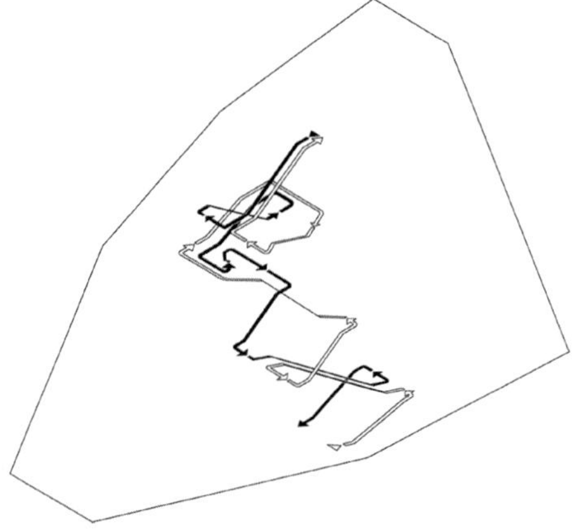

the Groninger Forum

" When reaching the house, the staircase invites the visitor to ascent on the roof and encounter' the horizon that appears on the distance, extended in a way by the flat part of the roof all the way to where the viewer is.

집에 도착하자 마자 계단은 방문객을 지붕으로 인도하여 멀리 보이는 수평선과의 '만남'을 주선한다. "

Long Answer

Casa Malaparte, built on the eastern side of the island of Capri by Curzio Malaparte, is a unique design in many different ways. One of them is the stairway on the back of the house, which leads to its patio. The stairway, which is in fact also the 'roof' of the north-west part of the house, has a prismatic shape that extends the main, rectangular volume of the house. It is the first element one encounters physically when approaching the house from the land, which can be done only on foot through a rough, mountainous landscape. When reaching the house, the staircase invites the visitor to ascent on the roof and 'encounter' the horizon that appears on the distance, extended in a way by the flat part of the roof all the way to where the viewer is. The roughness of the landscape the visitor had to walk through is reflected in the staircase: no handrail or other protective element is present on the sides of the stairs, something that is repeated on the patio. That creates a sense of danger, greatly enhanced by the surrounding landscape, but at the same time a sense of freedom; the illusion that one can connect with the horizon across him/her.

The dramatic effect of the staircase has been captured in a spectacular way by Jean-Luc Godard on his 1963 film Le Mépris. In one of his final scenes, Paul Javal (portrayed by Michel Piccoli) ascents the staircase in search of his wife Camille Javal (portrayed by Brigitte Bardot). Godard frames the staircase in an almost absolute symmetrical way. The long shape of the staircase – and in extension of the house – comes in direct opposition to the wide format of the film, dividing the screen in two. And along with Piccoli, the spectator also ascends the stairs in order to finally meet the horizon as the camera pans upwards.

The staircase in Casa Malaparte manages to become a defining element of the building. It is no longer an element that connects two different levels; it is instead an architectural landscape that exceeds any distinction between separate architectural elements in order to create a unified, spatial experience.

Casa Malaparte

© Peter Schüle

OPA

" To emphasize this swirling, there is a dramatic change in both scale and geometry as the space is 'sucked' downwards.

소용돌이 형상을 강조하기 위해 마치 공간이 아래로 '빨려 들어가는' 것처럼 스케일과 형태에 극적인 변화들을 주었다. "

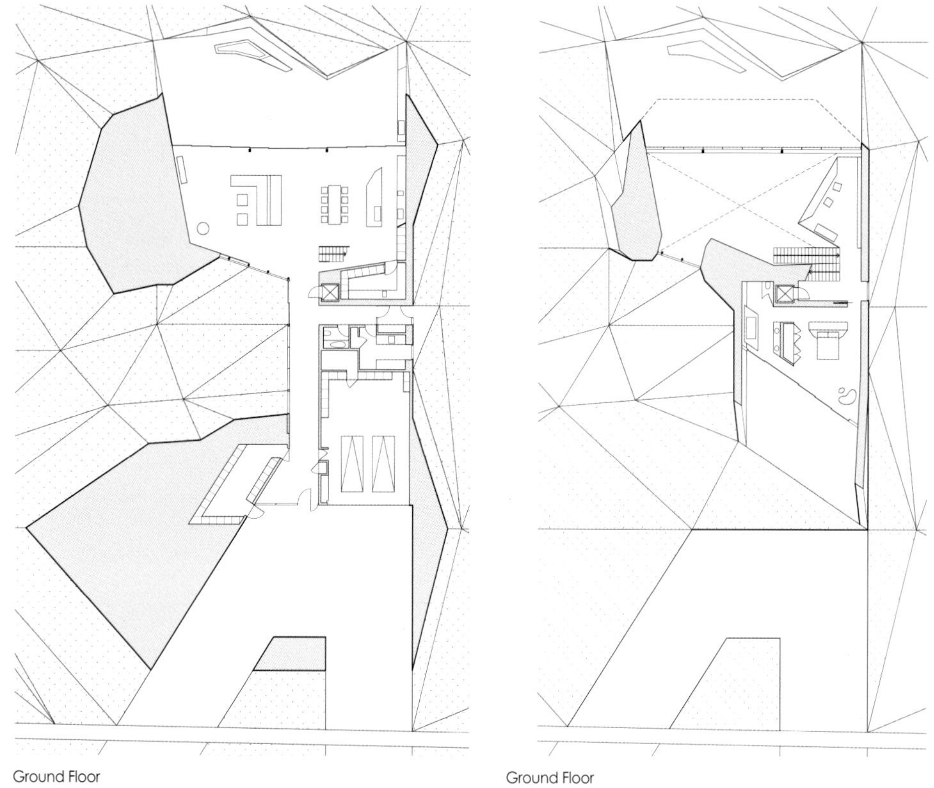

Ground Floor

Ground Floor

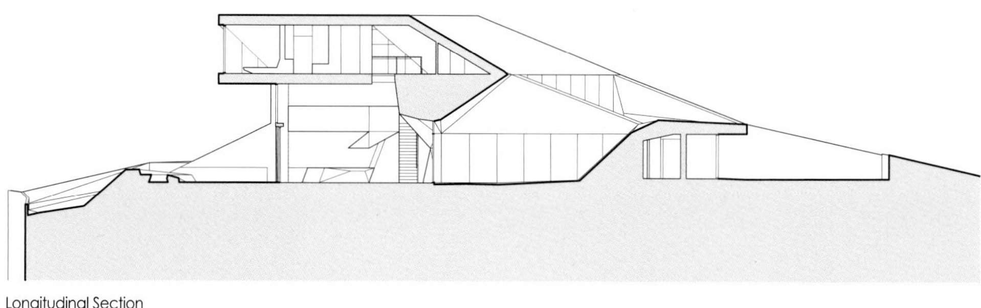

Longitudinal Section

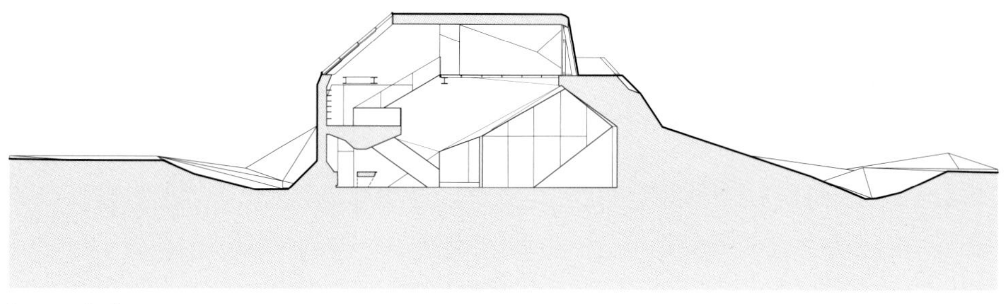

Transverse Section

Long Answer

The design of the main stair at Shapeshifter was particularly memorable. At some moment during design development we recognized that we could integrate several previously distinct elements into a single swirling composition fabricated entirely of thick plate steel. To emphasize this swirling, there is a dramatic change in both scale and geometry as the space is 'sucked' downwards.

Shapeshifter

SLOT STUDIO

"In this way, the pragmatics of a stairway opened the way to address an important aspect of life in the plant.

이 공공장소는 계단의 실용성이 만들어낸 공장의 활력소가 되었다."

Long Answer

In one of our industrial projects we needed to connect two volumes standing on ground with a difference of five meters because of the uneven topography of the site. In this problem we recognized an opportunity to create a significant public space where employees from every area of the plant could intermingle. In this way, the pragmatics of a stairway opened the way to address an important aspect of life in the plant.

Stefano Corbo Studio

"I enjoy designing staircases when these can function as threshold, as a real filter between different spatial conditions.

나는 여러 공간적 환경에서 실질적 필터의 역할을 하는 문턱의 기능을 가진 계단을 즐겨 디자인한다."

Long Answer

I enjoy designing staircases when these can function as threshold, as a real filter between different spatial conditions. I imagine any staircase as a bridge: it connects, unifies, but at the same time emphasizes differences and peculiarities.

TOUCH Architect

" Creating a step-like not only for easily being seen from outside which will attracts more people, but also allows more privacy for those who are dining on the terrace.

이 공간은 외부로 잘 드러나 있기 때문에 사람들이 쉽게 모이는 계단형 공간을 조성하며, 동시에 테라스에서 식사를 하는 손님들에게는 보다 더 사적인 공간을 제공한다. "

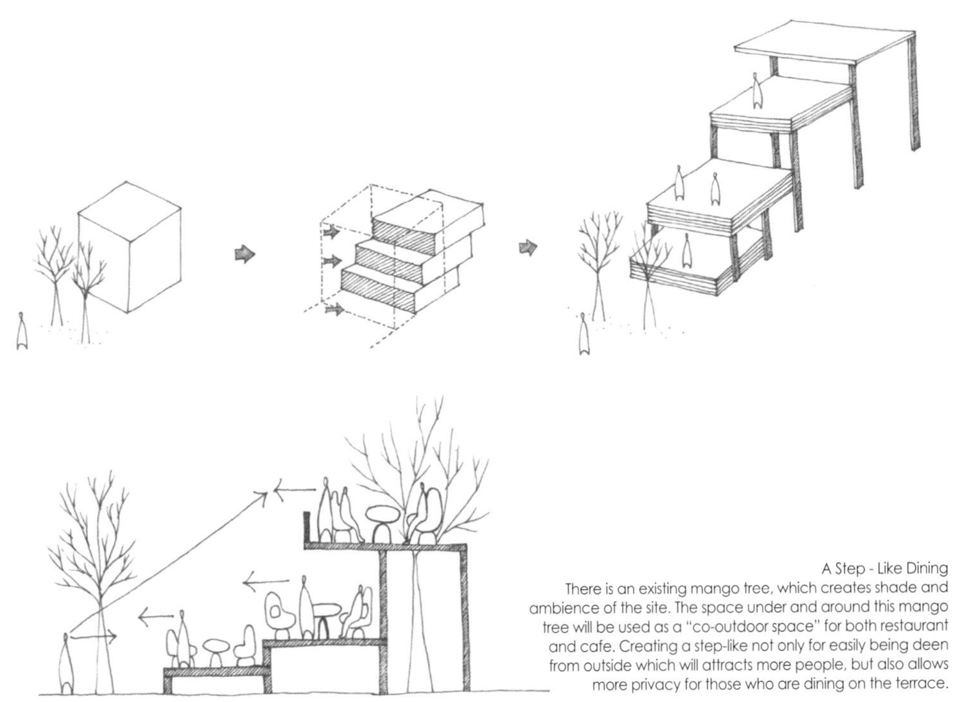

A Step - Like Dining
There is an existing mango tree, which creates shade and ambience of the site. The space under and around this mango tree will be used as a "co-outdoor space" for both restaurant and cafe. Creating a step-like not only for easily being deen from outside which will attracts more people, but also allows more privacy for those who are dining on the terrace.

PLAA-GUT

© Chalermwat wongchompoo

Long Answer

It is a Southern-Thai Cuisine named "PLAA-GUT" which is located at CBD in Bangkok. There is an existing mango tree, which creates shade and ambience of the site. The space underneath this mango tree will be used as a "co-outdoor space" for both restaurant and cafe. Creating a step-like not only for easily being seen from outside which will attracts more people, but also allows more privacy for those who are dining on the terrace.

TROPICAL SPACE

" The client wants to see an active space that showing chicken movement.

건축주는 닭의 활동이 보이는 동적인 공간을 기대했다. "

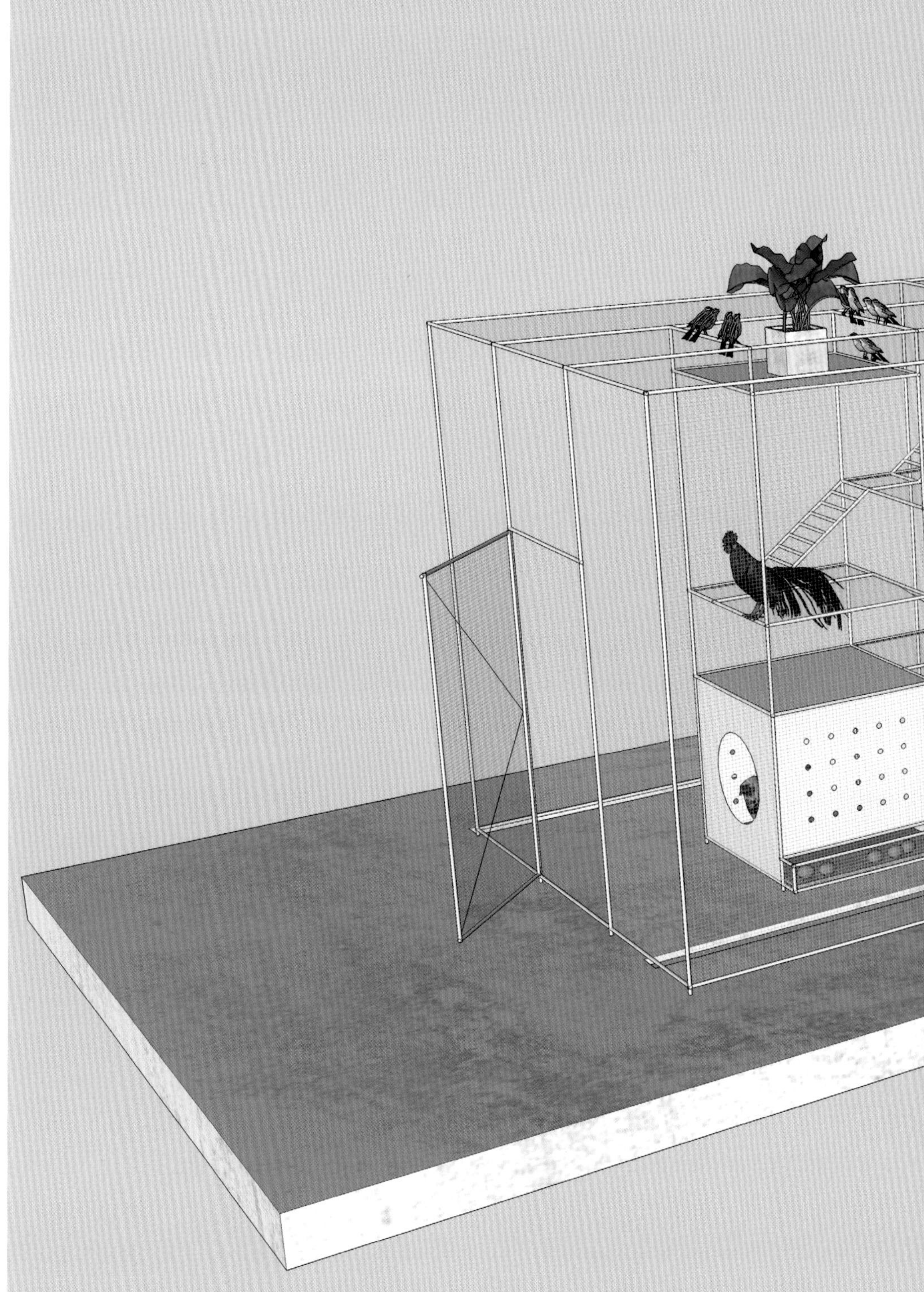

Long Answer

A memorable moment comes to my mind is when constructing stairs for a chicken cage in the Long An House. The client wants to see an active space that showing chicken movement. Thus we have to change the position of those stair so many times after watch the way how chicken move, jump, and fly.

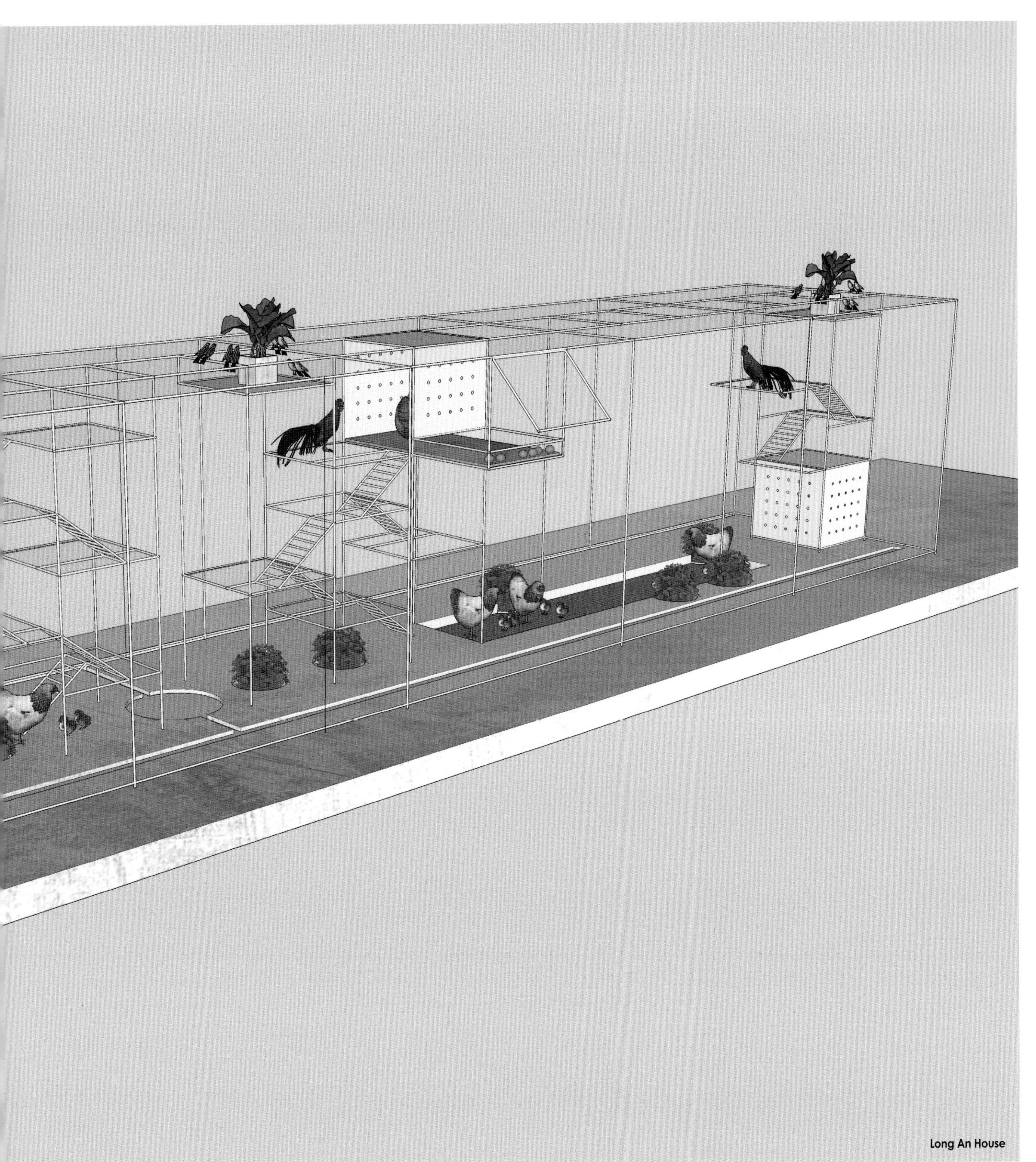

Long An House

계단 설계 과정에서 기억나는 에피소드가 있는가?
(ex. 클라이언트의 요구에 의한 독특한 계단 디자인 또는 공간 제약에 따른 디자인 등)

LGSMA_

In post-war Rome, many architects redefined the typology of residential buildings.The Roman Palazzina was an occation for a very interesting experimentation on stairs. One of the most beautiful examples can be found in Casa del Girasole by Luigi Moretti.

The main staircase defines essentially the atrium of the building making it a unique place.

Wonderful are also the structural solutions thought by the Engineer Pier Luigi Nervi for the football Stadium Artemio Franchi in Florence.

전쟁 후 로마에는 많은 건축가들에 의해 주거 건물들의 유형이 재정의되었다. 로마의Palazzina(작은 주택)에는 매우 흥미로운 실험적인 계단들이 있다. 그 중 가장 아름다운 사례들을 루이지 모레티가 설계한 Casa del Girasole (카사 델 지라솔레)에서 볼 수 있다. 여기서 메인 계단은 본질적으로 건물의 아트리움이 되어 독특한 장소를 형성한다.

플로렌스의 아르 미오 프란끼 축구장의 계단에서 엔지니어 피에르 루이지 네르비가 고안한 구조적 해결법도 훌륭하다.

P.060

복잡한 로마 대지에 위치한 2층짜리 오래된 주택의 구조적 리뉴얼 작업을 던 치열한 시점이다. 우리는 돌로 된 기존 계단을 철거하고 철과 나무로 만든 새로운 계단으로 교체하였다. 한쪽 벽면에만 위치한 일층 창문을 가장 용이하게 사용할 수 있도록 계단 참 구조를 변형하였다. 시공 중에 내진보호 국가 규정이 여러모로 변경 되었다. 새 규정에 따르면 건축물의 모든 신축된 부분이나 재구성된 부분은 기존의 방위벽과 떨어진 상태로 고립되어야 했다. 그래서 우리는 새로운 방안을 모색하여 계단 실 지붕 슬라브까지 전적으로 강철 케이블로 계단을 지탱하였고, 이렇게 함으로써 구조도 쉽게 강화되었다. 그리고, 계단을 얇은 스페이서 브래킷 하나만으로 벽과 연결하였다. 무거운 벽돌 구조로 된 주변 벽들과 직접적으로 맞닿지 않는 매우 가벼운 계단이 주는 최종 건축적 효과에 우리는 매우 신이 났다. 강철 빔과 벽사이의 공간 안에 섬세한 조명 시스템 삽입을 선택한 것도 탁월했다.

b4architects

P.064

사무실 STAR(건축설계 및 전략기업)와 함께 로테르담에 높이 3m, 너비 1.97m, 길이 3.6m 규모의 아주 작은 주택을 설계하였다. 우리는 이 집을 "작은 별장"이라고 불렀다. 총 6.89m² 규모이다. 아마 세상에서 가장 작은 집일 것이다. 집은 부엌 딸린 거실, 샤워장이 있는 화장실, 수납공간이 많은 침실 그리고 스파의 4개 공간으로 구성된다. 설계를 마친 후, 우리는 집이 너무 작아 2층 침실로 올라갈 수 있는 제대로 된 계단이 들어갈 공간이 충분하지 않다는 것을 알게 되었다. 그래서 우리는 즉흥적으로 안전하게 올라갈 수 있을 정도로 튼튼하면서 샤워실이 있는 화장실로 옮겨 걸어 둘 수 있을 정도로 가벼운 철제 사다리 계단을 디자인하였다.

BOARD

P.066

나에게 있어 사다리나 램프를 설계하는 일은 늘 특별한 도전이다. 그 이유는 대개 이것들이 우리 프로젝트의 주된 요소이가 되기 때문이다. 나는 여러 수직 공간들을 연결하는 통로(circulation)적 요소를 중심으로 공간을 설계한다. 베를린 독일의회의 방문자 센터에 디자인한 램프가 그에 적합한 예이다. 건축주는 건물 자체 보안상 방문자들이 서로 엉키지 않도록 입구와 출구가 다른 두 종류의 통로를 원하였다. 그래서, 두개의 램프를 이용해서 두 종류의 필터를 만들기로 하였다. 첫 번째 램프는 중앙으로의 접근과 동시에 보안모드와 같은 역할을 하며, 두 번째 램프는 의회 방문 후 중앙을 벗어나 출구로 나가는 램프이다. 이렇게 함으로써 통로로 인해 하나이면서 서로 다른 두 영역이 생겨난다. 두 램프 사이에서는 모두가 모두를 볼 수 있지만 자신이 정확히 어디에 있는지 알 수 없는 특이하면서도 강렬한 시각적 관계가 일어난다.

ELA - Edu Lopez Architects

P.067

아트 콜렉터의 제일 첫 요청은 계단을 유리로 만들 달라는 것이었다. 그런 계단을 한번도 설계해 본적이 없는 우리에게는 큰 도전이었지만, 결론적으로 우리는 재료와 미학은 별개라는 것을 깨달었다. 우리는 초기부터 스타일에 대해 너무 회의적이었던 것이다.

Ezequiel Farca + Cristina Grappin

P.068

기억에 남는 계단은 홈오피스 같은 작은 사무실인 소호라는 또 다른 프로젝트의 계단이다. 이 사무실은 층이 나눠진 원룸 형태로 다양하게 사용할 수 있다. 각 층을 연결하는 4개의 계단이 있다. 계단 아래(공공공간)에서 위로(사적공간)갈수록 경사도가 변하여 계단을 오르는 게 리드미컬하다.

Katsuhiro Miyamoto & Associates

P.069

대개 계단은 형태적으로나 구조적으로 까다롭다는 사실 이외에 계단의 디자인은 주변 환경과 가장 큰 연관성이 있는 것 같다. 기억나는 인상적인 순간은 공중에 떠 있는 조립식 강철 구조물을 계단 바닥에서 꼭대기까지 삽입하기 위해 어쩔 수 없이 계단 꼭대기의 콘크리트 벽 일부를 부숴야 할 때였다.

Moussafir Architectes

P.070

현재 우리는 그로닝겐 포럼을 시공 중에 있다. 이 '정보와 토론을 위한 센터'는 가지처럼 뻗은 수평 공간들과 야외 광장이 에스컬레이터로 연결되는 커다란 아트리움을 중심으로 구성된다. 이동의 방향을 조작함으로써 건물을 둘러보는 즐거움을 증대 시킬 수 있기를 기대한다: 위로 움직일지 아래로 움직일지 결정하는 디제이처럼.

NL Architects

P.071

쿠르치오 말라파르테가 설계한 카프리 섬 동쪽에 위치한 Casa Malaparte(카사 말라파르테)는 여러 방면으로 독특한디자인을 선보인다. 파티오(집 후면 테라스)로 올라가는 계단도 그 중 하나이다. 계단은 북서쪽 거주 공간의 지붕이기도 하다. 각기둥 모양으로 직육면체 형태를 한 가장 큰 주거 동으로 뻗어 있다. 이 계단은 섬에서 집으로 진입할 때 가장 먼저 물리적으로 맞닥뜨리는 곳으로, 험한 산지 지형을 지나 단지 걸어 서만 도달할 수 있다. 집에 도착하자 마자 계단은 방문객을 지붕으로 인도하여 멀리 보이는 수평선과의 '만남'을 주선한다. 마치 수평선이 방문객이 서 있는 평평한 지붕까지 뻗어 있는 것 같다. 방문자는 거친 지형을 계단처럼 걸어 올라와야 한다. (거친 지형처럼) 계단 양 옆에는 손잡이나 다른 안전 장치가 없으며, 파티오도 마찬가지다. 위험해 보이고, 주변 환경은 그 불안을 더 고조시킨다. 하지만, 동시에 자유를 느낄 수 있다. 바다를 가로지르는 수평선과 일체가 될 것 같은 착각을 일으킨다.

영화감독 장 뤽 고다르는 1963년 영화 '경멸'에서 계단의 극적인 효과를 과감하게 보여줬다. 이 영화의 마지

막 장면 중에 폴 자발(미셸 피콜리)이 그의 부인 카밀 자발(브리지트 바르도)을 찾기 위해 계단을 오르는 장면이 있다. 고다르는 계단을 거의 완벽한 대칭으로 화면에 담았다. 집 전반으로 뻗어 있는 계단의 기다란 형태는 영화의 와이드한 포멧과는 대비되는 방향으로 솟아 있어 스크린을 둘로 나눈다. 그리고 영화 관람객들은 피콜리를 따라 계단을 올라가며 높아지는 카메라 앵글이 만드는 수평선과 만나게 된다.

카사 말라파르테의 계단은 더 이상 두 개의 층을 잇는 요소가 아니라 건물의 성격을 결정짓는 요소이다. 계단은 분리된 건축적 요소들 사이에서 차이를 극복하는 건축적 조경이다.

object-e architecture

P.072

Shapeshifter의 메인 계단 디자인이 각별히 기억에 남는다. 설계 단계 어느 시점에서 우리는 분리된 두꺼운 강철 판들을 조립하여 하나의 소용돌이 구조로 통합시킬 수 있음을 알게 되었다. 소용돌이 형상을 강조하기 위해 마치 공간이 아래로 '빨려 들어가는' 것처럼 스케일과 형태에 극적인 변화들을 주었다.

OPA

P.074

우리가 작업한 산업디자인 프로젝트 중 고르지 못한 지형 때문에 5m 높이의 오차를 두고 두 건물을 연결해야 하는 과제가 있었다. 우리는 이 문제를 공장 모든 직원들이 서로 섞일 수 있는 중요한 공공장소의 생성 기회로 보았다. 이 공공장소는 계단의 실용성이 만들어낸 공장의 활력소가 되었다.

SLOT STUDIO

P.076

나는 여러 공간적 환경에서 실질적 필터의 역할을 하는 문턱의 기능을 가진 계단을 즐겨 디자인한다. 나는 연결, 융합됨과 동시에 다양성과 특이성이 강조되는 브릿지와 같은 계단을 상상한다.

Stefano Corbo Studio

P.077

방콕 CBD 지역에 있는"PLAA-GUT"이라는 명칭의 태국 남부식 음식점이 있다. 거기에 망고 나무 한 그루가 있는데 땅으로 그늘을 드리우며 특유 분위기를 자아낸다. 이 망고 나무 아래 공간은 음식점과 카페를 위한 "공공 외부 공간"으로 활용 될 수 있다. 이 공간은 외부로 잘 드러나 있기 때문에 사람들이 쉽게 모이는 계단형 공간을 조성하며, 동시에 테라스에서 식사를 하는 손님들에게는 보다 더 사적인 공간을 제공한다.

TOUCH Architect

P.078

기억에 남는 순간은 Long An House의 닭장 안 계단을 만들 때이다. 건축주는 닭의 활동이 보이는 동적인 공간을 기대했다. 그래서, 우리는 닭이 움직이고 점프하고 날아다니는 것을 관찰하면서 반복적으로 계단을 재배치해야 했다.

TROPICAL SPACE

Are there any stairs you are inspired by?
What was **inspirational** about it?

b4architects

> "The extreme visual lightness reached with the use of concrete usually known as an heavy material causes in the observer a great sense of astonishment.
>
> 일반적으로 무거운 재료로 알려진 콘크리트를 사용해서 이뤄낸 극단적인 시각적 가벼움은 보는 이에게 큰 놀라움을 선사한다."

Long Answer

We take in mind a series of masterpieces of the modern architecture where also the role of an architectural element as a stair is so great.

For example we think to Niemeyer's Itamaraty Palace, Brasilia, with its fantastic spiral concrete stair: the extreme visual lightness reached with the use of concrete usually known as an heavy material causes in the observer a great sense of astonishment.

The stair from the terrace to the waterfall of Kauffmann House of Wright with its suspended steps: the poetry with few architectural words with no age.

The great expressionist episodes of Mendelsohn's stairs like in De la Warr Pavillion, in UK, where each detail is thought as part of a whole as in an alive organism.

We look with great attention to the work of Morphosis: the sculptural stairs in all their public works become often a public architectural events inside and outside the buildings where people love to stay. The stairs become in every sense a place, not only a path or functional expedient to connect two different levels.

The graphic and 'fluid dynamic' sense of space in all the work about stairs of Zaha Hadid: the stairs become a materialization of poetics of flow lines starting from far, crossing all the building and continuing in the landscape.

© G. Evels

Itamaraty Palace

" Where each detail is thought as part of a whole as in an alive organism.

영국의 De la Warr Pavillion에서 처럼 (에리히) 멘델손의 연속적인 계단 각각의 디테일은 살아있는 유기체처럼 전체를 이루는 요소처럼 매우 표현주의적이다. "

• De la Warr Pavilion, Bexill on sea - Mendelsohn
+ S. Chermayeff

© G. Evels

© Esther Westerveld

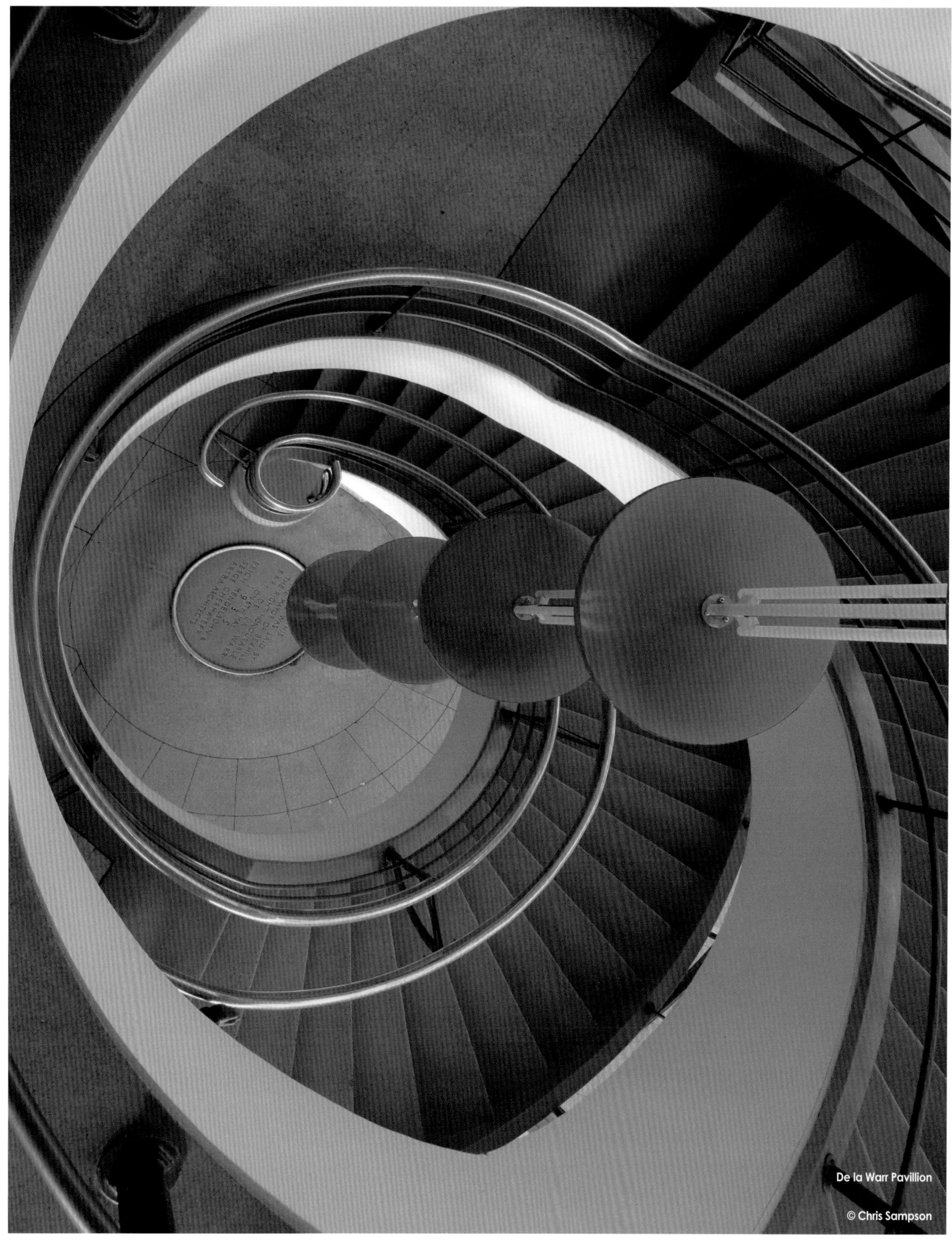

De la Warr Pavillion

© Chris Sampson

“The stairs become in every sense a place, not only a path or functional expedient to connect two different levels.

모포시스의 작품에도 관심이 크다: 건물 안팎에서 대중을 위한 건축 이벤트가 되기도 한다.”

Emerson College · Emerson College Los Angeles USA - Morphosis © G. Evels

“The graphic and ‘fluid dynamic’ sense of space in all the work about stairs of Zaha Hadid.

자하 하디드 공간의 그래픽적이고 `유체역학`적 감각은 그녀의 모든 계단에 스며들어 있다.”

© G. Evels

© G. Evels

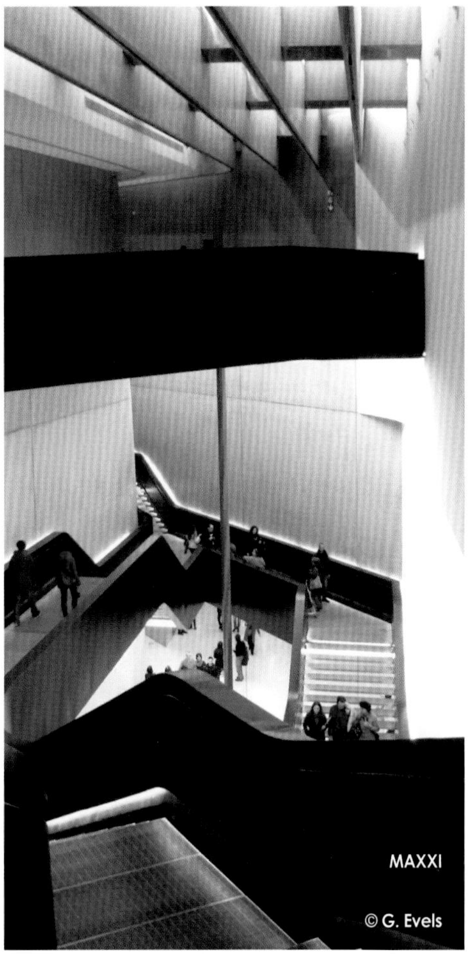

MAXXI

© G. Evels

> “There I realized what steps and stairs can do to a public space, which inspires me until today.
>
> 거기서 나는 계단이 공공 공간에게 무엇을 할 수 있는지 깨닫게 되었고 지금까지도 그 영향이 남아있다.”

Long Answer

During a school trip with my Latin class at the beginning of the 1990s, I traveled to Rome for the first time. Our accommodation was located very close to the Spanish Steps, a monumental stairway of 135 steps, which deeply impacted the way I perceive public spaces. As our budget did not allow us to go out during that trip, we spent almost every evening sitting on the steps of this gigantic stair that functioned like an outdoor theatre, watching the people pass by and enjoying the lively atmosphere that attracted hundreds of people every night. There I realized what steps and stairs can do to a public space, which inspires me until today. The abovementioned stair of the Estonian Academy of Arts in Tallinn is clearly inspired by the Spanish Steps.

Spanish Steps

© Nick Cook

ELA - Edu Lopez Architects

"From the highest part of the staircase a leaky cone is created which is really evocative for anyone.

계단 꼭대기에서 내려다보면 누구든지 구멍 뚫린 원뿔 모양을 연상할 수 있다."

Long Answer

Undoubtedly when designing our stairs or ramps I always have several examples such as the helicoidal staircase of the Vatican museum. It really is a stair-ramp, due to its large footprint and small riser. This makes it a very comfortable ladder to move through it, in addition the fact that it is helical, makes it much stronger spatially as it is escaping as you go up. From the highest part of the staircase a leaky cone is created which is really evocative for anyone. This leakage is also created in the lower zone of the same but in a less accentuated way since this leakage is fruit of the own perspective. To this must be added that the areas of risers are marked in white marble so the view from the top of the stairs is great that you see as you go down the regulated surface of the ramp itself.

Vatican museum

© Colin

Ezequiel Farca + Cristina Grappin

" Effect of floating platforms, I believe that it is an intention that transcends by its functionality and aesthetic cleaning.

떠있는 플랫폼 효과, 이는 계단의 기능성과 미적 단순함을 극복하기 위한 도전이 아닐까 생각한다. "

Long Answer

I find inspiration in the modern models of stairs of mid XX century residences, I admire the effect of floating platforms, I believe that it is an intention that transcends by its functionality and aesthetic cleaning.

MAX CETTO HOUSE sketch by EF+CG

Katsuhiro Miyamoto & Associates

"One of which is from India which is simple and beautiful.

그 중 인도에 있는 계단은 심플하면서도 아름답다."

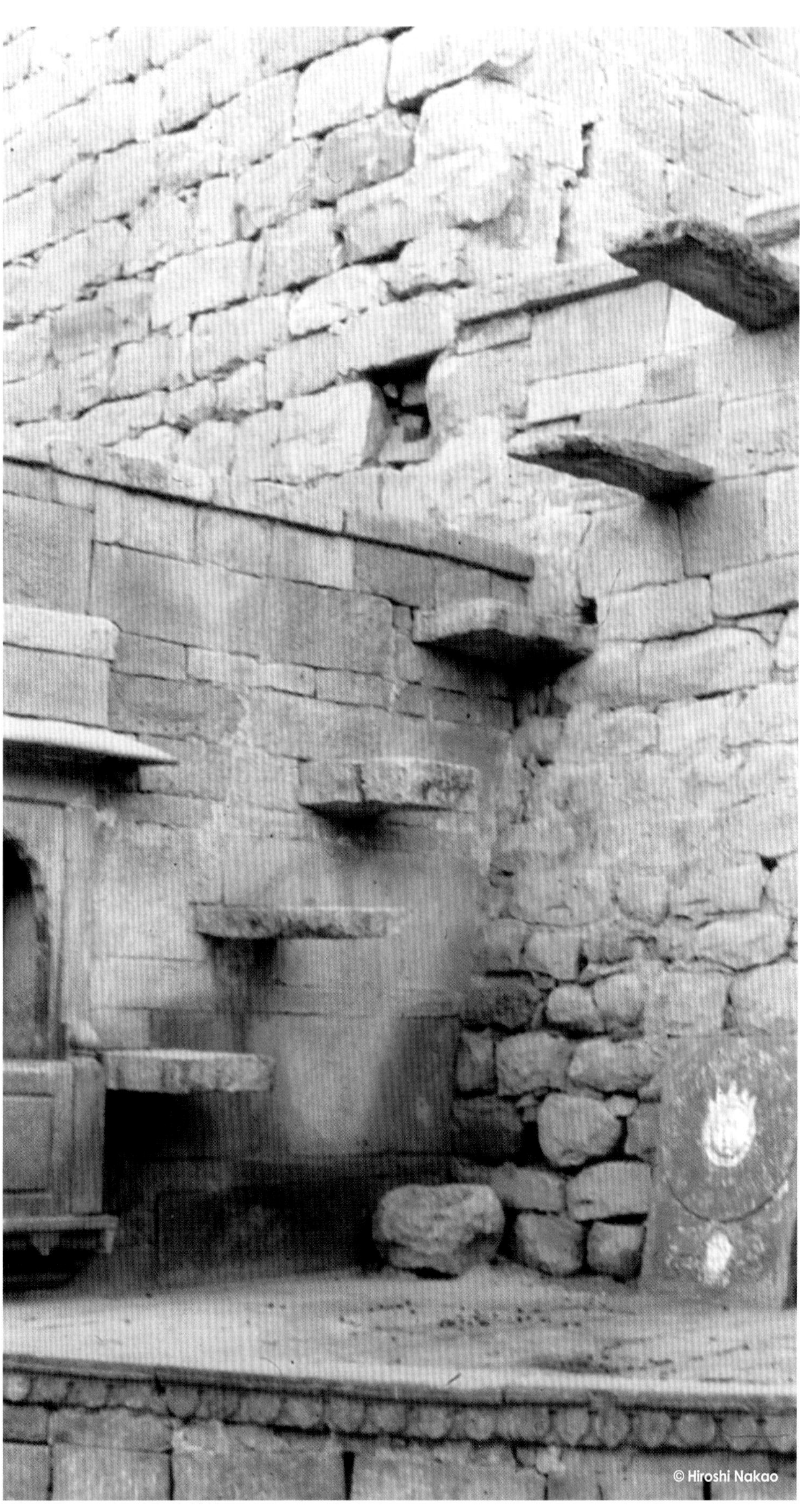

© Hiroshi Nakao

Long Answer

I have a large collection of interesting staircase images. One of which is from India which is simple and beautiful.

LGSMA

“ **This is one of the view of Rome that remained untouched.**

이런 모습은 여전히 훼손되지 않고 남아있는 옛 로마의 전경 중 하나이다. ”

Long Answer

Maybe the staircase that best represents our idea of infrastructural element is the one of the two stairs that connect Piazza Venezia to Rome to Piazza del Campidoglio and to Basilica of Santa Maria in Aracoeli. They are two stairs that don't claim any integration to the context but, on the countrary, they oppose to it.

This is one of the view of Rome that remained untouched.

Roma Campidoglio in「Vedute di Roma(1748)」

Miha Volgemut architect

“ **The lesson that those stairs taught me was that no matter how banal the task is, you can always be imaginative and playful and make an impact.**

그 계단에서 얻은 교훈은 아무리 평범한 것이라도 끊임없이 상상력과 창의력을 발휘한다면 그 영향은 엄청나다는 것이다. ”

Long Answer

First time I visited Peglezen (it is a building in Ljubljana, designed by famous Slovenian architect Jože Plečnik) I was inspired enormously by those stairs. The experience of those stairs was something strange and new, the feeling was strong, they caught me by surprise. Such a simple trick of geometry, and yet so powerful effect. The lesson that those stairs taught me was that no matter how banal the task is, you can always be imaginative and playful and make an impact.

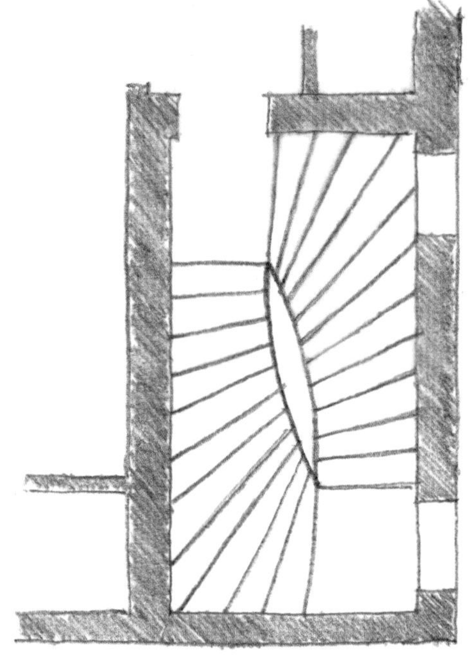

Peglezen Sketch

Moussafir Architectes

" By its shape, its scale and its relation with the surrounding space, this stair seems to flow downwards more than to raise upwards.

형태와 스케일 그리고 주변 공간과의 관계성 측면에서 이 계단은 위로 상승하기 보다는 아래로 흐르는 것처럼 느껴진다. "

Long Answer

The most inspirational stair that comes to my mind is the one by Michelangelo for the Laurentian Library vestibule in Florence. By its shape, its scale and its relation with the surrounding space, this stair seems to flow downwards more than to raise upwards. It is inspiring in the way it expresses masterfully the tensions of human condition.

Laurentian Library vestibule

object-e architecture

"They provide ways to think about architectural elements, the staircase in this instance, that can change our approach to their design and redefine our understanding of the functions that they perform both at the level of tectonics, as well as at the level of the occupancy that they accommodate.

소설이나 영화 속 계단은 우리의 디자인 접근 방향에 변화를 줄 만큼 계단을 포함한 건축적 요소에 대한 우리의 생각을 전환시킨다. "

Long Answer

"The emergency stairway lay before her a metal stairway painted gray. Plain, practical, functional. Not made for use by miniskirted women wearing only stockings on their otherwise bare feet. Nor had Junko Shimada designed Aomame's suit for use on the emergency escape stairs of Tokyo Metropolitan Expressway Number 3. Another huge truck roared down the outbound side of the expressway, shaking the stairs. The breeze whistled through gaps in the stairway's metal framework. But in any case, there it was, before her: the stairway. All that was left for her to do was climb down to the street."

In Haruki Murakami's novel 1Q84, in the opening pages, one of the main characters, Aomame, is forced to take an emergency stairway in order to escape a traffic jam on the highway and manage to accomplish her current mission on time (which is to murder someone). However, when she climbs down that stairs she enters into a different world. Not a totally different one, she cannot even tell the difference at the beginning, but one that has nonetheless some differences from the one she used to live; for example, a world that has two moons instead of one. At the end of the novel, she climbs the same stairway back up, managing to escape back into her original world.

Somehow, examples like the one above, as the ones from film mentioned earlier, are more inspirational for us than actual stair designs in architectural projects. They provide ways to think about architectural elements, the staircase in this instance, that can change our approach to their design and redefine our understanding of the functions that they perform both at the level of tectonics, as well as at the level of the occupancy that they accommodate. If we manage to design a staircase for example that succeeds to impose to the user the feeling that he or she travels from one reality to another that is just slightly altered, like the staircase in Murakami, it would be a great accomplishment indeed.

The stairs in a novel 1Q84

OPA

" **These stairs are symmetrical copies of each other, with the mirror line rotated off of the expected centerline. Through this deceptively simple move, Olgiati produces an uncanny space that feels like a dream.**

이 계단은 뚜렷이 인지되는 센터라인을 중심으로 갈라지며 서로를 대칭으로 복제한다. 올지아티는 언뜻 보기엔 간단한 움직임으로 꿈 같은 묘한 공간을 만들어냈다. "

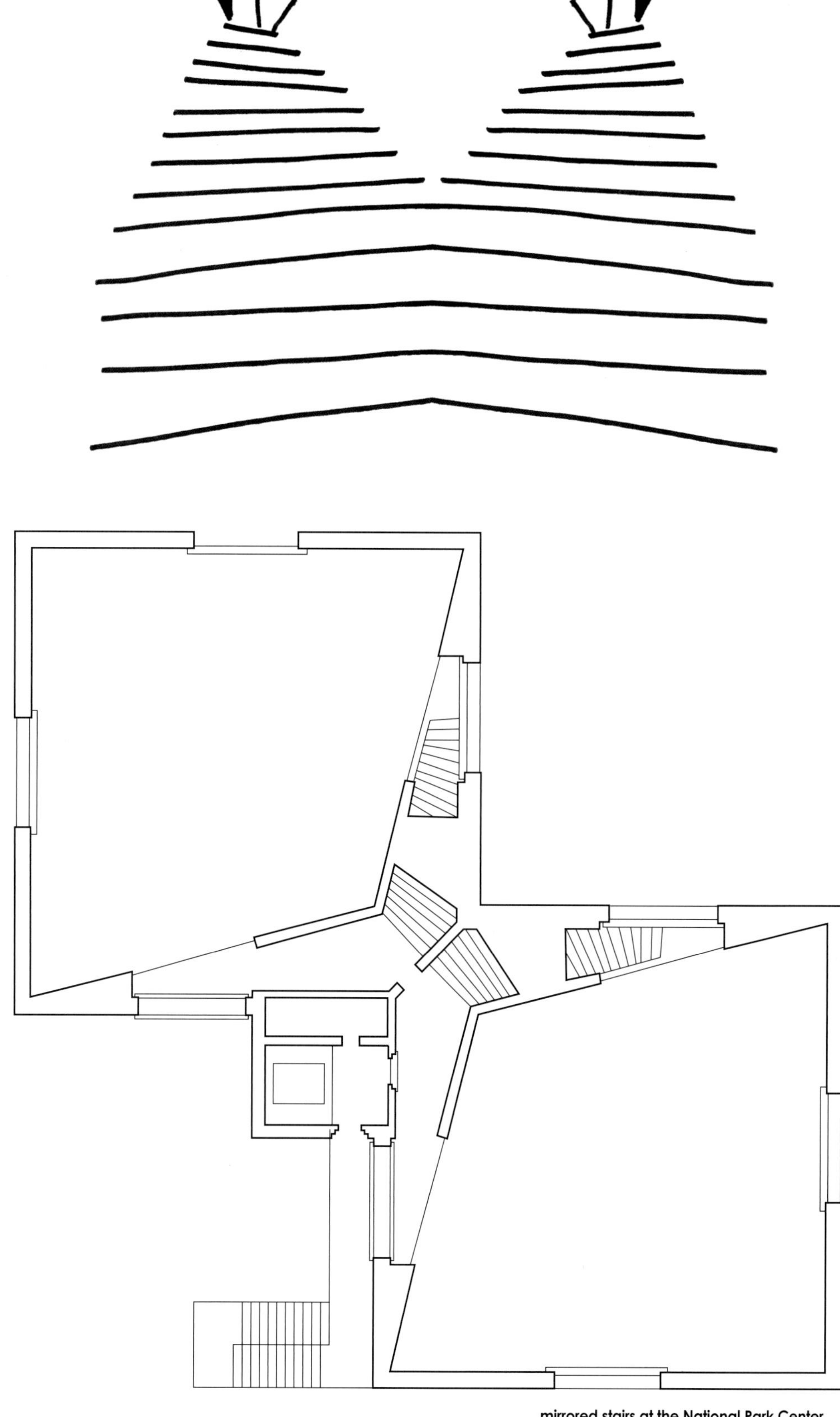

mirrored stairs at the National Park Center

Long Answer

Valerio Olgiati's mirrored stairs at the National Park Center in Zernez, Switzerland are an inspiration. These stairs are symmetrical copies of each other, with the mirror line rotated off of the expected centerline. Through this deceptively simple move, Olgiati produces an uncanny space that feels like a dream.

"Because of its relationship with the exterior and the space it creates inside the building, making it the central experience when entering the bank building.

그가 창안한 기술적 해결책 때문이 아니라 건물의 외면과 계단이 가지는 관계성 그리고 건물 내부에서 계단이 만들어내는 공간의 성격이 그 이유이다. 이 계단은 은행을 들어가는 행위 그 중심에 있다."

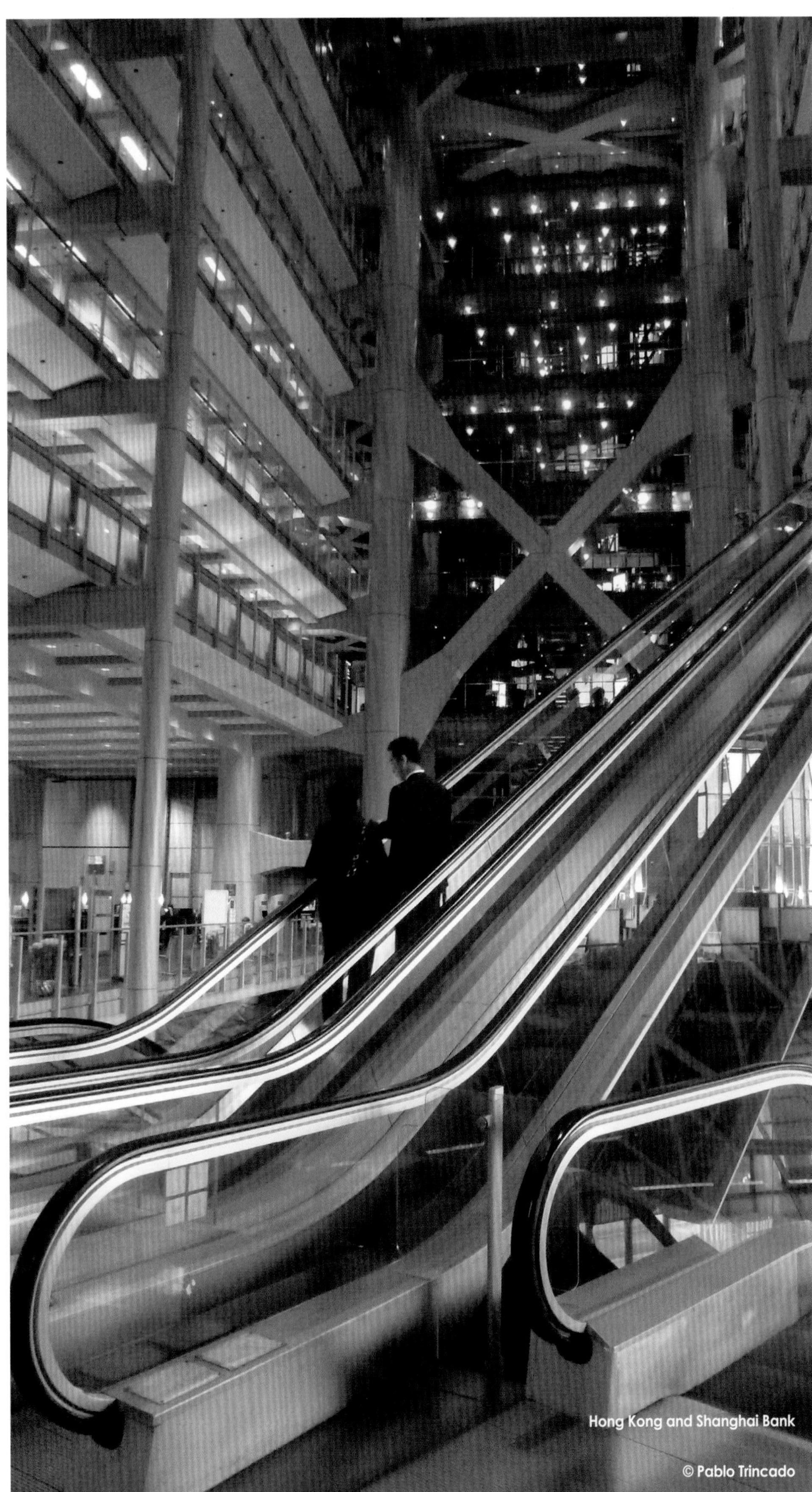

Hong Kong and Shanghai Bank

© Pablo Trincado

Long Answer

There are so many examples and benchmarks in architecture, but one that really poses questions about how we look at stairways is the one designed by Norman Foster for the Hong Kong and Shanghái Bank, and not because of the technical solution it offers, but because of its relationship with the exterior and the space it creates inside the building, making it the central experience when entering the bank building.

Stefano Corbo Studio

Long Answer

I've always admired the iconic and sculptural character of Arne Jacobsen's staircases. In his projects, staircases represent the only visible element immerged within an abstract and metaphysical space.

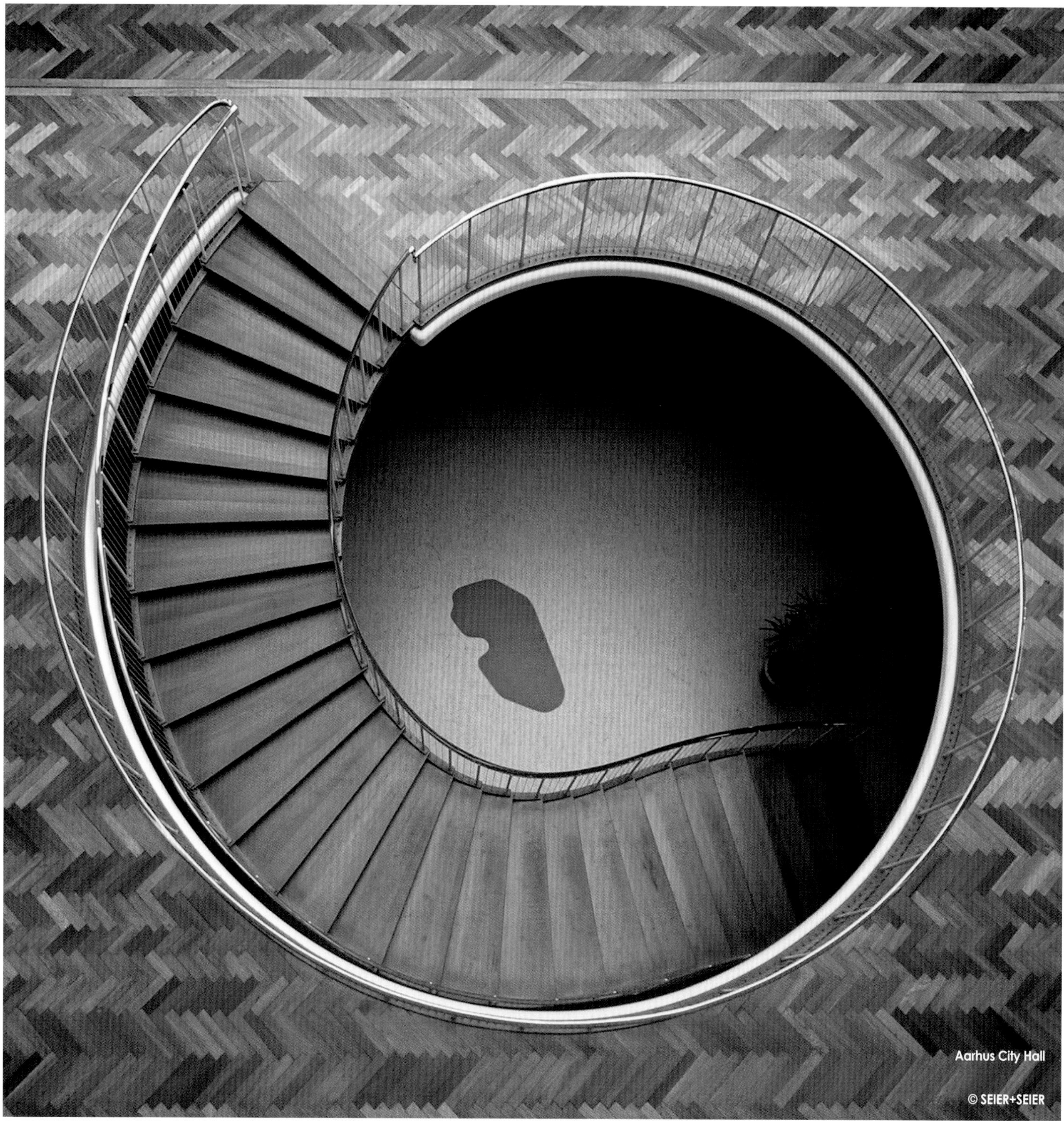
Aarhus City Hall

© SEIER+SEIER

TOUCH Architect

" While using the simple white clean wall of corridor to emphasize the element of the stairway.
 It represents the feeling of wound during the war, which created an integration into the consciousness and memory of the city of Berlin.

 깨끗한 흰 색의 심플한 복도 벽은 이러한 계단의 특징을 부각시킨다.
 이 계단은 시민들의 의식과 베를린 도시의 기억속에 남아있는 전쟁의 상처를 표현한다. "

JEWISH MUSEUM

© Parpis Leelaniramol

Long Answer

The stairs inside JEWISH MUSEUM, Berlin, designed by Daniel Libeskind is not just a simple staircase, but there is another element which is a set of disorderly concrete beam while using the simple white clean wall of corridor to emphasize the element of the stairway. It represents the feeling of wound during the war, which created an integration into the consciousness and memory of the city of Berlin.

" It harmornizes with the size to create a whole natural university where people can truly admire the beauty of the landscape.

계단은 완전히 자연으로 뒤덮인 주변환경과 규모적으로 조화를 이루며 사람들로 하여금 자연 경관의 아름다움에 흠뻑 빠질 수 있도록 해준다. "

Long Answer

The stair lead to the entrance of Gia Long Tomb in Hue is the one which insprited me a lot. It harmornizes with the size to create a whole natural university where people can truly admire the beauty of the landscape.

영감을 받은 계단 디자인이 있는가? 어떤 부분에서 영감을 받았나?

NL Architects

The magnificent transformer stairs in Harry Potter's Hogwarts Castle of course! "The Grand Staircase, often known as Hogwarts Stairways, was invented by Rowena Ravenclaw (fl. c. 993–1000), a Scottish witch, who lived in the early Middle Ages. Noted for her intelligence and creativity and regarded as one of the greatest witches of the age, Ravenclaw was one of the four founders of Hogwarts School of Witchcraft and Wizardry. "Wit beyond measure is man's greatest treasure." Harry Potter Wiki

But also the dizzying omni-directional M.C. Escher inspired stairs in Monument Valley (indie puzzle game developed by Ustwo Games).

당연히 해리포터의 호그와트 성의 움직이는 웅장한 계단이다! "호그와트 계단이라고 흔히 알려진 큰 계단은 중세 초기에 살았던 스코틀랜드 마법사 로웨나 래번클로(fl.c.93-1000)에 의해 개발되었다. 총명함과 창의력으로 유명한 그녀는 이 시대의 가장 훌륭한 마법사 중 한명으로 알려져 있다. 래번클로는 호그와트 마법 학교 창립자 4명 중 한 명이었다. "지혜는 인간의 가장 큰 보물이다." 해리포터 위키피아

Monument Valley(Ustwo Games사가 개발한 인디 퍼즐게임) 속 계단도 M.C. Escher(모리츠 코리넬리스 에셔)의 어지러운 전방위성에 영향을 받은 경우이다.

P.084

건축적 요소로써 매우 훌륭한 계단을 가진 현대 건축의 대작들을 떠올려본다. 예를 들어, 브라질리아(브라질의 수도)에 있는 니마이어의 itamaraty 궁전의 환상적인 나선형 콘크리트 계단이 생각 난다: 일반적으로 무거운 재료로 알려진 콘크리트를 사용해서 이뤄낸 극단적인 시각적 가벼움은 보는 이에게 큰 놀라움을 선사한다.

프랭크 로이드 라이트의 카우프만 저택(낙수장)에서 테라스에서 폭포까지 이어지는 떠 있는 계단은 시대를 뛰어넘는 흔치 않은 시적인 건축언어이다. 영국의 De la Warr Pavillion에서 처럼 (에리히) 멘델손의 연속적인 계단 각각의 디테일은 살아있는 유기체처럼 전체를 이루는 요소처럼 매우 표현주의적이다.

모포시스의 작품에도 관심이 크다: 이들의 모든 공공 작품에서 볼 수 있는 조각 같은 계단은 사람들이 머물기 좋아하며 그 자체만으로도 건물 안팎에서 대중을 위한 건축 이벤트가 되기도 한다. 자하 하디드 공간의 그래픽적이고 '유체역학'적 감각은 그녀의 모든 계단에 스며들어 있다: 계단은 먼 곳에서 시작되어 건물을 가로질러 주변 환경으로 확장되는 선의 흐름과 같이 시적으로 구현 된다.

b4architects

P.089

1990년도 초반에 라틴 수업에서 간 학교 현장학습 때 처음으로 로마 여행을 하게 되었다. 우리가 묵은 숙소는 거대한 135계단으로 이뤄진 스페인 광장과 광장히 가까웠는데, 이 계단은 공공장소에 대한 나의 생각을 크게 변화시켰다. 여행동안 예산이 충분치 않아 외출을 할 수 없어서 대부분 매일 저녁 외부 극장 같은 이 거대한 계단에 앉아서 지나다니는 사람들을 구경하고 매일 밤 수 백명의 사람들이 모이는 생동감 넘치는 분위기를 즐기며 시간을 보냈다. 거기서 나는 계단이 공공 공간에게 무엇을 할 수 있는지 깨닫게 되었고 지금까지도 그 영향이 남아있다. 앞에서 언급한 탈린의 에스토니아 미술 학교의 계단은 명백히 스페인 광장에서 영감을 받은 디자인이다.

BOARD

P.090

당연히 우리가 직접 디자인한 계단이며 우리에게는 늘 바티칸 박물관의 나선형 계단과 같은 좋은 예들이 있다. 바티칸 박물관의 경우 계단의 단이 넓고 낮기 때문에 실제로는 계단-램프라고 말 할 수 있다. 형태는 오르내리기 쉬운 편안한 사다리 같다. 게다가 나선형이기 때문에 계단을 오르면 마치 계단이 달아나는 것 같은 느낌이 들어 더 역동적인 공간이 연출된다. 계단 꼭대기에서 내려다보면 누구든지 구멍 뚫린 원뿔 모양을 연상할 수 있다. 계단 아래 부분에도 이런 구멍이 있지만, 보는 각도에 따라 달라 두드러지지 않는다. 경사면이 흰 대리석으로 되어 있어 계단 꼭대기에서 걸어 내려오며 보이는 규격화된 계단의 광경은 근사하기까지 하다.

ELA - Edu Lopez Architects

P.092

우리는 20세기 중반 주거공간의 모던한 디자인의 계단에 영감을 받는다. 특히, 떠있는 플랫폼 효과를 좋아하는데 이는 계단의 기능성과 미적 단순함을 극복하기 위한 도전이 아닐까 생각한다.

Ezequiel Farca + Cristina Grappin

P.093

특이한 계단 이미지들을 많이 수집하고 있다. 그 중 인도에 있는 계단은 심플하면서도 아름답다.

Katsuhiro Miyamoto & Associates

P.094

계단은 하부구조 요소라는 우리의 생각을 아마도 가장 잘 드러내는 계단이 다음 중 하나일 것이다. 베네치아 광장에서 로마로 이어지는 계단과 캄피돌리오 광장에서 로마 산타마리아 인 아라　리 성당으로 이어지는 계단이다. 이 두 계단은 주변 환경과의 상호적 관계가 전혀 없다. 반대로 주변환경에 대적한다. 이런 모습은 여전히 훼손되지 않고 남아있는 옛 로마의 전경 중 하나이다.

LGSMA_

P.094

처음 Peglezen(류블랴나에 있는 건축물로 유명한 슬로베니아 건축가 요제 플레츠니이 디자인 하였다.)을 방문했을 때 계단을 보고 크게 감동했다. 그 계단을 걷는 경험은 왠지 낯설고 새로웠으며 그 느낌은 놀라울 정도로 강했다. 아주 간단한 형태적 트릭이지만 그 효과는 매우 강력했다. 그 계단에서 얻은 교훈은 아무리 평범한 것이라도 끊임없이 상상력과 창의력을 발휘한다면 그 영향은 엄청나다는 것이다.

Miha Volgemut architect

P.095

가장 인상에 남는 계단은 플로렌스에 있는 미켈란젤로의 라우첸치아나 도서관 입구 계단이다. 형태와 스케일 그리고 주변 공간과의 관계성 측면에서 이 계단은 위로 상승하기 보다는 아래로 흐르는 것처럼 느껴진다. 인간사의 긴장감을 거장답게 표현한 점이 인상적이다.

Moussafir Architectes

P.096

"비상 계단은 눈 앞에 있다. 회색으로 도장한 철제계단이다. 간소하고 실용적이며 철저히 기능성만을 추구한 계단. 스타킹만 신은 발에 타이트한 미니스커트 차림의 여자가 오르내리라고 만든 건 아니다. 아모마메가 입은 준코 사마다의 정장도 수도고속도로 3호선의 비상계단을 내려갈 것을 염두에 둔 디자인은 아니다. 대형 트럭이 반대 차선을 지나가며 계단을 부르르 흔들었다. 바람이 비명을 지르며 철골 틈새를 뚫고 지나갔다. 하지만 계단은 어쨌든 그곳에 있다. 이제 남은 건 지상에 내려갈 일 뿐이다."

무라카미 하루키 소설 1Q84의 서두에 나오는 내용으로, 주인공 아오마메는 누군가를 살해해야 하는 그녀의 임무를 제때 완수하려면 고속도로의 교통체증에서 벗어나기 위해 비상계단을 내려가야 하는 상황에 놓여 있다. 하지만, 그녀가 계단을 내려갈 때 그녀는 다른 세계로 들어가게 된다. 완전히 다른 세계는 아니다. 그녀도 처음에는 달라진

걸 느낄 수 없다. 그렇지만, 그녀가 살던 세계와는 어딘가 다르다. 예를 들어, 달이 하나가 아닌 둘이 있는 세계. 소설 마지막 부분에서 그녀는 그녀가 살던 세계속으로 다시 도피하기 위해 똑같은 계단을 거꾸로 올라간다. 이 소설의 계단은 왠지 앞서 언급한 영화의 계단과 같다. 건축 프로젝트의 실제 계단 디자인보다 더 우리에게 영감이 된다. 소설이나 영화 속 계단은 우리의 디자인 접근 방향에 변화를 줄 만큼 계단을 포함한 건축적 요소에 대한 우리의 생각을 전환시킨다. 또한 건축 요소들의 기능에 대한 우리의 생각을 구조면으로나 사용성면으로 재정립해준다. 무라카미 소설의 계단처럼 단지 조금이라도 현실에서 벗어남을 느낄 수 있는 계단을 설계한다면 우리는 큰 성과를 거두는 거다.

object-e architecture

P.098

스위스 체르네츠 국립공원에 발레리오 올지아티가 디자인한 대칭 계단이 인상깊다. 이 계단은 뚜렷이 인지되는 센터라인을 중심으로 갈라지며 서로를 대칭으로 복제한다. 올지아티는 언뜻 보기엔 간단한 움직임으로 꿈 같은 묘한 공간을 만들어냈다.

OPA

P.099

벤치마크 하고 싶은 계단의 사례는 무지 많지만, 그 중 계단에 대한 우리의 관점을 의심하게 만든 계단이 있다. 그 계단은 노먼 포스터가 설계한 홍콩과 상하이 은행의 것으로 그가 창안한 기술적 해결책 때문이 아니라 건물의 외면과 계단이 가지는 관계성 그리고 건물 내부에서 계단이 만들어내는 공간의 성격이 그 이유이다. 이 계단은 은행을 들어가는 행위 그 중심에 있다.

SLOT STUDIO

P.100

나는 언제나 아르네 야콥센이 디자인한 계단의 상징적이고 조각적인 성향을 흠모해왔다. 그의 프로젝트에서 계단은 추상적이고 형이상학적인 공간안에 스며드는 유일한 시각적 요소로 표현된다.

Stefano Corbo Studio

P.101

다니엘 리베스킨트가 설계한 독일의 유태인 박물관 안의 계단은 단순한 계단이 아니다. 그 계단에는 무질서하게 연속되는 콘크리트 빔이라는 또 다른 요소가 존재한다. 깨끗한 흰 색의 심플한 복도 벽은 이러한 계단의 특징을 부각시킨다. 이 계단은 시민들의 의식과 베를린 도시의 기억속에 남아있는 전쟁의 상처를 표현한다.

TOUCH Architect

P.102

베트남 후(Hue)에 있는 자롱릉의 입구로 진입하는 계단은 나에게 큰 영감을 주었다. 계단은 완전히 자연으로 뒤덮인 주변환경과 규모적으로 조화를 이루며 사람들로 하여금 자연 경관의 아름다움에 흠뻑 빠질 수 있도록 해준다.

TROPICAL SPACE

What was

most memorable

stairs design

you've seen and why?

b4architects

Long Answer

Here in Rome we have different great historical architectural episodes expressed by stairs examples.

Borromini's helicoidal stair of Palazzo Barberini, a baroque spatial invention that marked the birth of spatial continuum with great consequence in Architecture, until the modern era: a concept today still alive.

A great precedent was Palazzo Farnese, in Caprarola,a little city few kilometers out of Rome: a perfect example of a Reinassance architecture of sixteenth century, Vignola was the architect

On the urban side we have Michelangelo's staircase to Campidoglio Square, a great 'fusion' of solved technical complexities on the context before the construction with a monumental perspective effect with its false parallelism of the stone balustrades to exalt the façade of Palazzo Senatorio, urban scenery of the square.

Remaining in our age we were very impressed by the stair system of Souto de Moura's Braga Stadium in Portugal, both in the jutting concrete diaphragm series and in the space between the bleachers and the rock hill. The great impression is due not for the special design spent in the single elements of the stairs, rather ordinary, but in the rhythm of the composition and spatial assembly of all the elements thought for a rapid circulation and evacuation of people in a short time, like in an ancient arena evoking the visual mith of a labirinth (Myth of a labyrinth???).

A special sense of mystic space as pure architectural poetry we felt in the main entrance hall of the Kiasma Museum in Finland designed by Steven Holl Architects: the curved ramp occupies the hall with its sculptural presence and invites the people on the first level under a great skylight that diffuse a soft natural light all around and along the textile concrete white walls.

Palazzo Farnese

© G. Evels

"A great precedent was Palazzo Farnese, in Caprarola, a little city few kilometers out of Rome: a perfect example of a Reinassance architecture of sixteenth century, Vignola was the architect.

좋은 선례로 로마에서 몇 킬로미터 떨어진 작은 도시 카프라롤라에 있는 Palazzo Farnese가 있다: 건축가 비놀라의 작품으로 16세기 르네상스 건축의 완벽한 예이다."

© G. Evels

© G. Evels

Palazzo Farnese

© G. Evels

" **Souto de Moura :**
Braga Stadium
The great impression is due not for the special design spent in the single elements of the stairs, rather ordinary, but in the rhythm of the composition and spatial assembly of all the elements thought for a rapid circulation and evacuation of people in a short time, like in an ancient arena evoking the visual mith of a labirinth.

Souto de Moura의
Braga Stadium
큰 감동은 각 계단의 특유한 디자인에서 오는 것이 아니라 오히려 평범하지만 마치 고대 경기장의 미궁 신화를 시각적으로 떠올리듯 관람객의 빠른 순환과 급속한 대피를 위해 고안된 모든 요소들의 리듬 있는 구성과 공간적 조합에서 온다. "

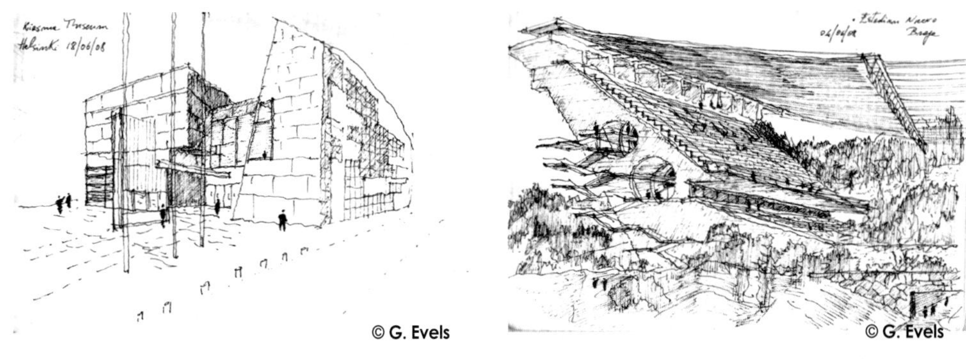
© G. Evels
© G. Evels

© S. Papitto

Braga Stadium
© S. Papitto

" Functioning as a kind of hinge and switch between two worlds, to an upper part of the piece.

두 세계 사이에서 경첩과 스위치 같은 중요한 역할을 성공적으로 수행하고 있었다. "

Long Answer

When I visited the Venice Art Biennale 2017 I was quite impressed by the work of Giorgio Andreotta Calò that was exhibited in the Italian Pavilion. There, a stair played a crucial role in the success of this installation, as it provided access for the audience, functioning as a kind of hinge and switch between two worlds, to an upper part of the piece. This dividing aspect and power of the stair I perceived as most appealing. Because the work was composed of two parts: in the lower part the visitor had to walk through a sequence of scaffolding in order to reach the stair leading to the upper part of the installation. Once upstairs, a view on a large surface, which turned out to be made of water, opened up, revealing a spectacular image that was composed by the old timber truss ceiling of the space above and its mirrored version below.

Giorgio Andreotta Calò's work at the Venice Art Biennale 2017

© Roberto Marossi

ELA - Edu Lopez Architects

Long Answer

One of the stairs that most impressed me was the inner staircase of the Cooper Union building by Morphosis. This stairway that starts from the lobby is a great space not only for vertical communication but also for the meeting all the students in the room. It is not a simple ladder that ascends gradually, but that said ladder acts as a singular and articulating element of the building. The power of this element resides in two aspects, the first of them in that it is not a purely linear element, but it is opening, closing, breaking and doubling in the different sections of the same. In turn, this ladder is framed by a structural mesh that covers it, marking its singularity. In the section that we show below you can see well the completeness of that ladder and all the visual relationships that are created in the interior. The sections of vestibulo and superiors are very well differentiated, in order to create this area of citizen encounter among the students that we have named above. In this staircase nothing is left to the chance, everything is thought with great care, to create a unique space in the building. Even the handrail that acts like a small backlit polycarbonate breastplate, follows in a stable way the lines of the staircase in all its sections. Undoubtedly this staircase is also a reference in our projects, for being the building's nerve center and its spectacular, as well as serve as a point of relationship between the users of the building. It is not a simple element connecting plant in height.

Cooper Union building

© Ci-Daemon

Ezequiel Farca + Cristina Grappin

"I really appreciate his work because of the encompasses of the concept in the entire project.

프로젝트 컨셉 전체를 아우르는 그의 작업방식을 우리는 정말 좋아한다."

Long Answer

The interplay of geometry that makes Carlo Scarpa is memorable. I recognize the composition and I can imagine lots of possibilities reflected in the integration of the staggering to vertical elements (walls) and other architectural elements. I really appreciate his work because of the encompasses of the concept in the entire project.

BRIONVEGACEMENTERYC SCARPA sketch by EF+CG

Katsuhiro Miyamoto & Associates

“Staircases in Fondazione Querini Stampalia, Venice by Carlo Scarpa for their elegance.

카를로 스파르카가 디자인한 베니스의 폰타치오네 퀘리니 스탐팔리아의 계단이 그 우아함에 가장 기억에 남는다.”

© Katsuhiro Miyamoto & Associates

"The main staircase defines essentially the atrium of the building making it a unique place.

여기서 메인 계단은 본질적으로 건물의 아트리움이 되어 독특한 장소를 형성한다."

Long Answer

In post-war Rome, many architects redefined the typology of residential buildings.The Roman Palazzina was an occation for a very interesting experimentation on stairs. One of the most beautiful examples can be found in Casa del Girasole by Luigi Moretti.

The main staircase defines essentially the atrium of the building making it a unique place.

Wonderful are also the structural solutions thought by the Engineer Pier Luigi Nervi for the football Stadium Artemio Franchi in Florence.

© Pier Luigi Nervi

The football Stadium Artemio Franchi in Florence

© Hans-juergen.breuning

Miha Volgemut architect

Long Answer

It was from the Fountainhead movie scene; at the opening of Howard Roark new building where Patricia Neal is coming down the stairs. These stairs really stuck in my mind forever, poetry of elegance.

Moussafir Architectes

Long Answer

I can think of many examples, but the stairs I like the most are the ones that interact with surrounding space and enhance the feeling of elevation or vertical movement. This can be the case with very elaborate and skillful examples as the Laurentian Vestibule, but it can also occur with very low tech constructions. I like for instance the stairs in the "H" house by Sou Fujimoto. They appear as fragile elements floating in the air and look like temporary stairs in a building site. They modify the perception of space and remind me of Piranesi's Prisons.

H House by Sou Fujimoto

Carceri n° VII Piranesi

NL Architects

"A lazy swirl elevates the visitors seemingly effortlessly to the next level.

완만한 나선은 마치 아무 노력없이 사람들을 위로 끌어 올리는 것처럼 보인다."

Long Answer

Itamaraty Palace by Oscar Niemeyer in Brasilia features one of the most the most jealousy evoking inventions in the history of our profession, the 2.3 meter-wide spiral staircase with NO handrail. A lazy swirl elevates the visitors seemingly effortlessly to the next level. As if gravity does not exist (but why would you need a stair in that case anyways?)

Itamaraty Palace

OPA

"At the auditorium your view is split by a knife edge and sheared both in plan and in section.

눈 높이에서 보이는 강당은 평면도와 단면상에서 칼날처럼 날카롭게 반으로 갈라져 있다."

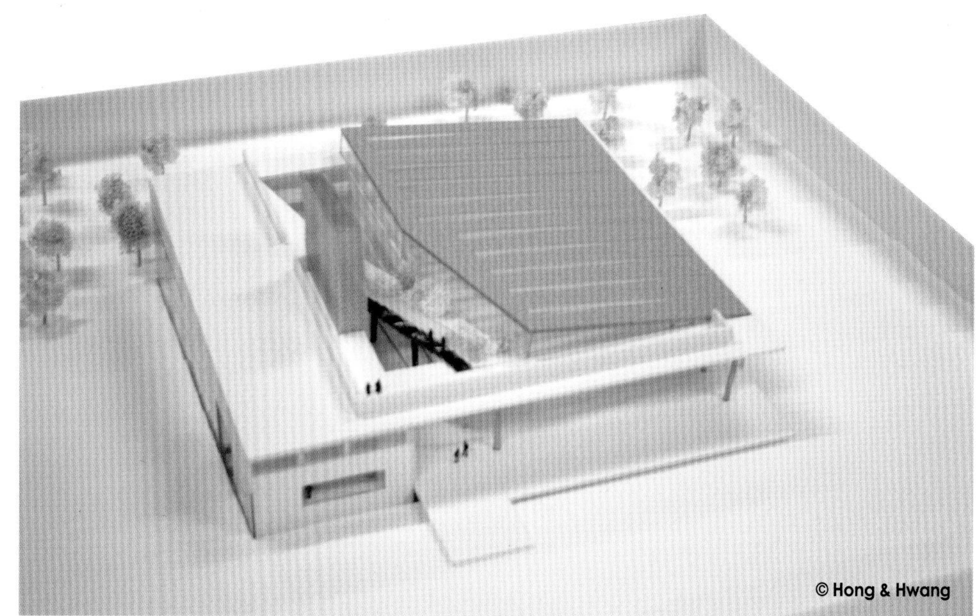
© Hong & Hwang

Long Answer

The stair at OMA's Kunsthal in Rotterdam is incredible. At the auditorium your view is split by a knife edge and sheared both in plan and in section. This is one of the best spatial effects I have ever personally experienced, as the entire building feels like it is ripping apart.

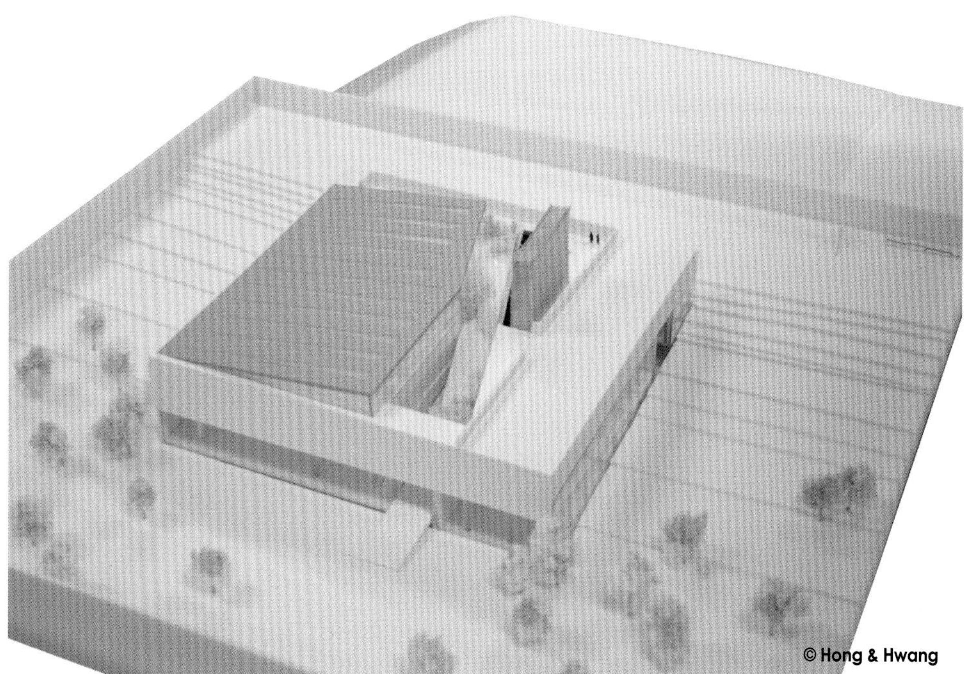
© Hong & Hwang

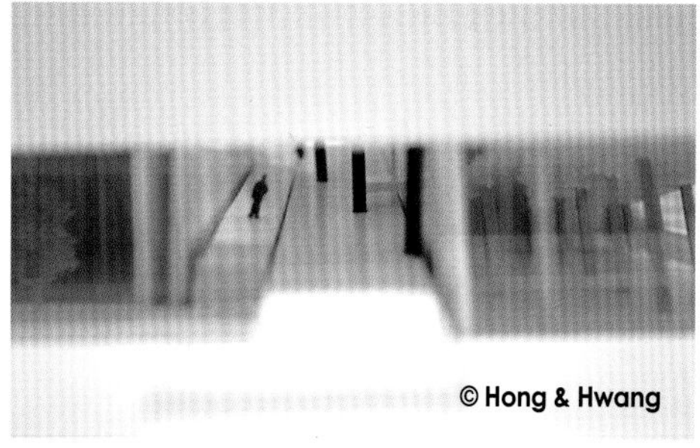
© Hong & Hwang

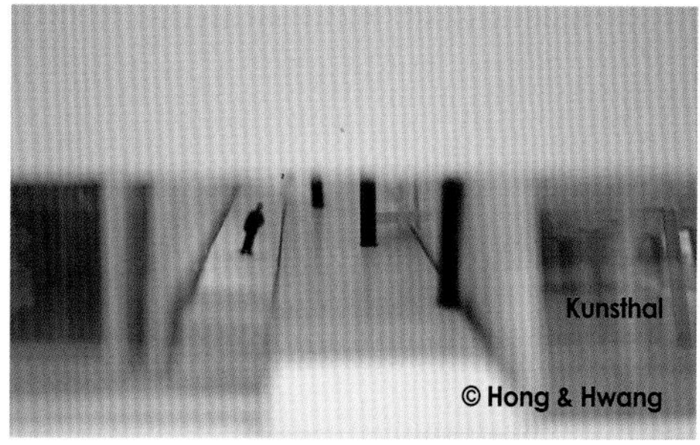
Kunsthal
© Hong & Hwang

SLOT STUDIO

Long Answer

To pick a single one is difficult, because in the field of architecture the stairway is in constant change. Moreover, as observers of the design around the globe it is difficult for us to point out one moment; nonetheless, in Mexico City there is a contemporary example of the use of the stairway as a concentrator of design decisions.

We are referring to the Jumex Museum staircase designed by David Chipperfield, who in addition to design it to fulfill the linking path function, also posited the stairways as a sculpture on display with painstaking attention to construction details and its relationship with users.

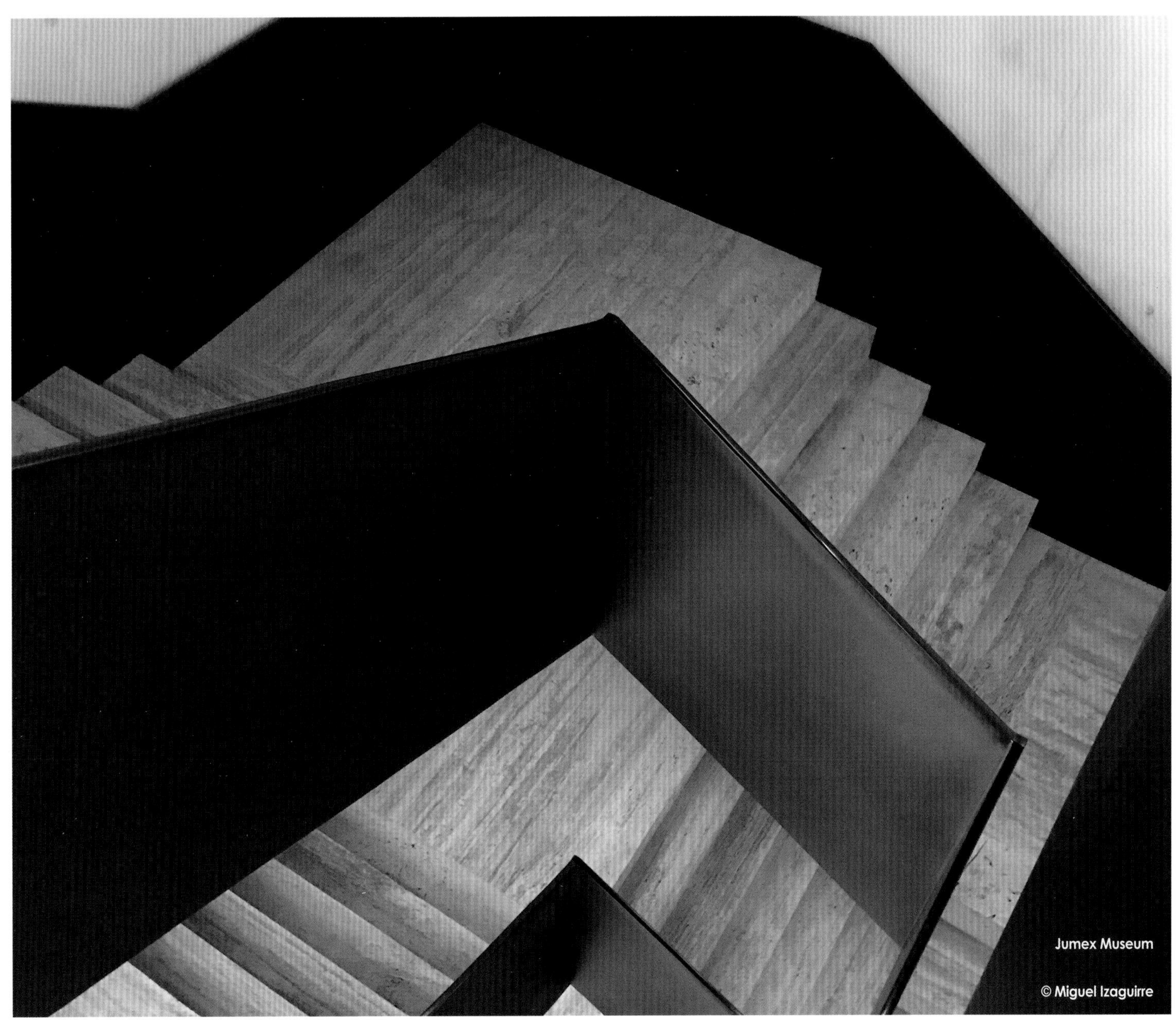

Jumex Museum

© Miguel Izaguirre

Stefano Corbo Studio

" It's a place where people can have a seat, take a rest, and meet with other visitors.

앉을 수 있고 휴식을 취할 수 있고 여러 사람들을 만날 수 있는 공간이다. "

Long Answer

One of the most fascinating staircases I've ever visited is part of David Chipperfield's project for the Neues Museum in Berlin. This staircase is a white elegant object, fulfilling different requirements at the same time. It's monumental, traditional, classical in its layout. And at the same time it works as a real communal space: it's a place where people can have a seat, take a rest, and meet with other visitors.

Neues Museum in Berlin

© Jean-Pierre Dalbéra

> "The shape and form of the steps has a gently curve and fold into an architectural topography.
>
> 이 계단은 부드러움 곡선형태로 건축 지형 위에 포개어져 있다."

Long Answer

Port of Yokohama is one of the most memorable stair design we have ever seen. It was designed by Farshid Moussavi and Alejandro Zaera-Polo which is located at waterfront side of Japan. The shape and form of the steps has a gently curve and fold into an architectural topography. Material using of the stairs' surface is a compilation of wooden decks which can be arrayed into a terrain line.

Port of Yokohama

© Setthakarn Yangderm

TROPICAL SPACE

" This space like a small social of it's region.

이 공간은 지역사회의 작은 소통의 장 같다. "

Long Answer

The most memorable stair i've seen is Chand Baori step water wells in India.

The stair can become a multi-function space depend on different occasion and different types of people. This space like a small social of it's region, it reflect multi-layer of cultural, history, life-styles that when admiring it I can see not only the beauty of its scale, its arrangement... but also the beauty of life in its region.

© NguyenLe

Chand Baori step water wells

가장 인상 깊었던 계단 디자인은 무엇이었나?

P.108

여기 로마에서 우리는 계단이 전달하는 위대한 역사적 건축 에피소드를 다양하게 경험한다. 보로미니가 설계한 Palazzo Barberini의 나선형 계단은 바로크 공간에서 발견되는 공간 연속체의 시발점으로 현재까지 위대한 건축적 성과로 인지된다: 오늘날까지 여전히 사용되는 컨셉이다.

좋은 선례로 로마에서 몇 킬로미터 떨어진 작은 도시 카프라롤라에 있는 Palazzo Farnese가 있다: 건축가 비뇰라의 작품으로 16세기 르네상스 건축의 완벽한 예이다.

도시에는 캄피돌리오 광장으로 이어지는 미켈란젤로의 계단이 있다. 이 계단은 석조 난간의 허구적 평행성을 통해 세나토리오 궁전의 외관을 상승시켜 기념비적 시각 효과를 냄으로써 건설이전에 대지가 가진 기술적 복잡성을 도시적 풍경의 광장으로 탈바꿈한 대단히 "융합"적인 해결책이다.

이 시대에 현존하는 것 중 우리가 가장 인상깊게 본 것은 포르투갈에 있는 Souto de Moura의 Braga Stadium의 계단 시스템이다. 이 시스템은 연속되는 돌출 콘크리트 가로막과 관람석과 바위 언덕사이의 공간에 모두 사용되었다. 큰 감동은 각 계단의 특유한 디자인에서 오는 것이 아니라 오히려 평범하지만 마치 고대 경기장의 미궁 신화를 시각적으로 떠올리듯 관람객의 빠른 순환과 급속한 대피를 위해 고안된 모든 요소들의 리듬 있는 구성과 공간적 조합에서 온다.

우리는 건축가 스티븐 홀이 설계한 핀란드의 키아스마 현대미술관의 중앙 진입 홀에서 순수 건축 서정시와 같은 특별한 신비로움을 느꼈다: 조각상 같이 홀을 점령하고 있는 램프 곡선은 1층에 있는 관람객들을 질감이 거친 흰색 콘크리트(텍스타일 콘크리드) 벽을 따라 자연광이 건물 전체로 부드럽게 퍼져 들어오는 채광창 아래로 이끈다.

b4architects

P.112

2017 베니스 비엔날레 전시회를 관람하였을 때 이태리관에 전시된 Giorgio Andreotta Calò의 작품이 상당히 인상깊었다. 설치 물 위로 이어지는 계단은 설치물 아래와 설치물 위 두 세계 사이에서 경첩과 스위치 같은 중요한 역할을 성공적으로 수행하고 있었다. 계단의 이런 분리적 역할의 힘이 나에게는 가장 매력적이었다. 설치물은 두 부분으로 구성되어 있었다. 아래부분에는 설치물 위 부분으로 이어지는 계단으로 진입하는 발판이 나열되어 있었고, 위 부분에 다다르면 넓은 수면위로 천장의 오래된 목재 트러스 구조가 거울처럼 비쳐 그 환상적인 모습을 드러냈다.

BOARD

P.113

가장 인상깊었던 계단 중에 하나는 모포시스가 디자인한 쿠퍼 유니온 대학건물 계단이다. 로비에서 시작되는 이 계단은 수직적 소통 뿐만 아니라 모든 학생들이 한 방에 모인 것과 같은 느낌을 주는 기대이상의 공간이다. 조금씩 상승하는 단순한 계단이 아니라 독립적인 연결요소이다. 이 계단의 힘은 두 가지 요인에서 나온다. 첫째로 단순한 선적인 요소가 아닌 위치에 따라 개방, 폐쇄, 단절, 증식의 요소가 된다는 것이며, 둘째로는 그물 구조로 둘러싸여 있어 그 존재감이 확실하다는 것이다. 아래의 단면도는 공간 내에서 생성되는 모든 시각적 관계가 드러나는 계단의 완결도를 보여준다. 로비 단면을 보면 계단은 층마다 철저히 차별화되어 있다. 이는 (앞에서 호명한) 학생들을 위한 다양한 만남의 장소를 생성한다. 이 계단은 독특한 내부공간을 조성하기 위해 모든 부분이 세심하게 디자인 되었다. 난간 조차도 작은 후면발광 폴리카보네이트 재질로 만들어져 브레스트 플레이트와 같은 역할을 하며 차분하게 계단 라인을 따른다. 건물의 중추부로써 극적인 외형을 지니고 있으며, 건물 이용자들 간의 관계 형성 시점이 되는 이 계단은 당연히 우리 프로젝트 작업에 참고자료로 활용된다. 다시 말하지만, 이 계단은 수직으로 층들을 연결하는 단순한 요소가 아니다.

ELA - Edu Lopez Architects

P.114

카를로 스카르파의 계단에 연출되는 형태적 상호작용이 인상 깊다. 우리는 수직적 요소들(벽)과 그 외 건축적 요소들을 구불거리는 계단으로 통합하는 그의 계단 구성방법을 뚜렷이 기억하며, 이런 계단 구성이 파생하는 수많은 가능성들을 상상해 본다. 프로젝트 컨셉 전체를 아우르는 그의 작업방식을 우리는 정말 좋아한다.

Ezequiel Farca + Cristina Grappin

P.115

카를로 스파르카가 디자인한 베니스의 폰타치오네 퀘리니 스탐팔리아의 계단이 그 우아함에 가장 기억에 남는다.

Katsuhiro Miyamoto & Associates

P.116

전쟁 후 로마에는 많은 건축가들에 의해 주거 건물들의 유형이 재정의되었다. 로마의Palazzina(작은 주택)에는 매우 흥미로운 실험적인 계단들이 있다. 그 중 가장 아름다운 사례들을 루이지 모레티가 설계한 Casa del Girasole (카사 델 지라솔레)에서 볼 수 있다. 여기서 메인 계단은 본질적으로 건물의 아트리움이 되어 독특한 장소를 형성한다.

플로렌스의 아르 미오 프란끼 축구장의 계단에서 엔지니어 피에르 루이지 네르비가 고안한 구조적 해결법도 훌륭하다.

LGSMA_

P.117

파운틴헤드라는 영화에서 본 계단이다; 영화 시작부분에 하워드 로크가 막 설계한 건물안에서 패트리샤 닐이 계단을 내려오는 장면이 있다. 그 계단은 정말 마치 우아한 시처럼 내 마음속에 영원히 남을 것이다.

Miha Volgemut architect

P.117

많은 계단이 떠오른다. 하지만, 가장 좋아하는 계단은 주변 공간과 소통하며 수직 상승 움직임의 느낌을 강화 시키는 계단이다. 라우첸치아나 도서관 입구 계단처럼 매우 정교하고 기술적인 경우도 있지만, 저차원적 기술로 시공된 계단도 있다. 예를 들어 후지모토 소우가 설계한 "H" 주택의 계단이다. 이 계단은 공중에 떠있는 연약한 구조물 같으며, 마치 건물 안에 임시로 만들어진 것처럼 보인다. 이 계단은 공간에 대한 인식의 변화를 주었으며, 조반니 바티스타 피라네시의 감옥 (Piranesi's Prisons)을 보는 듯 하다.

Moussafir Architectes

P.118

오스카 니마이어가 설계한 브라질리아의 이타마라티 궁전에는 우리 실무 역사상 가장 질투를 유발하는 건축물인 2.3m너비의 난간 없는 나선형 계단이 있다. 완만한 나선은 마치 아무 노력없이 사람들을 위로 끌어 올리는 것처럼 보인다. 마치 중력이 작용하지 않는 듯. (하긴, 중력이 없다면 왜 계단이 필요할까?)

NL Architects

P.120

OMA의 쿤스탈 로테르담은 믿을 수 없을 만큼 굉장하다. 눈높이에서 보이는 강당은 평면도와 단면상에서 칼날처럼 날카롭게 반으로 갈라져 있다. 이는 내가 개인적으로 경험한 최고의 공간 효과들 중 하나이다. 건물 전체가 마치 찢어진 것 같다.

OPA

P.121

계단은 건축에서 끊임없이 변화하고 있는 요소이기 때문에 하나만 고르기는 어렵다. 게다가 전 세계의 디자인을 탐방 하노라면 콕 집어 한 순간만을 고르는 것도 어렵다. 그럼에도 불구하고 디자인적 접근이 집중되어 있는 당대의 사례가 멕시코 시티에 있다. 바로 휴맥스 뮤지엄의 계단이다. 이 계단은 데이비드 치퍼필드가 설계한 것으로 통로적 기능과 더불어 관람객과의 관계를 형성하고 마치 전시 조각상 같이 구조 디테일에 세심한 공이 들여졌다.

SLOT STUDIO

P.122

내가 직접 본 계단 중 가장 매력적인 계단은 데이비드 치퍼필드의 작품인 베를린 신 박물관의 계단이다. 이 계단은 흰색의 우아한 오브젝트로, 동시에 여러 요건을 충족시킨다. 기념비적, 전통적, 고전적인 레이아웃으로 동시에 실용적 공동 공간으로 쓰인다: 앉을 수 있고 휴식을 취할 수 있고 여러 사람들을 만날 수 있는 공간이다.

Stefano Corbo Studio

P.123

요코하마 항구의 계단은 우리가 본 계단 중 가장 인상적이다. 파사드 모사비와 알레한드로 자에라 폴라의 디자인으로 일본 해안가에 위치해 있다. 이 계단은 부드러움 곡선 형태로 건축 지형위에 포개어져 있다. 계단의 외관은 해변가를 따라 데크들이 서로 엮여 있는 모습이다.

TOUCH Architect

P.124

가장 인상깊게 본 계단은 인도에 있는 찬드바오리, 계단식 우물이다. 계단은 경우와 사람에 따라 다양한 용도로 쓰인다. 이 공간은 지역사회의 작은 소통의 장 같다. 문화, 역사, 생활방식의 다중적인 면을 반영하고 있어 그 곳을 감상하다 보면 규모나 디자인이 주는 아름다움 외 그 지역의 삶의 아름다움도 느낄 수 있다.

TROPICAL SPACE

Are there **myths, stories or superstitions** about stairs in your country?

Italy

b4architects

In Italy there are different stories and superstition about stairs. All of them have origin in Middle Age Catholic popular culture full of superstition stories. The most known is that to pass under a ladder is a great misfortune: if a young unmarried girl pass under a ladder she will not marry. Instead if she stumbles on steps she will soon marry. But in general stumbling coming down is a presage of loss of money.

In Rome there is a Catholic great monument, the 'Holy Stairs', a set of 28 marble steps located in a great building complex. According to Roman Catholic tradition, they are the steps leading up to the praetorium of Pontius Pilate in Jerusalem on which Jesus Christ stepped on his way to trial during his Passion. The legend says that St. Helena, mother of the Emperor Constantine the Great, brought the Holy Stairs from Jerusalem to Rome covering them with a special roof to transform the new location in a place of pilgrimage. In the Renaissance the site was rebuild and the Pope Sixtus V ordered to place the steps starting from the top to the bottom to avoid they were not trampled by the foot of the bricklayers, but touched only by the knees of the pilgrims. Still today a lot of people climbs the steps on knees honoring the Passion and asking religious clemencies.

Holy Stairs

© Vlad Lesnov

Japan

Katsuhiro Miyamoto & Associates

There is an interesting tradition of the Suwa shrines called 'Onbashira' festival in which trees are felled and moved physically by manpower to respective shrines to be erected as the new sacred 4 post pillars. In the case of Iinuma branch of Suwa shrine, the logs have to be pulled up an incredibly long and steep stairs to the shrine which is surely a testament to the human spirit.

And there is another story about the height of one of Japan's most ancient shrine, Izumo-taisha. It was said to be a tower-like shrine rebuilt many times over due to typhoon and earthquake damages. In the year 2000, the bottom remains of a gigantic column made up of 3 cedar logs were excavated within the shrine grounds which proved that it was a tower-like shrine. The size of the column is estimated to be able to support a shrine up to 96 metres high. The height of such a shrine structure would require a magnificent staircase as shown in the image of the model.

Suwa shrine

© Katsuhiro Miyamoto & Associates

Izumo-taisha shrine

© Blue Lotus

Mexico

"In architectural terms, stairways fulfill diverse functions beyond the pragmatics of moving up and down.

건축적 측면에서 이런 계단은 오르내리는 실용적 기능을 넘어 다양한 기능을 충족시키는 요소이다."

SLOT STUDIO

Historically, stairways in Mexico were an important feature of pyramids, representing ascension of the gods to higher planes of existence, and as places of sacrifice for honoring these gods. In architectural terms, stairways fulfill diverse functions beyond the pragmatics of moving up and down.

Pyramid of Teotihuacan

© DIEGO DELSO

Netherlands

BOARD

There are some interesting stairs, which are in fact escalators made of wood that can be found in Rotterdam in the so-called "Maastunnel". The tunnel connects the northern with the southern part of Rotterdam under the river "Maas". About 75,000 motor vehicles and especially a large number of cyclists and pedestrians use the tunnel daily, making the Maastunnel an important part of Rotterdam's road network. The tunnel was opened to the public on 14 February 1942 and was the first car tunnel in the Netherlands. The fact that the escalators are made of wood is most intriguing, because that material creates a very domestic and homey atmosphere in this public space that is usually dominated by traffic and is thus everything but inviting.

Maastunnel

© Stichting Microtoerisme

본인 나라에 계단에 얽힌 미신이나 속담이 있으면 알려달라

France

Apart from the popular superstition according to which one should not walk under a ladder, (but is that typically French or European?) the major story I know is the Ladder giving way to heaven in Jacob's dream, synonymous with spiritual growth in the Old Testament.

Here are extracts from Wikipedia Encyclopedia: Jacob's Ladder (Hebrew: Sulam Yaakov סלום יעקב) is the colloquial name for a connection between the earth and heaven that the biblical Patriarch Jacob dreams about during his flight from his brother Esau, as described in the Book of Genesis. The significance of the dream has been somewhat debated, but most interpretations agree that it identified Jacob with the obligations and inheritance of the ethnic people chosen by God, as understood in Abrahamic religions. It has since been used as a symbolic reference in various other contexts.

The description of Jacob's ladder appears in Genesis 28:11-19 also called "Jacob's Dream":

And Jacob went out from Beer-sheba, and went toward Haran. And he lighted upon the place, and tarried there all night, because the sun was set; and he took one of the stones of the place, and put it under his head, and lay down in that place to sleep. And he dreamed, and behold a ladder set up on the earth, and the top of it reached to heaven; and behold the angels of God ascending and descending on it. And, behold, the LORD stood beside him, and said: 'I am the LORD, the God of Abraham thy father, and the God of Isaac. The land whereon thou liest, to thee will I give it, and to thy seed. And thy seed shall be as the dust of the earth, and thou shalt spread abroad to the west, and to the east, and to the north, and to the south. And in thee and in thy seed shall all the families of the earth be blessed. And, behold, I am with thee, and will keep thee whithersoever thou goest, and will bring thee back into this land; for I will not leave thee, until I have done that which I have spoken to thee of.' And Jacob awaked out of his sleep, and he said: 'Surely the LORD is in this place; and I knew it not.' And he was afraid, and said: 'How full of awe is this place! this is none other than the house of God, and this is the gate of heaven.'

— Genesis 28:10-17 Jewish Publication Society (1917)

Afterwards, Jacob names the place, "Bethel" (literally, "House of God"). "House of God" and "Heaven's Door" also relate to the Temple of Jerusalem.

민간 미신과는 관련 없지만, (통상적으로 프랑스나 유럽에서)사다리 아래를 걸어가면 안된다는 말이 있다. 가장 잘 알려진 이야기로는 구약성경에서 영적인 성장의 의미와 밀접한 구절로 야곱의 꿈에서 천국의 길로 인도한 사다리 이야기가 있다.

위키피디아 사전에서 발췌한 내용이다.

야곱의 사다리는 세상과 천국을 연결하는 구어적 명칭으로 창세기에 기록되었듯 성서의 총대주교 야곱이 형제에서를 방문하고 돌아오는 여행중에 꾼 꿈에 대한 이야기다. 이 꿈의 중요성에는 다소 논쟁이 있지만, 아브라함의 종교 대부분의 해석에 따르면 야곱은 아브라함의 하느님에 의해 선택된 소수 민족의 의무와 유산과 동일시 되며, 다른 여러 맥락으로 상징적으로 인용되고 있다.

야곱의 사다리는 "야곱의 꿈"으로도 불리며 창세기 28:11-19에 나온다:

야곱이 브엘세바에서 떠나 하란으로 향하여 가더니.

한 곳에 이르러는 해가 진지라 거기서 유숙하려고 그 곳의 한 돌을 가져 다가 베개로 삼고 거기 누워 자더니

꿈에 본 즉 사닥다리가 땅 위에 서 있는데 그 꼭대기가 하늘에 닿았고 또 본 즉 하나님의 사자들이 그 위에서 오르락내리락 하고

또 본 즉 여호와께서 그 위에 서서 이르시되 나는 여호와니 너의 조부 아브라함의 하나님이요 이상의 하나님이라 네가 누워 있는 땅을 내가 너와 제 자손에게 주리니

제 자손이 땅의 티끌 같이 되어 네가 서쪽과 동쪽과 북쪽과 남쪽으로 퍼져 나갈지며 땅의 모든 족속이 너와 네 자손으로 말미암아 복을 받으리라

내가 너와 함께 있어 네가 어디로 가든지 너를 지키며 너를 이끌어 이 땅으로 돌아오게 할지라 내가 네가 허락한 것을 다 이루기까지 너를 떠나지 아니하리라 하신지라

야곱이 잠이 깨서 이르되 여호와께서 과연 여기 계시거늘 내가 알지 못하였도라

이에 두려워하여 이르되 두렵도다 이 곳이여 이것은 다름 아닌 하나님의 집이요 이는 하늘의 문이로다 하고

창세기 28:10-17

그 후 야곱은 그 곳을 "벧엘"이라 하였다 (문자 그대로 "하나님의 집"이라는 뜻). "하나님의 집"과 "천국의 문"은 예루살렘 성전과도 연관된다.

Moussafir Architectes

Italy

이탈리아에는 계단에 대한 여러 이야기와 미신이 있다. 모두 중세 카톨릭 통속 문화에 기원을 두고 있다. 가장 잘 알려진 이야기는 사다리 밑을 지나가면 엄청난 불행이 따른다는 것이다: 젊은 미혼녀가 사다리 밑을 지나가면 결혼을 못 하게 된다. 대신 계단에 발이 걸리면 곧 결혼을 하게 된다. 하지만, 일반적으로 계단을 내려오다가 발이 걸리는 것은 돈을 잃는 다는 전조로 여겨 지기도 한다.

로마 대 저택 단지에는 28개의 대리석 계단으로 된 '신성한 계단'이라 불리는 카톨릭 유적이 있다. 로마 카톨릭교 전통에 따르면 이 계단은 예수 그리스도가 예루살렘에서 고난주에 본 디오 빌라도에게 재판을 받으러 궁으로 올라갔던 계단이라고 한다. 전설에 의하면 콘스탄티누스 황제의 어머니인 성 헬레나가 성지순례의 새로운 거처를 마련하기 위해 이 신성한 계단에 특별한 지붕을 씌워 예루살렘에서 로마로 옮겼다고 한다. 르네상스 시대에 이 지역은 재건되었고, 교황 식스토 5세는 벽돌공들의 발이 아닌 순례자들의 무릎만이 닿을 수 있도록 계단을 꼭대기에서 바닥으로 배치하도록 명령하였다. 여전히 오늘날에도 많은 사람들이 고난주를 경의하고 자비를 구하면서 무릎으로 계단을 오르고 있다.

b4architects (P.130)

Never walk under the stairs.

계단 밑으로는 절대 지나가면 안된다.

LGSMA_

Many are the stories about stairs: for instance, some believe that walking under stairs will bring you bad luck. The origin of this superstition may be due to the triangular shape that the ladder forms when placed against a wall, reminiscent of the Holy Trinity. Passing through the Trinity would be considered disrespectful, or blasphemous.

계단에 대한 이야기는 많다: 그 예로, 일부 사람들은 계단 밑을 지나가면 나쁜 운이 따를 거라고 믿는다. 이 미신은 아마도 벽에 기대어 세워진 사다리의 형태가 성 삼위일체를 연상하는 삼각형 모양이 되는 것에서 유래된 것 같다.

Stefano Corbo Studio

Japan

각 신사마다 새로운 신성한 4개의 기둥이 될 나무를 쓰러 뜨려 인력으로 직접 옮기는 '온바시라'라 불리는 스와신사의 특별한 전통축제가 있다. 이이누마에 있는 스와신사의 경우 엄청나게 높고 가파른 계단으로 나무를 끌고 올라가야 한다.

이는 분명 인간의 정신력을 입증하는 증거이다.

그리고 일본에서 가장 오래된 이즈모 타이샤 신사의 높

이와 관련된 또다른 이야기가 있다.

그것은 태풍과 지진으로 인해 여러번 재건된 탑과 같은 신사라고 전해진다. 2000년도에 세 개의 삼나무 통나무로 이루어진 거대한 기둥의 밑바닥이 신사 안에서 발견됐는데, 그것이 신사가 탑 모양이였을 것이라 예측하게 했다.

나무 기둥의 크기는 96미터 높이의 신사를 지탱할 수 있는 것으로 보였으며, 이러한 신사의 높이는 모델 이미지에 나타난 것처럼 멋진 계단이 필요했을 것이다.

Katsuhiro Miyamoto & Associates (P.131)

Mexico

Brings bad luck crossing underneath stairs, especially the work stairs located in the streets. This superstition possibly comes from a religion base, because a stair supported on a wall forms a triangle, symbol associated to Holy Trinity, to cross it represents desecrating therefore you will get bad luck in the future. The stairs are also associated with gallows and criminals, when the murders killed someone by hanging on a tree, nobody was enough brave to cross under to don't meet the dead person.

계단, 특히 길거리에 설치된 작업용 계단 밑으로 지나가면 나쁜 운이 따른다. 이는 아마도 종교에 기반한 미신일 것이다. 왜냐하면 벽에 기대어진 계단은 삼위일체를 의미하는 삼각형 모양을 만들기 때문에 그 곳으로 지나가는 것은 신성 모독을 의미하여 나쁜 운이 따른 다는 것이다. 또한, 교수형과 범죄 와도 연관된다. 살인자가 누군가를 나무에 목을 메어서 죽였다면 아무도 그 죽은 사람 밑으로 지나갈 용기를 내지 못하기 때문이다.

Ezequiel Farca + Cristina Grappin

역사적으로 멕시코에서 계단은 피라미드에서와 같이 더 높은 존재인 신들을 향한 승천을 의미하는 중요한 요소였다. 또한, 계단은 신들에게 경배의 재물을 바치는 장소이기도 했다. 건축적 측면에서 이런 계단은 오르내리는 실용적 기능을 넘어 다양한 기능을 충족시키는 요소이다.

SLOT STUDIO (P.132)

Netherlands

관심 가는 계단들이 몇 있다. 그 중 로테르담의 "마스 터널"이라고 불리는 곳에 실제로 나무로 만들어진 에스컬레이터가 있다. '마스' 강 아래로 로테르담의 북부와 남부 사이를 잇는 마스터널은 매일 약 75,000대의 자동차들과 자전거와 보행자들이 유난히 많이 지나다니는 로테르담의 중요한 도로망이다. 이 터널은 1942년 2월 14일 대중에게 개방되었고 네덜란드에서는 최초로 자동차 진입이 가능한 터널이었다. 사실 여기서 제일 흥미로운 점은 나무로 만들어진 에스컬레이터다. 주로 차량들로 꽉 차 있는 이 공공 장소에 나무라는 재료는 매우 익숙하고 편안한 분위기를 자아내기에 에스컬레이터는 사람들을 매료시키는 터널의 전부이다.

BOARD (P.133)

Dutch stairs are ladders.

네덜란드에서 계단이라고 하면 사다리를 의미한다.

NL Architects

Slovenia

I don't think there is a particular myth related to the stairs in my country, but the symbolism of the stairway is rather universal, it is about ascension into something new, better, transcendent..., or on the other side descension into the unconsciousness, darkness, hidden...

우리나라에는 계단에 대해 특별히 전해 내려오는 이야기는 없는 것 같다. 하지만, 계단은 대부분 일반적으로 더 나은 곳으로의 승천, 초월 등을 상징한다. 거꾸로 무의식으로의 하강, 어두움, 음침함 등을 상징하기도 한다.

Miha Volgemut architect architect

Thailand

. There are some superstitions about stairs in Thailand which is actually derived from Thai-Chinese culture. We believe that orientation of the stairs should not face straight to the main entrance, unless residents who lives in this house will run out of money.

태국에는 실제로 중국계 태국인들에 의해 전해오는 계단에 대한 미신들이 몇 개 있다. 계단의 방향이 메인 입구를 바라봐서는 안되다고 믿는다. 그렇지 않으면, 집 주인은 돈을 잃게 된다.

TOUCH Architect

USA

None that I know of, other than it is best to avoid the stairs to the basement in a horror film.

알고 있는게 없다. 그것보다 공포 영화에서는 지하로 내려가는 계단은 피하는게 최선이다.

OPA

Vietnam

Vietnamese have a fairy tale about a "kim thang" - "triangle stair" use for traditional vietnamese game and also for making a frame for convolve. When people play the game or three types of convolve grow in "kim thang", it appears connections between each element. Thus we can say the story imply the balance and the connection of everything in the naturals.

베트남에는 "킴탕"에 관한 동화가 있다. - 베트남 정통 놀이를 할 때 사용하거나 굴레 프레임을 만들 때 사용하는 "삼각 모양 계단"이다. 사람들이 이 놀이를 하거나 "킴탕" 안에 세 종류의 굴레가 나타나면 각 요소들이 연결된다. 즉, 이 이야기는 모든 것이 자연안에서 균형을 이루고 하나로 연결된다는 것을 의미한다고 할 수 있다.

TROPICAL SPACE

PROFILE

b4 architects

The b4architects is an architect firm based in Rome. The firm will provide architectural services using a specific design process for each customer providing greater additional value and enhanced design and construction.

The principals architects and co-founders are Gianluca Evels and Stefania Papitto and the firm utilizes a tested working team and a professional external network of consultants.

Our approach to any project is to involve all parties in a creative collaboration to define the objectives of the project with a balanced combination within critical readings of the local context and the "outsider" perspective of us. The work on preexistent spaces and the interior design projects try to explain all the available elements in a new synthesis: the traces of the history of the building, the expectations of the client, psycho-sensorial aspects of the architecture fused in a continuous spatial and visual tale.

Measuring us from urban and landscape design until restoration, interior design and object design, in a process that involve specific competences, always respecting the environmental characteristics.

We are interested in producing works that contribute to the debate of the complexity of modern life.

We also dedicate to further activities, like some different experiences at the university of Rome or taking part at some international workshops, with the aim to be active in the debate about contemporary architecture. The office attend to building energy consulting both for new construction and for renewal of existing building as Climate-House-Expert-Planner.

BOARD

BOARD (Bureau of Architecture, Research, and Design) was founded in Rotterdam in 2005 and is active in many fi elds: as an architecture, urban design, and design practice, as a research board and as a platform for comparative analysis on urban issues through its bi-annual journal MONU – Magazine on Urbanism. BOARD won several prizes recently in prestigious international architecture and urban design competitions.

Bernd Upmeyer is the founder of BOARD and editor in chief of MONU – Magazine on Urbanism. He studied architecture and urban design at the University of Kassel(Germany) and the Technical University of Delft (Netherlands). From 2004 until 2007 he taught and did research as Assistant Professor at the department of Architecture, Urban Planning and Landscape Planning at the University of Kassel. In 2010 he taught as Adjunct Professor at the department of Urban Design at the Hafen-City University Hamburg. In 2012 he was a guest critic at the Berlage Institute's fi rstyear postgraduate research studio "Anarcity".

In 2013 he lectured and participated in a discussion about architecture, urbanism and media at Strelka's Urban Studies Session in Moscow. Upmeyer frequently writes for international publications and magazines. He holds a PhD (Dr.-Ing.) in Urban Studies from the University of Kassel(Germany). Upmeyer is the author of the book Binational Urbanism – On the Road to Paradise. The book examines the way of life of people who start a second life in a second city in a second nation-state, without saying goodbye to their fi rst city.

Upmeyer coined the term "binational urbanism".

BOARD employs an international team of architects and planners and collaborates with national and international external consultants and specialists.

ELA-Edu Lopez Architects

ELA is an architectural design firm headquartered in Madrid, Spain with diversified services including architectural design, urban planning and interior design. Since the firm´s founding in 2010.

ELA´s mission is to deliver exceptional design ideas and solutions through the creative blending of human need, environmental stewardship, value creation, science and art, involved in a diverse portfolio including office, civic, cultural, healthcare, residential, academic, transportation, landscape and mixed-use projects.

ELA's approach to utilizing digital tools and technologies, contemporary theory, innovative building practices and advancements in engineering solutions and environmental sustainability have afforded the practice a broad and powerful perspective on all aspects related to architectural building design and city planning

With each project the firm explores new ways to integrate an organizing idea with the programmatic and functional essence of a building. Rather than imposing a style upon different sites and climates, or pursued irrespective of program, the unique character of a program and a site becomes the starting point for an architectural idea. While anchoring each work in its specific site and circumstance, ELA endeavors to obtain a deeper beginning in the experience of time, space, light and materials.

ELA: Edu Lopez Architects.
www.elarchitect.net
https://www.facebook.com/ELA.EduardoLopezArchitects/

Ezequiel Farca + Cristina Grappin

Ezequiel Farca Nacach
July 25, 1967.

Cristina Grappin Flores
November 16, 1988.

Ezequiel began his career at the Universidad Iberoamericana studying a bachelor in Industrial Design (1988-1991). He received a scholarship from Western Washington University in Washington State to continue his studies in Industrial Design (1991-1992). He obtained a Master's Degree in Architecture at Large Scale and Other Environments at the Polytechnic University of Catalonia in Barcelona, Spain, and in 2012 he completed an MBA at UCLA, Los Angeles. In 1995, Farca started the design firm, and shortly thereafter a furniture showroom in Mexico City.

Cristina Grappin, with a degree in Architecture from the Technological and Higher Studies Institute of Monterrey, joins the firm as a business partner to manage the office in Mexico City and to expand internationally with another office in Los Angeles and Milan, the last one specialized in developing projects of interior design and furniture design for yachts.

Ezequiel Farca® + Cristina Grappin® represent the perfect synergy between design and functionality, a clean aesthetic taking care of the details and the use of natural and local materials. In its trajectory, the firm has developed more than 80 projects of different scales and typologies such as residential, commercial and hotels as well as various special projects related to design.

Katsuhiro Miyamoto & Associates

Katsuhiro Miyamoto

1961-Born in Hyogo

1984-Bachelor of Architecture from the University of Tokyo

1987-Master of Architecture from the University of Tokyo

1988-Established Atelier Cinquiéme Architects

1995-Lecturer, Department of Architecture, Osaka University of Arts

1999-Associate Professor, Department of Architecture, Osaka University of Arts

2002-Reorganized to Katsuhiro Miyamoto & Associates

2005-Associate Professor, Department of Environmental Design, Osaka University of Arts

2008-Professor, Graduate School of Engineering and Urban Research Plaza, Osaka City University

Belongings
- Architectural Institute of Japan
- The Japan Institute of Architects
- Osaka Association of Architects & Building Engineers
- JAPAN INTER-DESIGN FORUM

LGSMA_

Luca Galofaro - Stefania Manna

Luca Galofaro_Stefania Manna e Associati (LGSMA_) is founded by Luca Galofaro and Stefania Manna in 2016.

Asocciate: Gianluca Fontana

The office sets up on the twenty-year experience of its partners and associated working as IaN+.

LGSMA works on the inseparable relationship between architectural thinking and construction. Architecture is seen as a test field of ideas and very different research tools, which ultimately aims at the Project in every kind of form.

Luca Galofaro has intensely pursued in teaching, writing and research, activities which have been an integral part of the office's engagement with architecture.

Stefania Manna has focused on the technical and material complexity of the project as a tool to transfer its ideal substance into build reality under any given circumstances.

Gianluca Fontana. His experience matures through the involvement in many international competitions as well as final designs, working plans and construction site managements.

Miha Volgemut architect

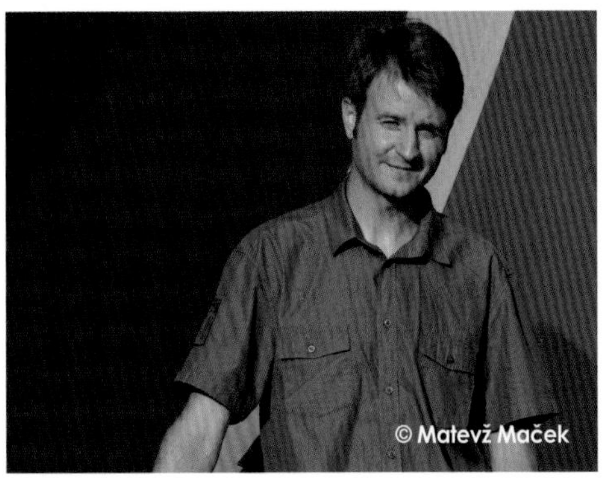

Miha Volgemut architect graduated in 2004 at Faculty of Architecture in Ljubljana and received his Master of Science in Urban Strategies under the mentorship of Wolf D. Prix from the University for Applied Arts Vienna in 2008. He also received certificate for the summer school under the mentorship of Aaron Betsky from Rotterdam Academy of Architecture and Urban Design in 2005. Prior to founding Volgemut Architects in 2008 he worked five years as a project designer at the Office for Architecture in Ljubljana, two years on interior design at Monochrome architects and also as a freelance architect. In 2005/06 he was employed at the Faculty of Architecture in Ljubljana.

Miha is winner of the Trimo research award 2005 and of the candidacy for Archiprix international 2005. He participated in international workshops in Glasgow, Rotterdam, Vienna and national ones.

Since May 2009 he is registered architect in the Chamber of Architecture and Planning Slovenia and has designed and realized numerous projects since then. On March 2013 he received Municipality Bronze Award for architectural achievement in Kamnik town.

Moussafir Architectes

Jacques Moussafir studied Architecture at the Ecole d'Architecture de Paris-Tolbiac and Art History at the Sorbonne. He founded his firm in 1995 after completing his training over a period of 10 years as project manager for Christian Hauvette, Henri Gaudin, Dominique Perrault and Francis Soler. After some early interior design work, he took part in a number of culturally oriented projects such as Music Venues and Art Museums as well as private houses and social housing programs.

Jacques Moussafir has also lectured at several European schools and at the Pavillon de l'Arsenal and Cité de l'Architecture in Paris. He was guest professor and associate lecturer at the Ecole Spéciale d'Architecture in Paris from 2003 to 2007 and at the Ecole d'Architecture, de la Ville et des Territoires at Marne-la-Vallée in 2011-2012. He was a founding member of the "French Touch" collective created in 2007 which represented France at the 11th Venice Architecture Biennale in 2008.

Our projects form part of an experimental approach whose chief themes are the relationship between interior and exterior, the idea of substance and materiality, and the mnemonic dimension of architectural space. For us, architecture is less a question of image than of 'sense', in both meanings of the word: 'making sense' by encouraging a process of meaningful inquiry, and experiencing space via the five senses.

NL Architects

© Jean Pierre

NL Architects is an Amsterdam based office. The three principals, Pieter Bannenberg, Walter van Dijk and Kamiel Klaasse, officially opened practice in January 1997, but had shared workspace already since the early nineties. All were educated at the Technical University in Delft.

NL Architects aspires to catalyze urban life. The office is on a constant hunt to find alternatives for the way we live and work. How can we intensify human interaction?

We understand architecture as the speculative process of investigating, revealing and reconfiguring the wonderful complexities of the world we live in. Can we compress banality into beauty; squeeze the sublime out of the obvious? How can we transform, twist, bend, stack, stretch, enhance or reassemble the components that constitute our environment into new and better configurations?

Some of our projects include Parkhouse/Carstadt (an attempt to integrate auto-mobility and architecture), WOS 8 (a seamless Heat Transfer Station) and the Mandarina Duck Store in Paris. The BasketBar (a grand café with basketball court on the roof) and A8ernA, the redevelopment of the space under an elevated highway, have become emblematic contributions to contemporary culture.

Currently the office is involved in 'numerous projects in various stages of development', including residential projects, cultural facilities and sports buildings. Early 2007 the office won the prestigious competition for the so-called Groninger Forum: an exhilarating mixture of library and cinema and museum. Construction has begun, the Forum will be completed in 2019.

The renovation of Kleiburg, a super-sized apartment block in the Bijlmermeer in Amsterdam was granted the EU Mies Award 2017.

object-e architecture

Object-e architecture is an architectural practice currently based in Thessaloniki, Greece and directed by Katerina Tryfonidou and Dimitris Gourdoukis. It started in 2006, in St. Louis, USA, as a platform with the intention to explore new territories in architecture with the aid of computational tools and techniques. Through time, object-e moved beyond the borders of computation and engaged design at large, trying to graft the new media with the social, political and ecological issues that architecture is facing today. It has won a number of prizes in international competitions, and its works has been published, exhibited and presented internationally.

Object-e is based on several collaborations with people coming from different backgrounds, with different design intentions and agendas. The outcome of object-e, being in most cases collaborative, is therefore defying any concept of style; Identity is formed through difference and constant transformation.

Object-e engages architecture and design in three different - but always connected - levels: Through specific design projects that are answers to specific design questions; private projects or competitions. Through experimental research projects that are aiming to extend our understanding of space, digital media and fabrication. Through teaching; either in established institutions or independently, sharing of knowledge is always the core that allows the rest to happen.

http://object-e.net
https://www.facebook.com/object.e

OPA

Ogrydziak Prillinger Architects (OPA) is an idea-driven office committed to finding design solutions that both expand the possibilities inherent in architecture and resonate within their particular context.

While every project originates as a response to specific requirements of site, program and client, each evolves as an exploration of its own internal potential rather than reflecting a predetermined style.

In all the work, there is an emphasis on communicating architectural meaning by creating powerful emotional and perceptual resonances. Shaping and choreographing spatial experiences through the consideration of movement and formal logic results in work that is distinctive for its conceptual clarity and physical presence.

Luke Ogrydziak and Zoë Prillinger received BA and M. Arch degrees from Princeton University and have taught at Harvard University and the University of California, Berkeley. OPA has been featured in publications including MARK magazine, The New York Times, Metropolis, Wallpaper*, Architecture, Architectural Record, and GA Houses, and in multiple exhibitions at the GA Gallery in Tokyo. They are currently exhibiting an installation at the University of Chicago coinciding with the 2017 Chicago Biennial. OPA has received numerous American Institute of Architects San Francisco and California awards and the Architectural League of New York's 'Emerging Voices' award.

www.oparch.net

Stefano Corbo Studio

Stefano Corbo (1981) is an Italian architect, researcher, and Assistant Professor at RISD (Rhode Island School of Design).

He holds a Ph.D and an M.Arch. II in Advanced Architectural Design from UPM-ETSAM Madrid (Escuela Técnica Superior de Arquitectura).

Stefano is currently Assistant Professor at the Rhode Island School of Design (RISD), and has taught at several academic Institutions: Nanjing University; LAU Beirut (Lebanese American University); The Faculty of Architecture in Alghero, Italy; ETSAM Madrid. He has been a guest lecturer at SAC Städelschule Frankfurt, Deakin University in Melbourne, College of Design Minnesota, ESALA Edinburgh, The University of Miami, and The University of Wisconsin.

Stefano has contributed to several international journals (OASE, Domus, Mark, CLOG, Il Giornale dell'Architettura, etc.), and has published two books.

In December 2014, his first book was published by Ashgate / Routledge: "From Formalism to Weak Form. The Architecture and Philosophy of Peter Eisenman."

In July 2016 his new book has been published by Images: "Interior Landscapes. A visual atlas", a journey through the interior - exterior dichotomy in modern and contemporary architecture.

In 2012, after working at Mecanoo Architecten, Stefano founded his own office SCSTUDIO (www.scstudio.eu), a multidisciplinary network practicing architecture and design, preoccupied with the intellectual, economical and cultural context.

SLOT STUDIO

SLOT is an active and interdisciplinary architectural design studio. People from diverse professional disciplines contribute to this project.

Our work has reached a profound understanding of the human needs, enabling us to intertwine the constructive and philosophical sides of building.

As architects, we push design to its ultimate material consequences and aim for cultural connectivity: sense of usability, mathematics of space and a wide aesthetic research.

The founders of the company, Juan Carlos Vidals (Mexican) and Moritz Melchert (German), are two young architects with a fresh and contemporary vision of architecture, urbanism and interior design. Our design criteria is not based or limited by shapes or elements, instead we create plenty strategies that enable us to adapt our projects to the special needs and requirements of our clients.

Throughout our experience, we have come to realize that a strong preliminary research of the surroundings is decisive for each one of our designs. This step allows us to create a cohesive and meaningful design beyond its physical features; in other words, our formal proposals are always the result of a comprehensive analysis of the context, this enables our projects to excel in terms of their uniqueness and authenticity.

Partners
Moritz Melchert
Juan Carlos Vidals

TOUCH Architect

TOUCH Architect Co.,Ltd. was first established since 2014. It was changed from TOUCH STUDIO Architect partnership, with four years experiences into a company. With a great chance of an improvement, we have two main co-founders consist of Mr. Setthakarn Yangderm as an architect and leader of our firm and Ms. Parpis Leelaniramol as an architect, which will corporate together in design, construction, and management.

SETTHAKARN YANGDERM
Architect // Managing Director // Founder
Bachelor of Architecture
(Department of Architecture, Major in Thai Architecture)
Faculty of Architecture, Chulalongkorn University. (1st top rank of Thailand's university)
Honor in best architectural design in 2007.

PARPIS LEELANIRAMOL
Architect // Co-founder
Bachelor of Science
(International Program in Design and Architecture),
Faculty of Architecture, Chulalongkorn University. (1st top rank of Thailand's university)
Master of Science in Real Estate Business (MRE),
Faculty of Commerce and Accountancy, Thammasat University. (1st top rank of business program)
Teaching Assistant - MRE Thammasat Personal Consultant - Mini-MRE at Ananda Development (Real Estate Listed Company in Thailand)

TROPICAL SPACE

Tropical Space is located in Ho Chi Minh city, which was established in 2011 by two founders: Architect Nguyen Hai Long - Master degree of Architecture at Ho Chi Minh City University of Architecture - Principal Architect Achitect Tran Thi Ngu Ngon - Bachelor degree of Architecture at Ho Chi Minh City University of Architecture - Director Design philosophy: Architecture with simple shapes, focus on ventilation solutionand natural lighting which is suitable with the tropical climate.

Meanwhiles, encourage clients using raw materials which are economical and substainable.

Award

- Fritz Hoger Award 2017 | Termitary House | Gold Winner | Semidetached House |
- Monsoon Architecture Award 2017| LT House | Winner |Single Family Residential Projects
- A+ Awards 2017:Terra Cotta Studio | Concepts-Architecture +Workspace |Jury Winners & Popular Choice Winners
- AR Emerging Architecture 2016 | Terra Cotta Studio | Finalist
- Brick Award 2016 | Termitary House | Winner | Residential Use Category
- FuturArc Green Leadership Award 2016 | Termitary House | Winner | Single Residential Category
- AZ Award 2016 | Termitary House | Best Residential Architecture
- Arcasia Award for Architectecture 2015 | Termitary House | Honorable Mention | Single Family Residential Projects
- Architectural Review House 2015 | Termitary House | Finalist •
- Talk : In Feb 2017, Ngon and Long have given a guest lecture at Cornell University with the topic: "Nests in the Tropic"
- Talk: In July 2017, lecture at living Asian with the topic: "Modern Tropical"

A Case Study of **Contemporary Stairs**

Haus am Weinberg, Germany

UNStudio

10 degree house, U.S.A

HYA architecture

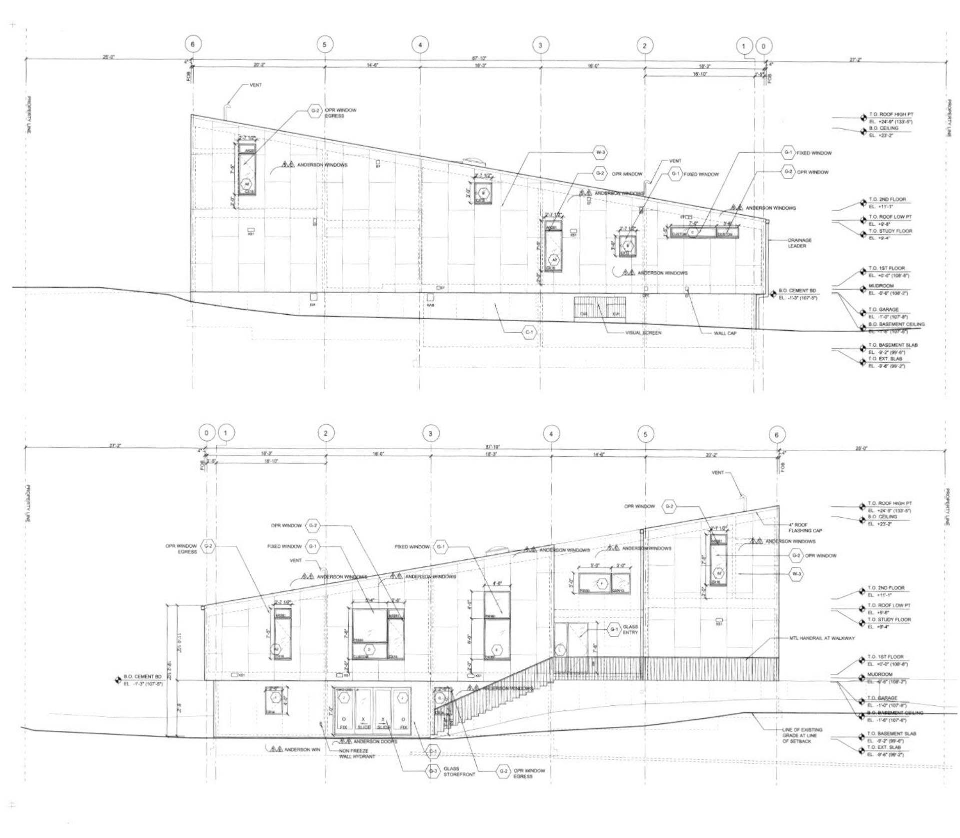

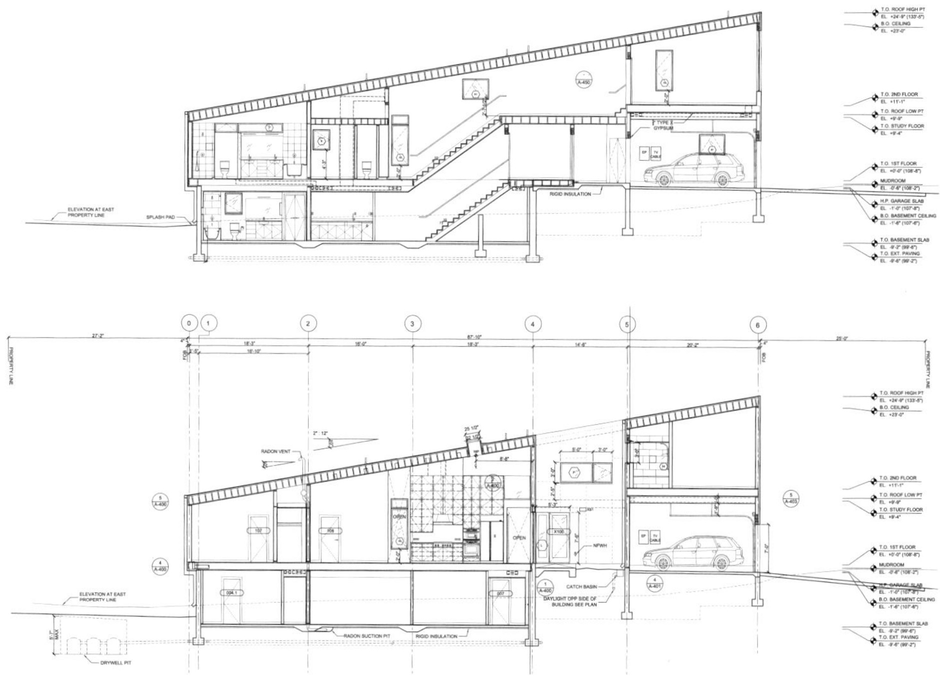

8House, Denmark
BIG

A House in Tojiin2, Japan

DAI NAGASAKA / MGA

© Kei Sugino

A&G, Cyprus
vardastudio

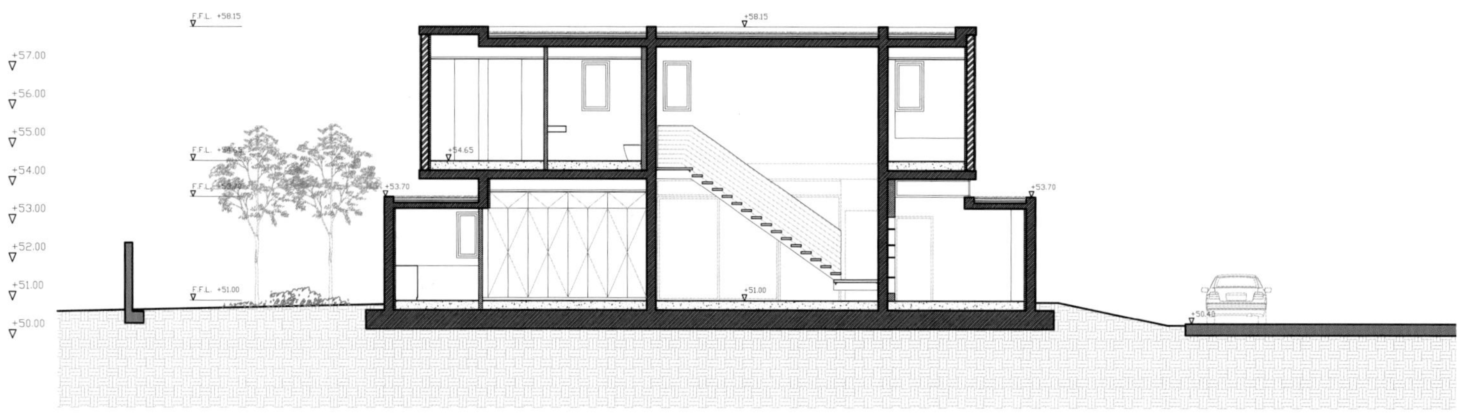

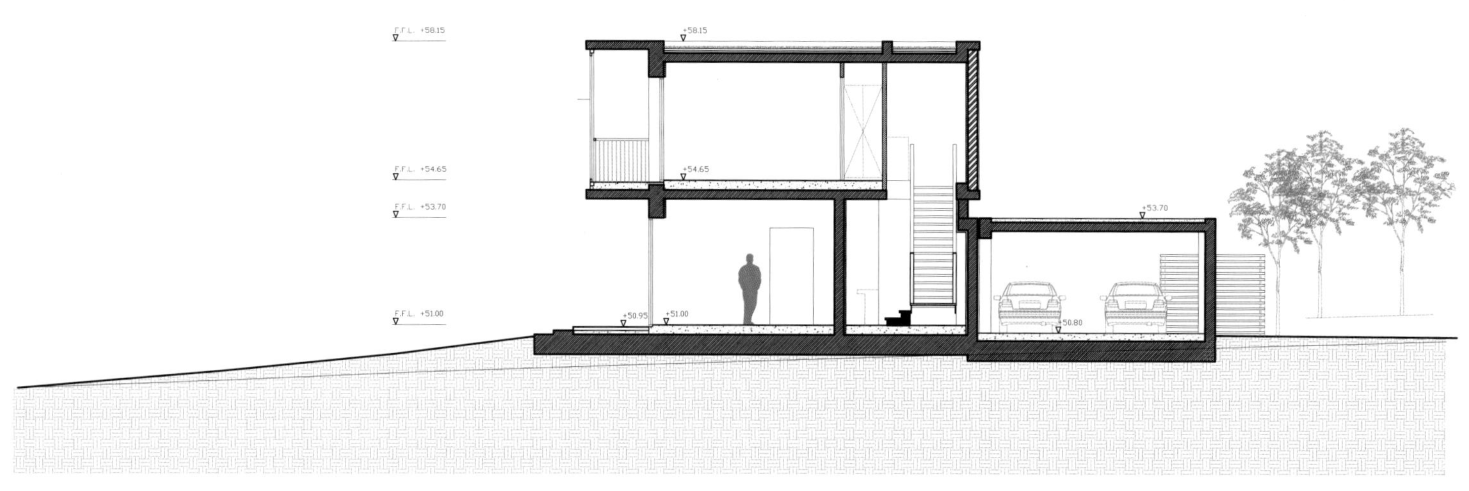

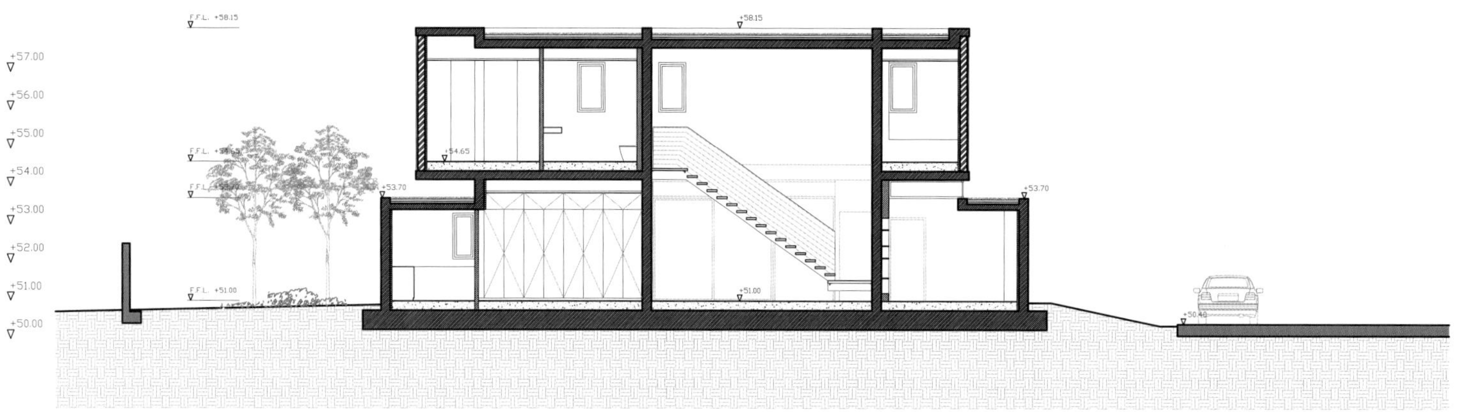

© CREATIVE PHOTO ROOM

© CREATIVE PHOTO ROOM

Anglesea, Australia

ANDREW MAYNARD ARCHITECTS

1. Existing house
2. Boat Shed
3. Trampoline

© Peter Bennetts

ÁTICO INVERSO, Spain

XPIRAL

© DAVID FRUTOS/BIS IMAGES

© DAVID FRUTOS/BIS IMAGES

© DAVID FRUTOS/BIS IMAGES

av house, Mexico

BGP Arquitectos

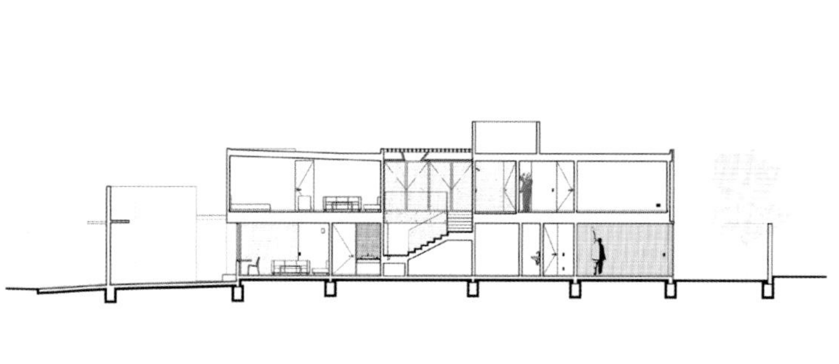

Longitudinal section A-A'

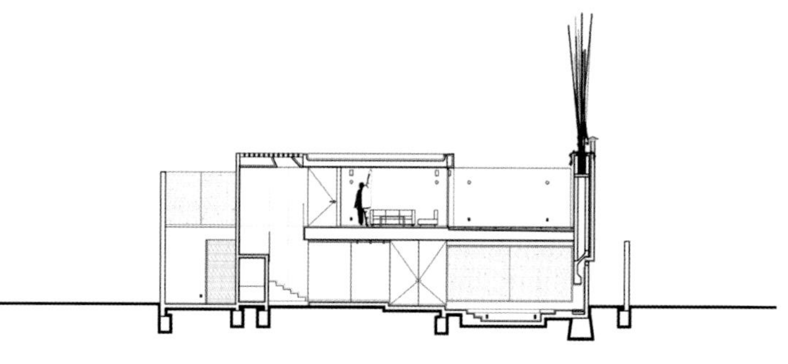

Transversal section B-B'

© Rafael Gamo

© Rafael Gamo

BARAUM, Korea
Lee Ki Ok

BARCELOS, Portugal
Rui Grazina
© Nelson Garrido

bird house, Japan

Katsuhiro Miyamoto & Associates

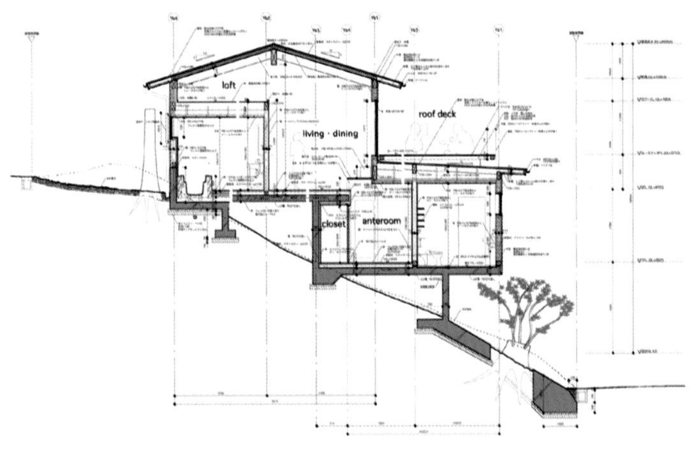

A-A' Section s=1:100

Blooming House with wild flowers, Korea

studio-GAON

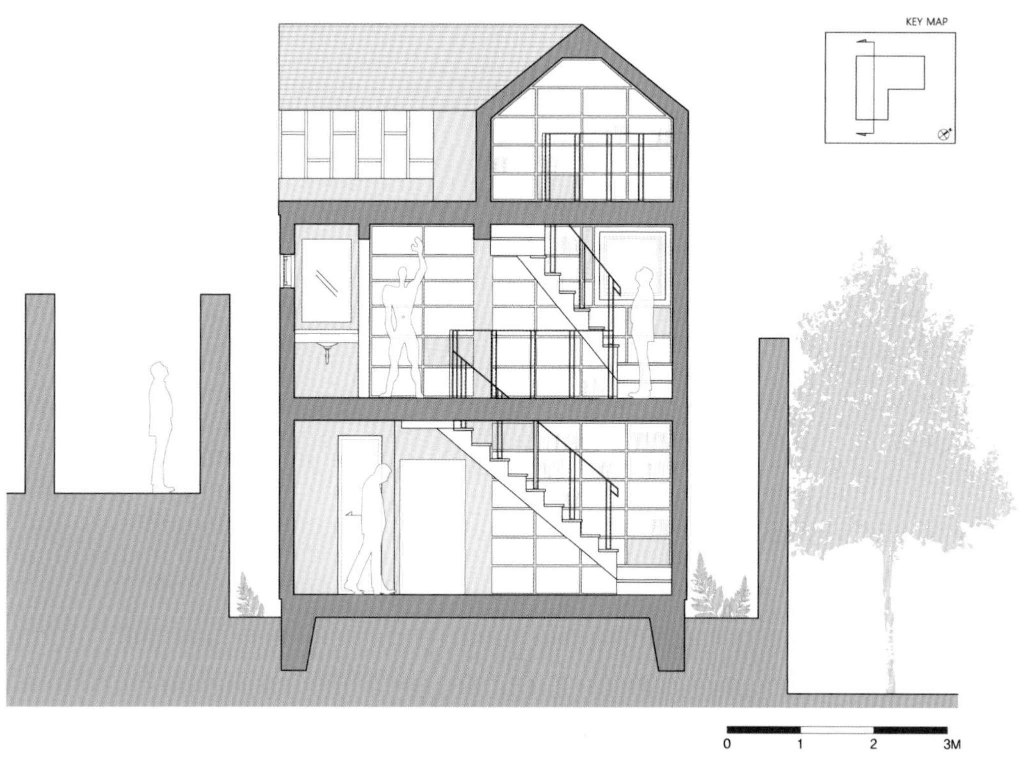

© Youngchae Park

Casa Osa, Costa Rica

OBRA Architects

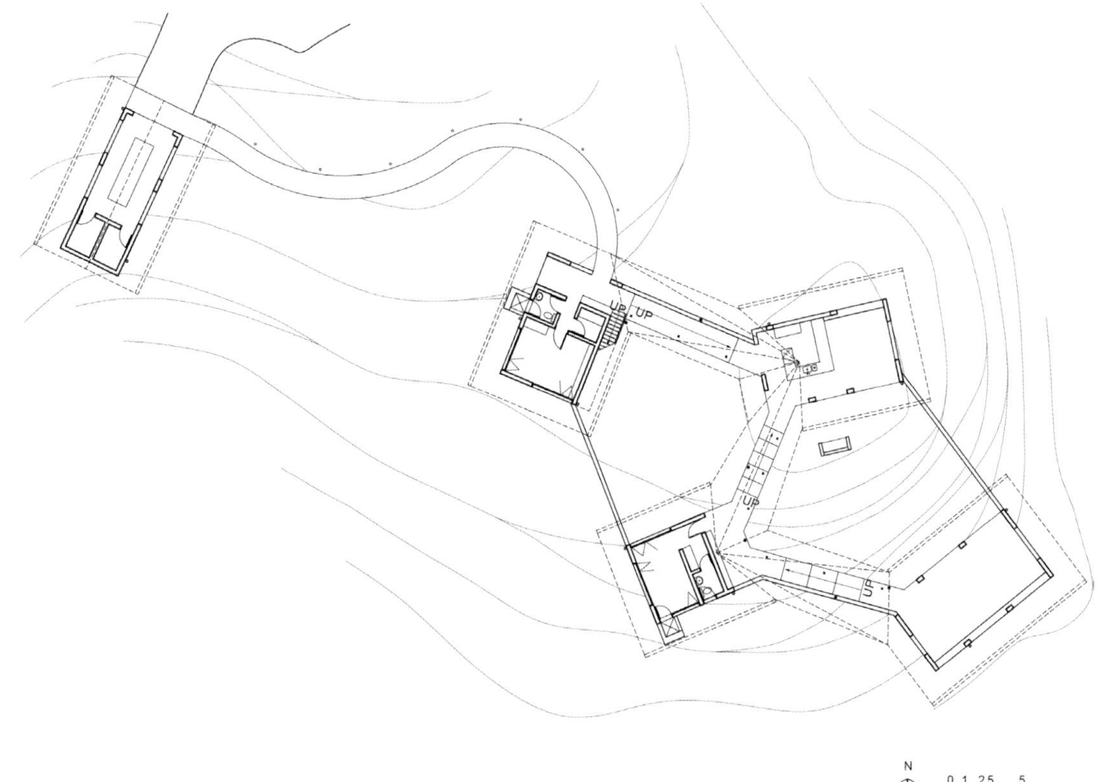

Butler House, Australia

ANDREW MAYNARD ARCHITECTS

© Kevin Hui

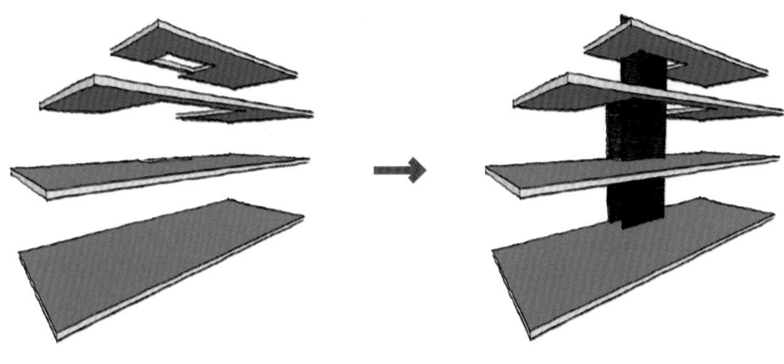

Timber louvers
sheives and operable louvers flanking stairs act as a sound barrier. carpet aloing the wall increses sound absorption

Carriage House, U.S.A
YOSHIHARA, MCKEE, ARCHITECTS

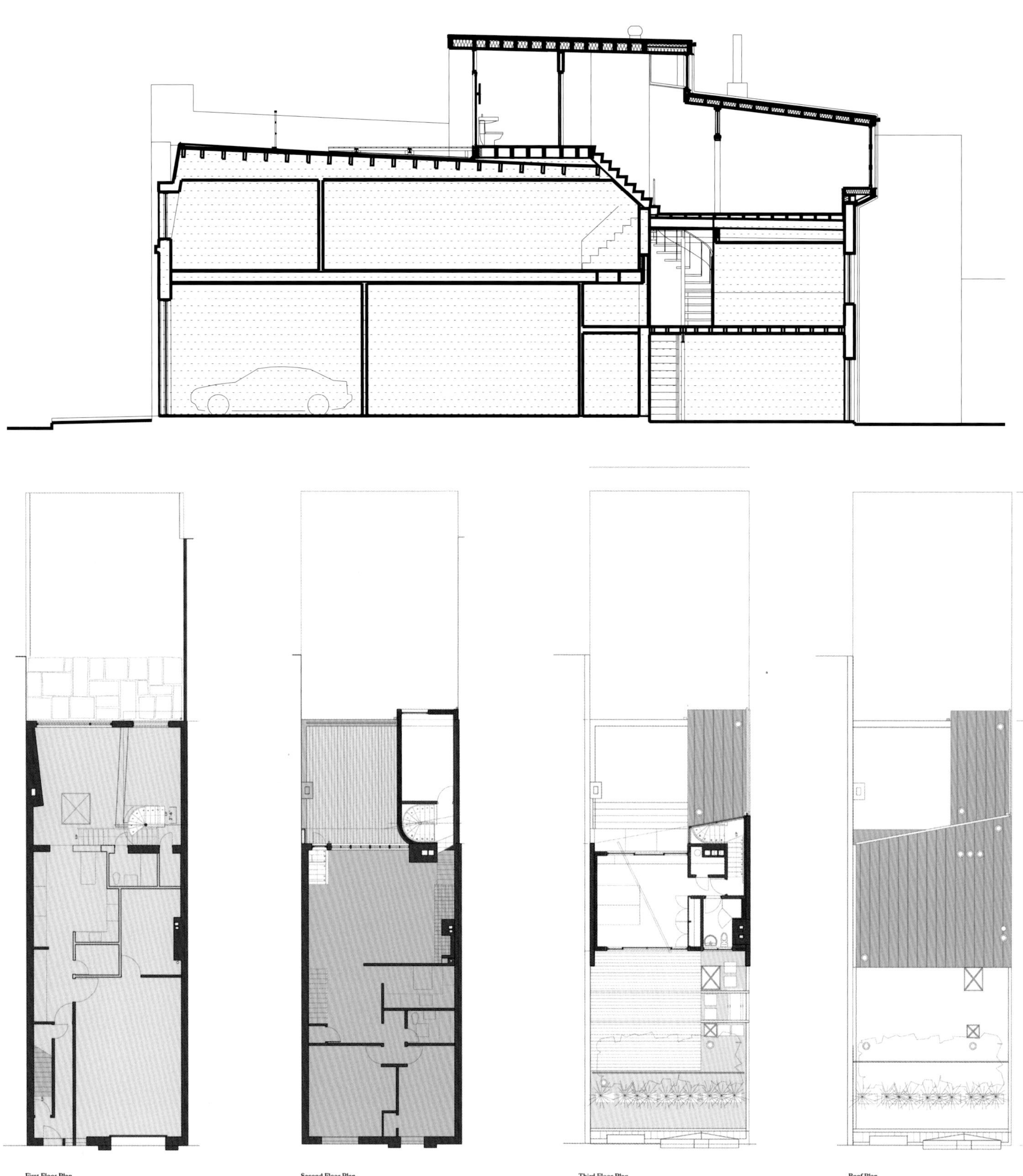

© Courtesy of the Archite

© Courtesy of the Architects

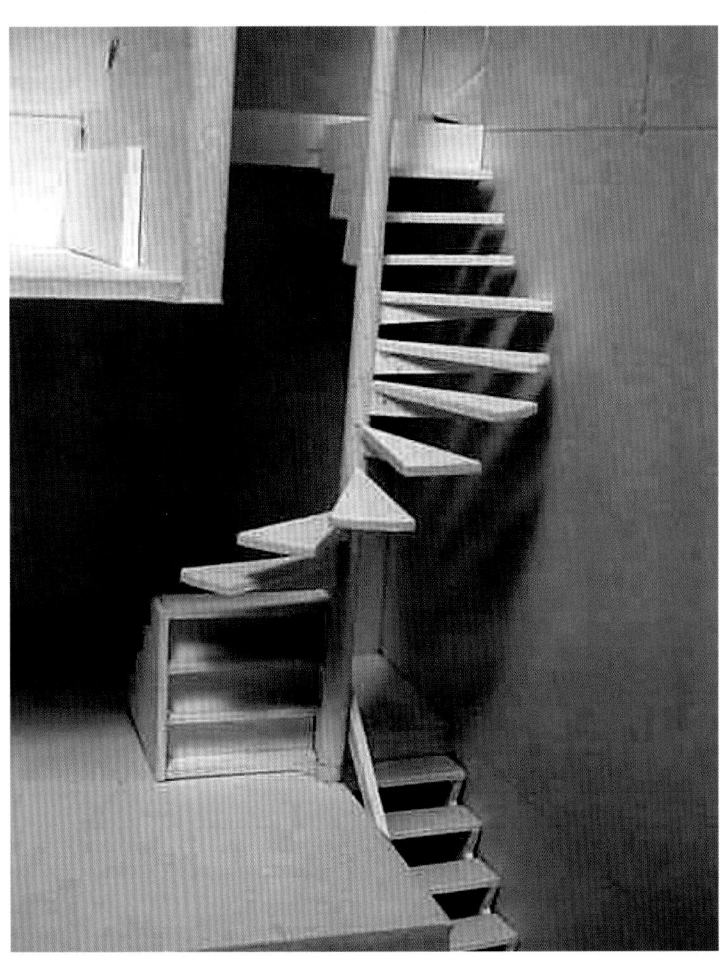

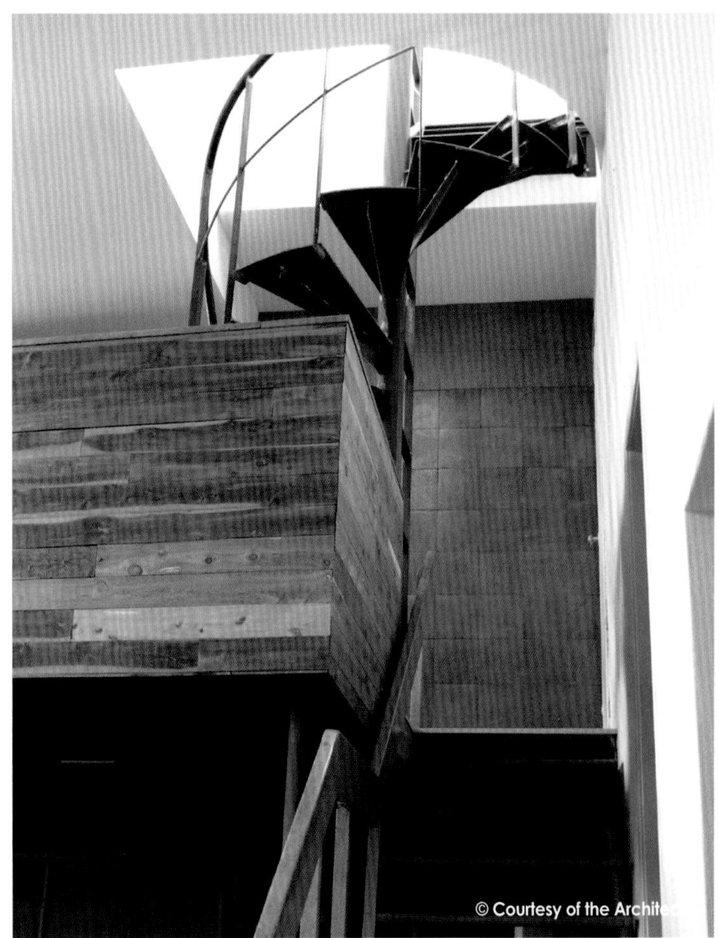

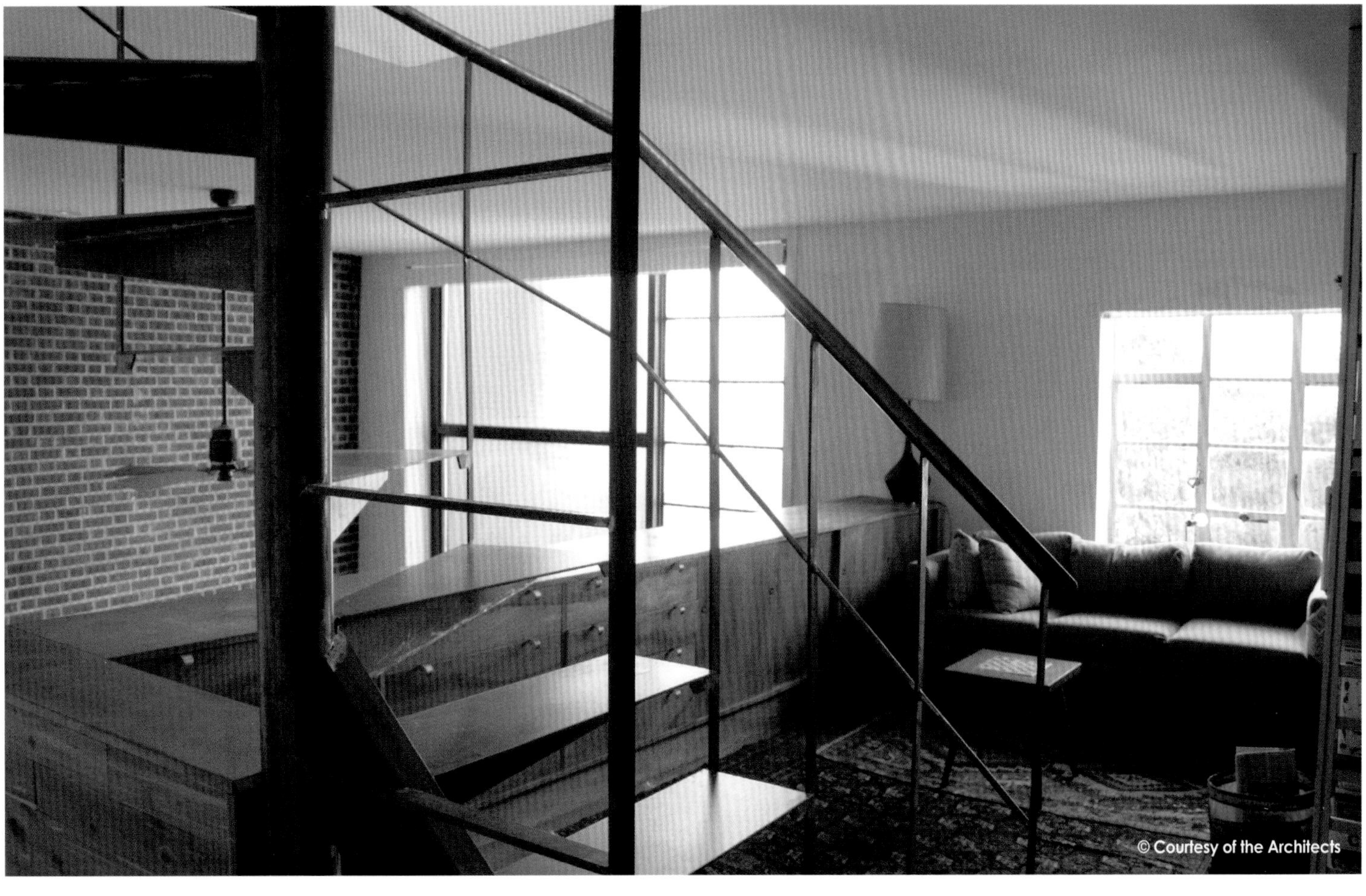

Cliffhanger, Ireland

KEVIN VALLELY DESIGN

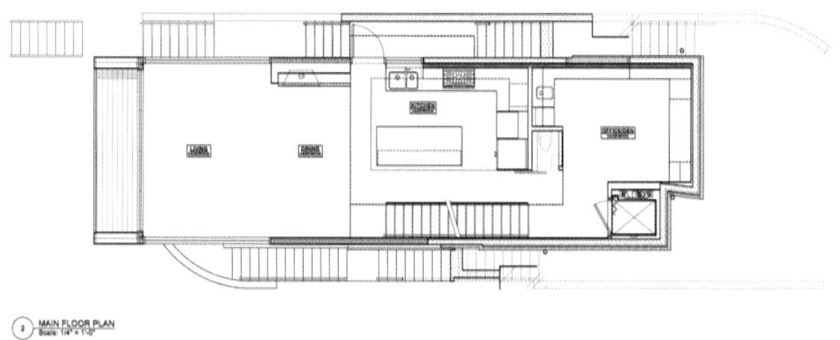

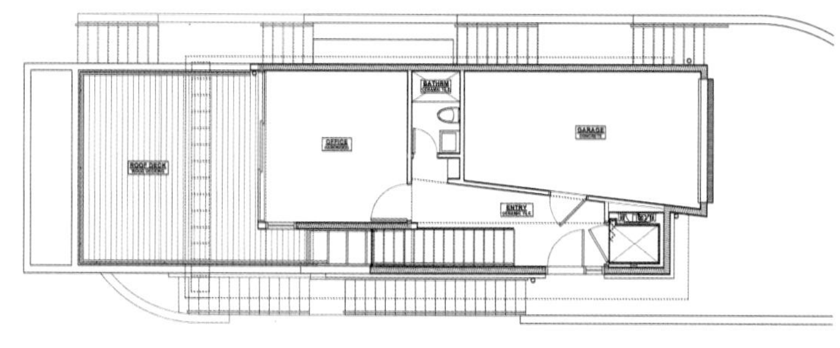

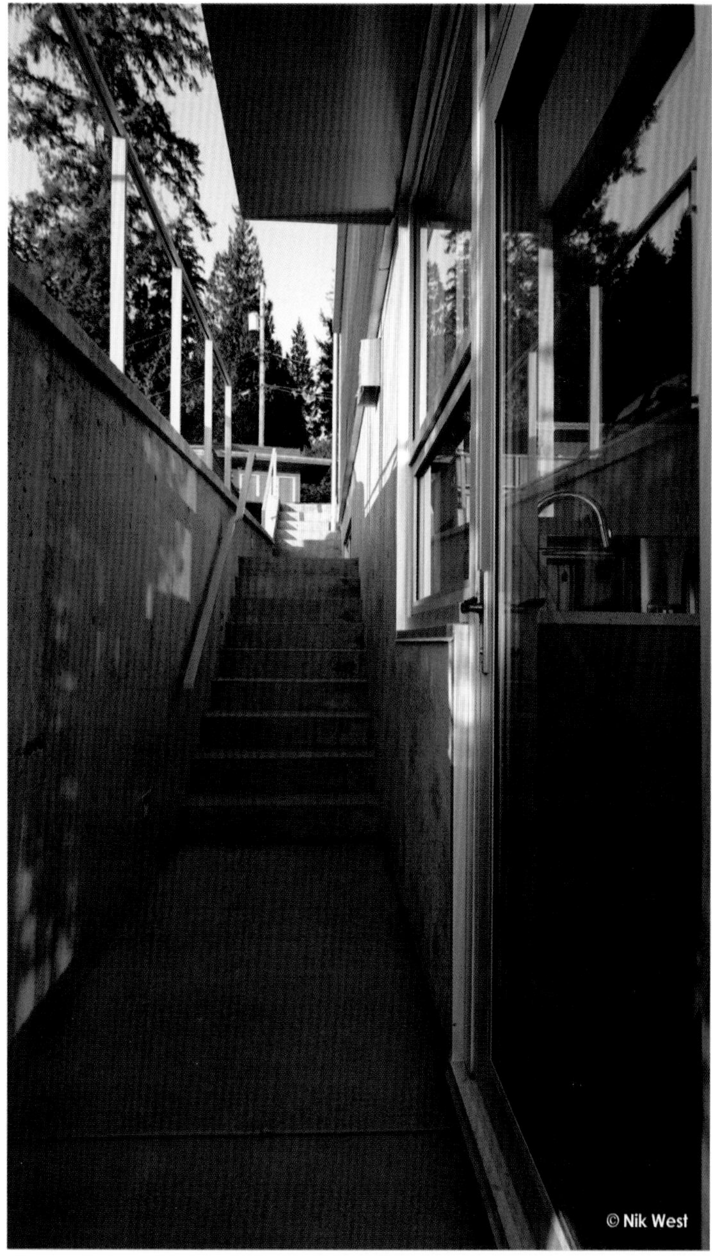
© Nik West

© Nik West

© Nik West

CLONE HOUSE, France

MOUSSAFIR ARCHITECTES

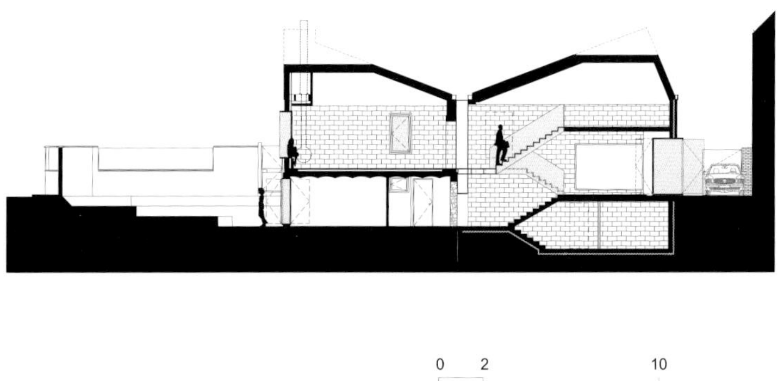

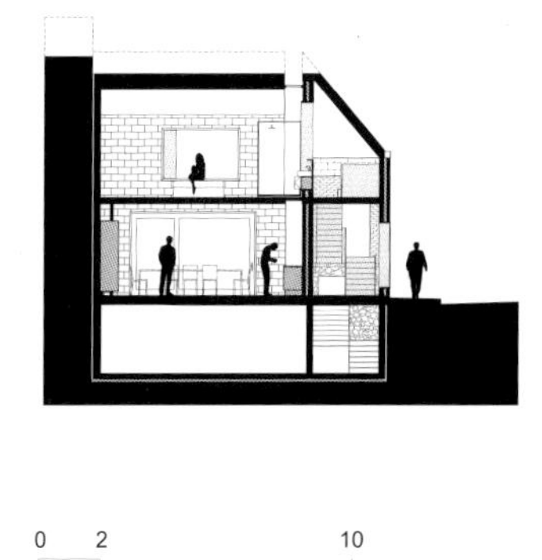

Eriso House, Mexico

Agraz Arquitectos

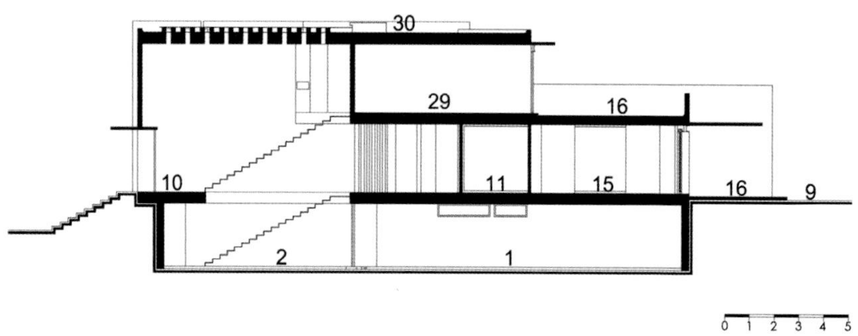

© Mito Covarrubias

Frame Box House, Indonesia

Delution Architect

© Anand Rambey

Floating Staircase, UK

Zaha Hadid Architects

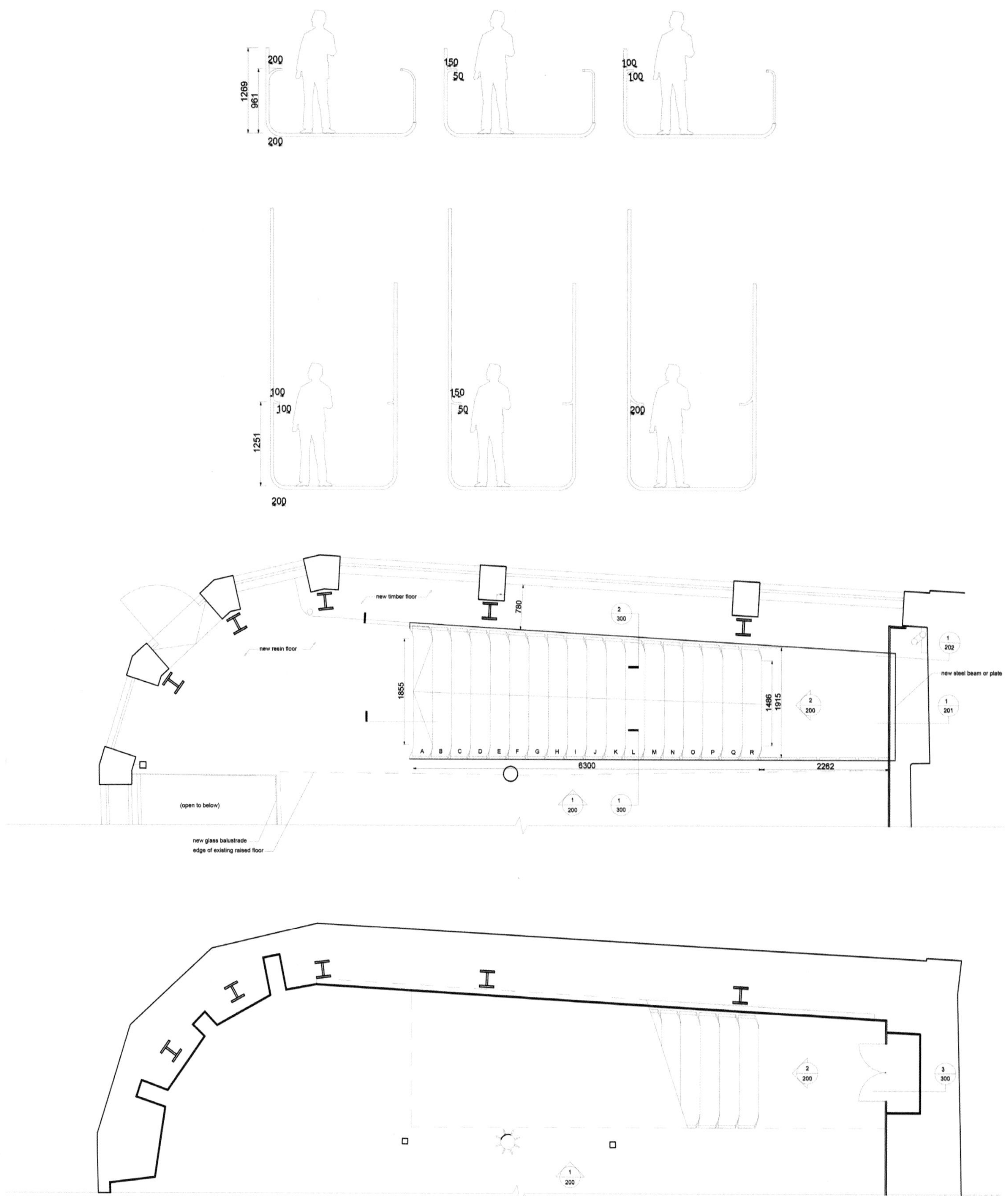

© Zaha Hadid Architects

© Zaha Hadid Architects

© Zaha Hadid Architects

© Zaha Hadid Architects

G55, Germany
adoptions

Gather, Japan

KATUHIRO MIYAMOTO & ASSOCIATES

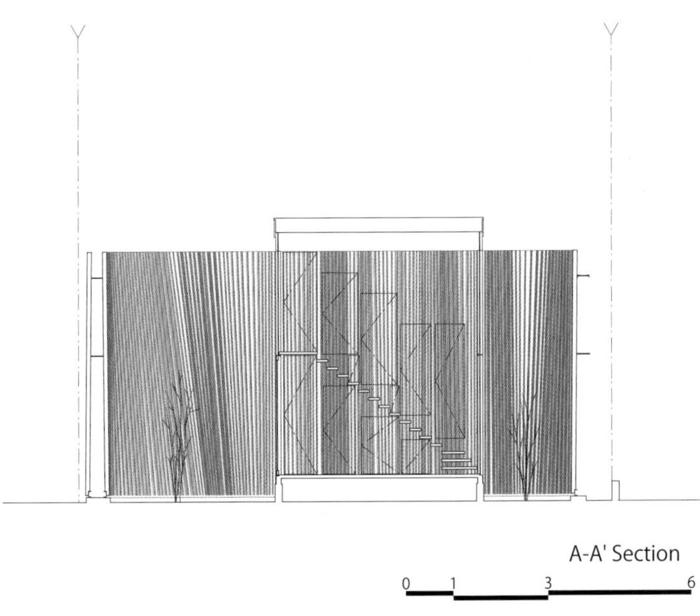

© Courtesy of the Architects

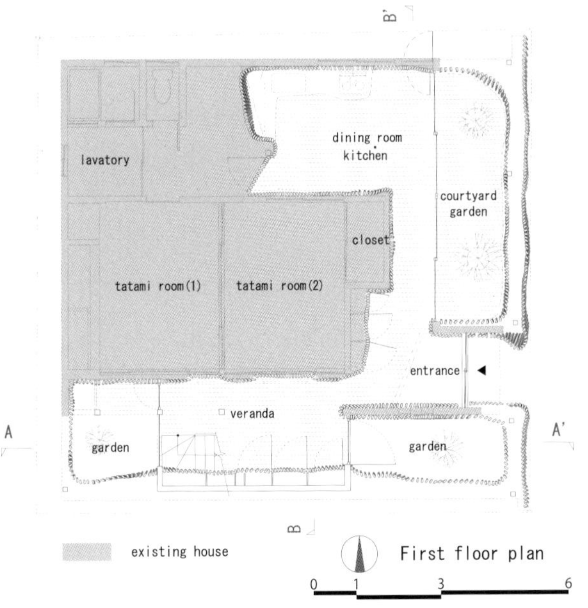

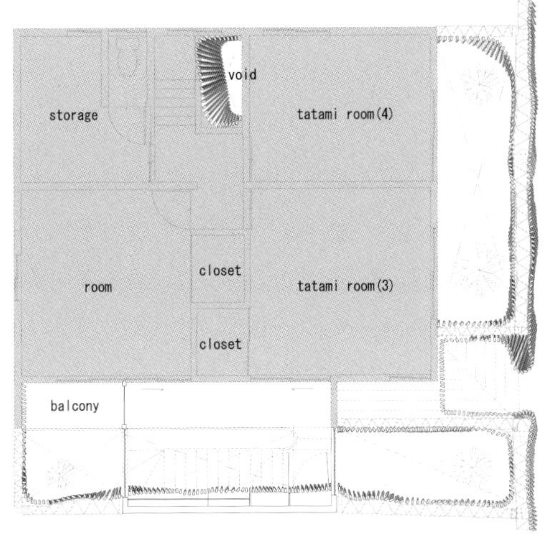

Second floor plan

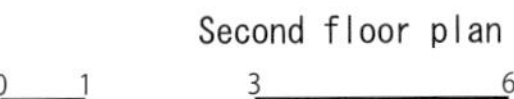

© Courtesy of the Architects

Galleria Foret Penthouse, Korea

Jay is working

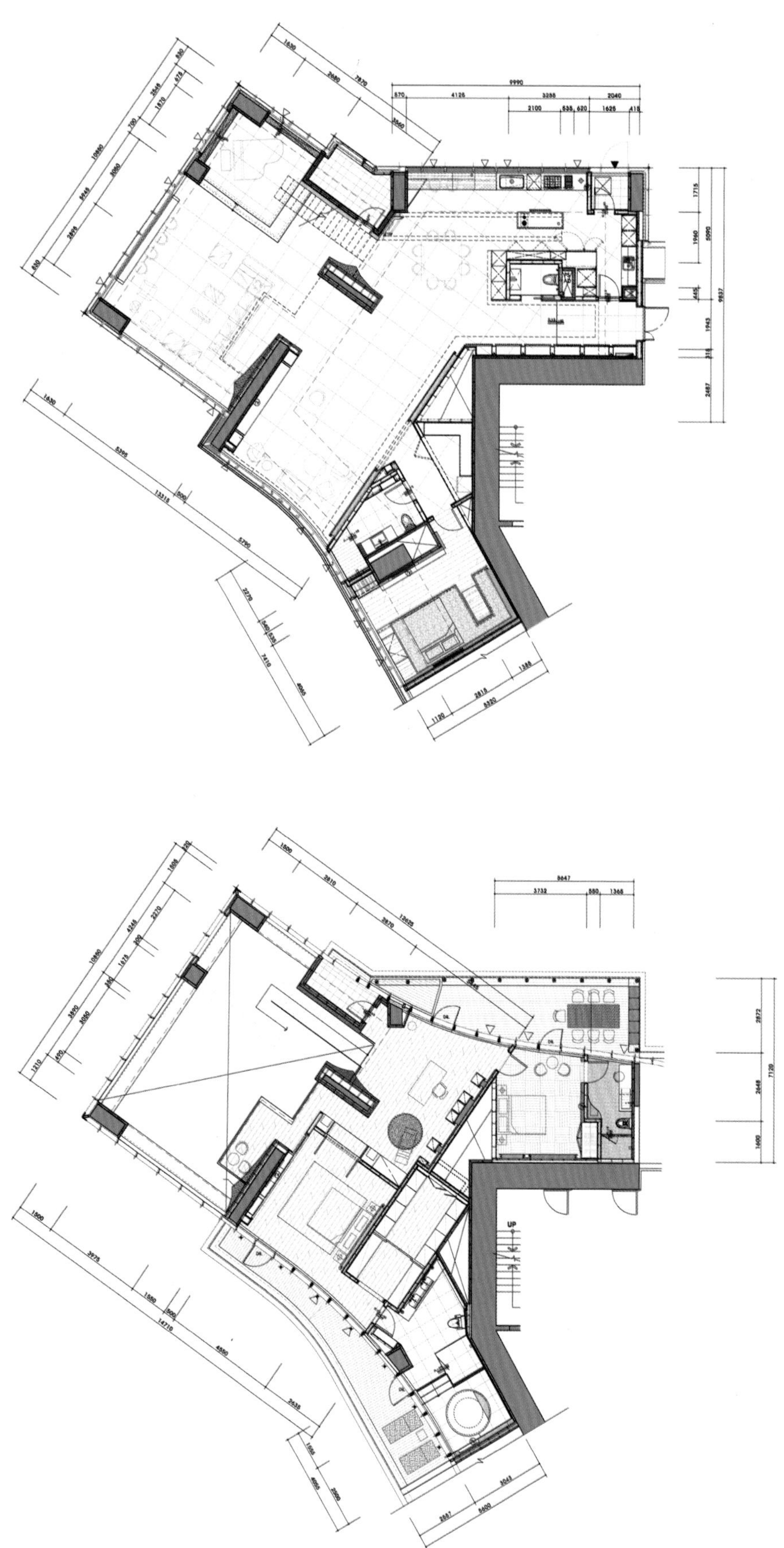

HAUS+, Germany

Anne Menke

© Aloys Kiefer

Haus D, Austria

Caramel architekten with architect Günther Litzlbauer

Hayashi Building, Japan

KEICHI HAYASHI ARCHITECT

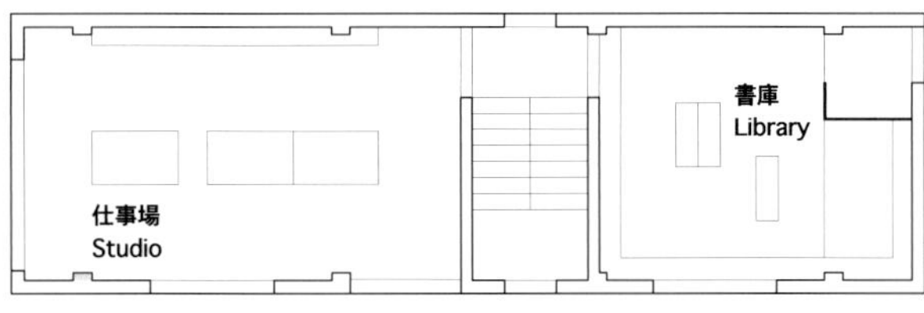

2階平面
1st Floor
1/150

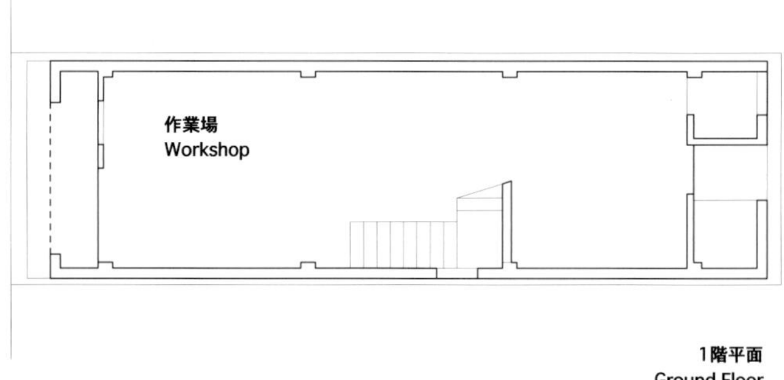

1階平面
Ground Floor
1/150

© Yoshiyuki Hirai

© Yoshiyuki Hirai

© Yoshiyuki Hirai

Hegianwandweg Housing Project, Swiss

EM2N

Hill House, Australia

ANDREW MAYNARD ARCHITECTS

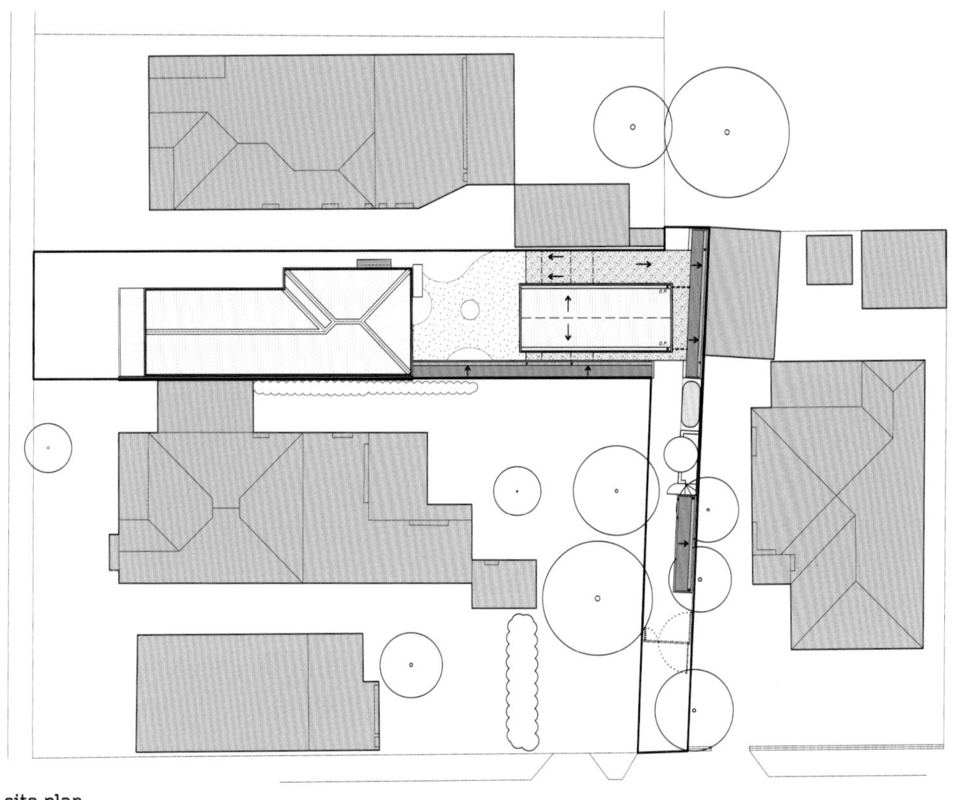

site plan

© Peter Bennetts

© Peter Bennetts

HONEYCOMB APARTMENTS, Slovenia

OFIS ARCHITECTS

© Tomaz Gregoric

© Tomaz Gregoric

© Tomaz Gregoric

holiday cottage in the swiss alps, Swiss

EM2N

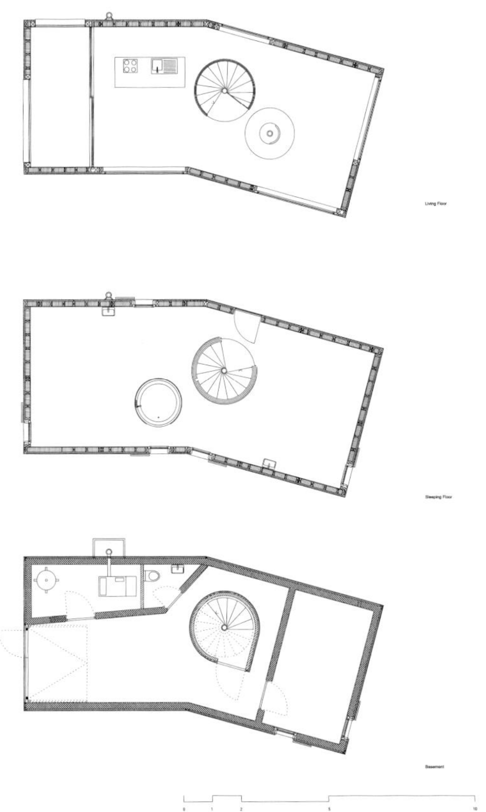

Honighaus, U.S.A

OGRYDZIAK / PRILLINGER ARCHITECTS

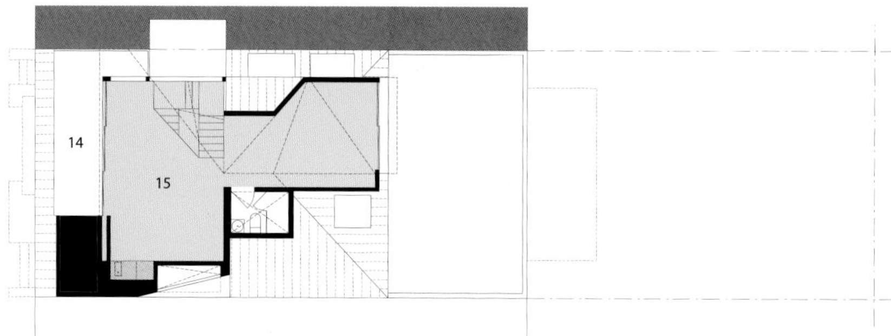

Third Floor Plan

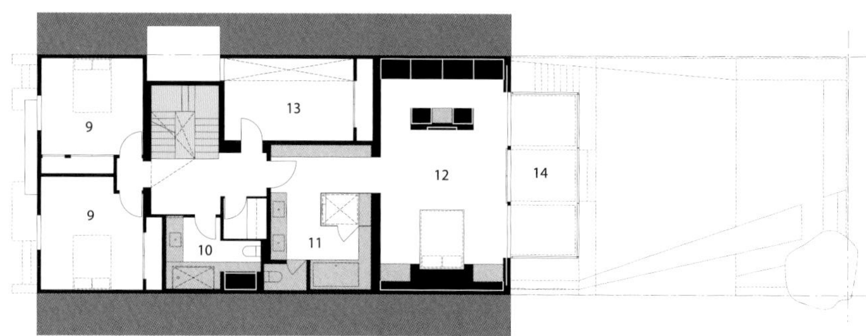

Second Floor Plan

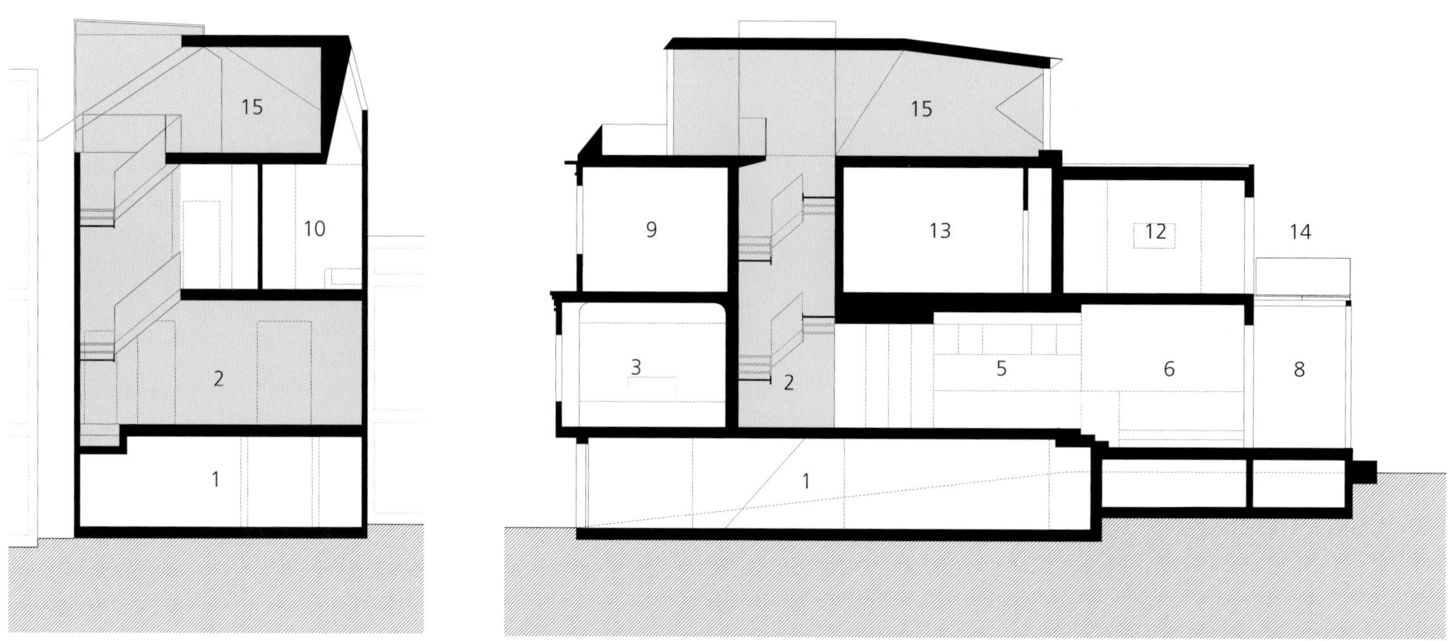

Cross Section

Longitudinal Section

contemporary areas

© Tim Griffith

© Tim Griffith

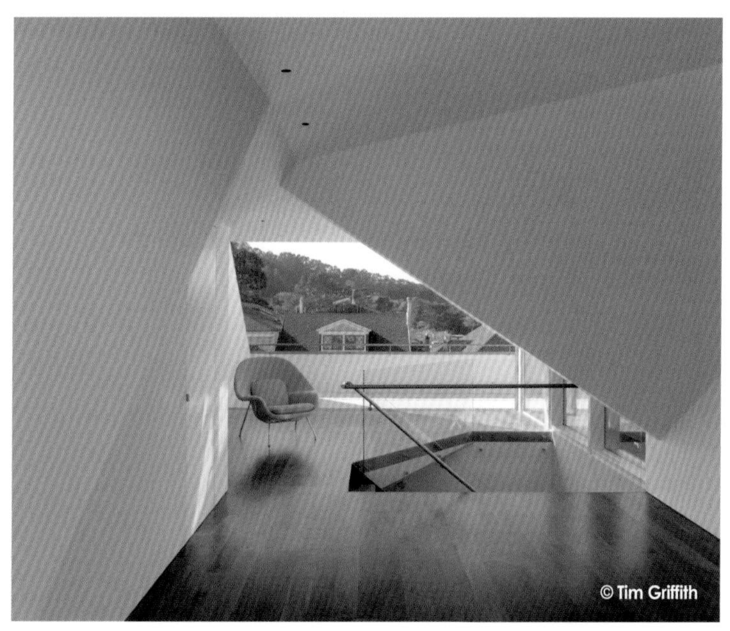

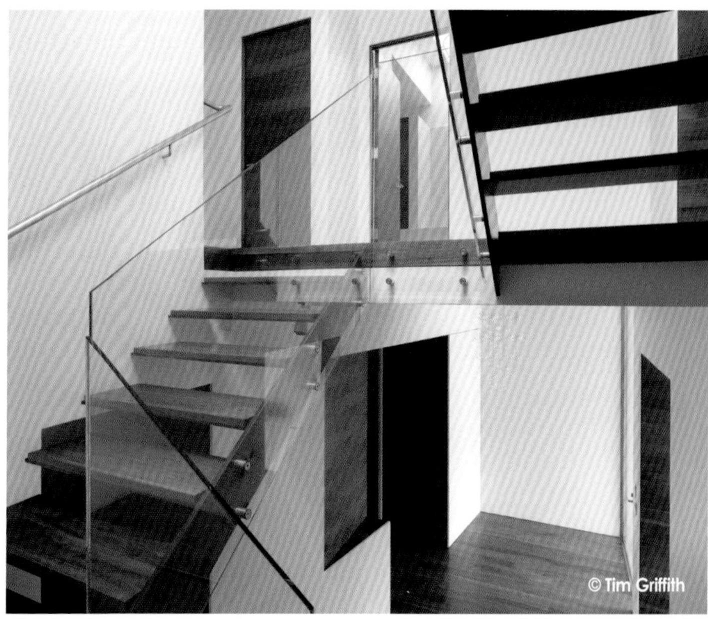

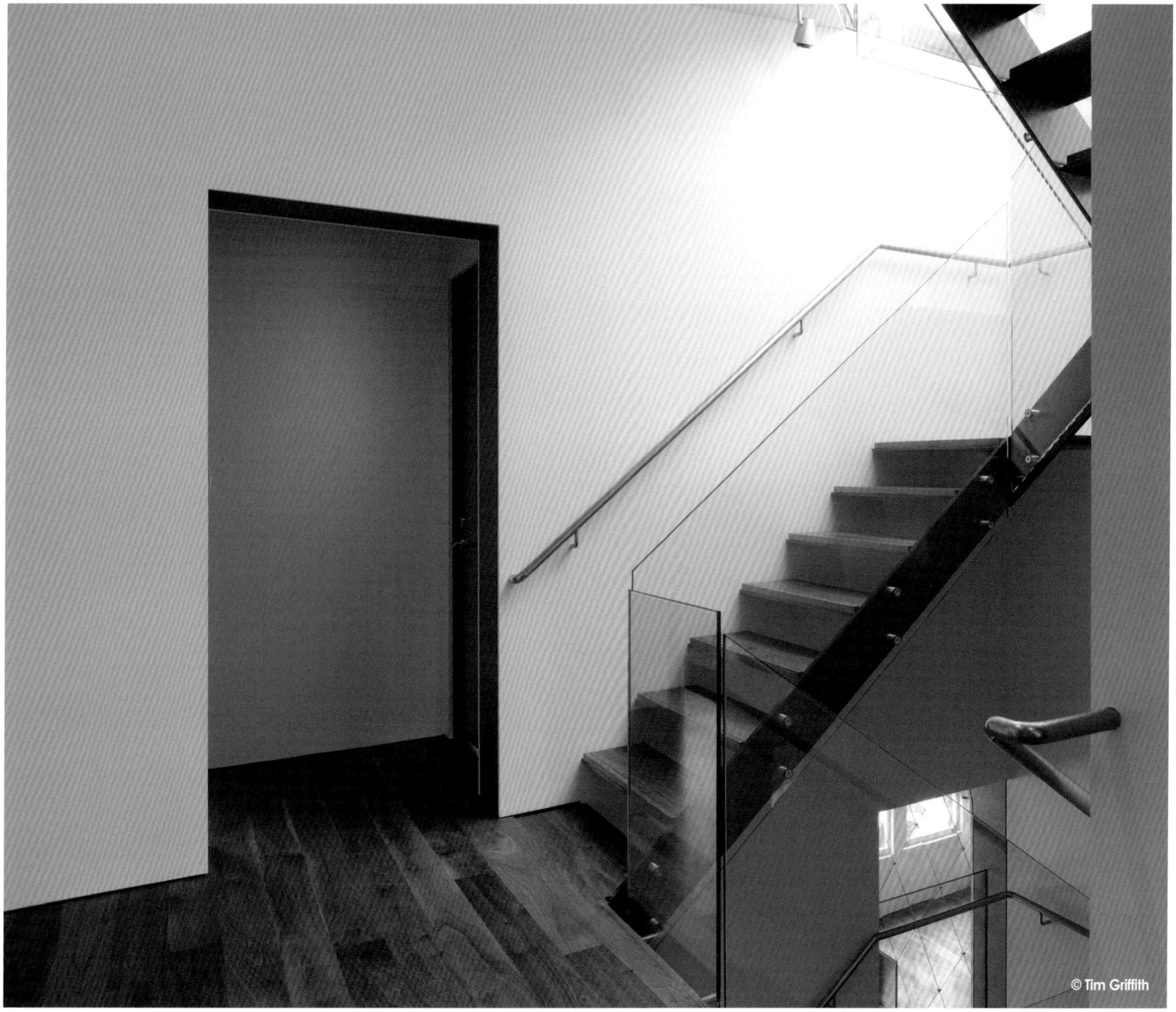

© Tim Griffith

house in a loft, U.S.A

Z-A studio

House in Macheon, Korea

studio-GAON

© Youngchae PARK

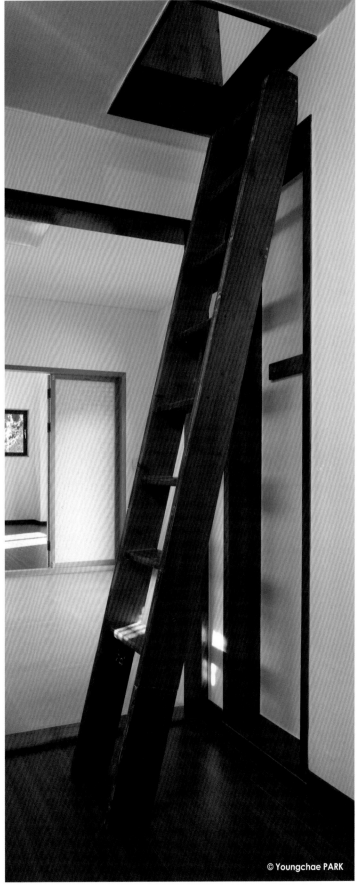

© Youngchae PARK

house of almond, Spain

Leon11

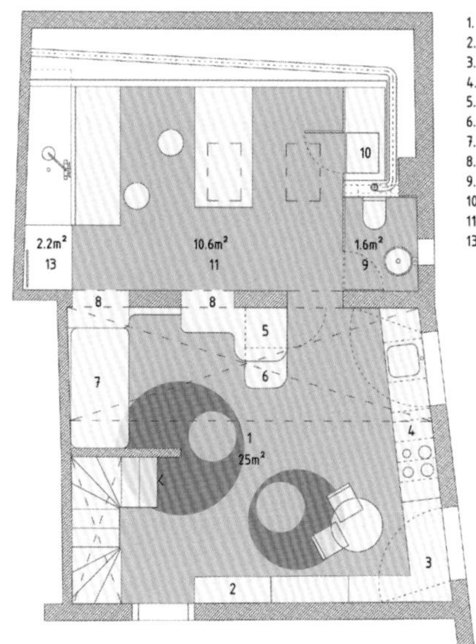

1. living room
2. shelves
3. bench
4. kitchen
5. fridge
6. foldaway table
7. sofa
8. wardrobe
9. toilete
10. washing/dry machine
11. studio
13. shower

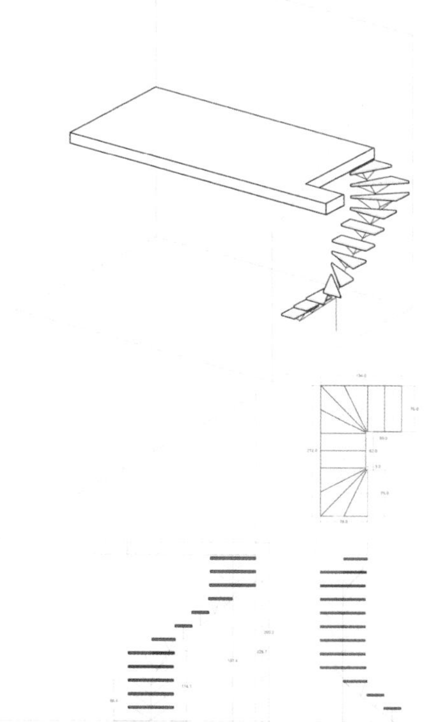

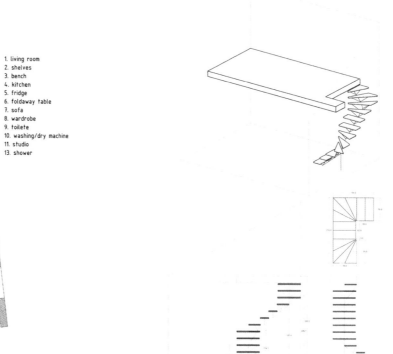

HOUSE ON THE BEACH, Anywhere

UGO architecture & design

House P, Korea

SUPA Schweitzer SongLitzlbauer

© Jaekeyng Kim

House_v, Croatia

3LHD

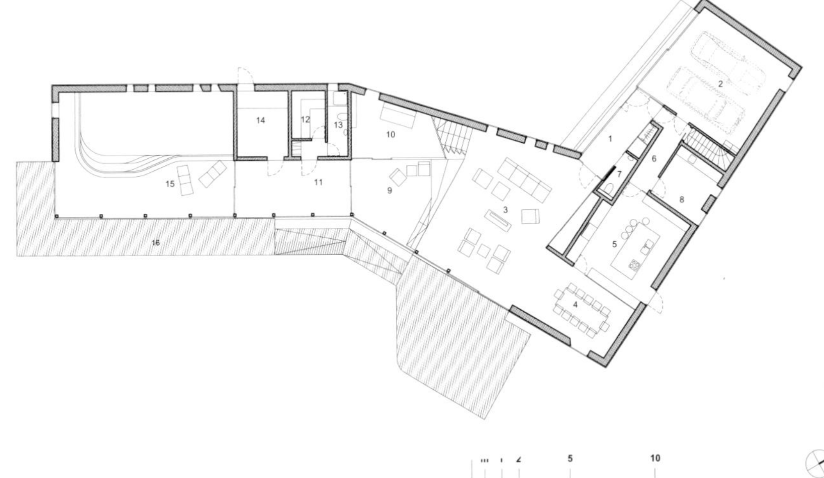

© Damir Fabijanic

House with Chapel, Austria

Architekten LANZ, Mutschlechner

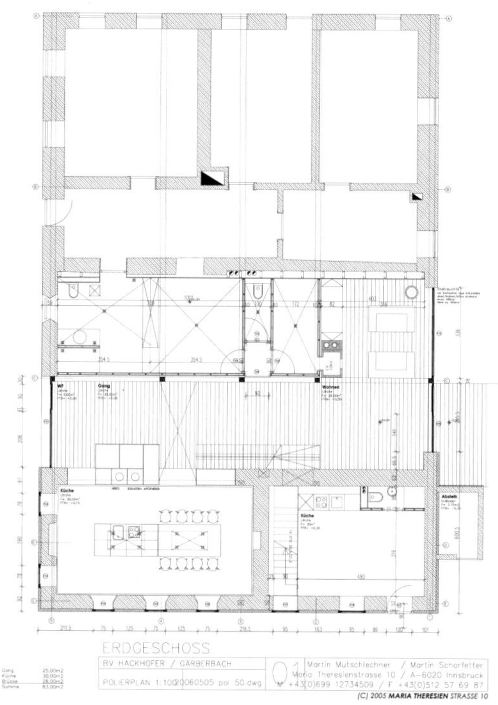

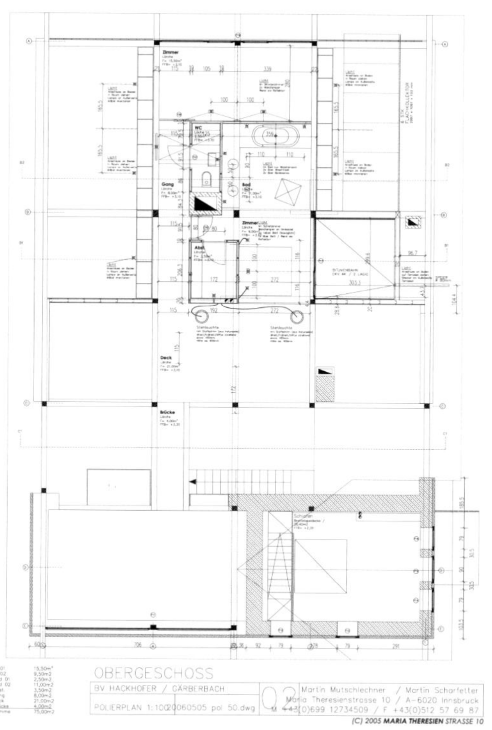

© Günter Richard Wett

© Günter Richard Wett

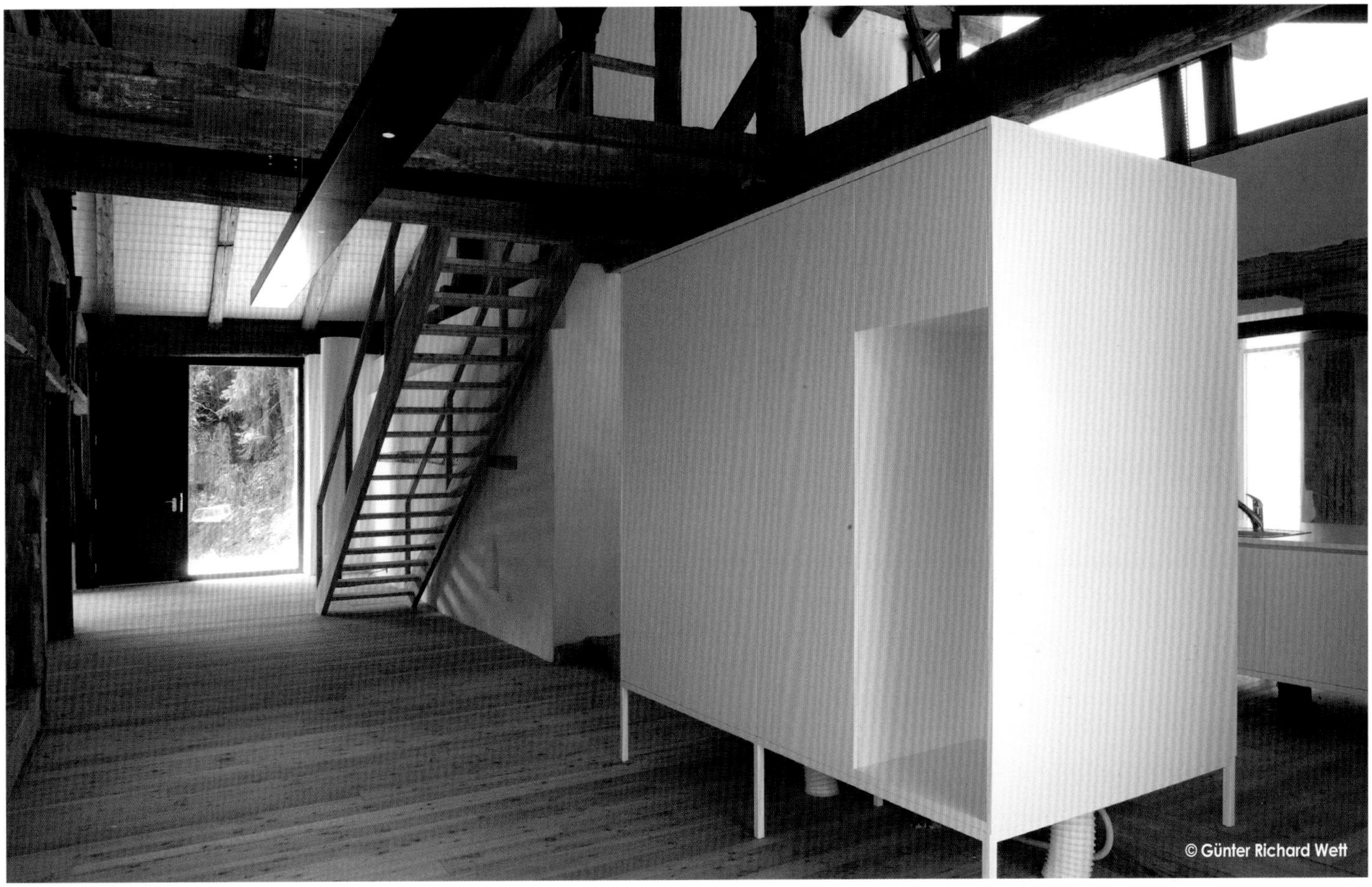

© Günter Richard Wett

Klein Bottle House, Australia

mcbride charles ryan architecture

Lake Side Residence No.113, Thailand

Ayutt and Associates design

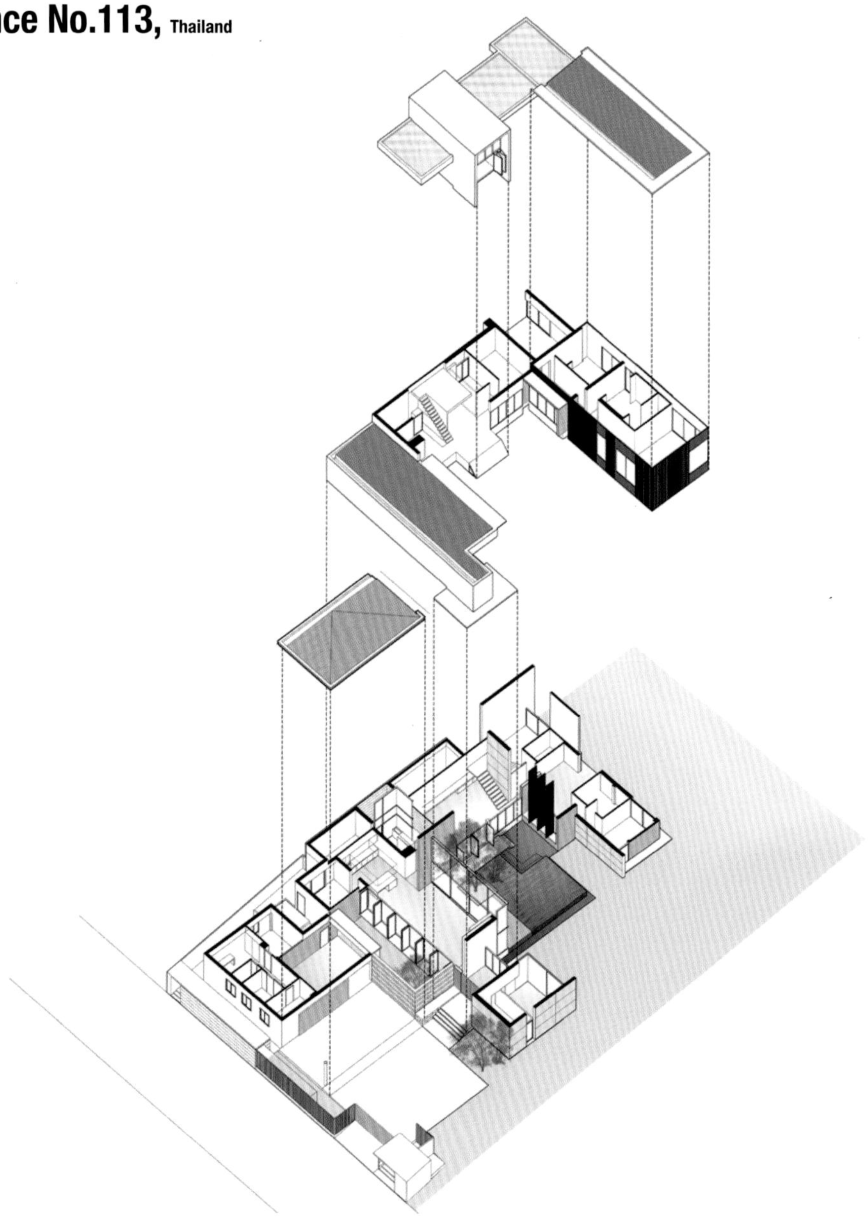

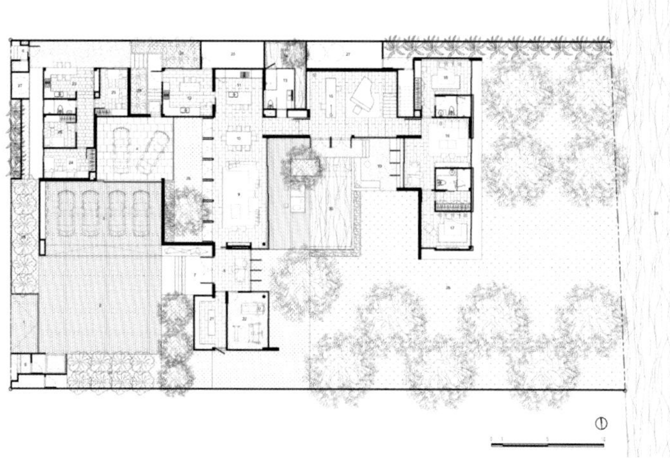

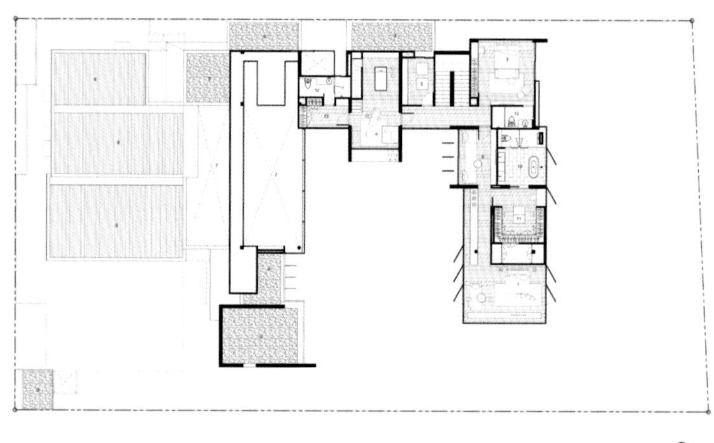

© Soopakorn Srisakul, Ayutt Mahasom
© Soopakorn Srisakul, Ayutt Mahasom
© Soopakorn Srisakul, Ayutt Mahasom

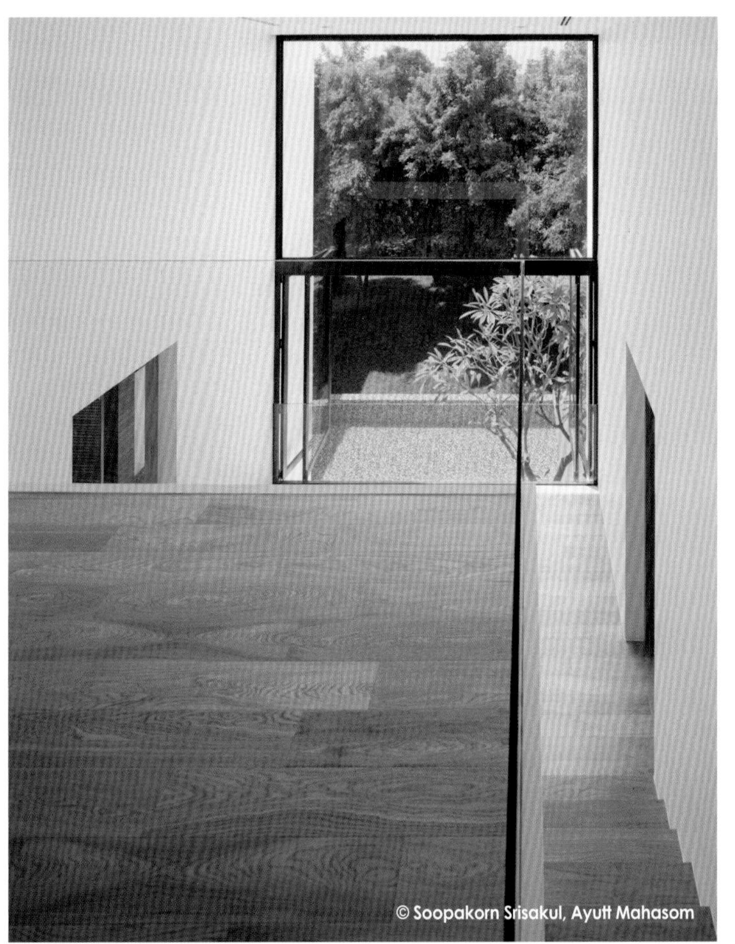

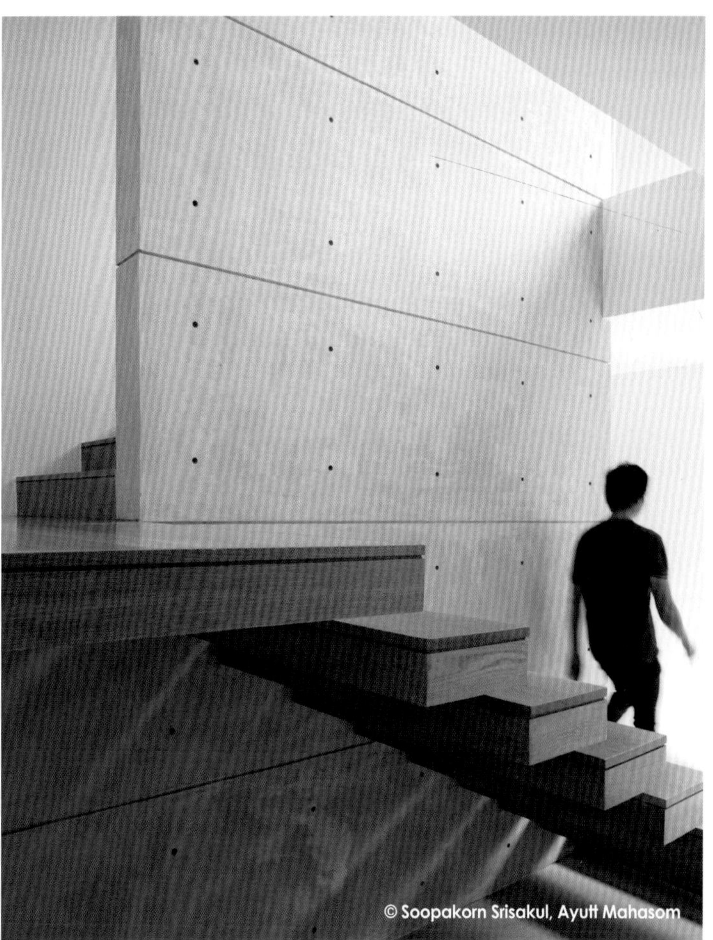

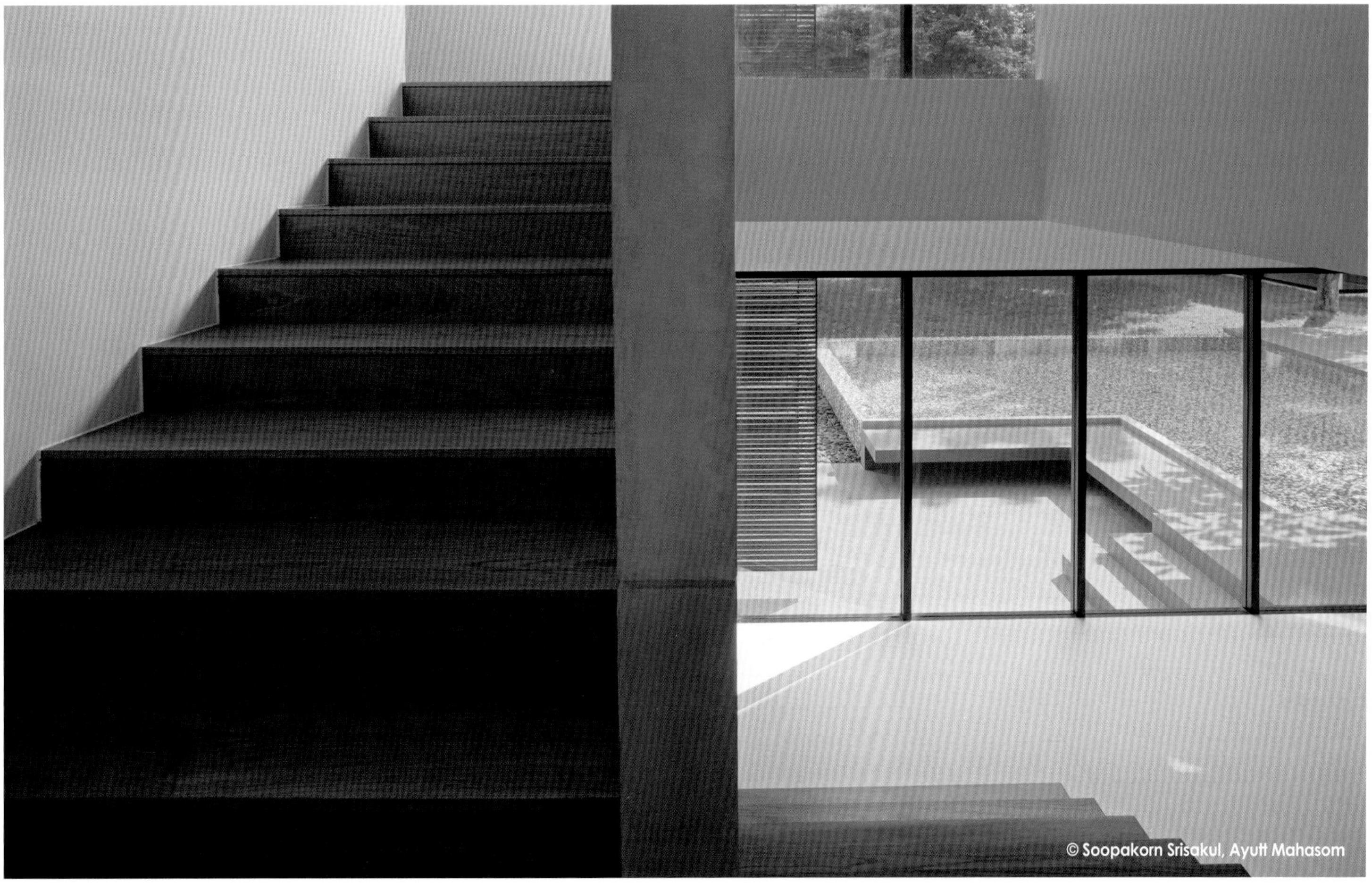

love house, Spain

nodo17 Architects

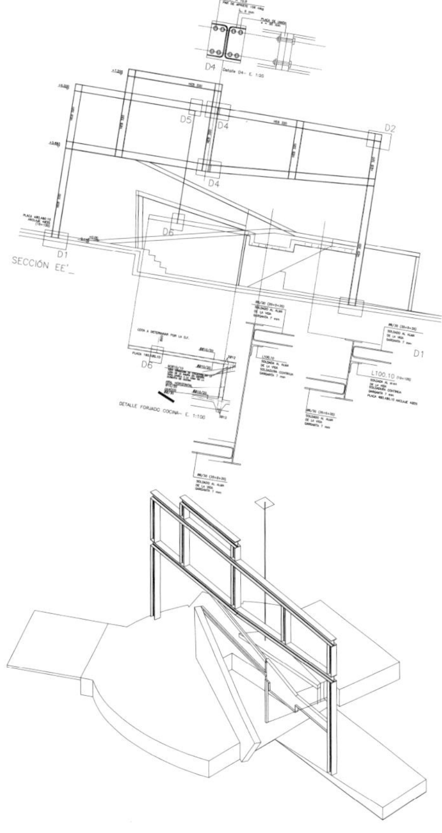

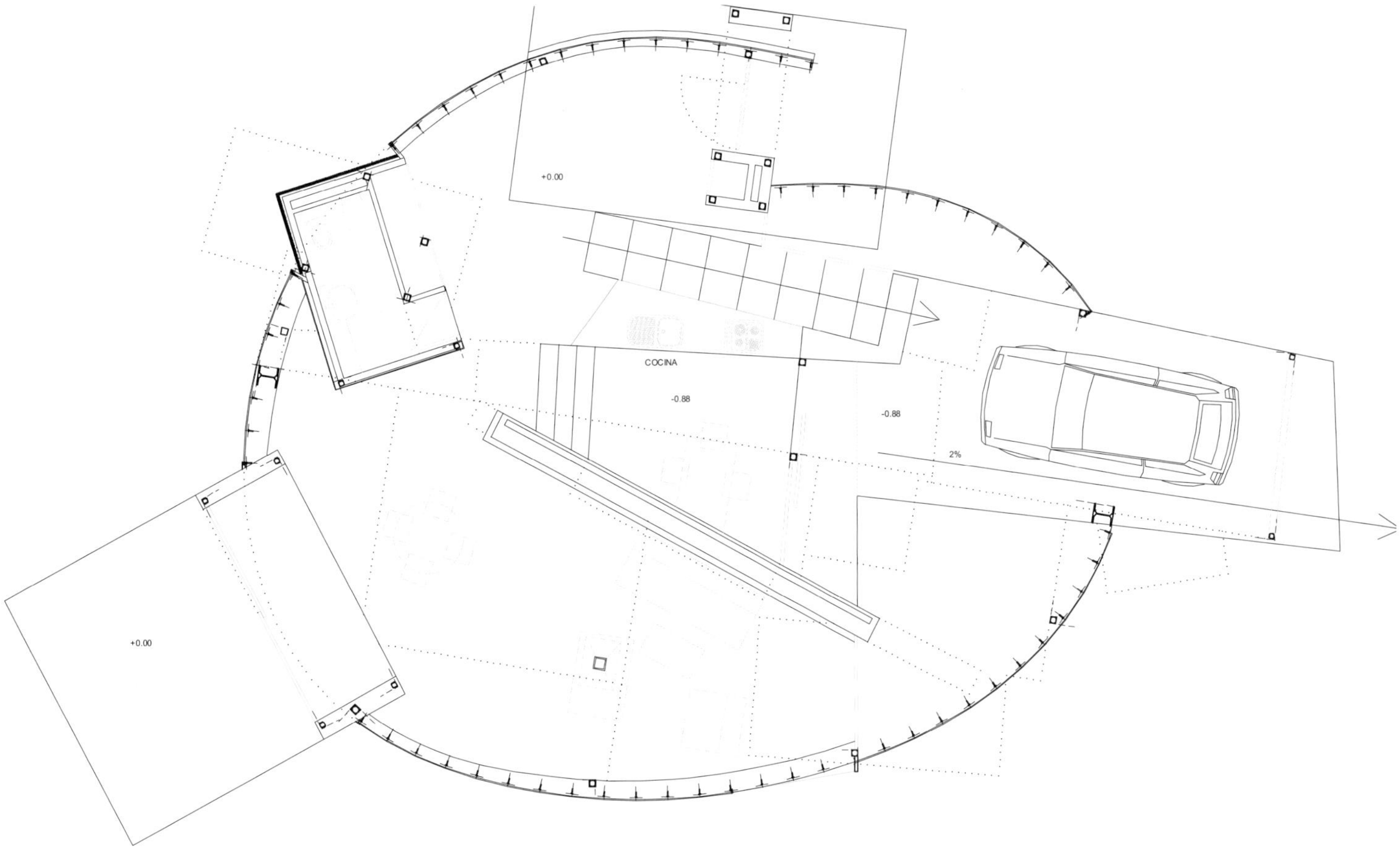

Hunsett Mill, UK

ACME

© Courtesy of the Architect

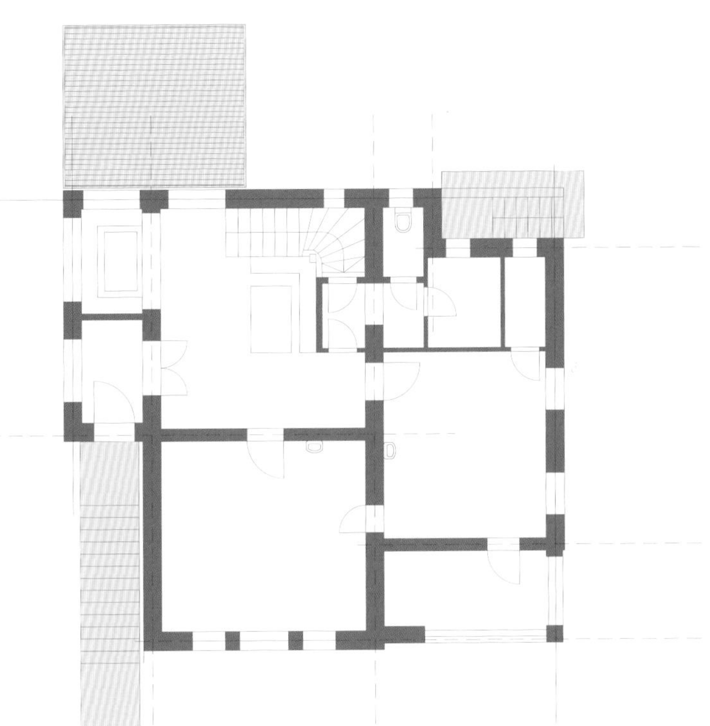

© Marko Zoranovič

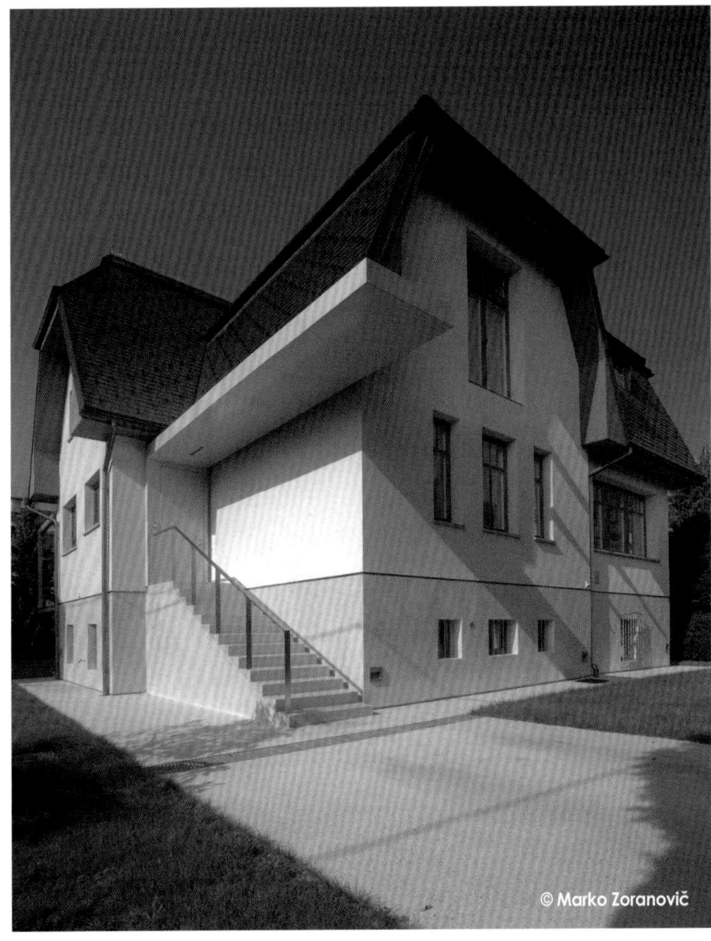
© Marko Zoranovič

MATERIALITY M HOUSE, Spain

MDBA

© ADRIÀ GOULA

m-country house

b4 architects

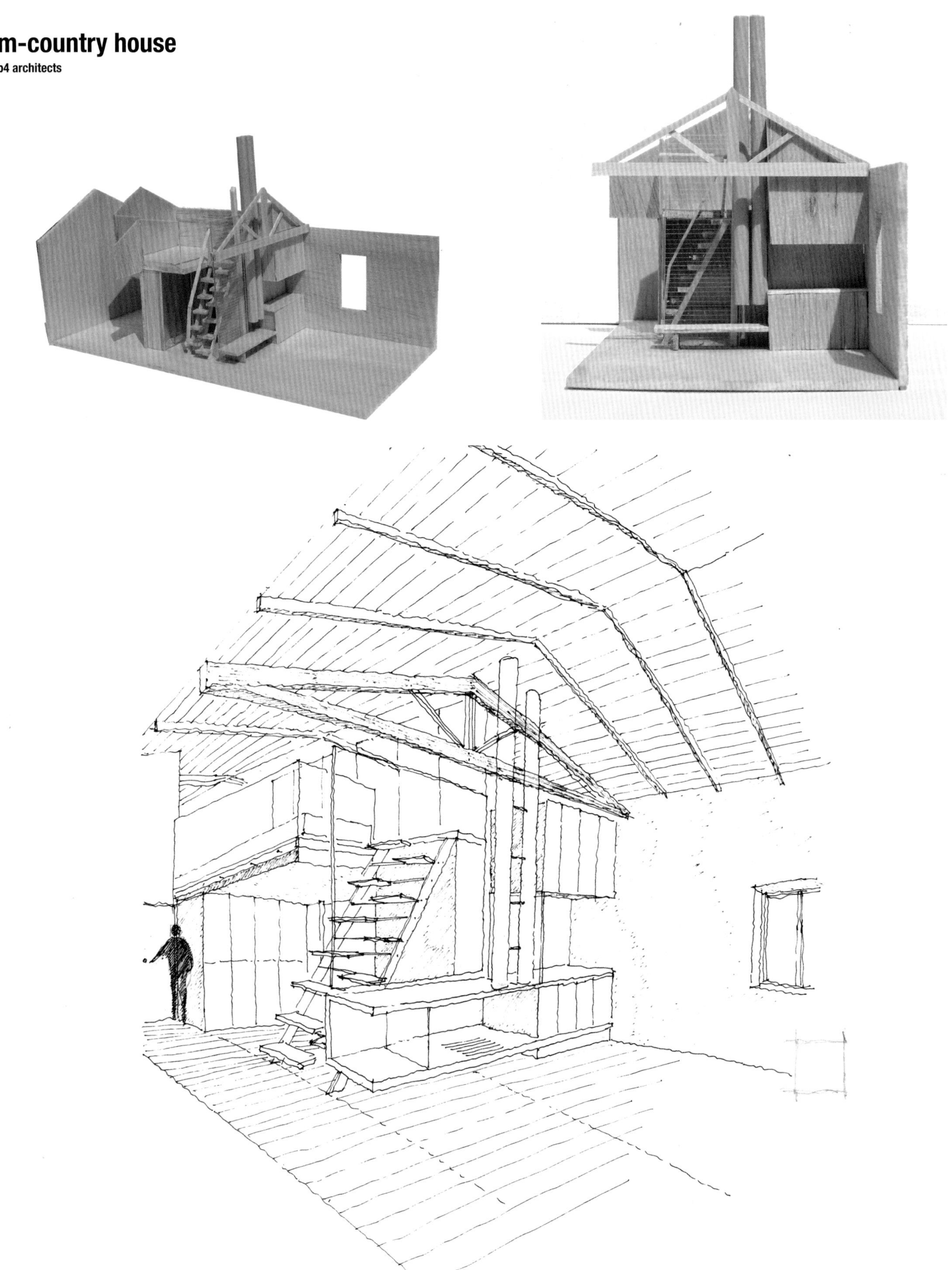

Maison Leguay, France
MOUSSAFIR ARCHITECTS ASSOCIÉS

Natalia House, Mexico

Agraz Arquitectos

© Mito Covarrubias

North Face [illegible]use, Spain
nodo17 group

© Pablo Cruz

Niz House, Mexico

Agraz Arquitectos

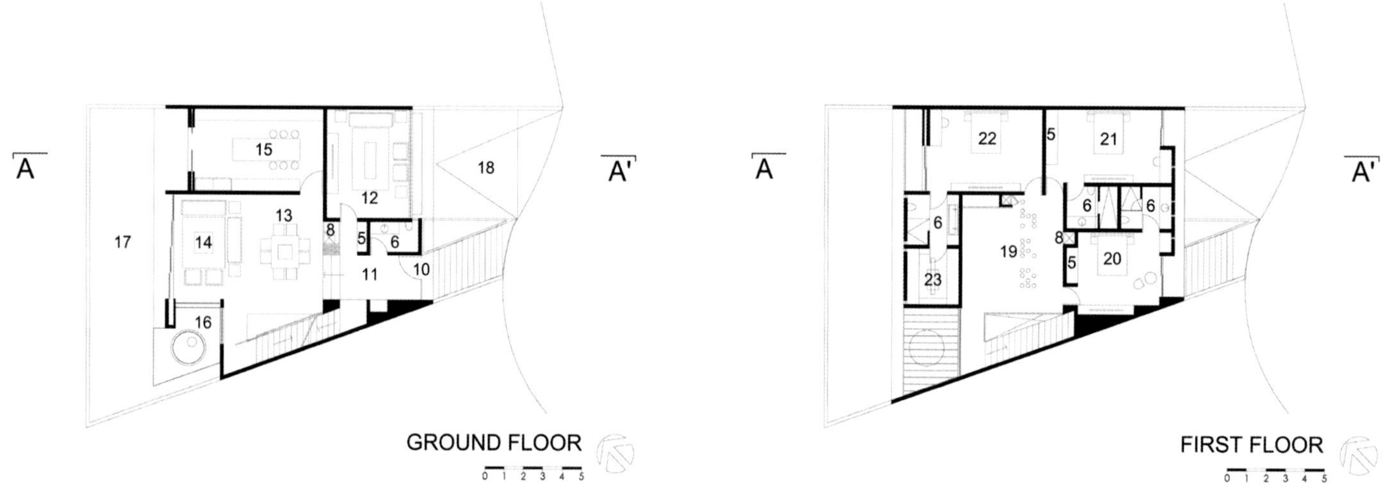

© Mito Covarrubias

© Mito Covarrubias

© Mito Covarrubias

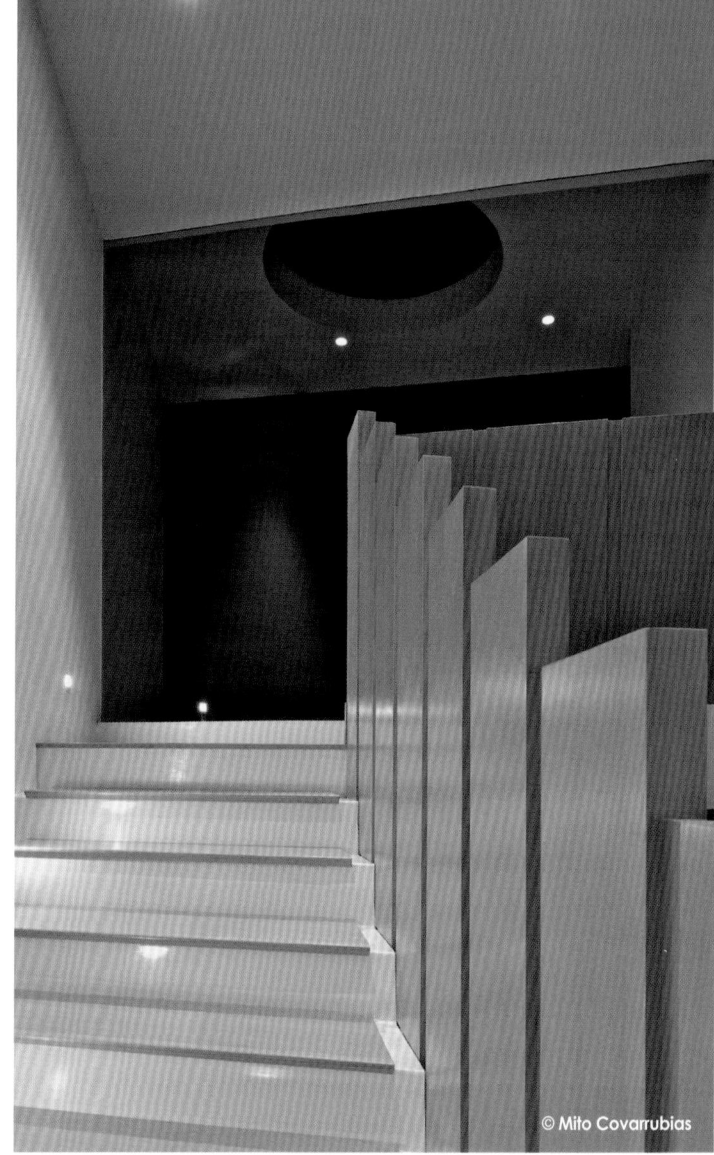
© Mito Covarrubias

Petchkasem 79 residence, Thailand

Ayutt and Associates design

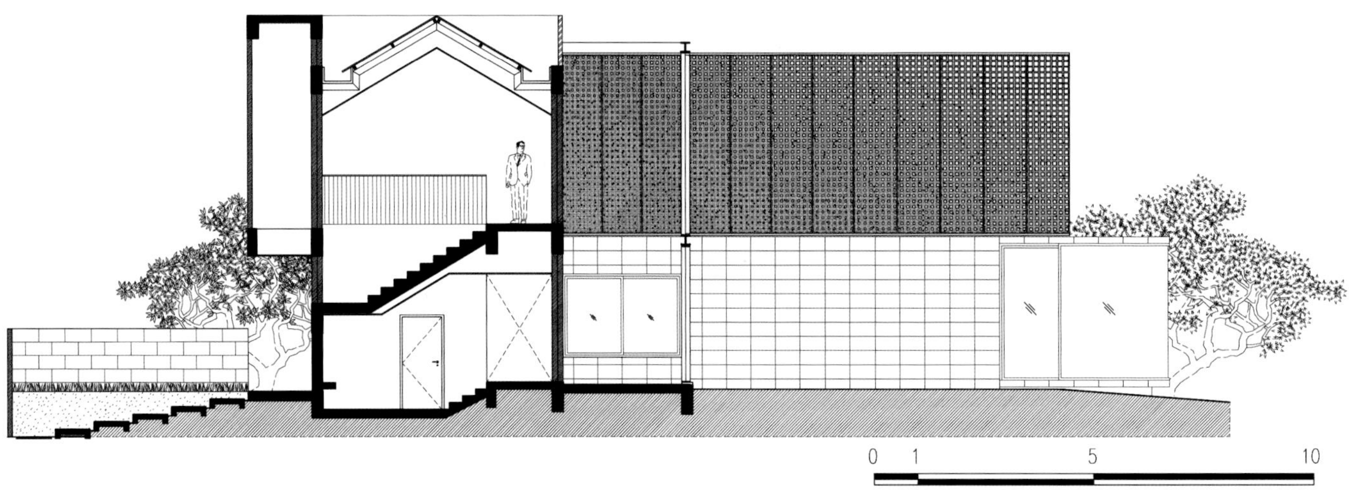

© Soopakorn Srisakul, Ayutt Mahasom

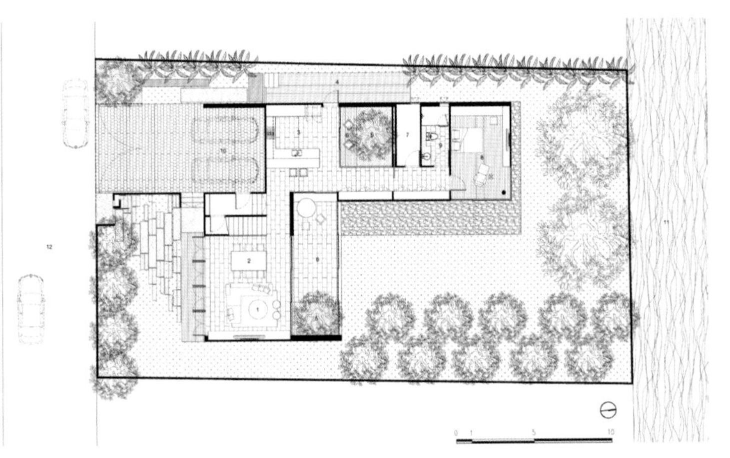

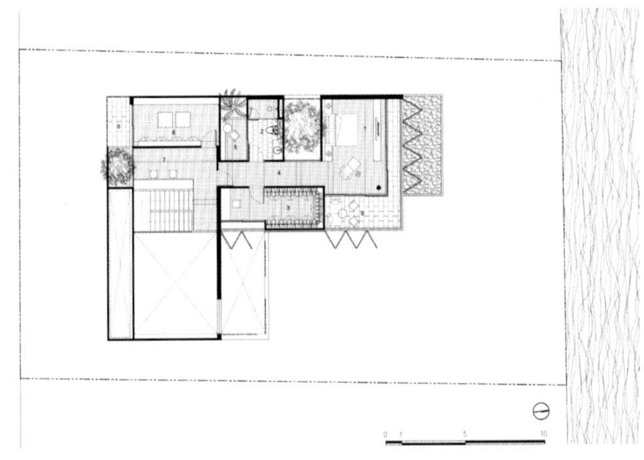

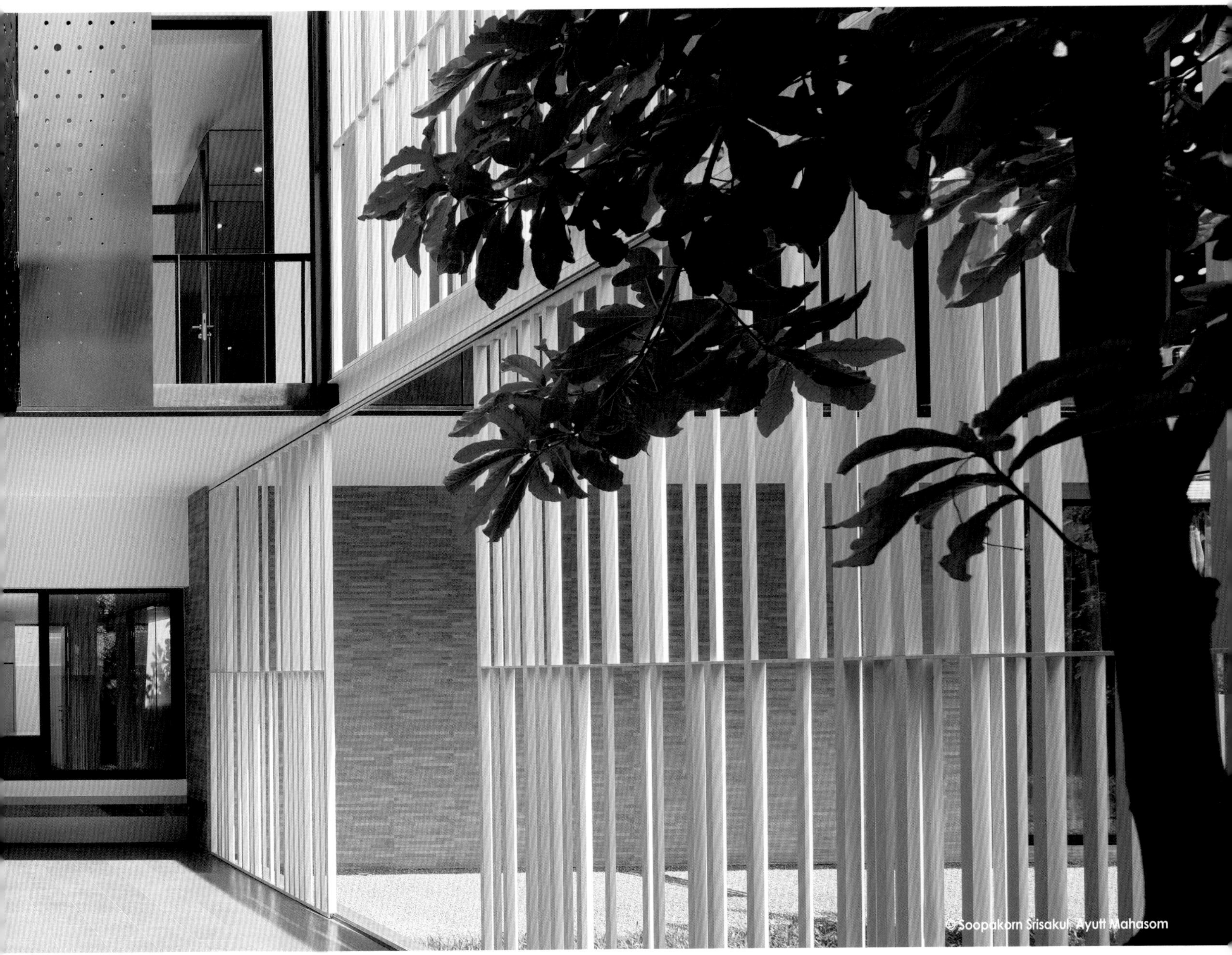

Peter's Room, U.S.A

YOSHIHARA, MCKEE, ARCHITECTS

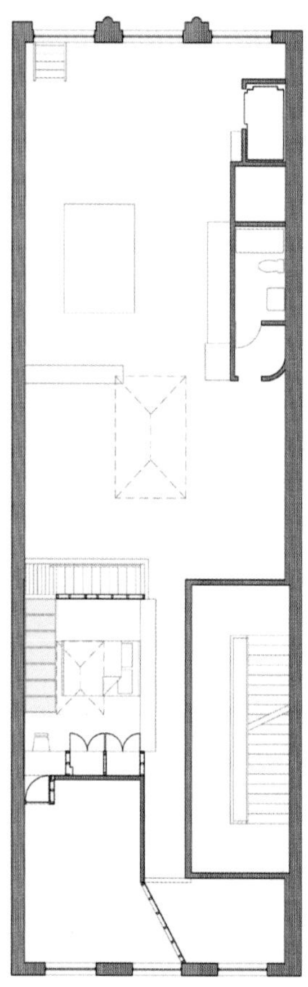

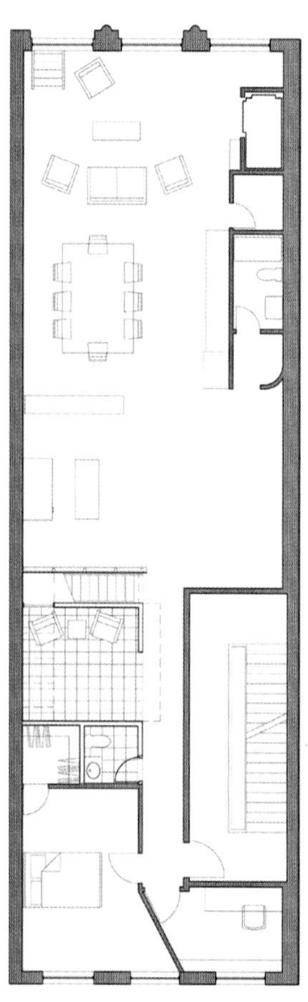

© Courtesy of the Architects

© Julian Wass

Petrucelli House, UK

mcbride charles ryan architecture

SlrSrf, U.S.A

Chandler Ahrens

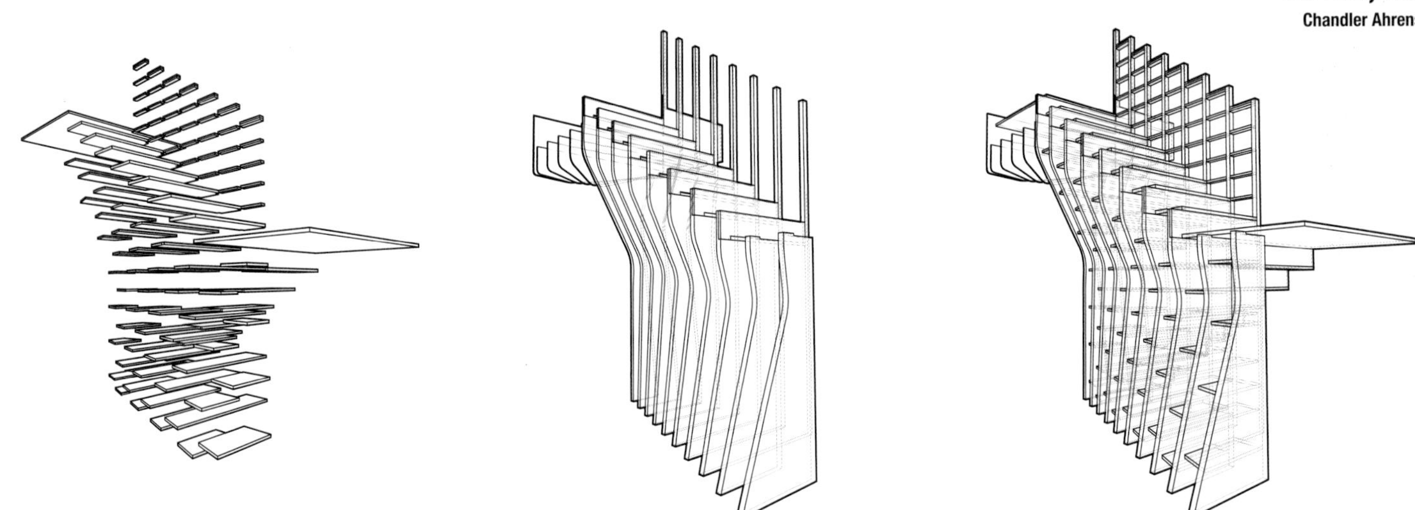

Splow House, Indonesia

Delution Architect

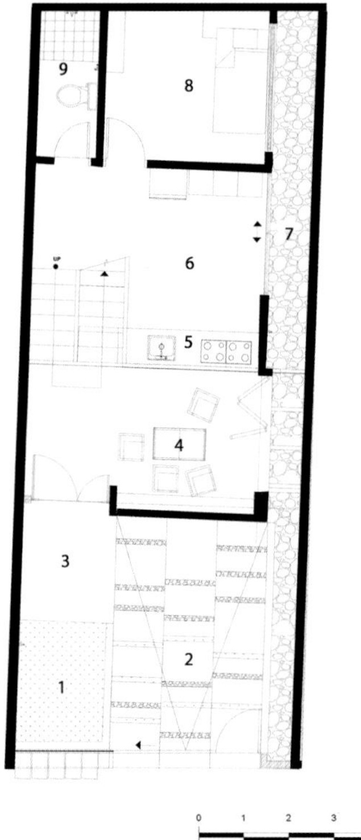

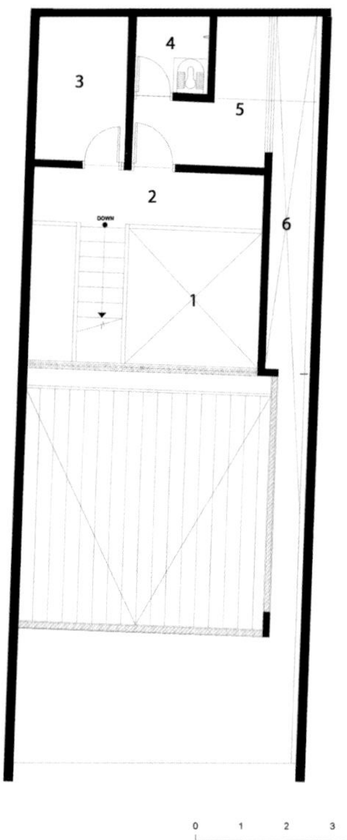

STAV, Germany

adoptions

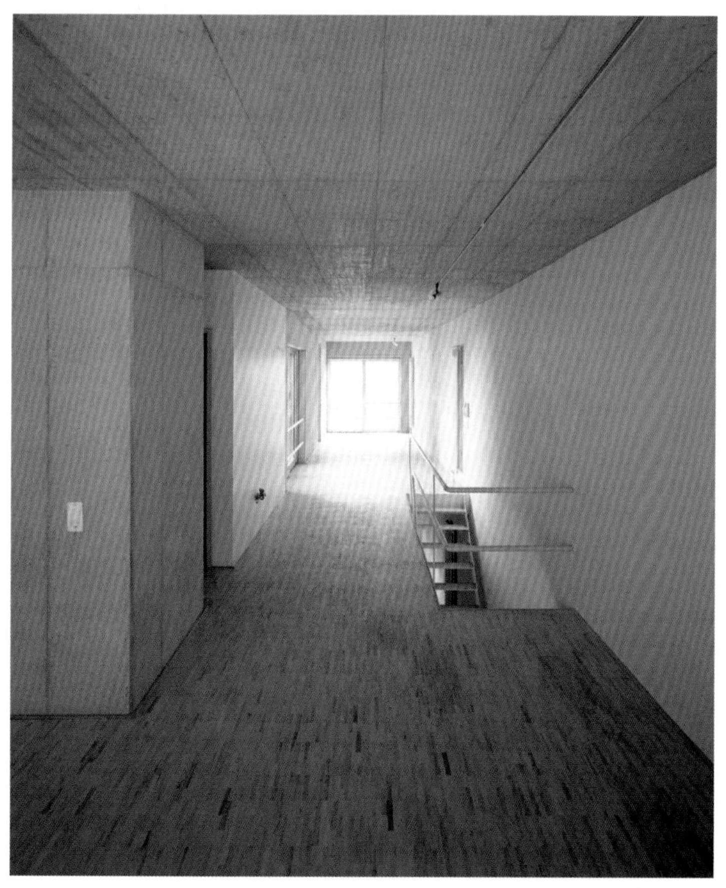

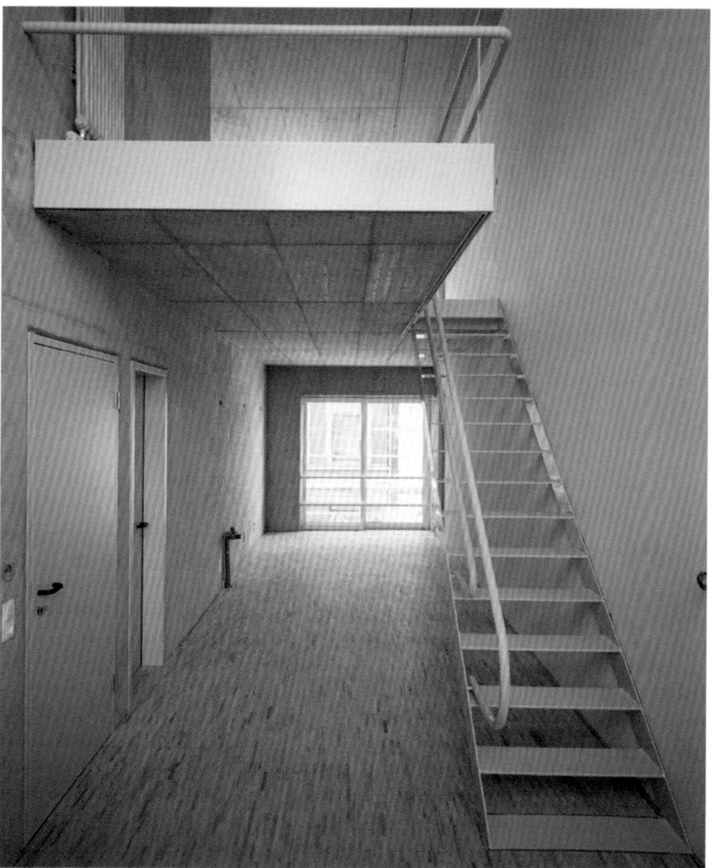

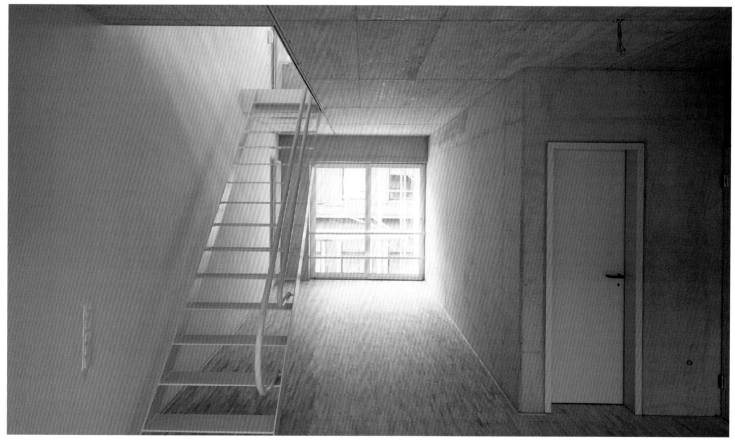

Swan Street Residence, Australia

IREDALE PEDERSEN HOOK ARCHITECTS

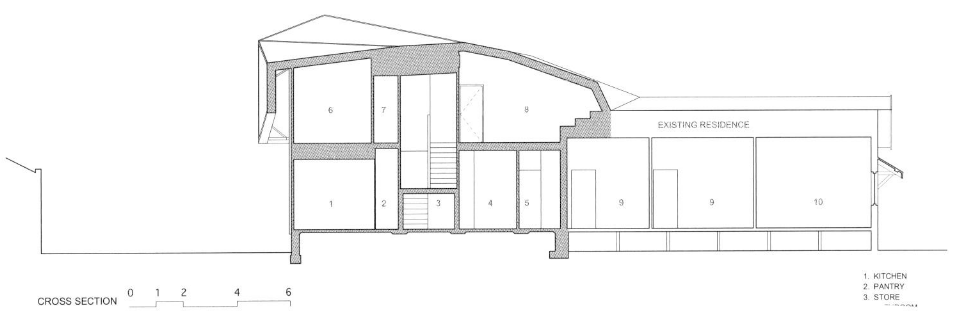

TUNING HOUSE, Spain

XPIRAL

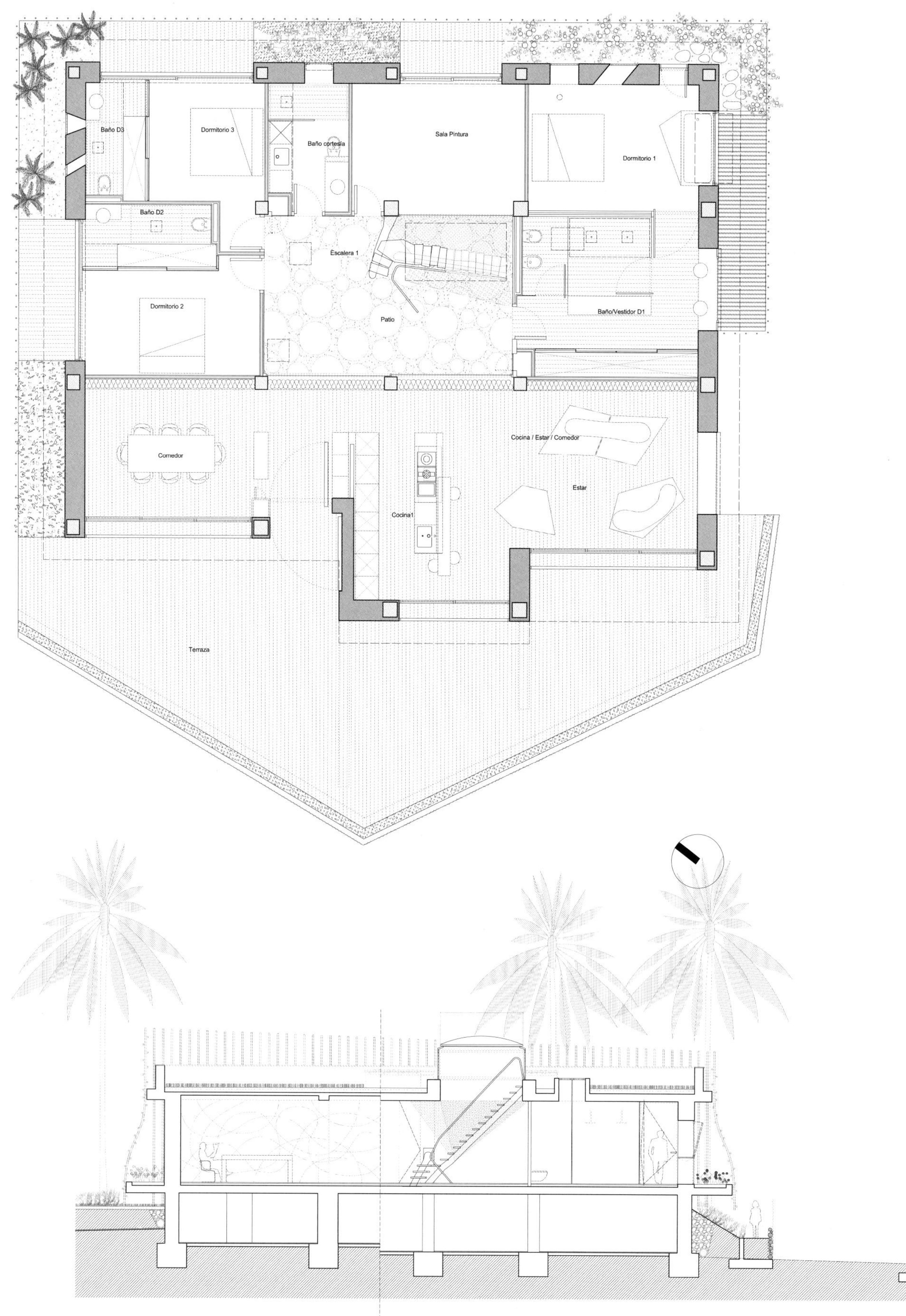

© DAVID FRUTOS/BIS IMAGES

© DAVID FRUTOS/BIS IMAGES

T11 & T13 RESIDENCES & ARTIST'S STUDIO, Cyprus

AA & U FOR ARCHITECTURE, ART AND URBANISM

Transformation in Charrat, Swiss

Clavienrossier Architects

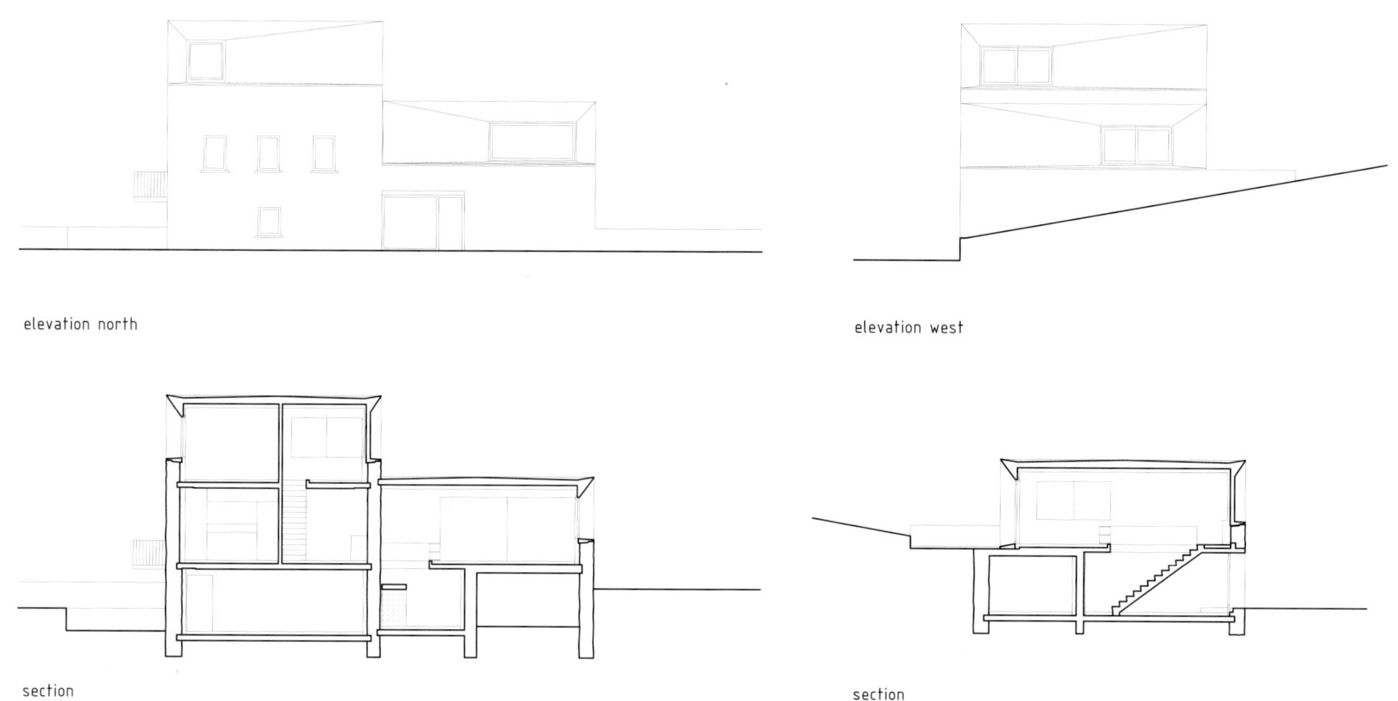

© Roger Frei

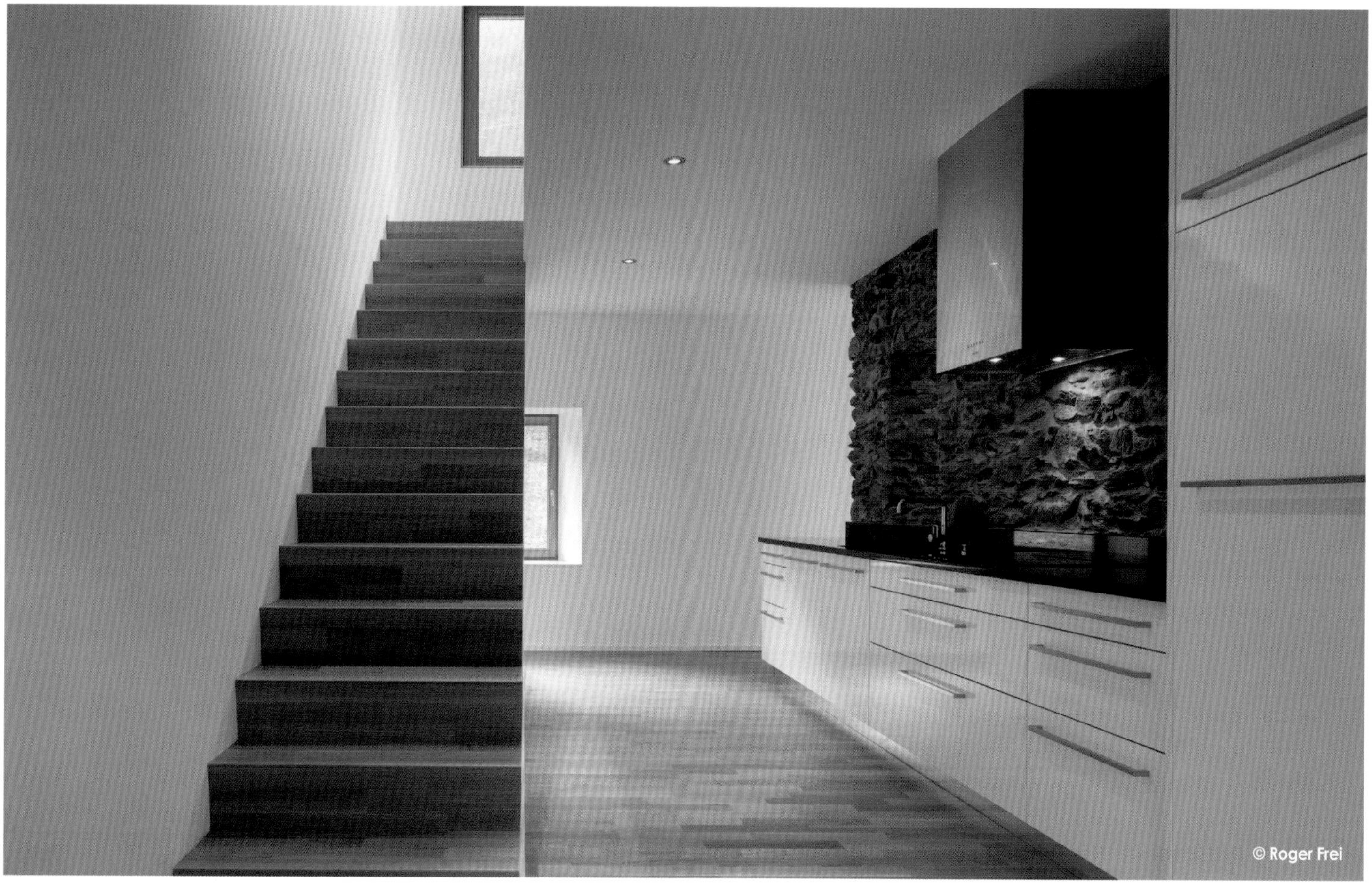

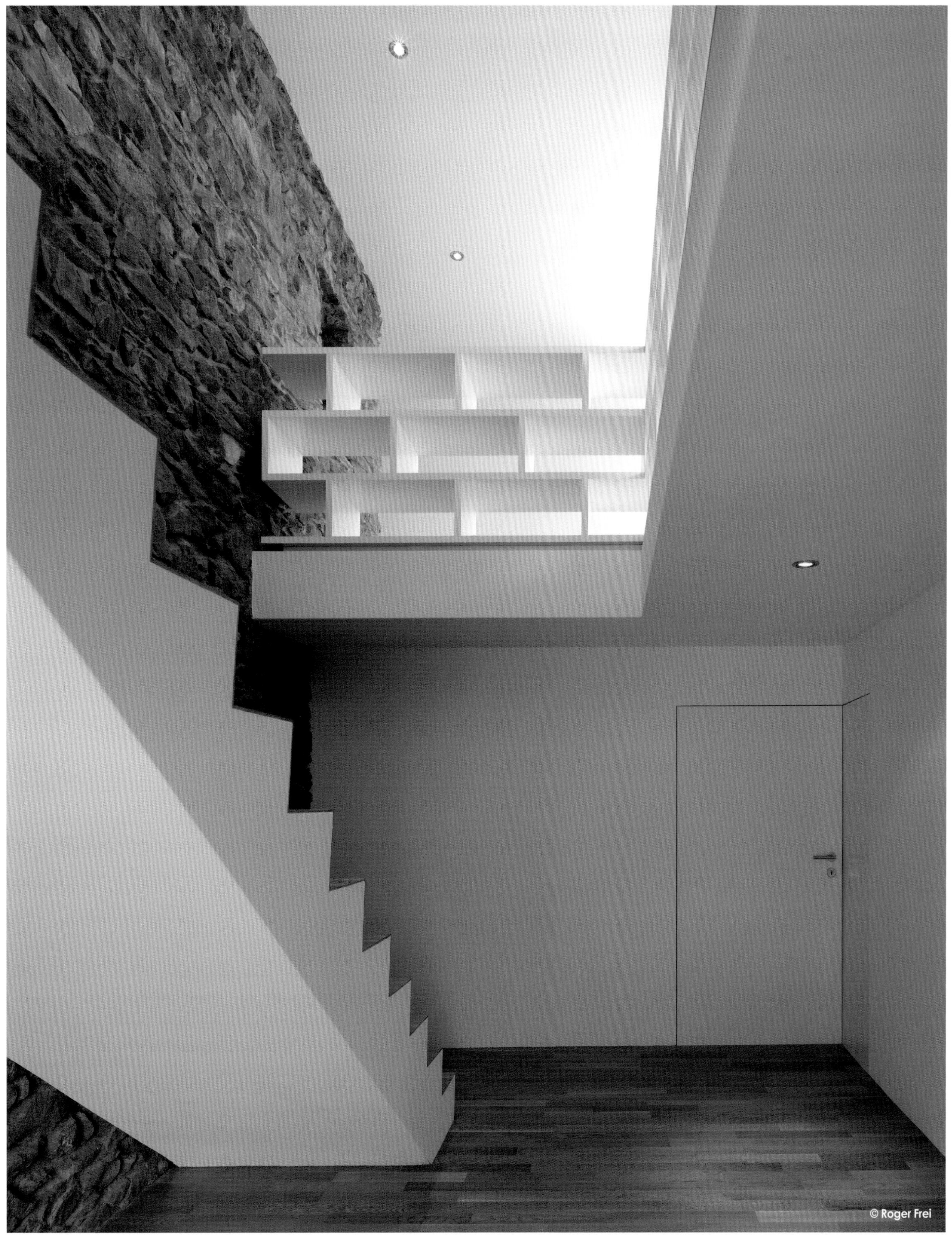
© Roger Frei

TURJEMAN, Israel

Pisou Kedem office

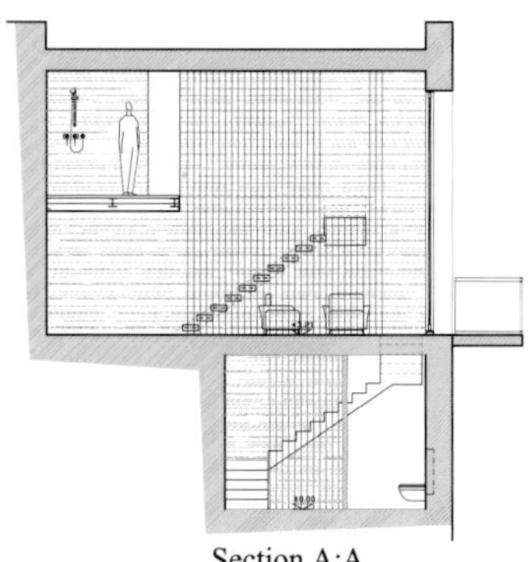

Section A:A

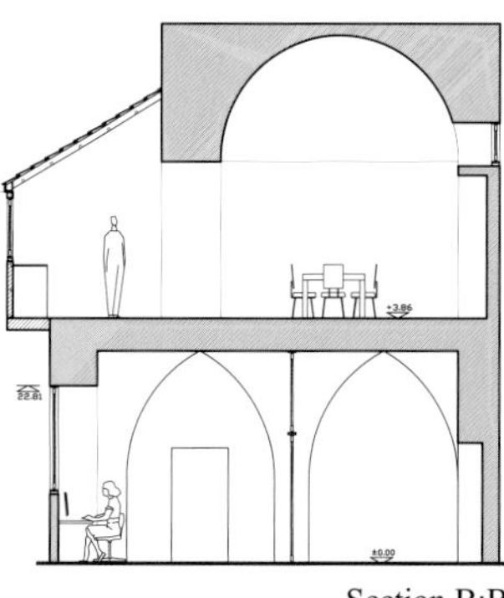

Section B:B

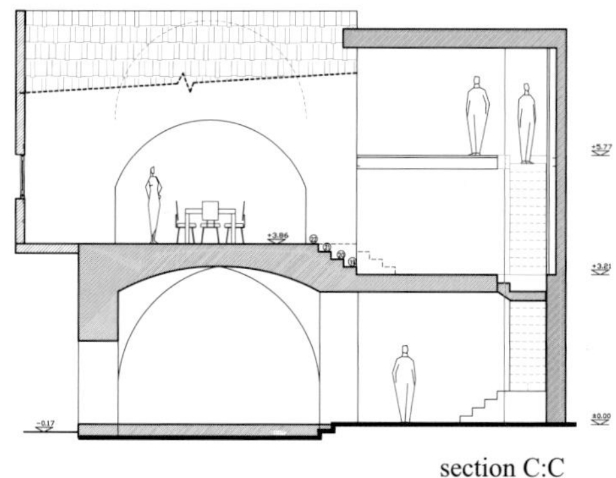

section C:C

urbia furniture system for small apartments in big cities, U.S.A

OBRA Architects

© OBRA Architects Pablo Castro & Jennifer Lee

© OBRA Architects Pablo Castro & Jennifer Lee

© OBRA Architects Pablo Castro & Jennifer Lee

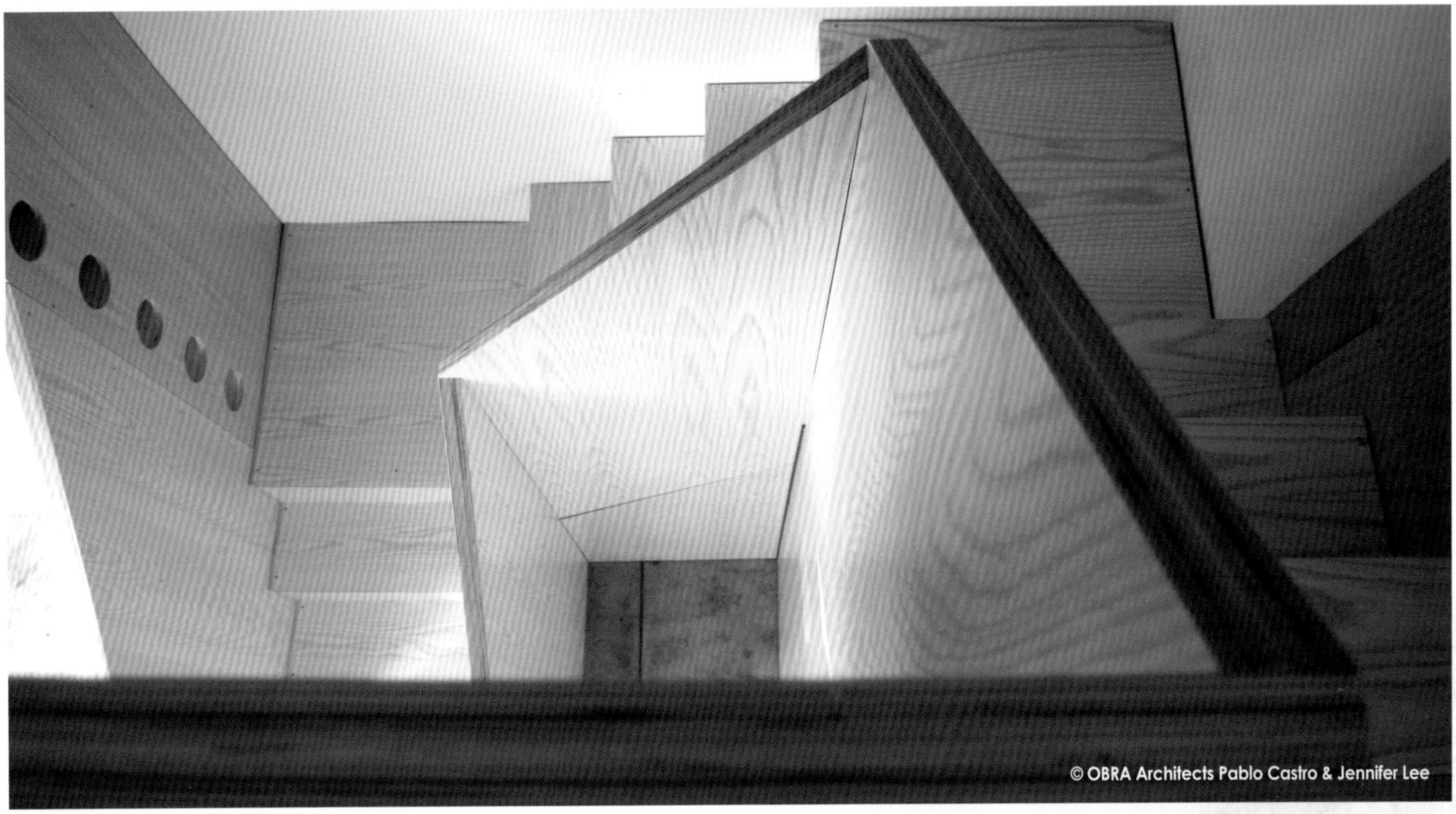

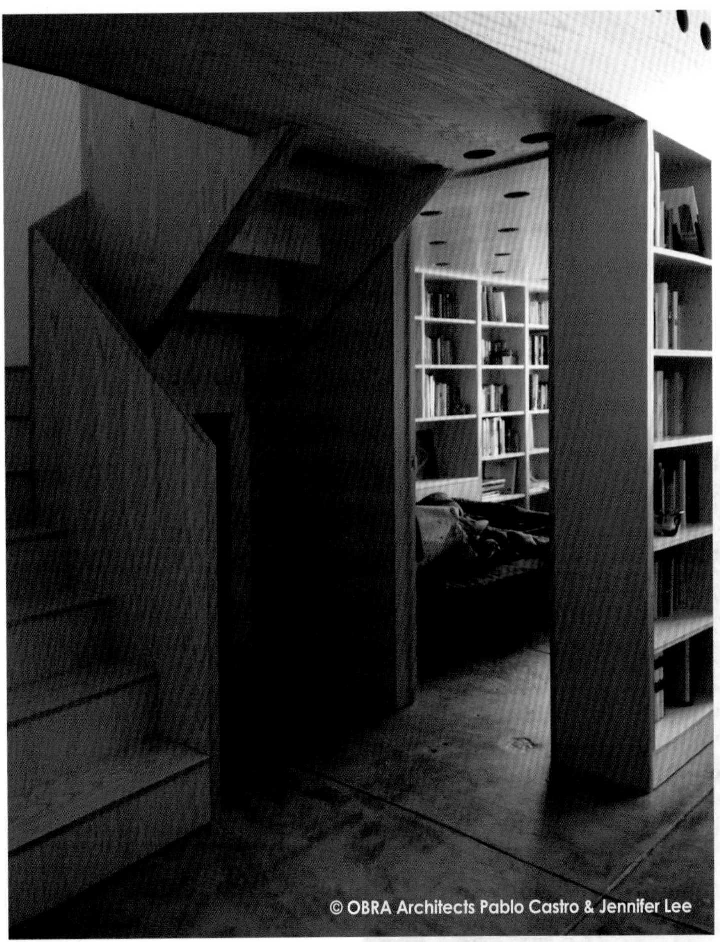

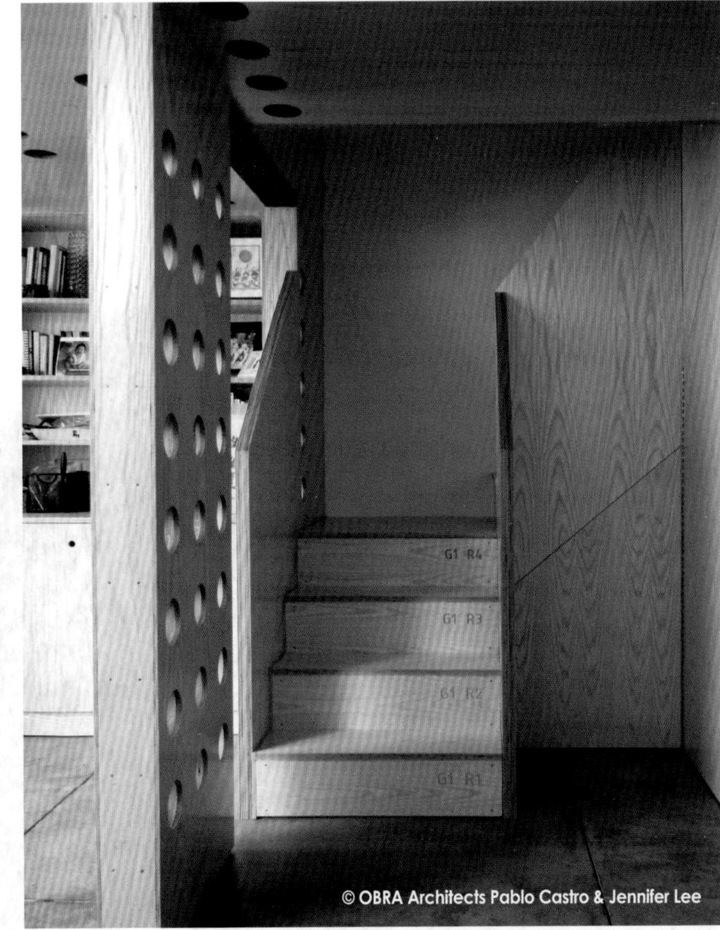

v-house, Norway

SPACEGROUP

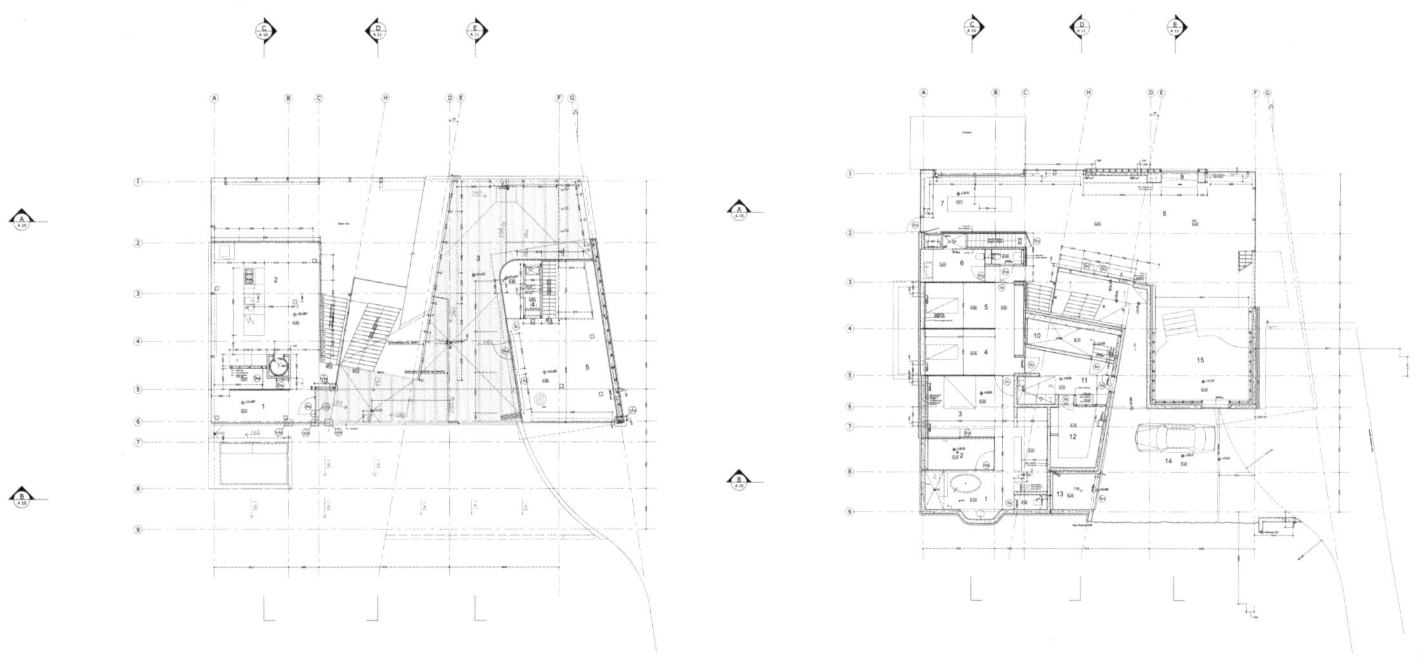

© Jeroen Musch & Ivan Brodey

Vila Nika, Serbia

sinestezia

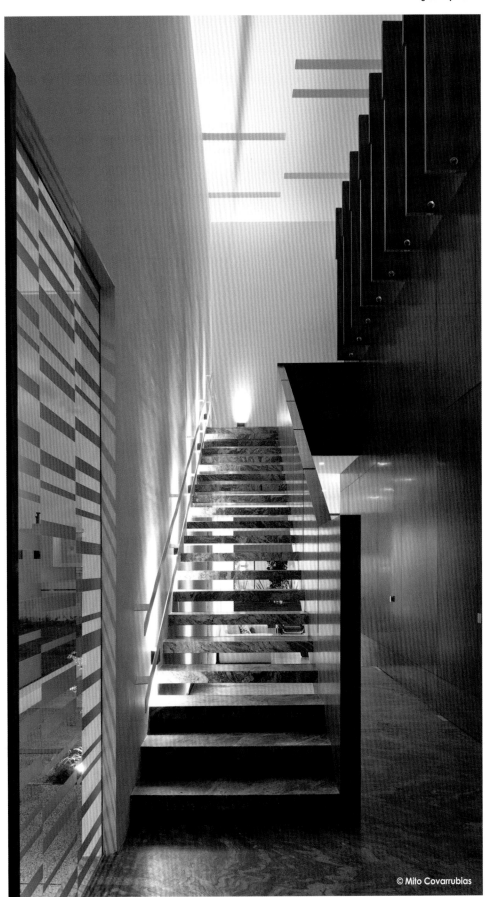

Wind House, Mexico

Agraz Arquitectos

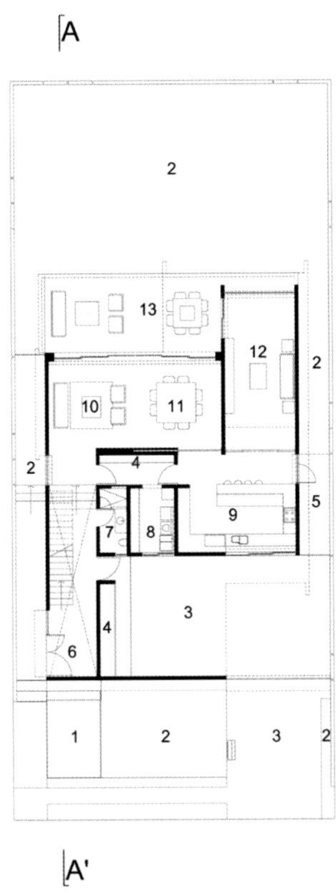

GROUND FLOOR

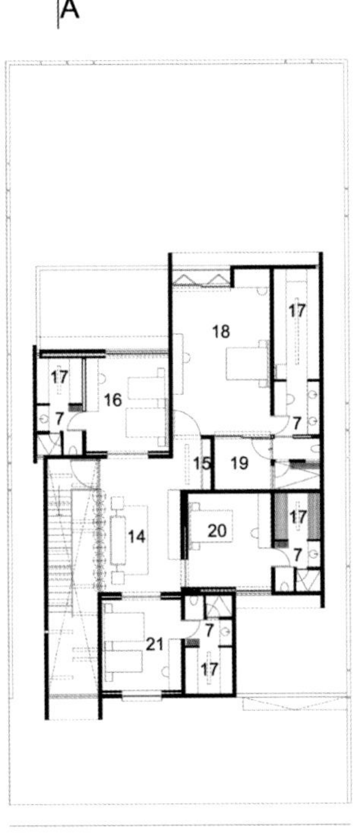

FIRST FLOOR

© Mito Covarrubias

w-house, Netherlands

VMX Architects

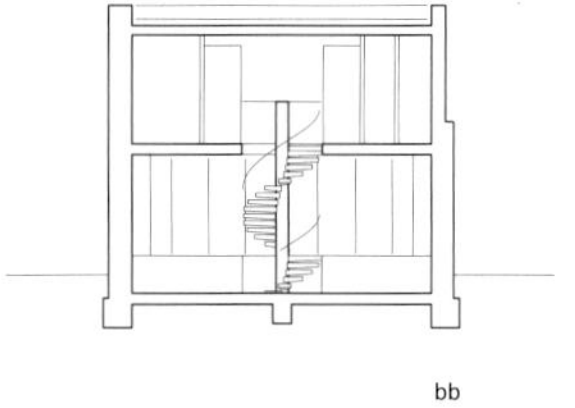

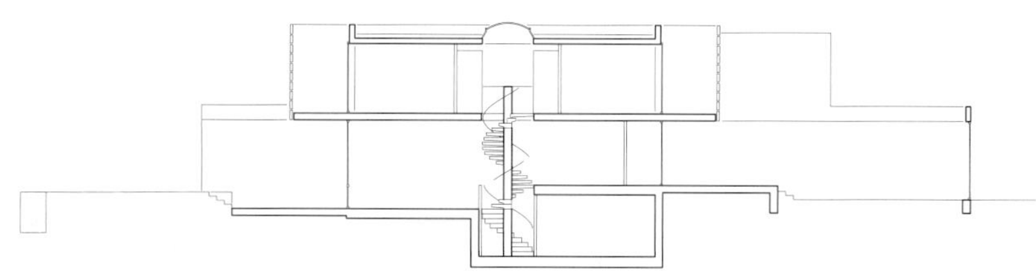

windowhouse, Japan

Yasutaka Yoshimura Architects

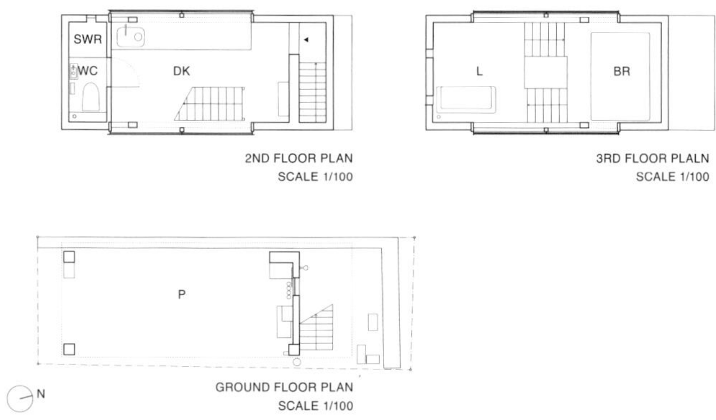

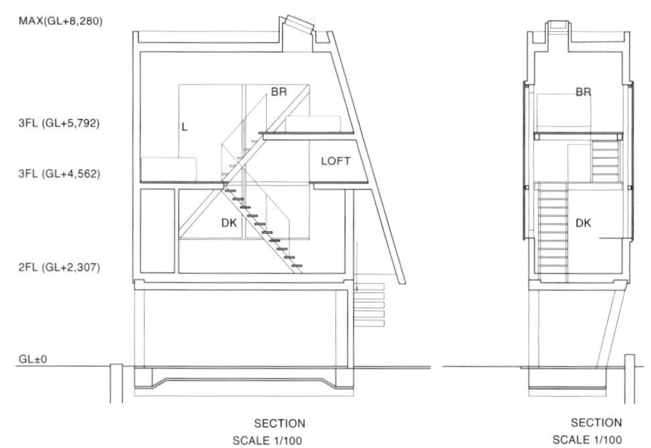

© Yasutaka Yoshimura

© Yasutaka Yoshimura

© Yasutaka Yoshimura

© Yasutaka Yoshimura

Y House, China

Beijing Matsubara and Architects

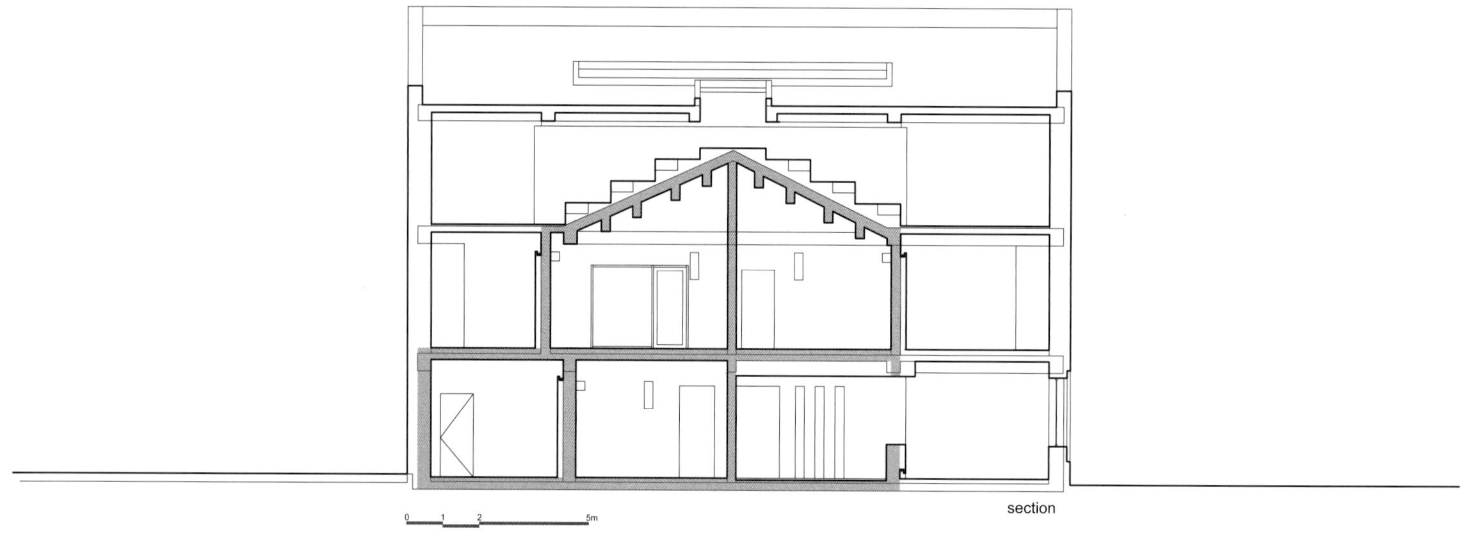

section

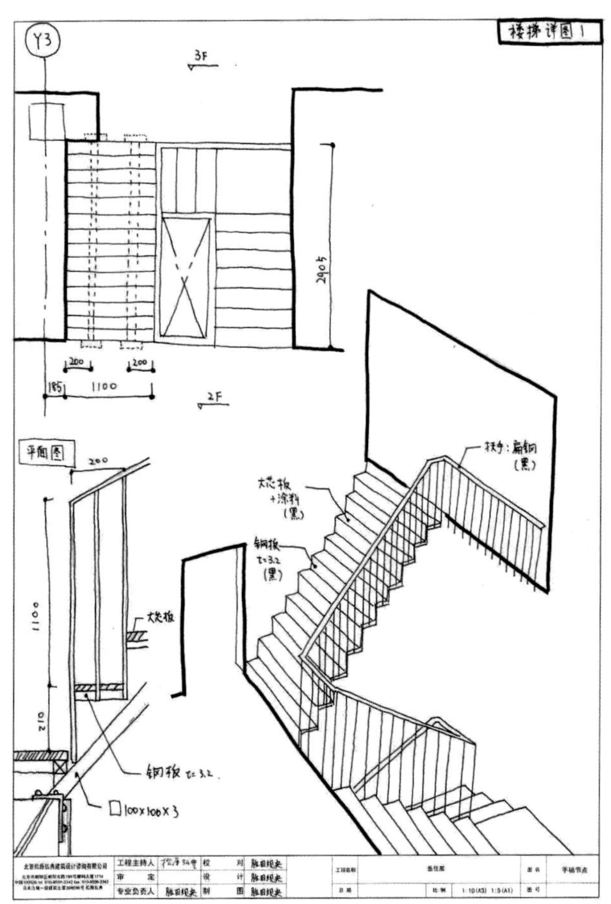

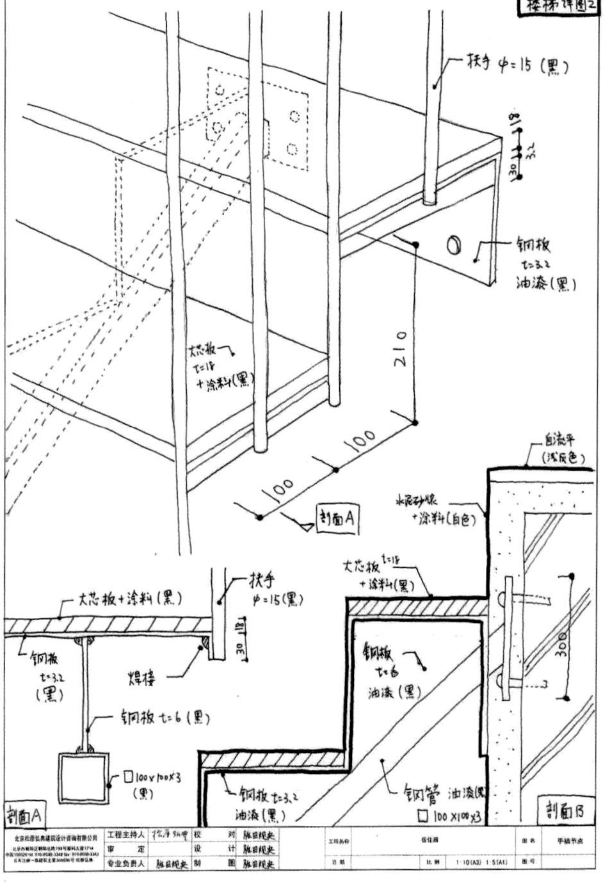

© Misae Hiromatsu

© Misae Hiromatsu

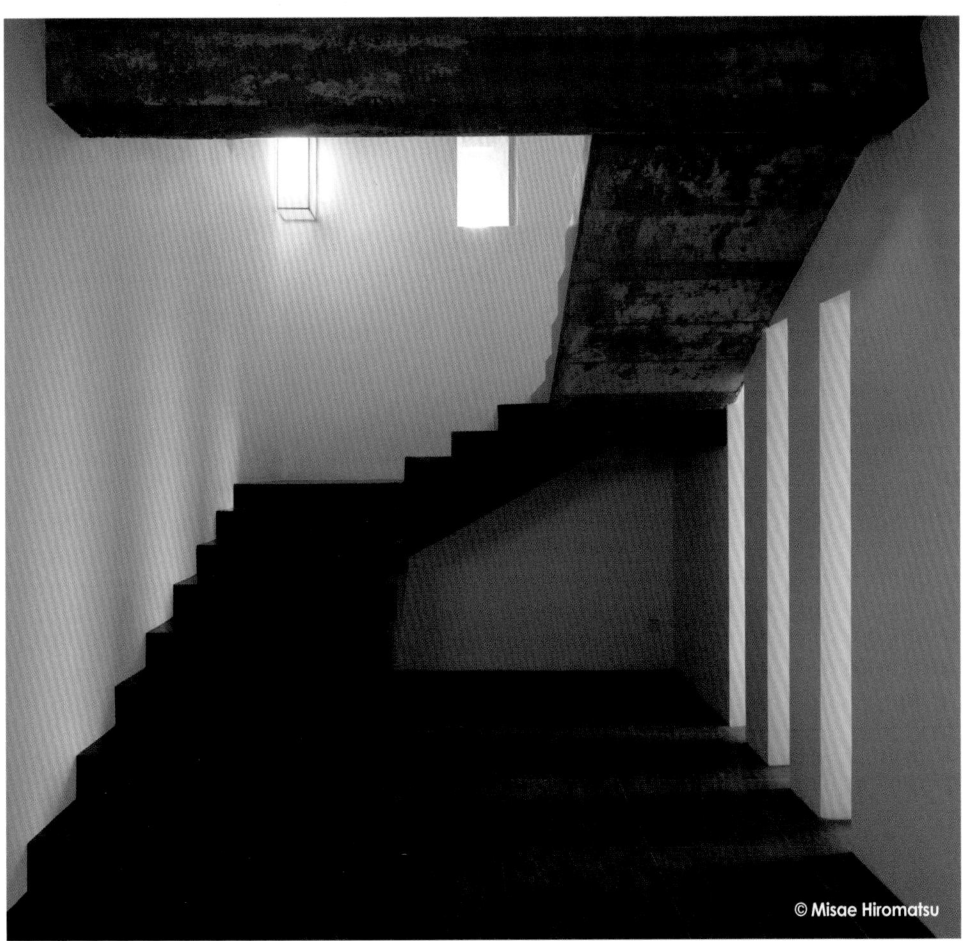

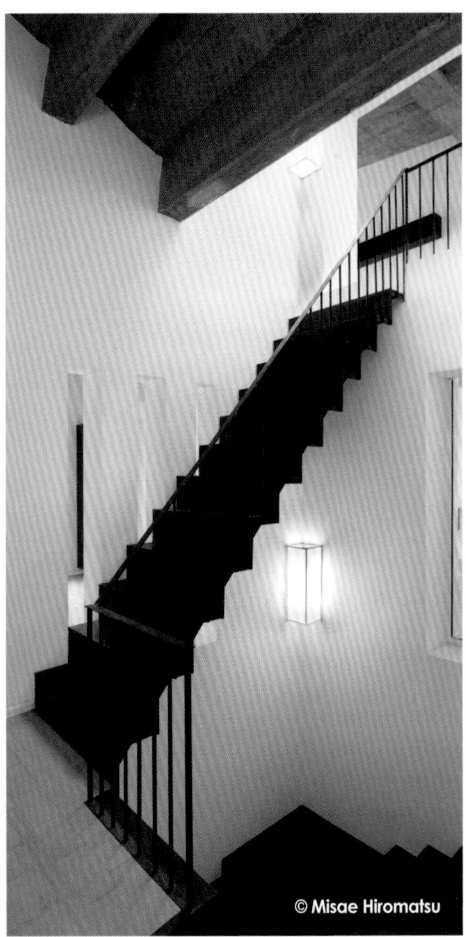

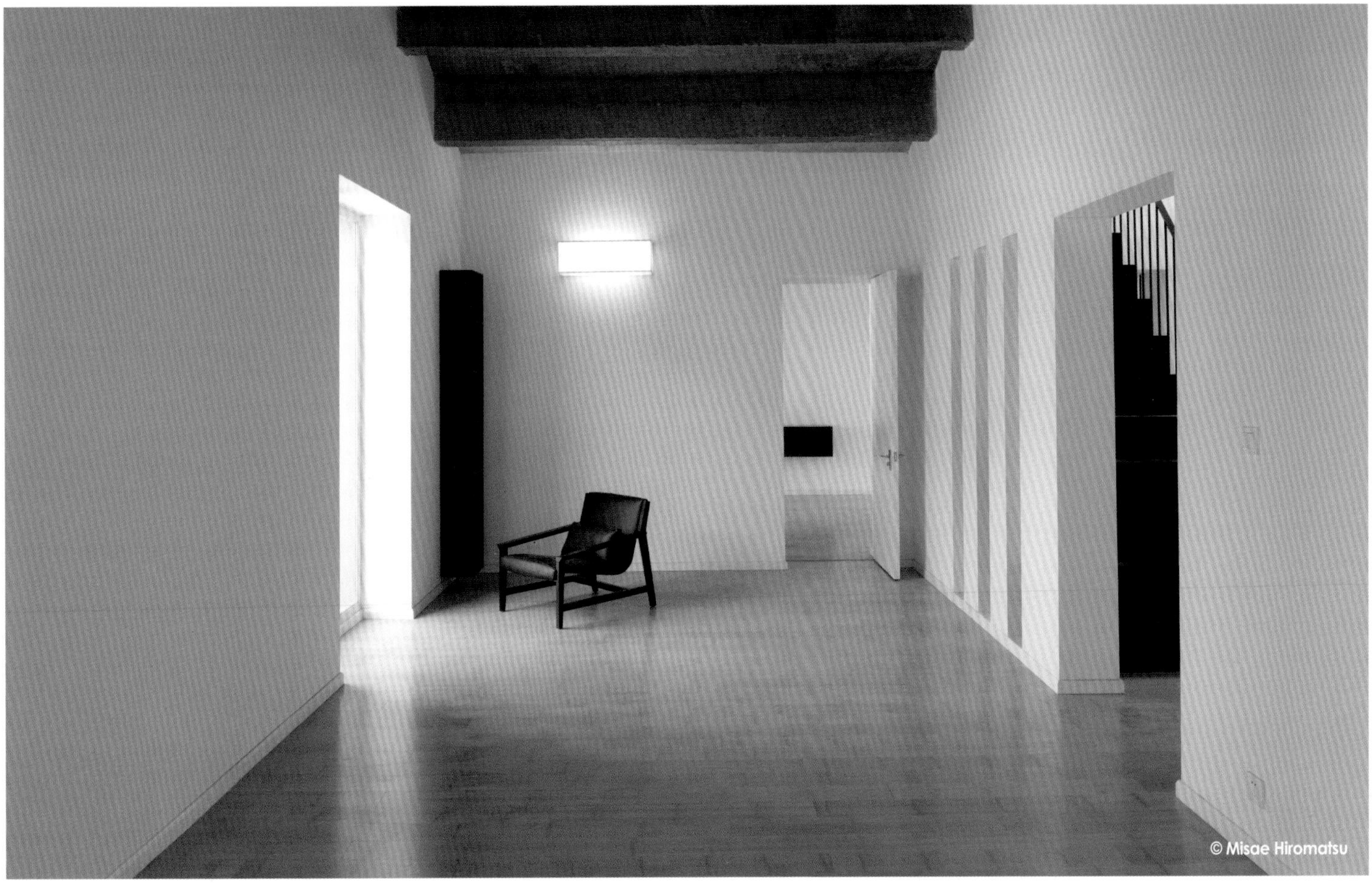

© Misae Hiromatsu

Yoojeongheon, Korea
studio-GAON

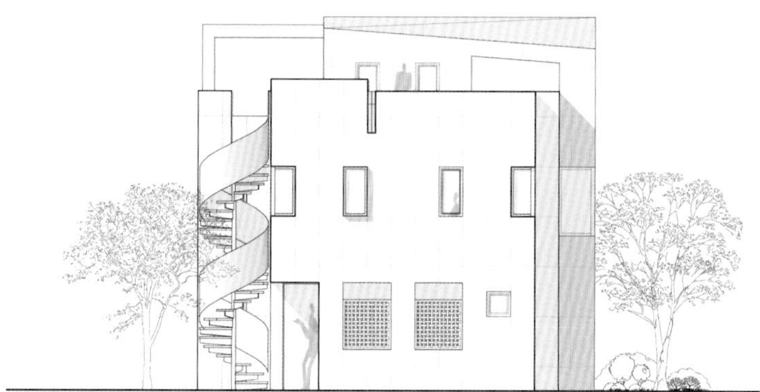

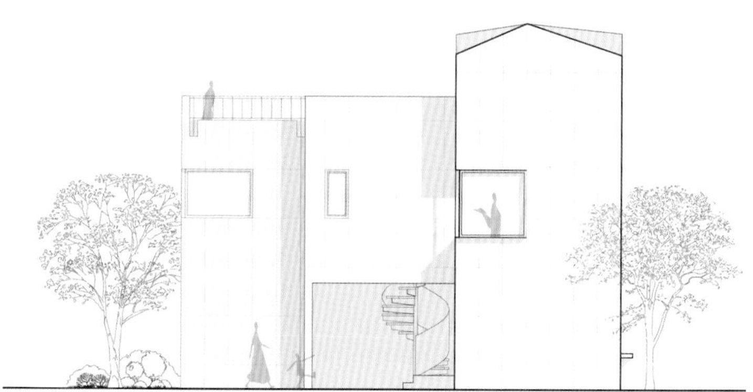

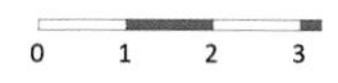

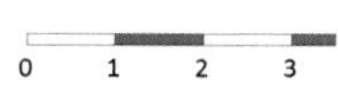

© Youngchae Park

oungchae Park

© Youngchae Park

Arequipa Hadcrafts Market, Peru

LABORATORIO URBANO DE LIMA

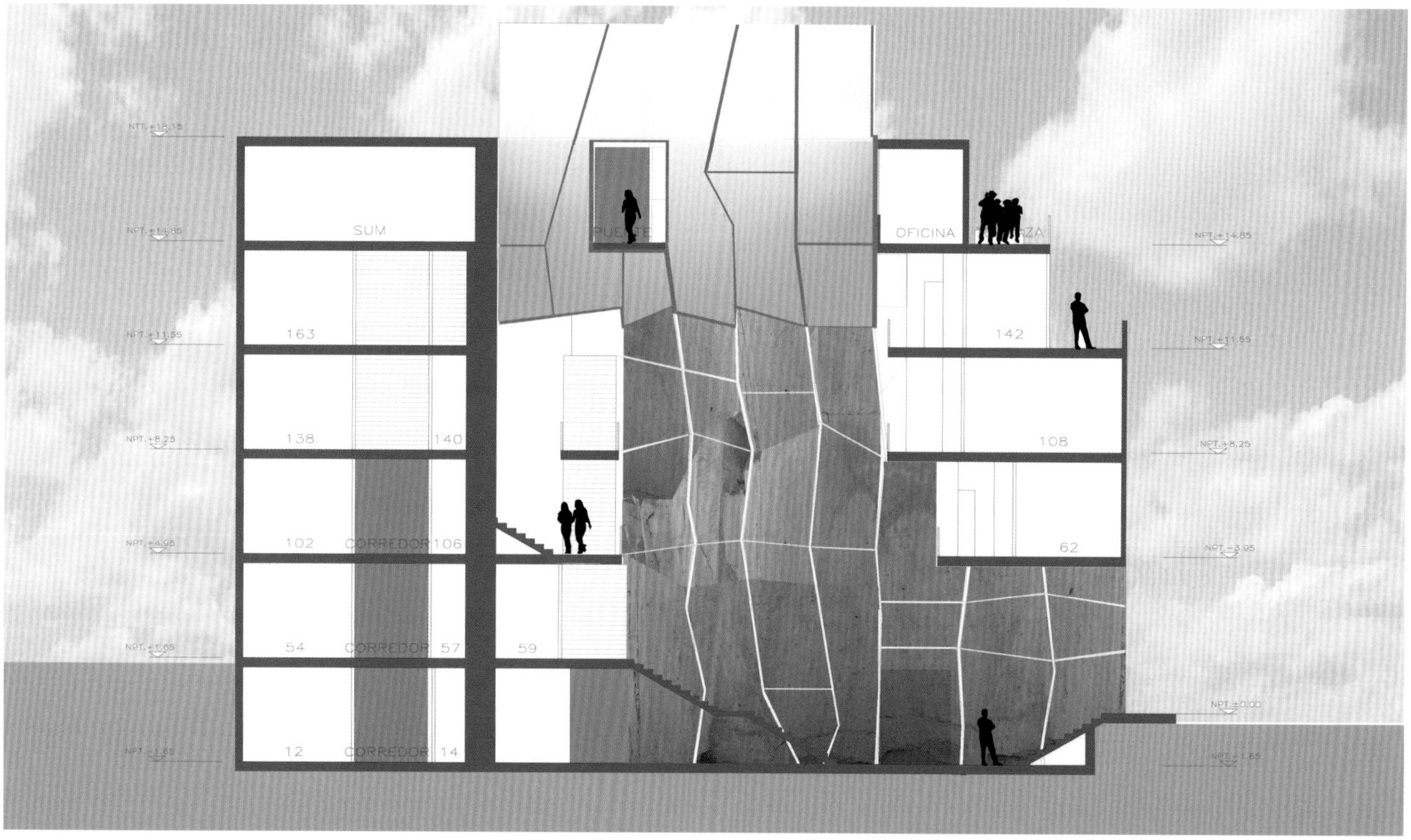

BLEUNORI / VINOTHÈQUE, U.S.A

ARQUIPELAGO

chasm, Korea

studio asylum

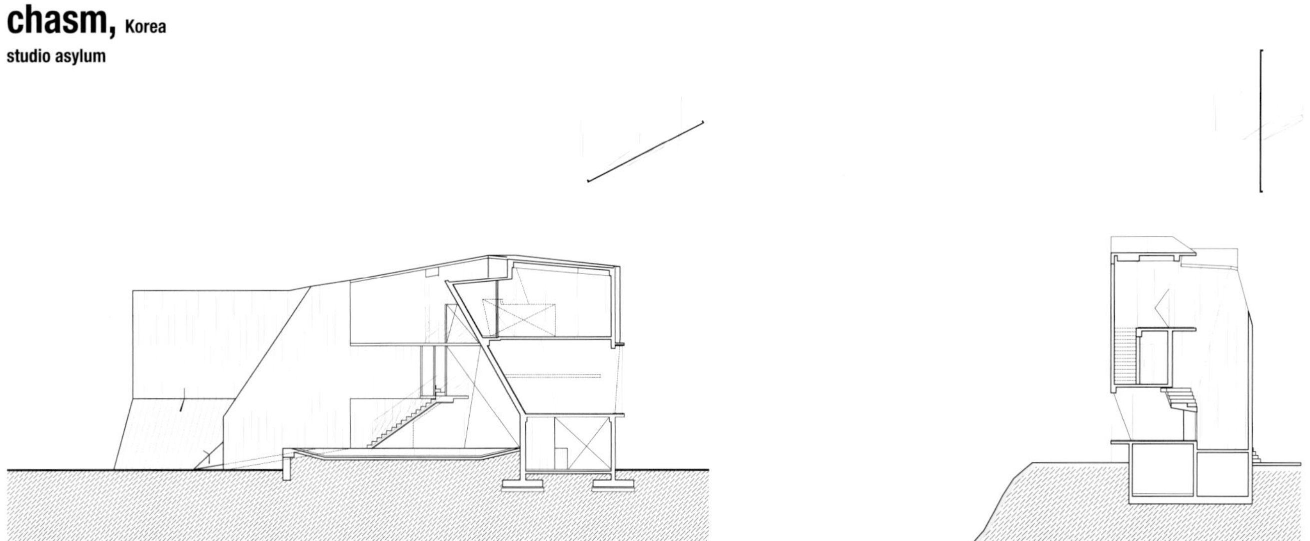

© Park Wan-soon

© Park Wan-soon

delicatessen 2, Israel

Z-A studio

© Fram Petit

café '-ismo', Greece
Point Supreme Architects

Dance House for Teenagers, Korea

studio-GAON

© Youngchae Park

© Youngchae Park

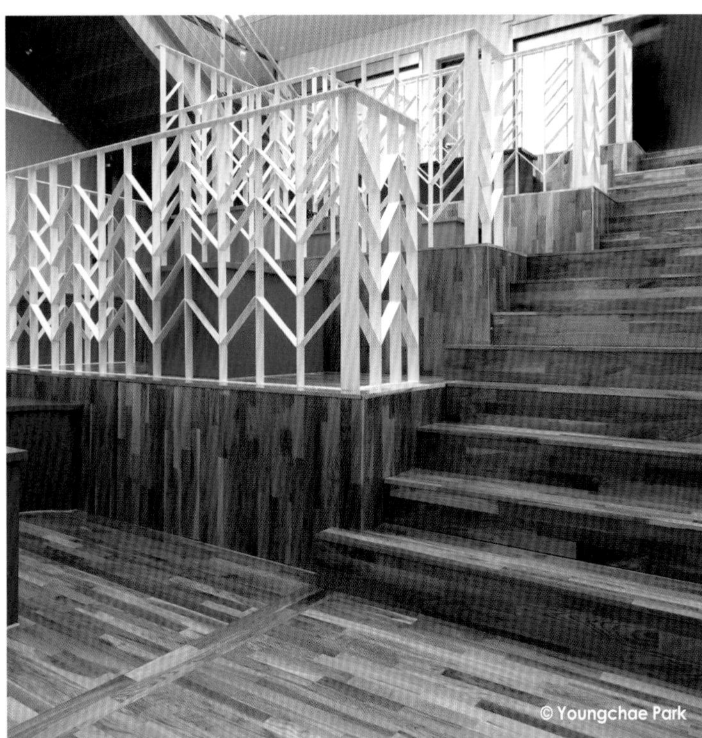

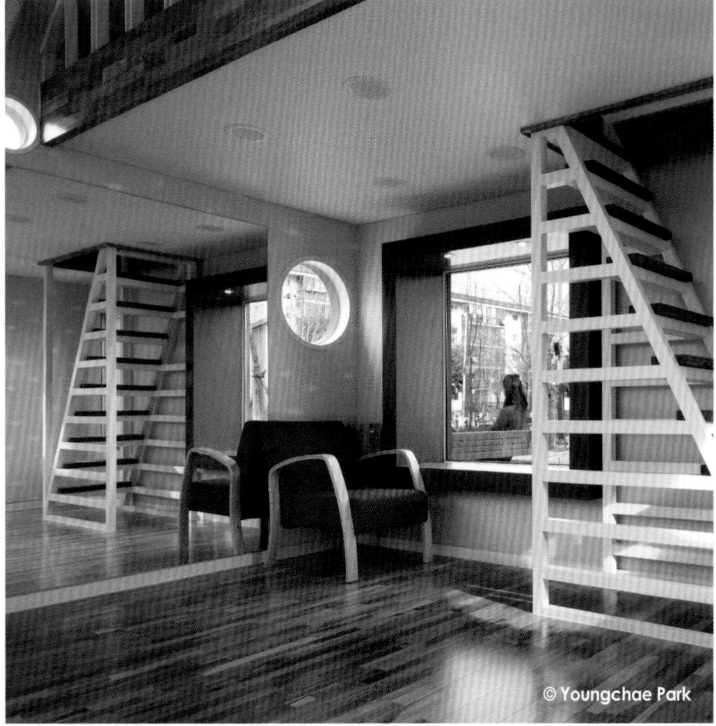

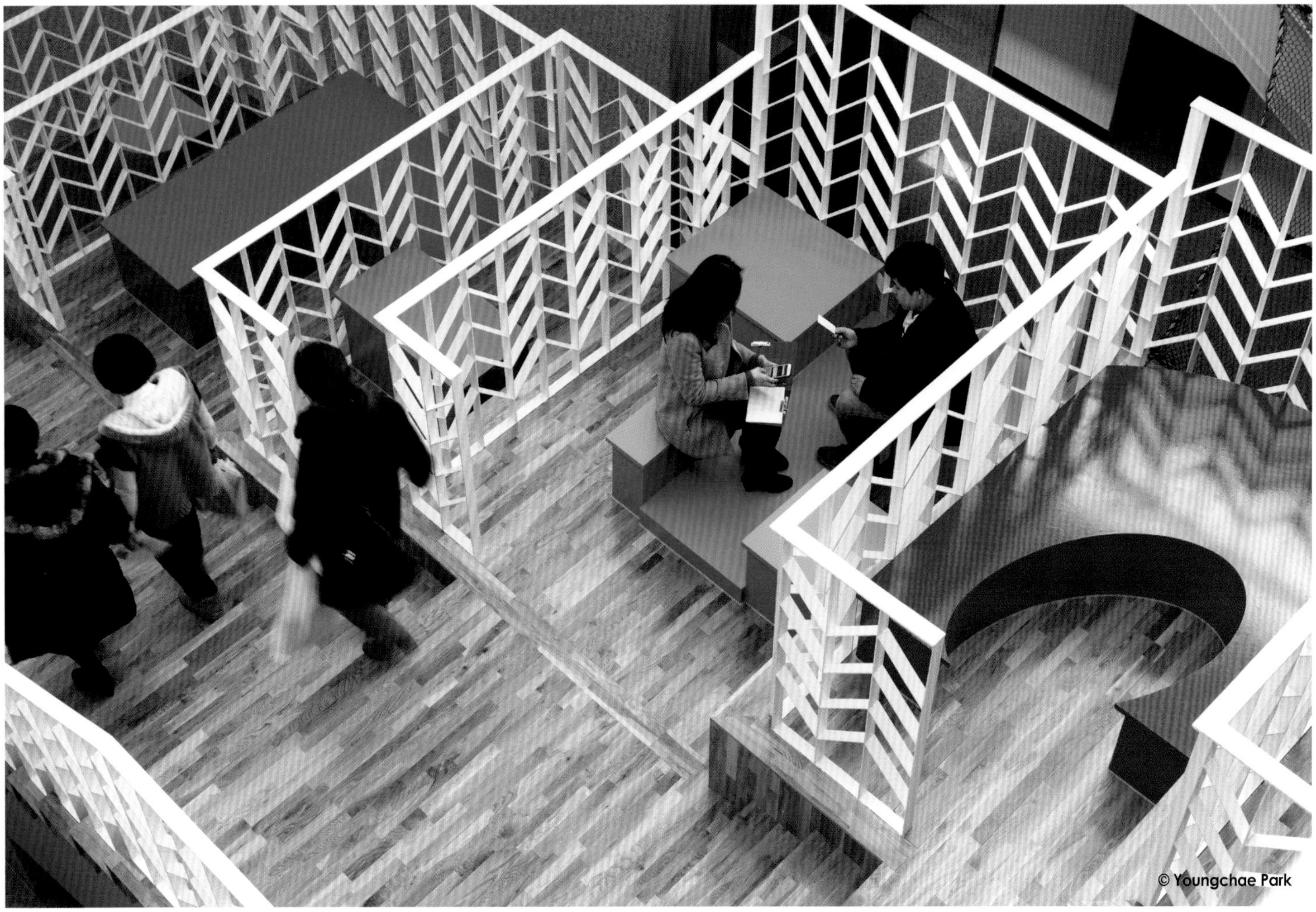

© Youngchae Park

dashing diva, China

MoHen Design International

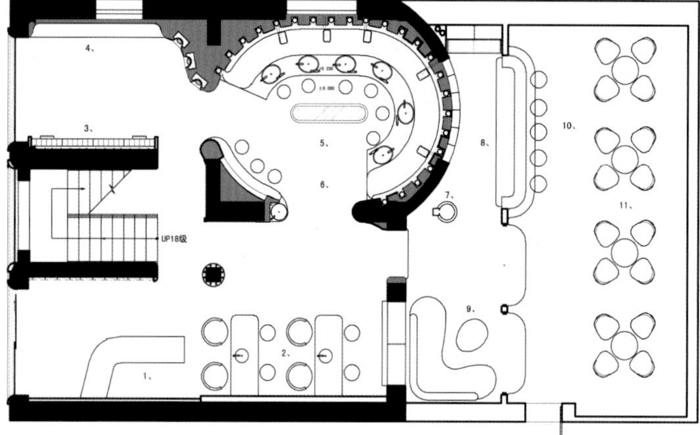

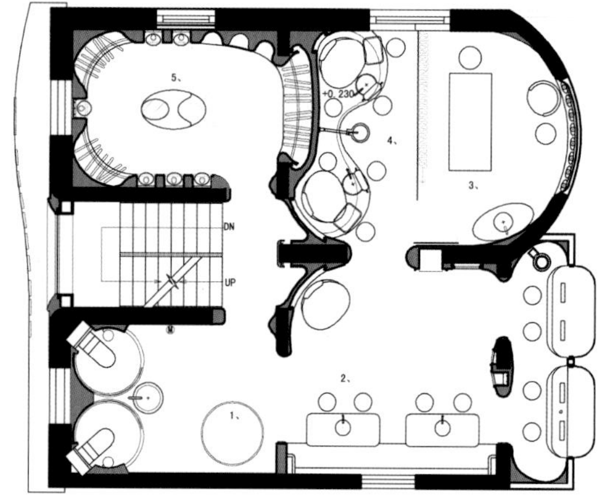

© Maoder Chou / MoHen Design International

© Maoder Chou / MoHen Design International

doosan arts quare, Korea

jay is working

© Park Wan soon

Enghelab Food Court Restaurant, Iran

DIBA Tensile Architecture

© Mohammad Hassan Ettefagh

espresso-fabriek, Netherlands

Studio Ramin Visch

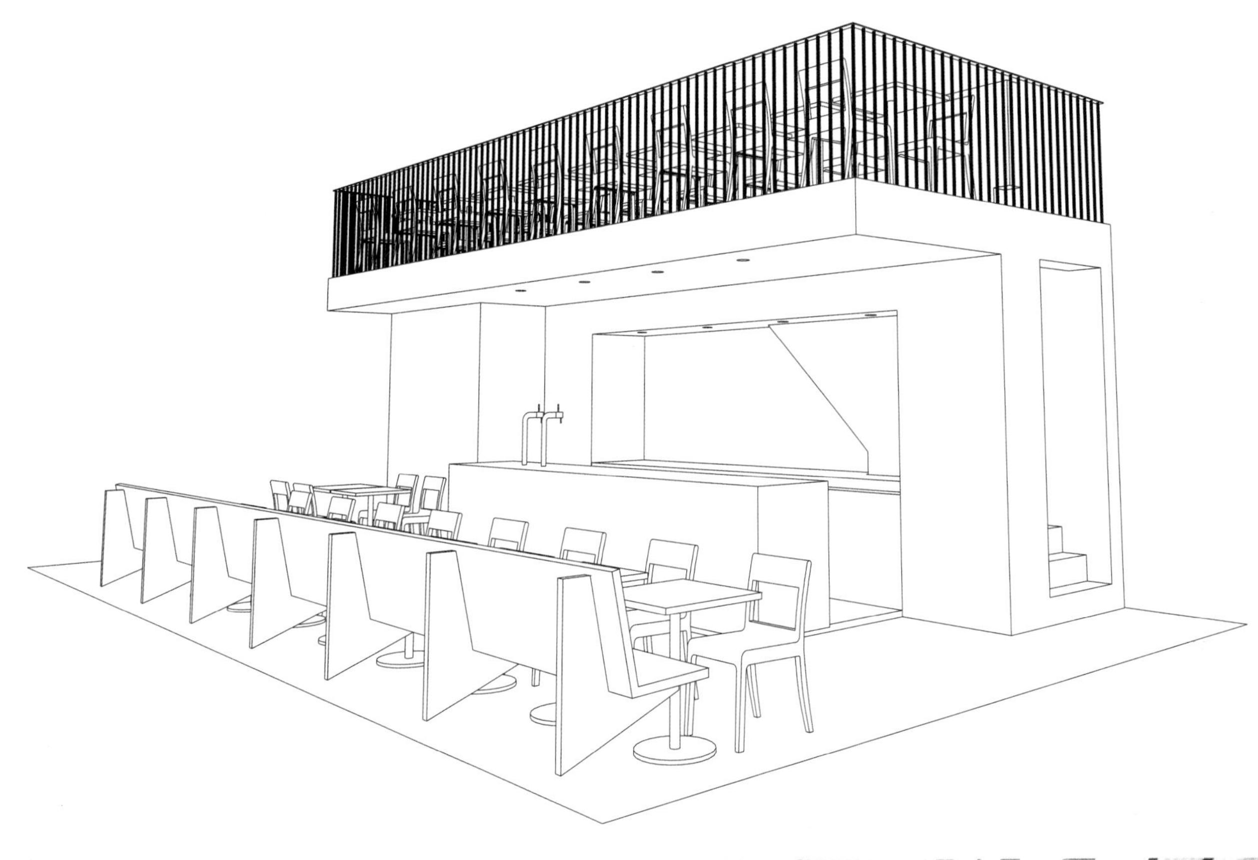

erics paris salon, China
GRAFT

爱丽克·巴黎

Groninger Forum, Netherlands

nARCHITECTS

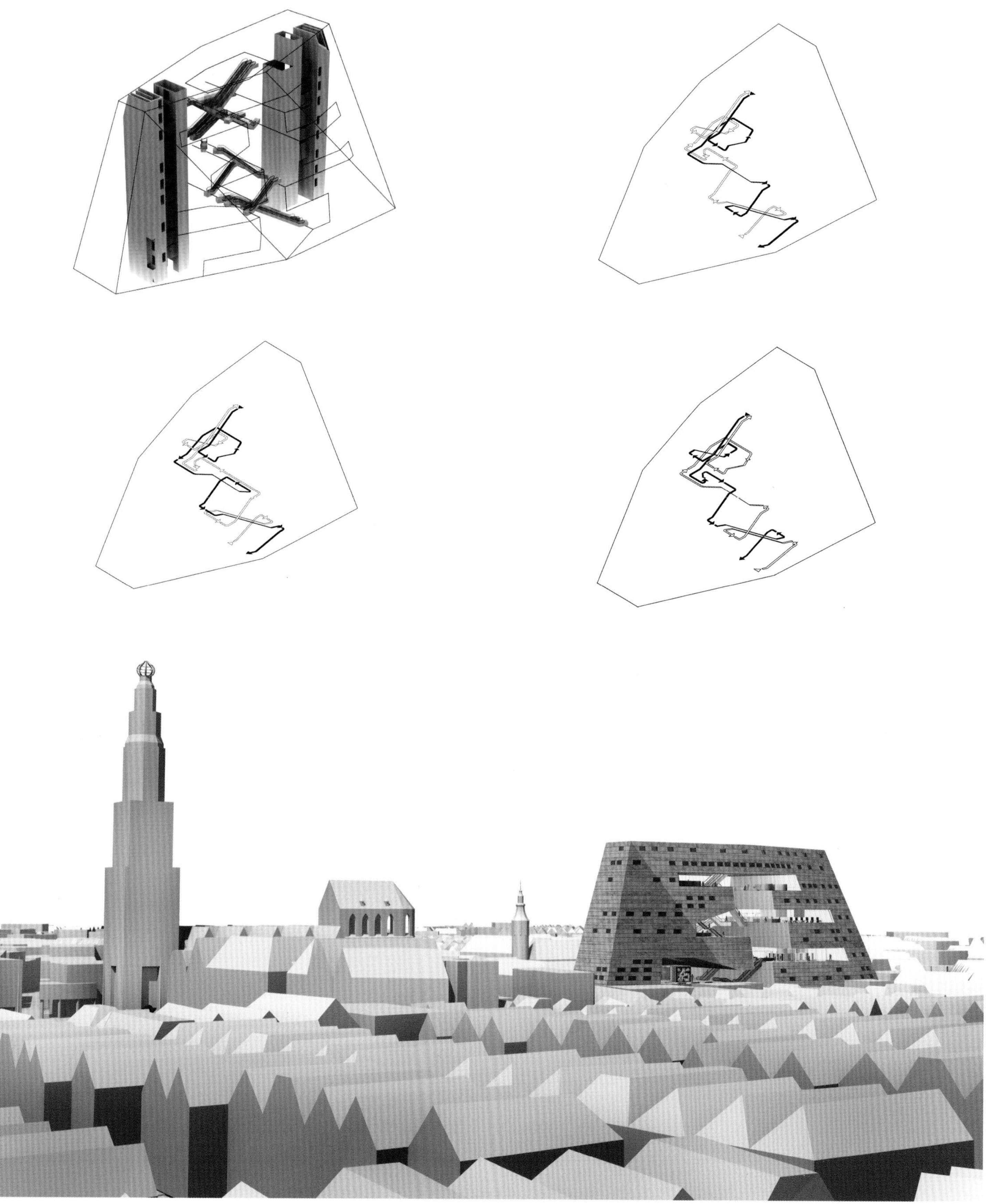

Han's Gallery cafe, Korea

Koo Seungmin

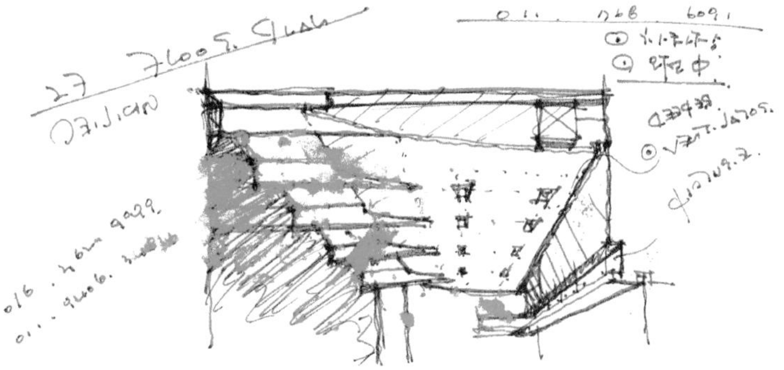

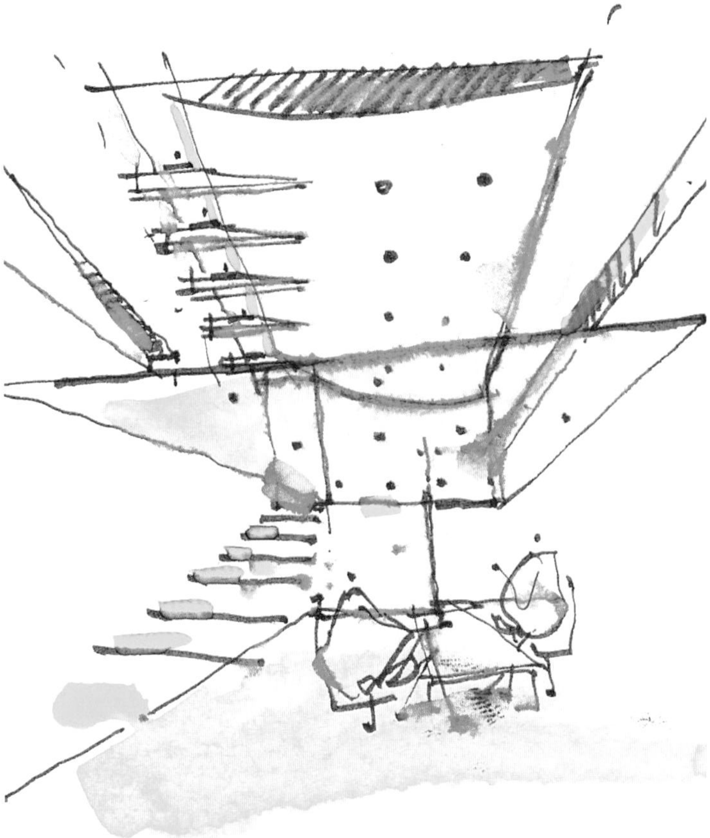

© Park Wan soon

Hangilsa Publishing Company, Korea

studio asylum

© Park Wan soon

Hotel Pro Forma, Denmark

ONE ARCHITECTURE

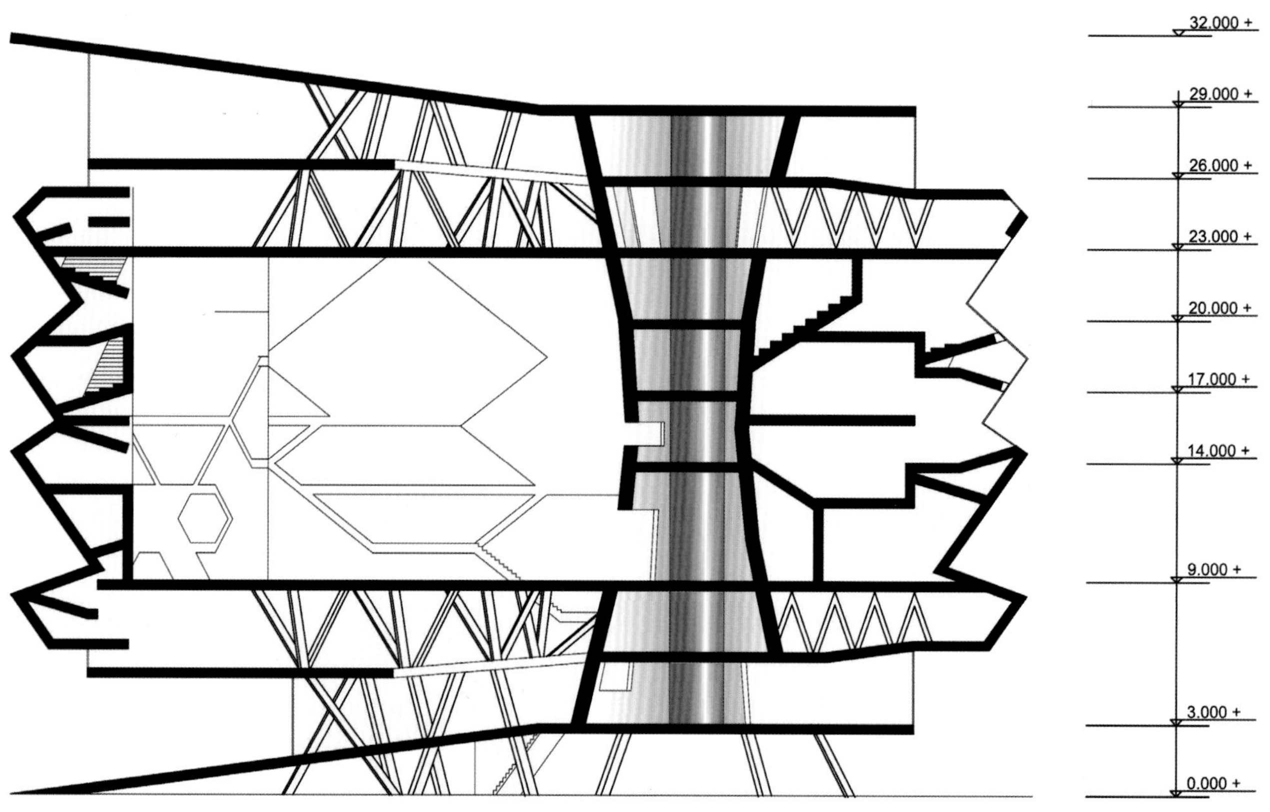

jonoyahonmachi, Japan
Inly Design

ibidem, Korea
studio asylum

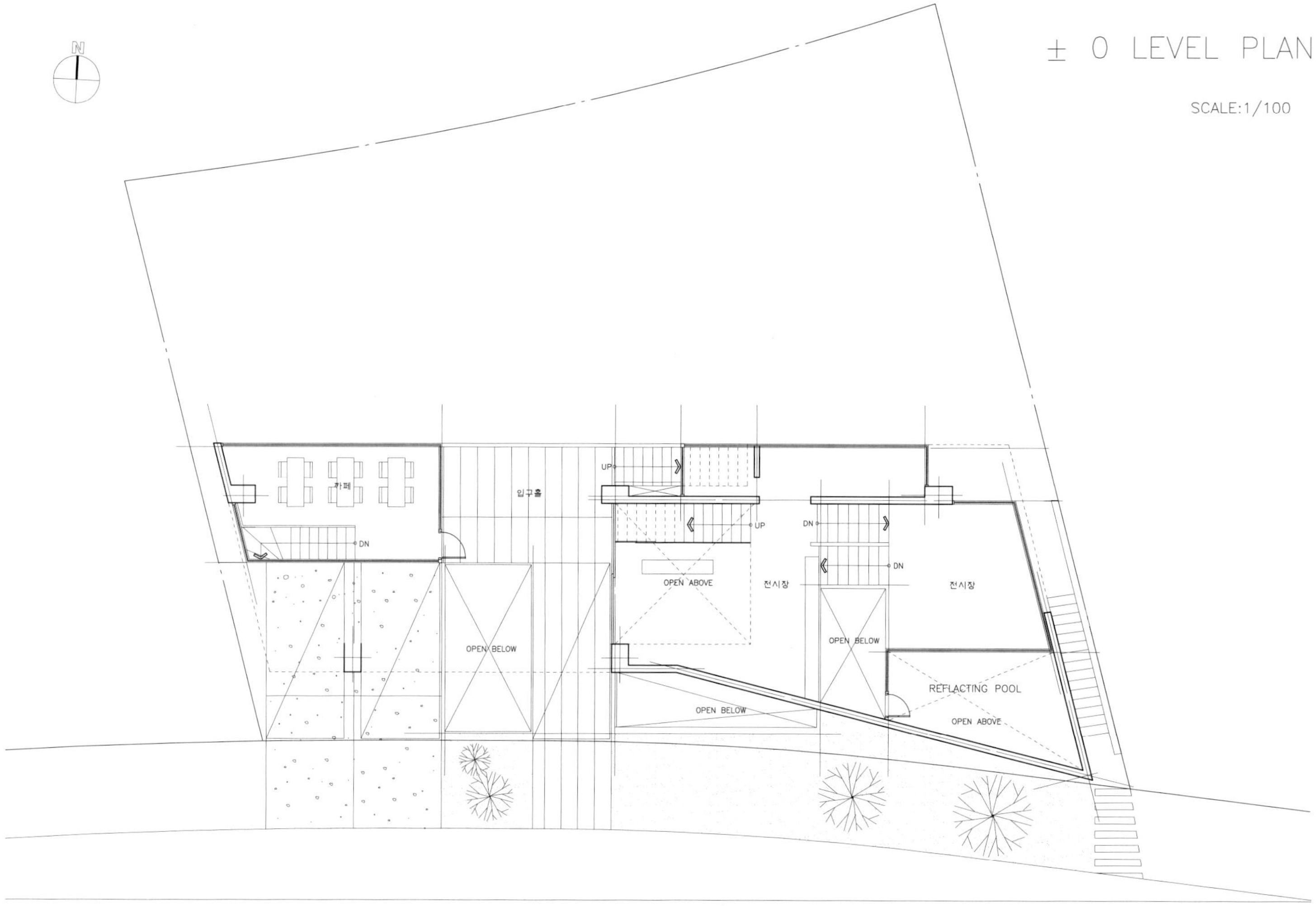

± 0 LEVEL PLAN

SCALE:1/100

N

카페

입구홀

UP

DN

UP

DN

DN

OPEN ABOVE

전시장

전시장

OPEN BELOW

OPEN BELOW

OPEN BELOW

REFLACTING POOL

OPEN ABOVE

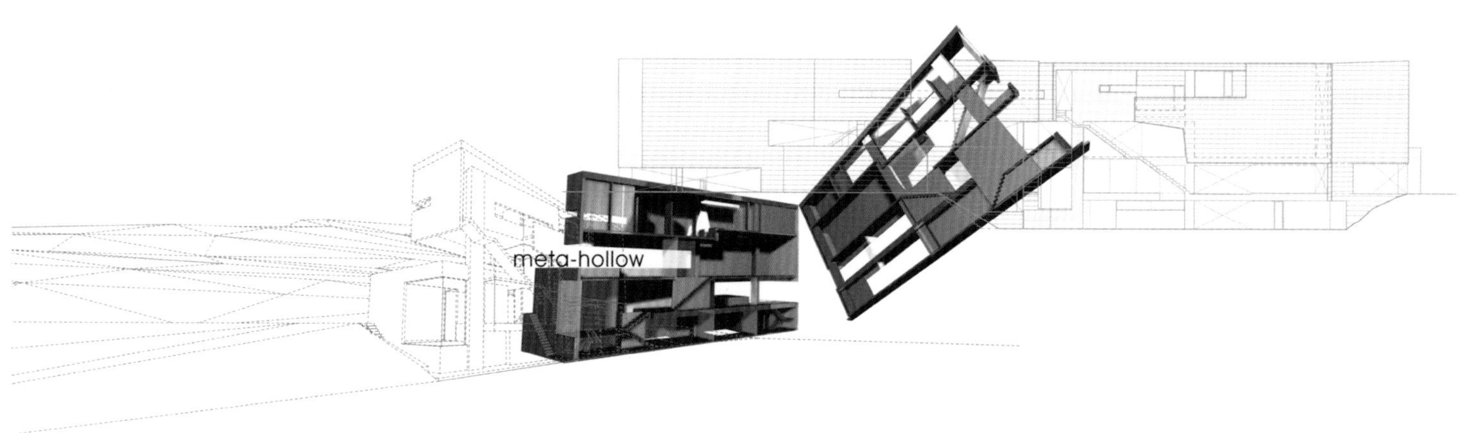

© Park Wan-soon

Inter White, Korea
Architects Group Raum

© Joonhwan Yoon

© Joonhwan Yoon

© Joonhwan Yoon

© Joonhwan Yoon

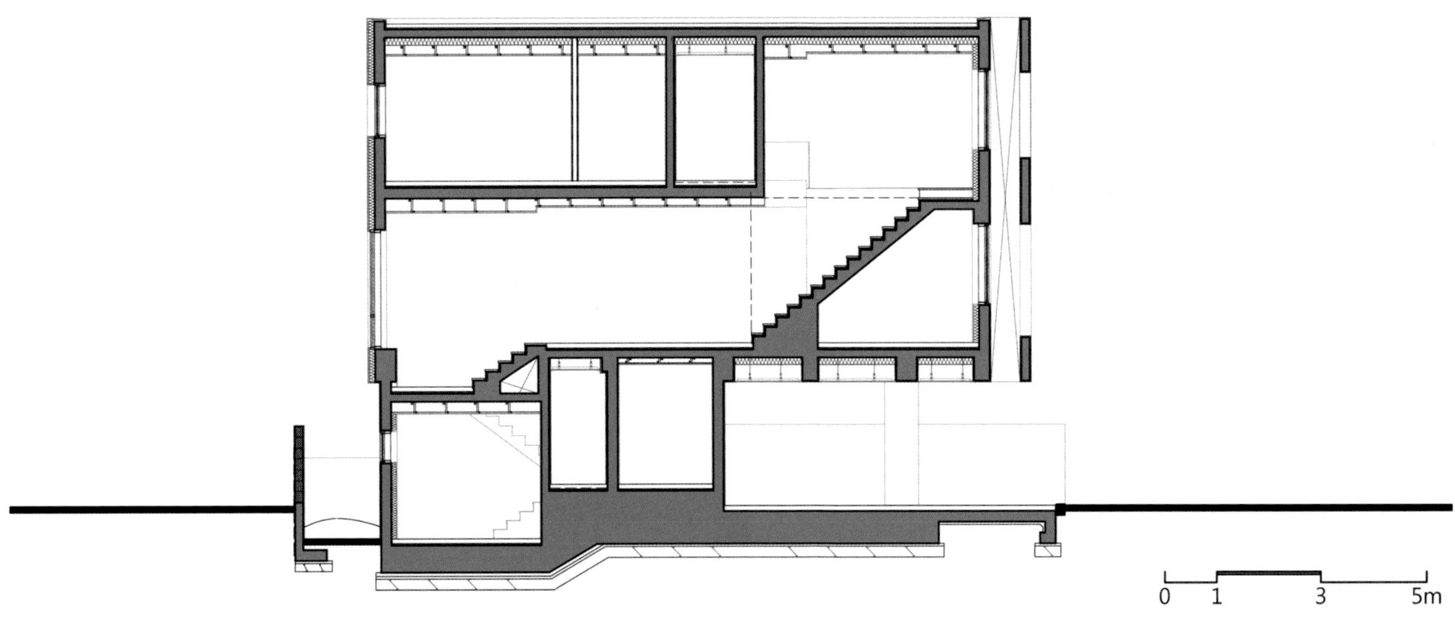

© Joonhwan Yoon

K8, Japan
Florian Busch Architects
© Nacasa + Partners

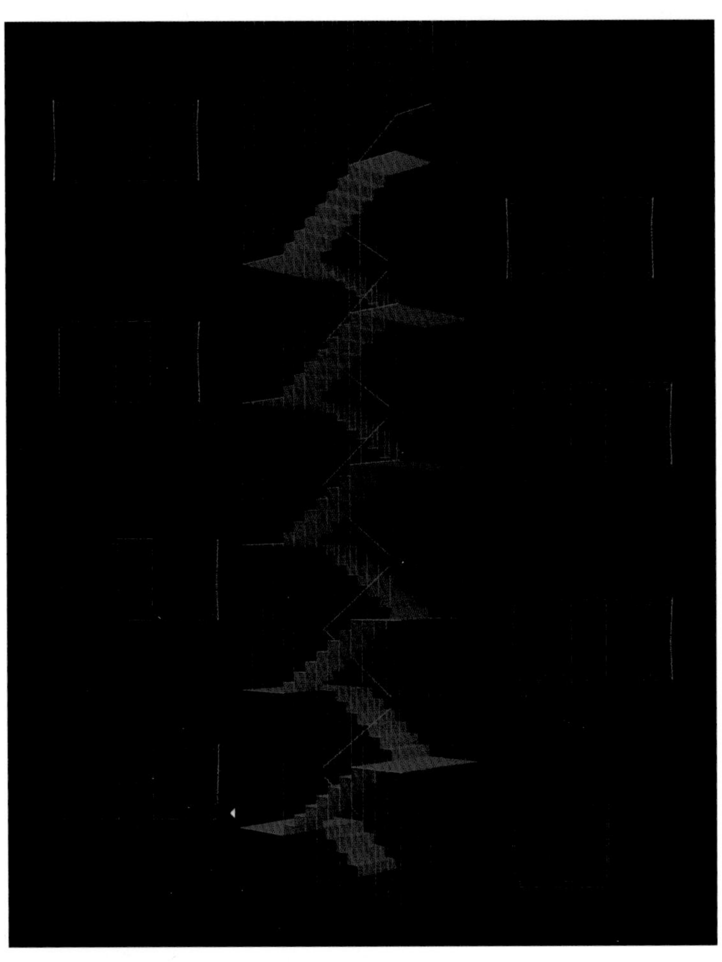

© Nacasa + Partners

© Nacasa + Partners

kantoor dupon, Netherlands

Studio Ramin Visch

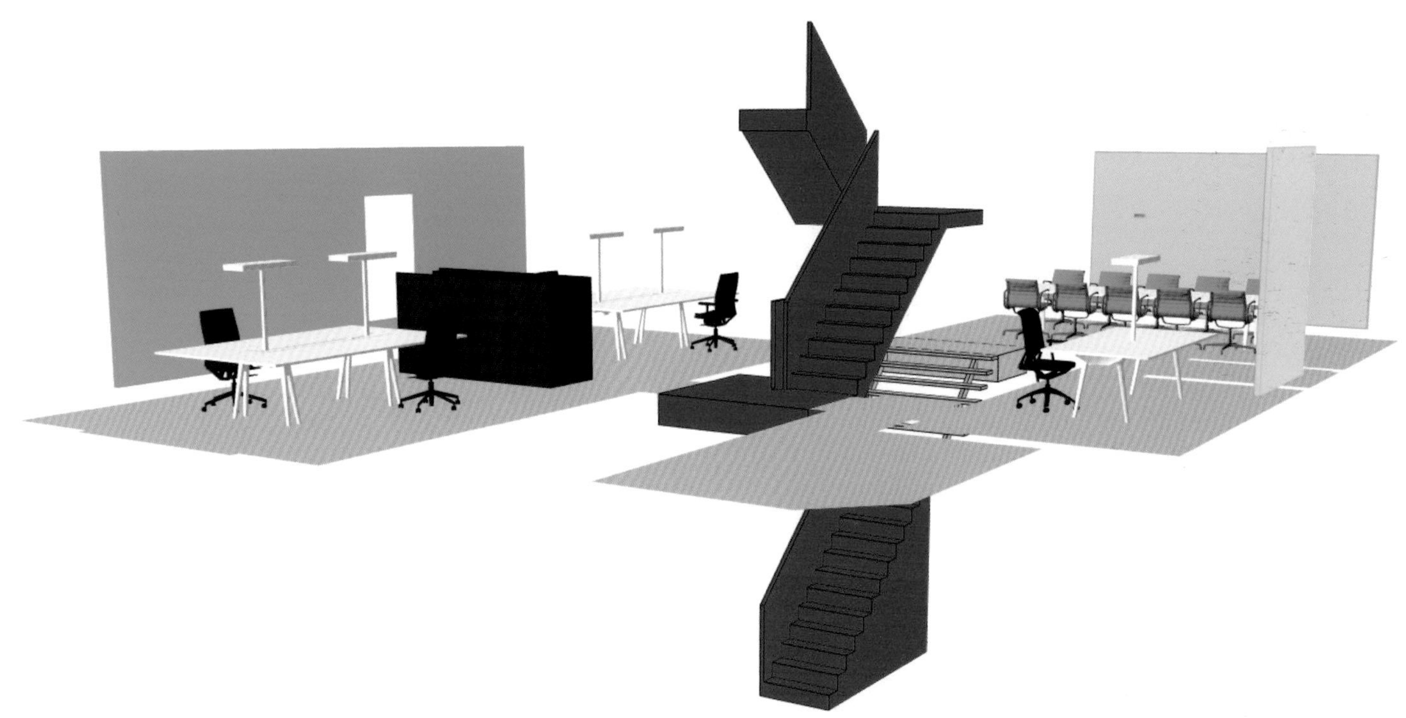

© Jeroen Musch

© Jeroen Musch

Kyoto Silk, Japan
KEICHI HAYASHI ARCHITECT

© Yoshiyuki Hirai

m studio, Spain

nodo17 Architects

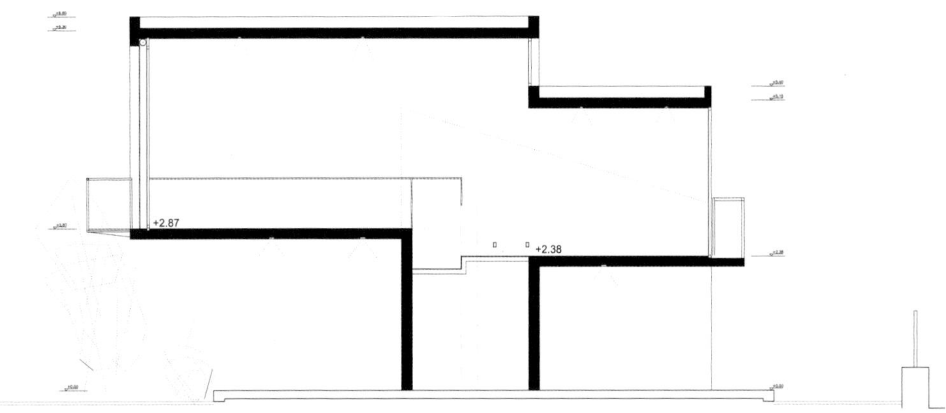

© Iván Ballesteros and Roberto Armas

Les Halles, France

PERIPHERIQUES

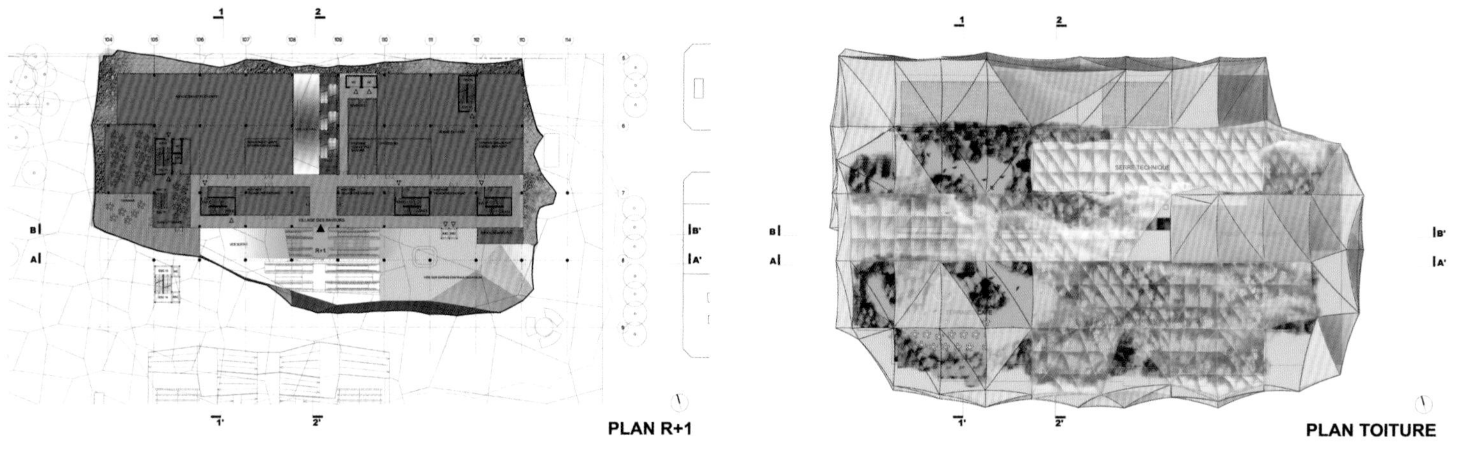

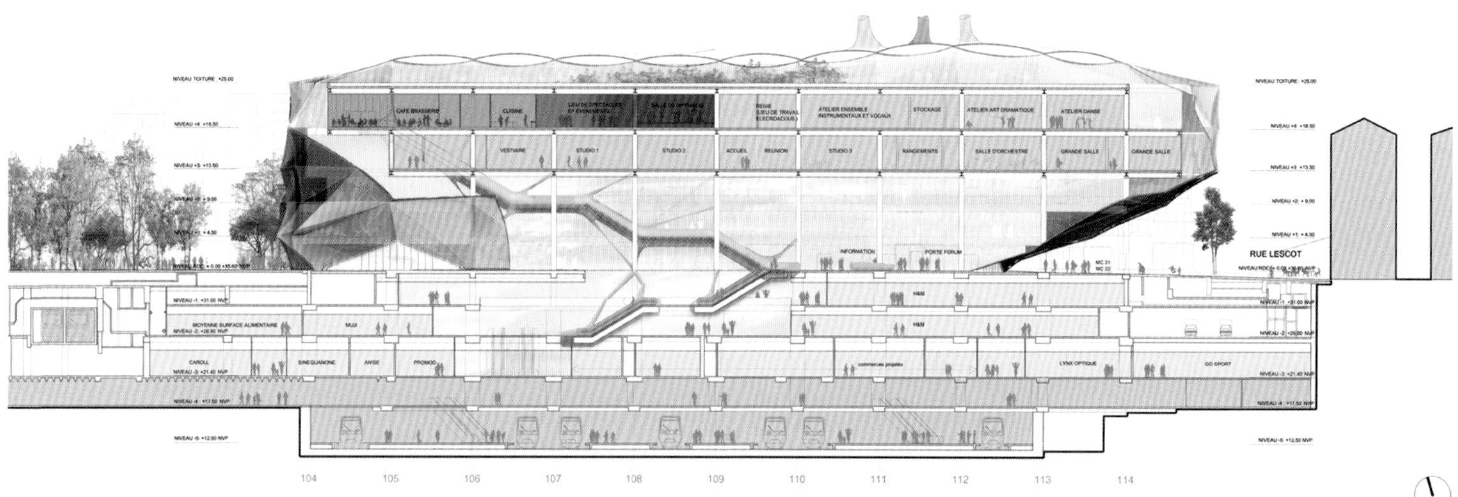

Coupe Longitudinale Nord/Sud

Madrid Metro Headquarters, Spain

SMAR Architecture Studio

Mercedes Salzburg, Austria
kadawittfeldarchitektur

music theatre, Austria
UNStudio

© Iwan Baan

© Iwan Baan

© Iwan Baan

© Iwan Baan

Mirae Medical Foundation Health Improvement Center, Korea

Jay is working

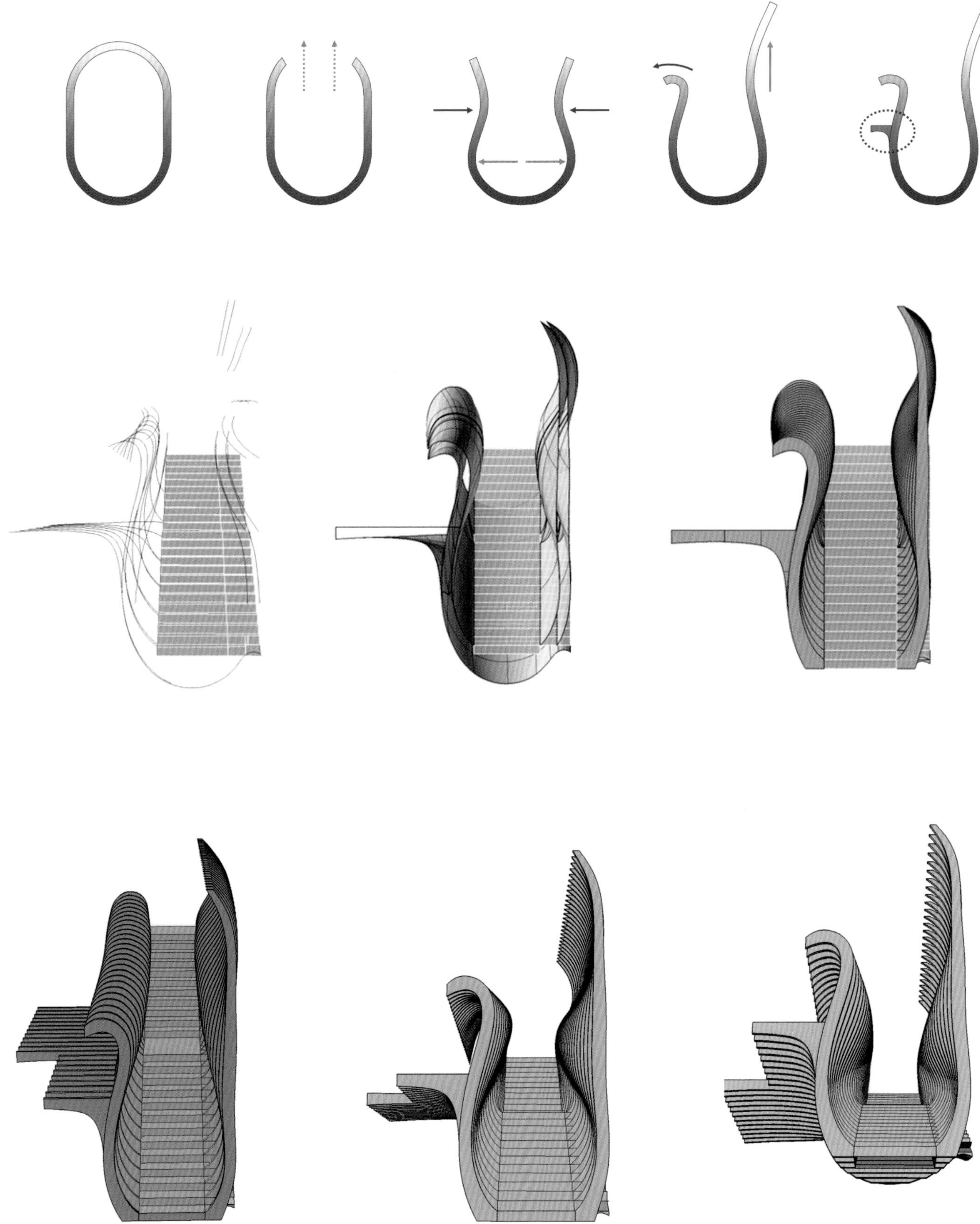

Namsan Patio, Korea

Architects Group Raum

Nedregate Culture District, Norway

SPACEGROUP

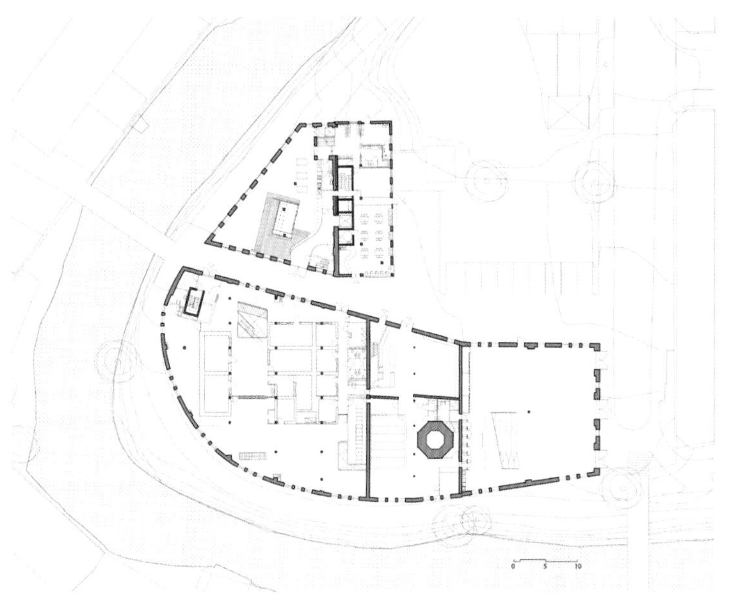

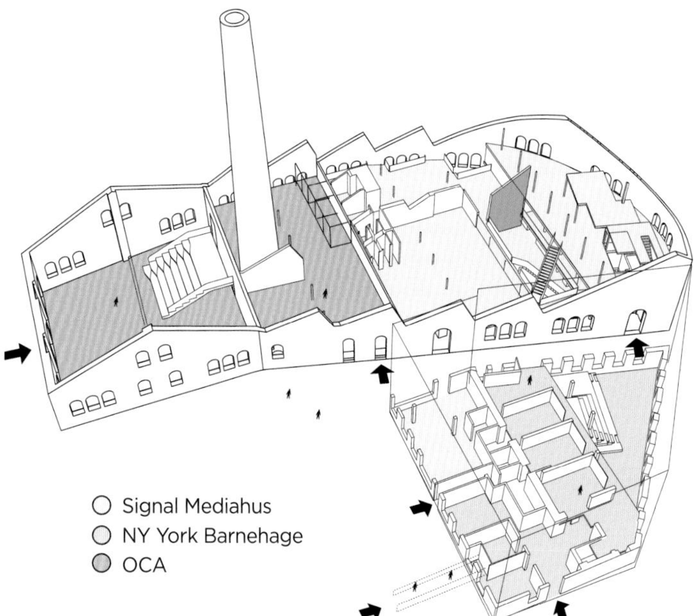

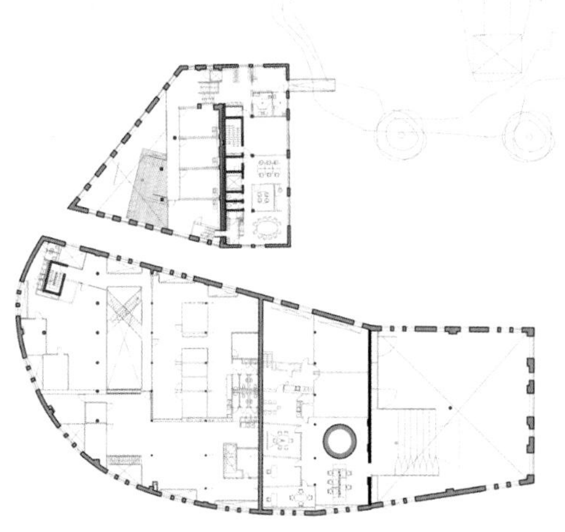

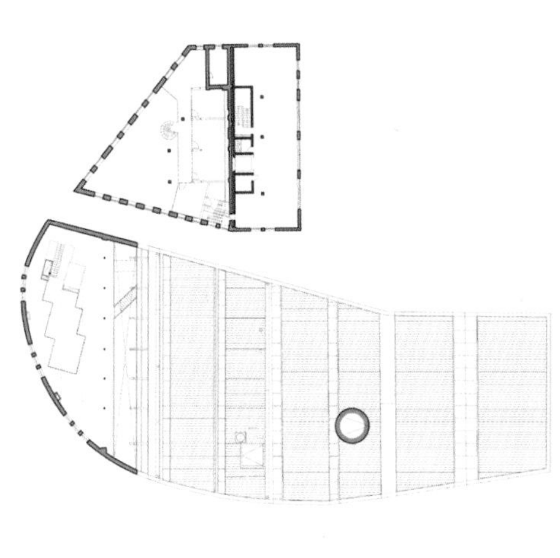

© Ivan Brodey

NFFC Training Institute, Korea
Kimm and Lee Architects
© Park Wan soon, Kimm and Lee Architects

nouveau casino, France

PERIPHERIQUES

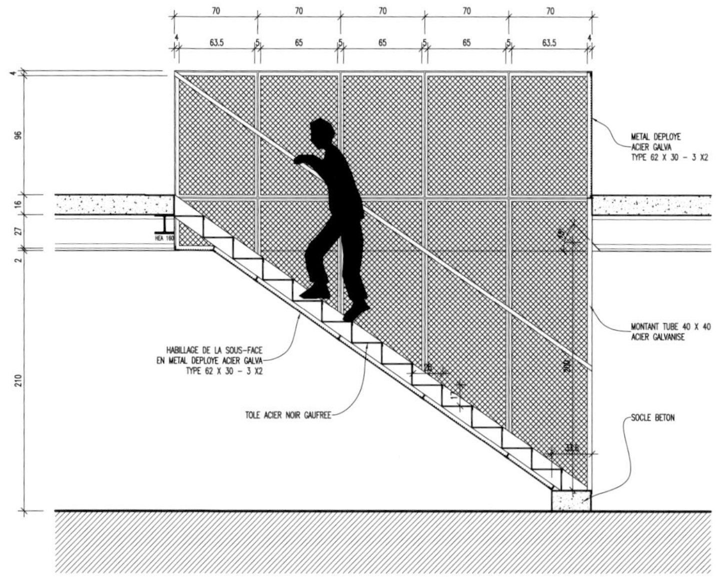

O+A Building, Korea

Architects Group Raum

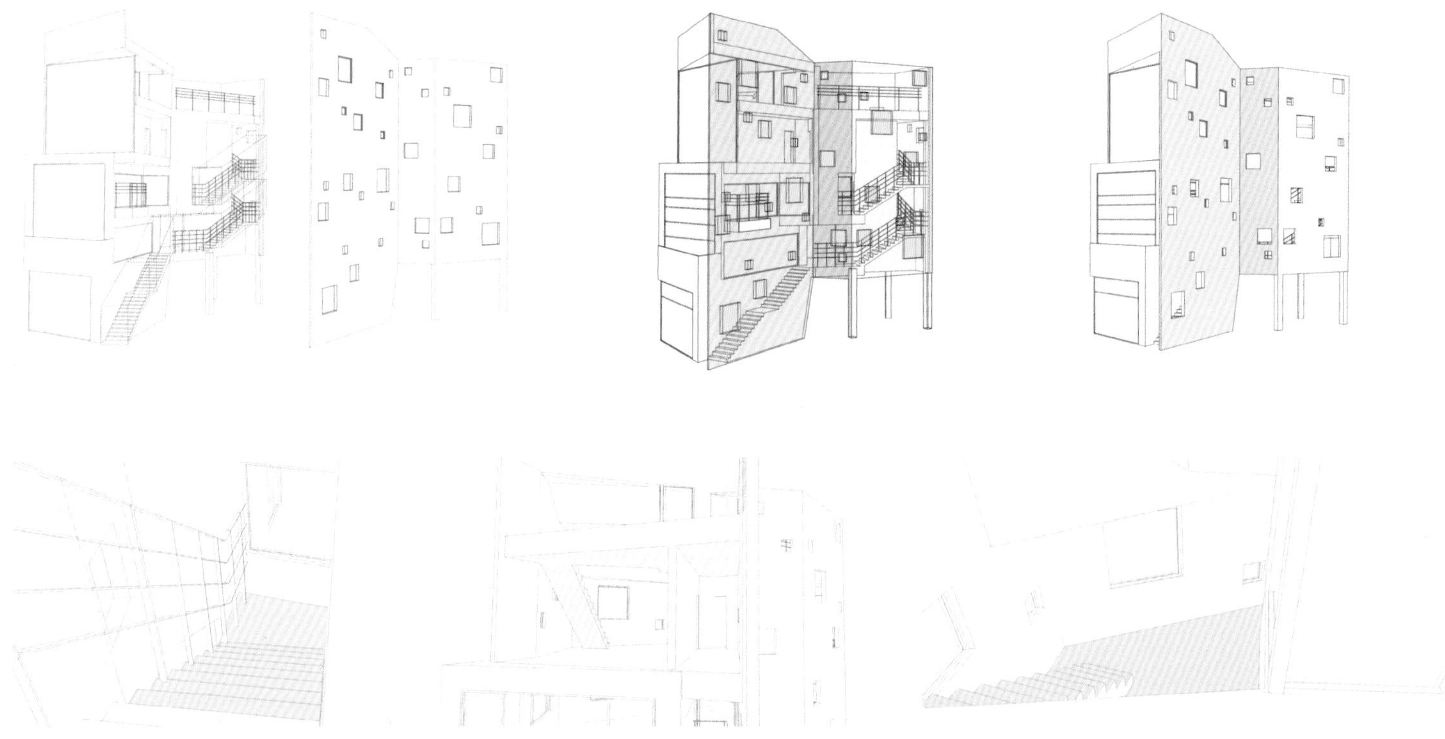

© Joonhwan Yoon

© Joonhwan Yoon

penumbra, Korea

studio asylum

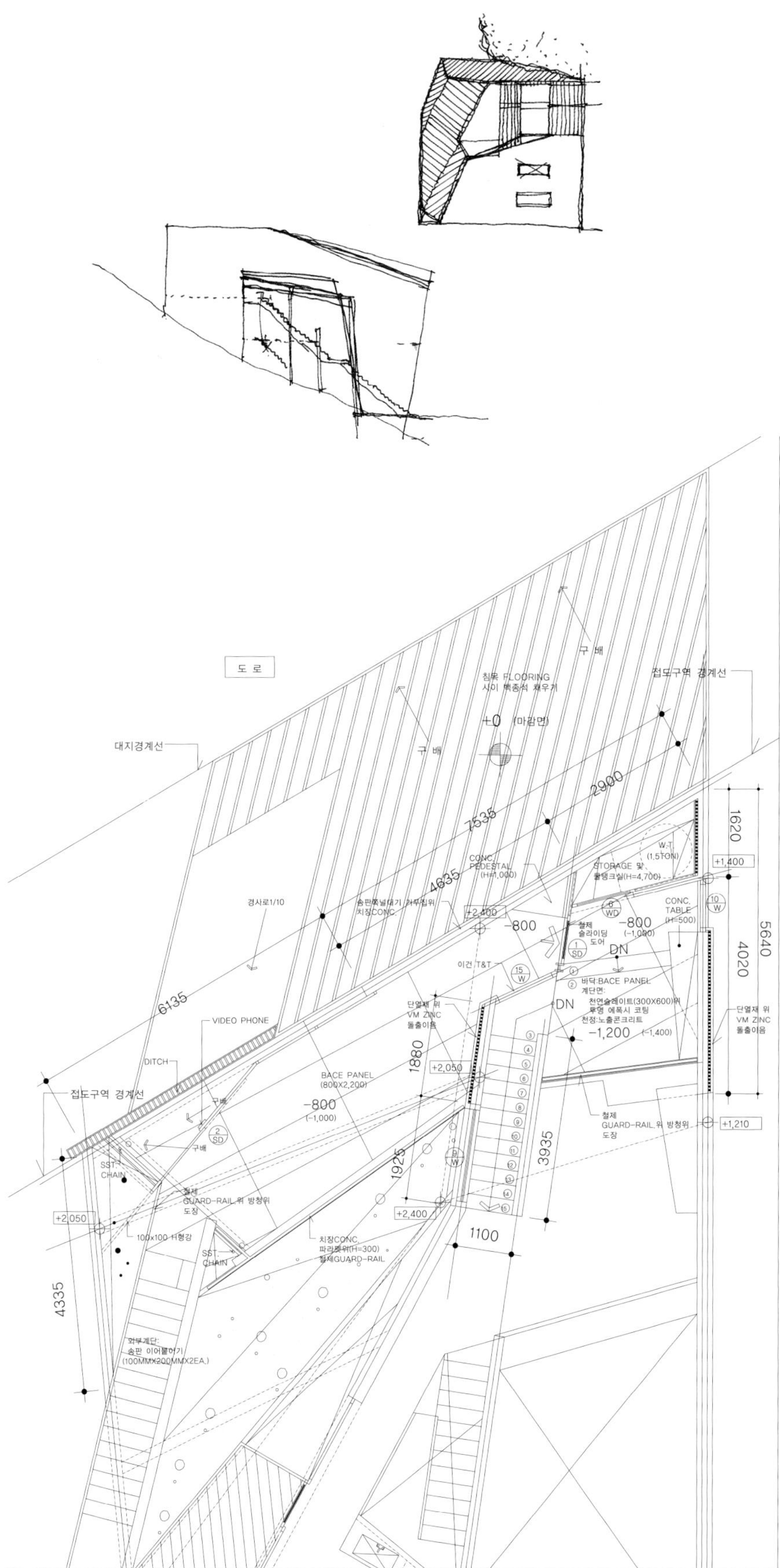

Public Records Office, Swiss

EM2N

SONNENHOF, Germany

J. Mayer H.

© David Franck

SPZ, Austria

kadawittfeldarchitektur

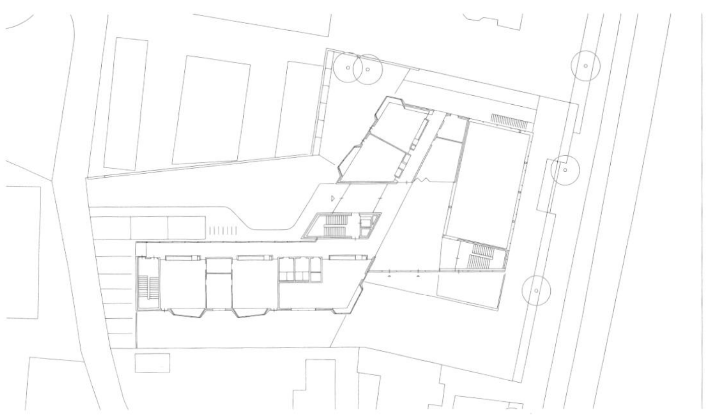

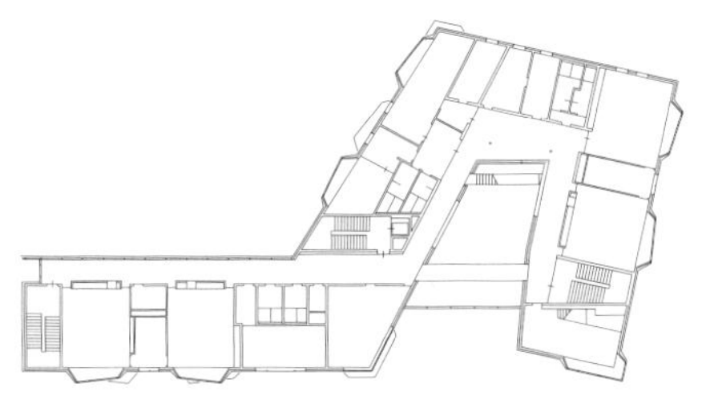

STAVANGER CONCERT HALL, Norway

JDS Architects

syllepsis, Korea
studio asylum

© Park Wan soon

supperclub singapore, Singapore
Concrete Architectural Associates

swiss club road, Singapore

Antonio Eraso Co

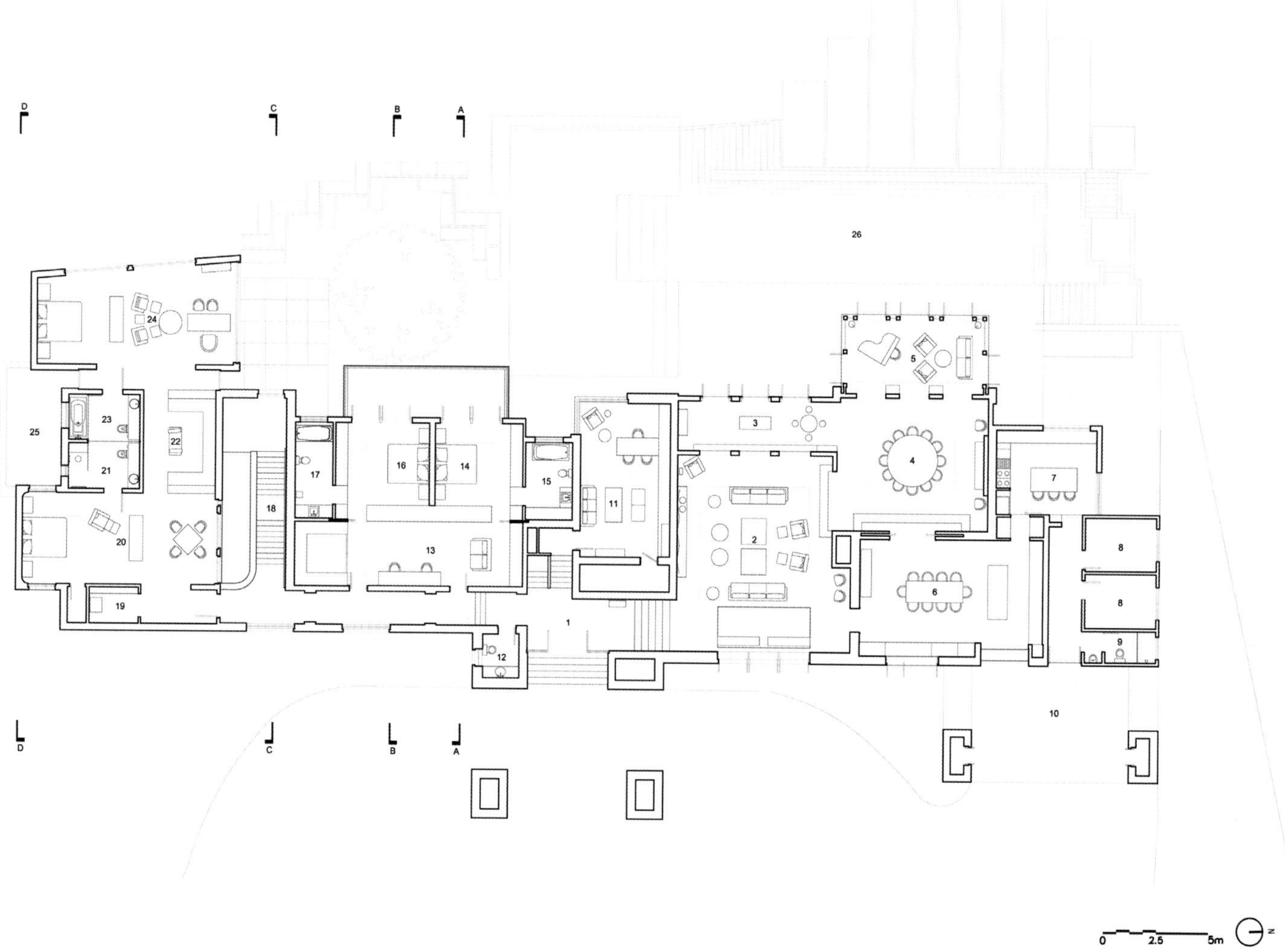

Switch Building, U.S.A

nARCHITECTS

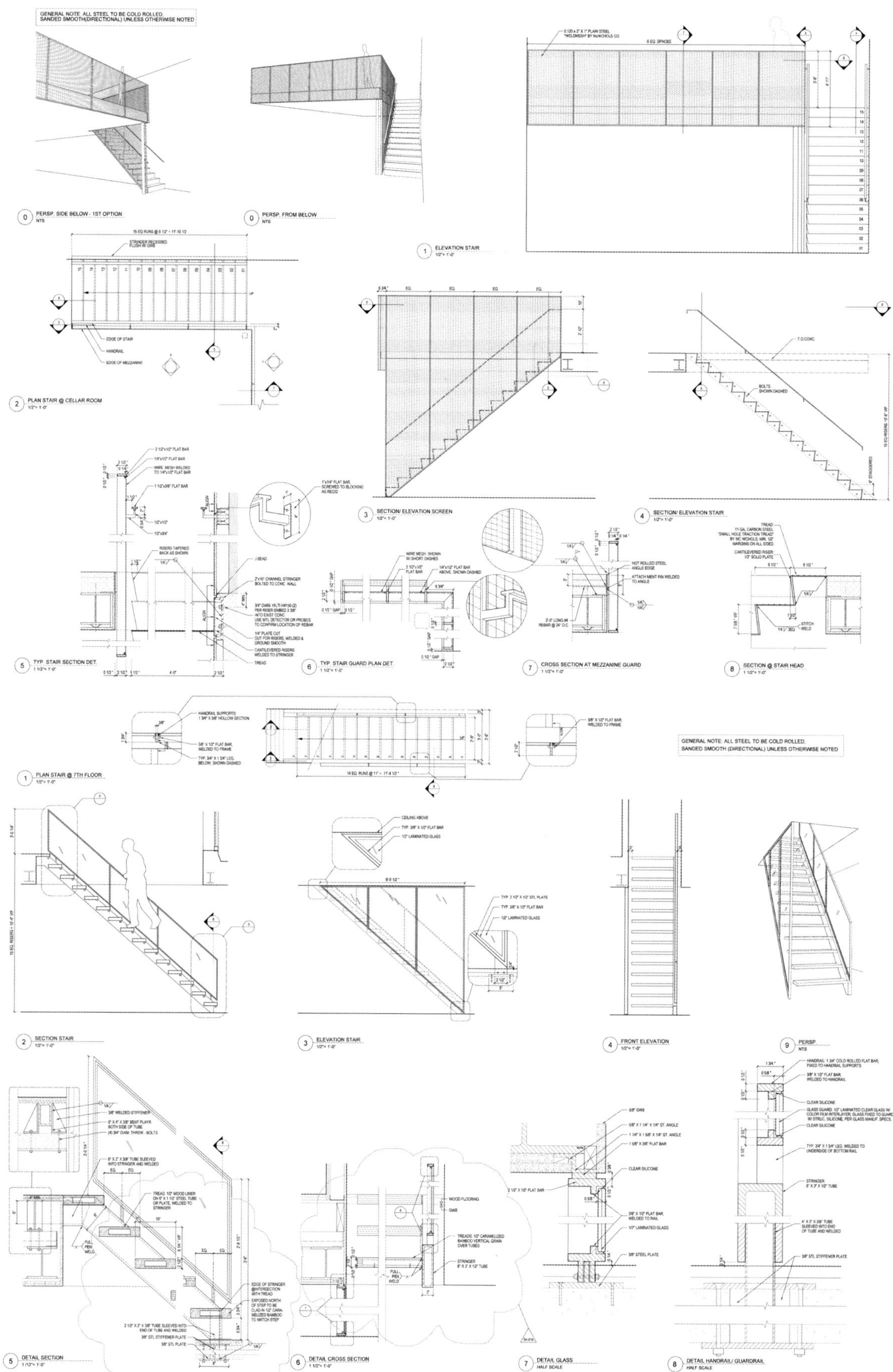

The Yisang's House, Korea

WISE ARCHITECTS

© Courtesy of the Architects

© Courtesy of the Architects

© Courtesy of the Architects

Uluru, Netherlands

AMID[cero9]

SYSTEM OF PUBLIC SQUARES AND STREETS

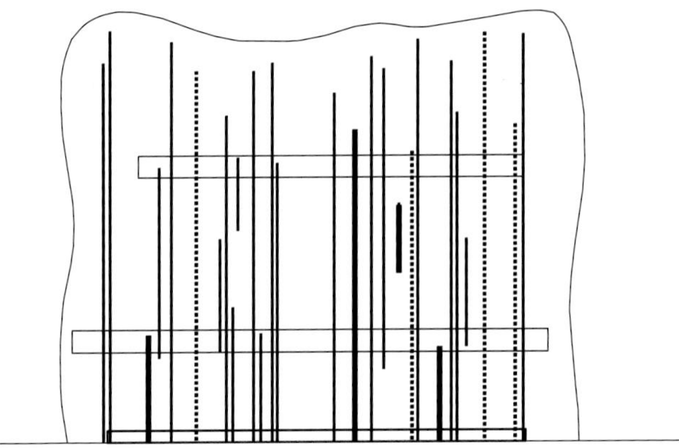

VERTICAL CONNECTIONS. ELEVATORS

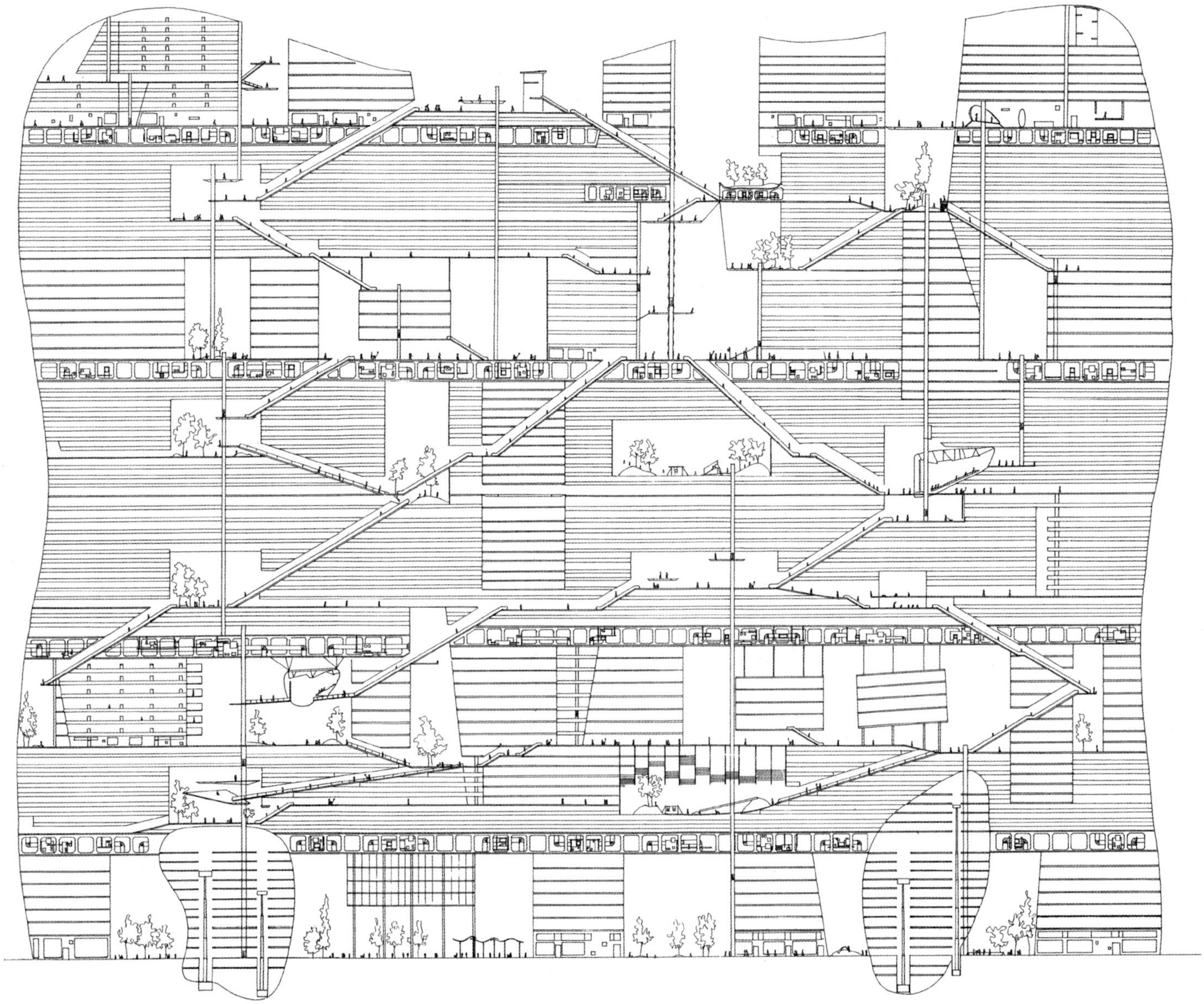

urban gallery I, U.S.A

Axi:Ome llc

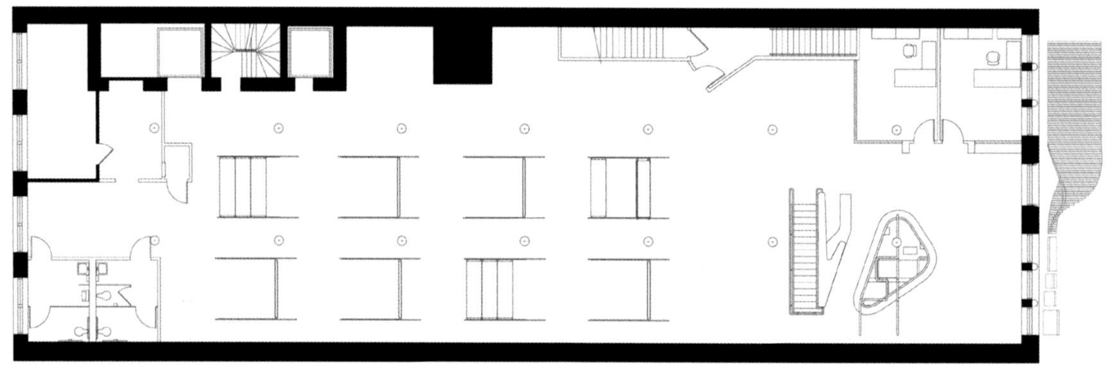

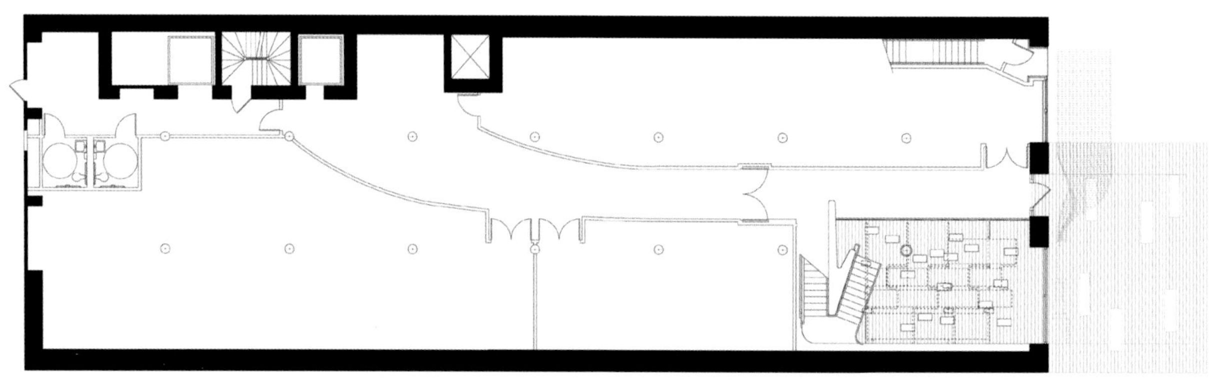

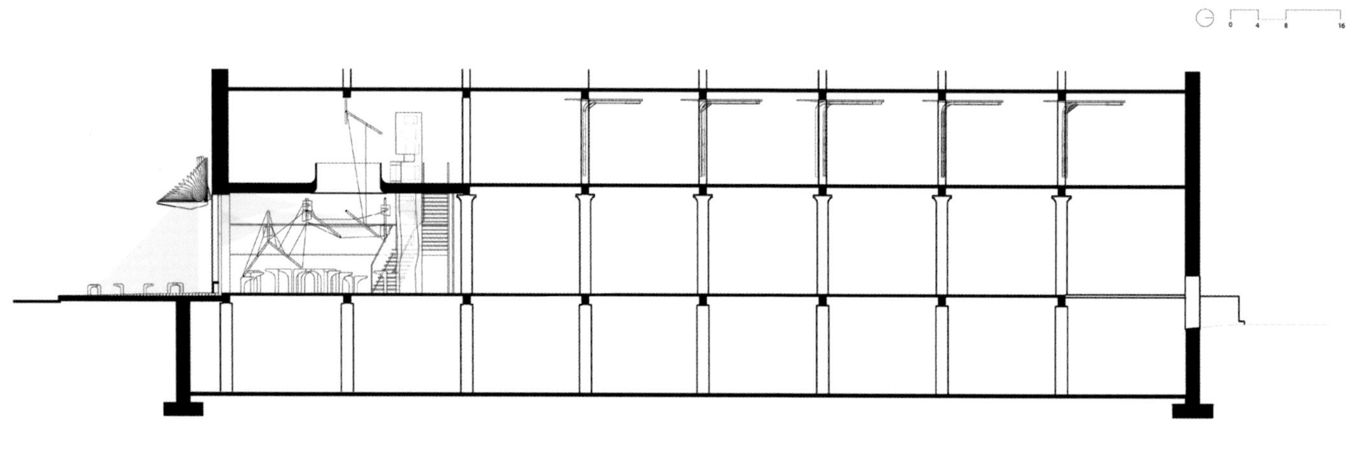

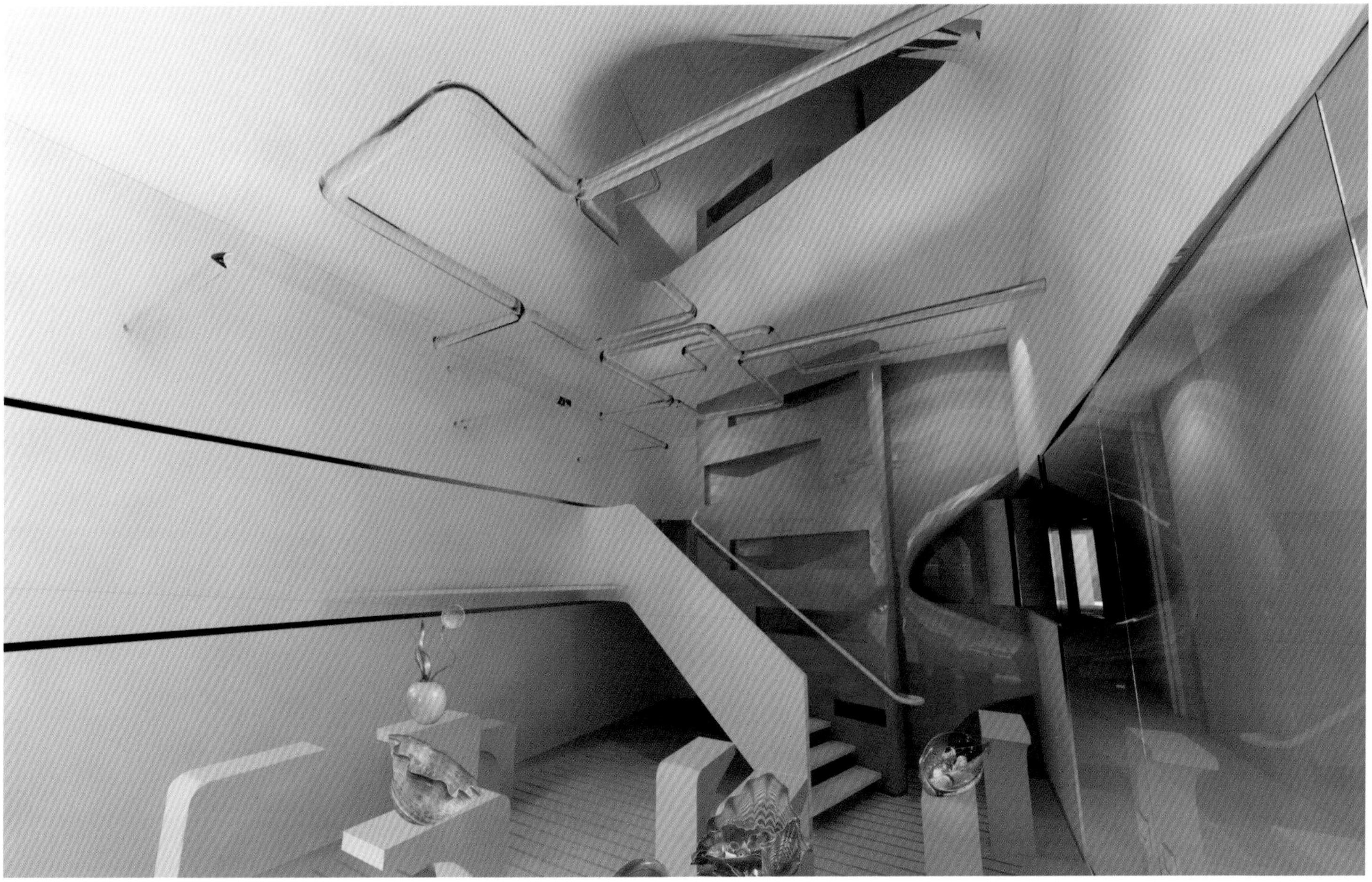

Watches Shop, "Via X Giornate - Orologi Da Collezione", Italy

STUDIOARTEC

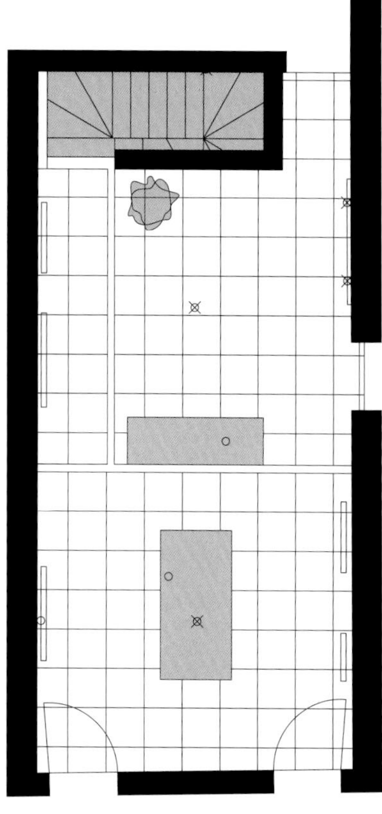

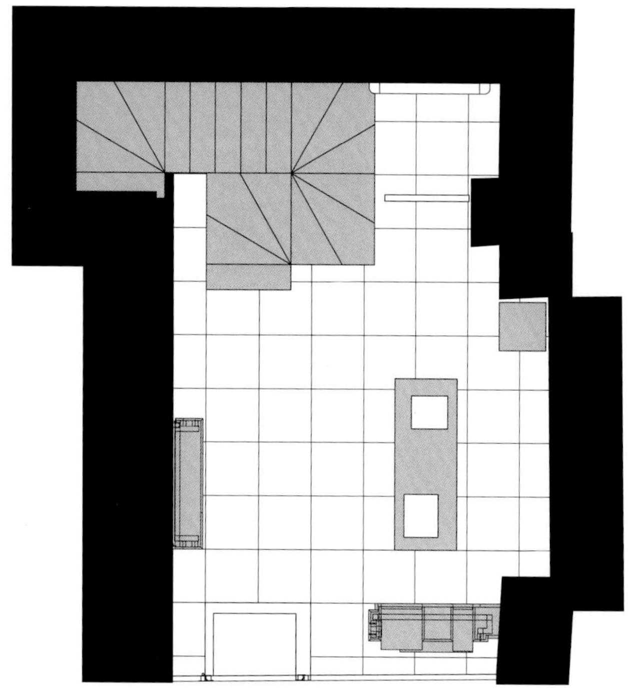

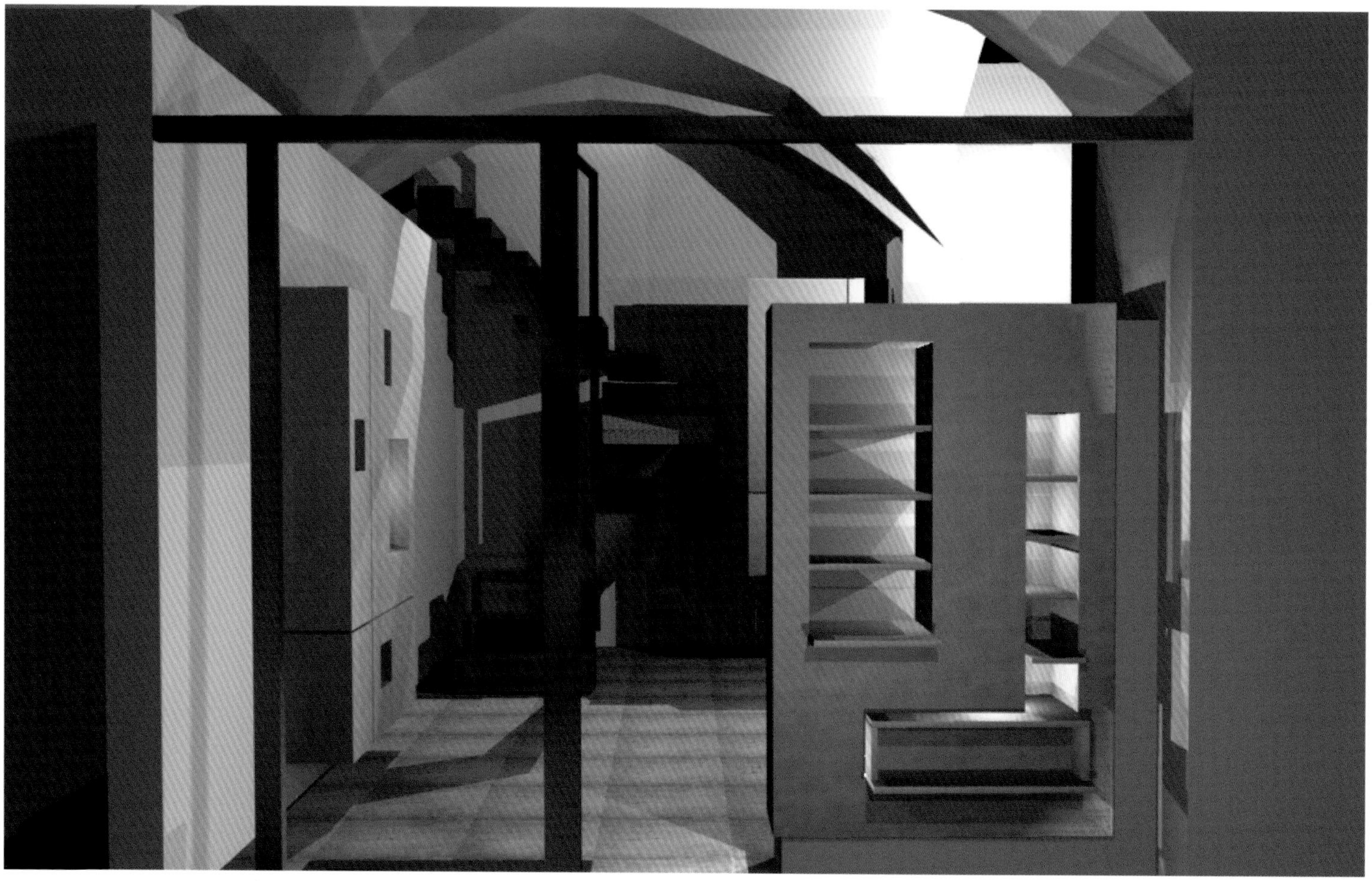

Zagreb Dance Center, Croatia

3LHD

ZAGREBAČKI
PLESNI
CENTAR
DVORANA
GARDEROBA

community centre aussersihl part 2, Swiss

EM2N

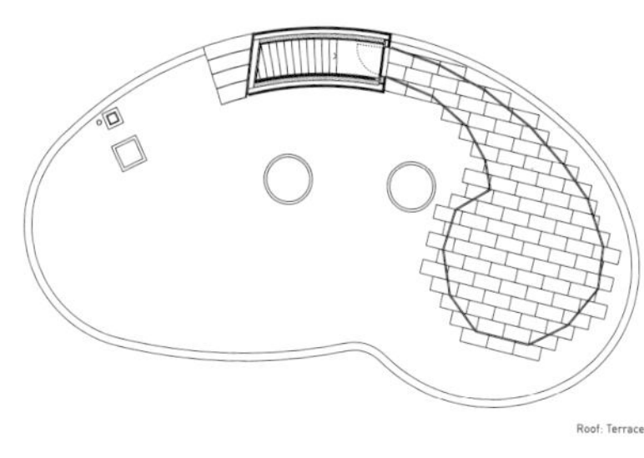

Roof: Terrace

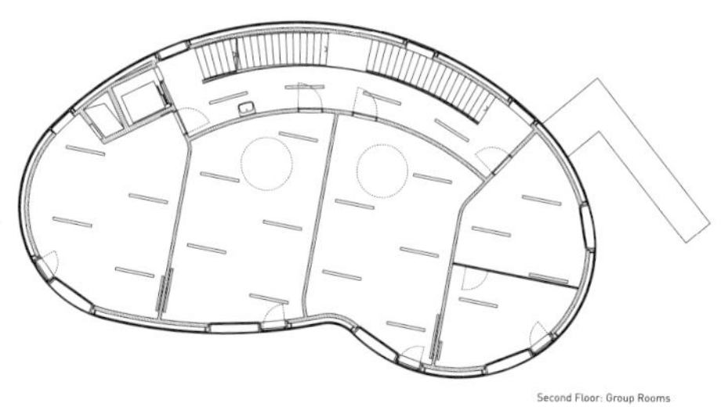

Second Floor: Group Rooms

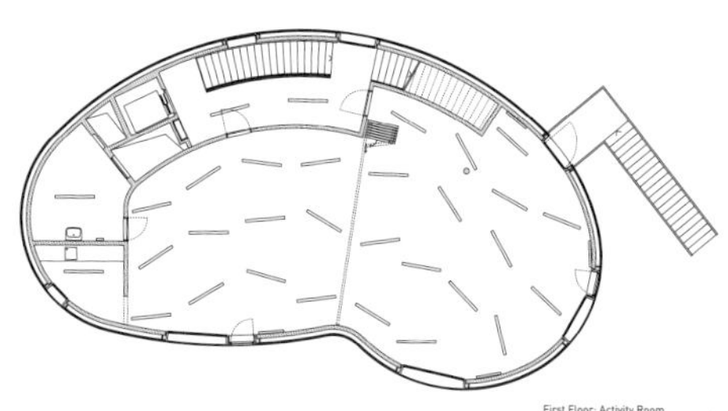

First Floor: Activity Room

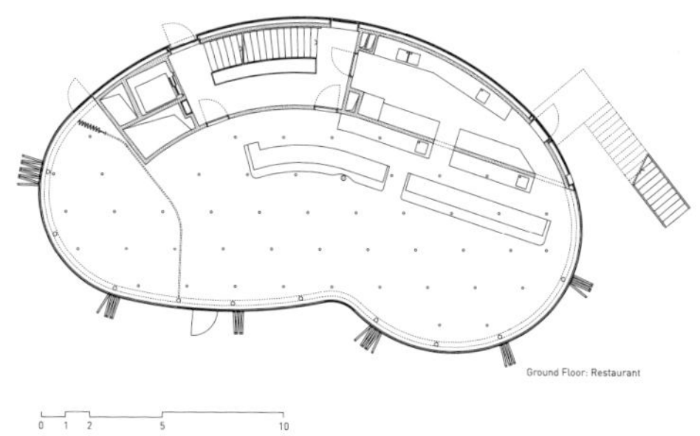

Ground Floor: Restaurant

CAPE PALOS, MARITIME PATH, Spain

XPIRAL

COPENHAGEN HARBOUR BATH, Denmark

JDS Architects

Faaborg, Denmark

Urban Agency

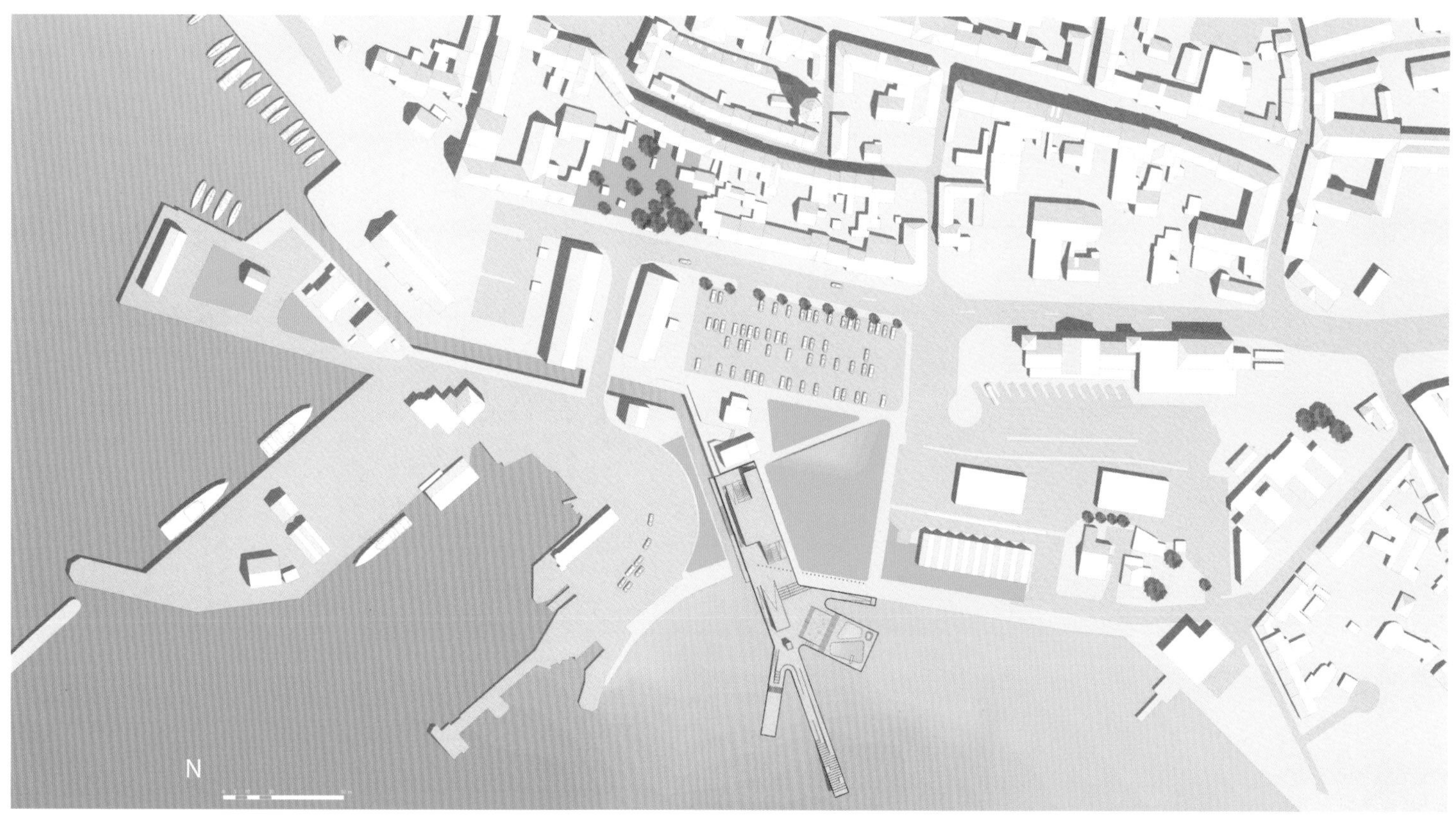

© UrbanAgency

FREESTAGE, Anywhere

AZC

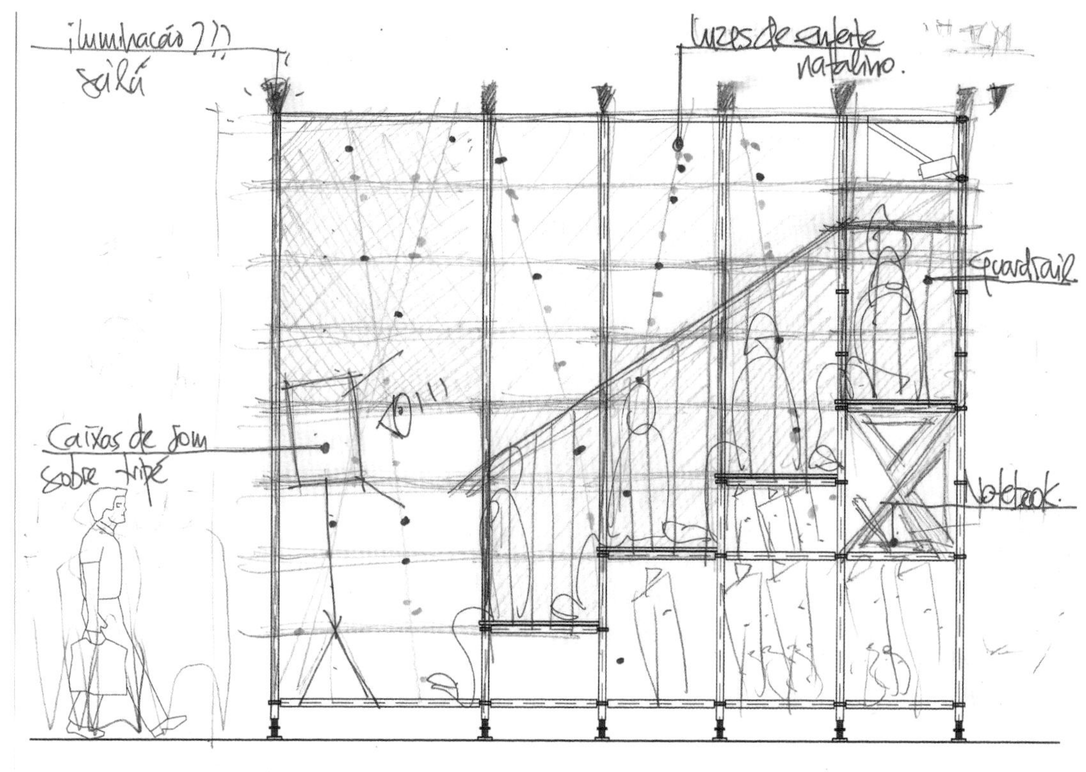

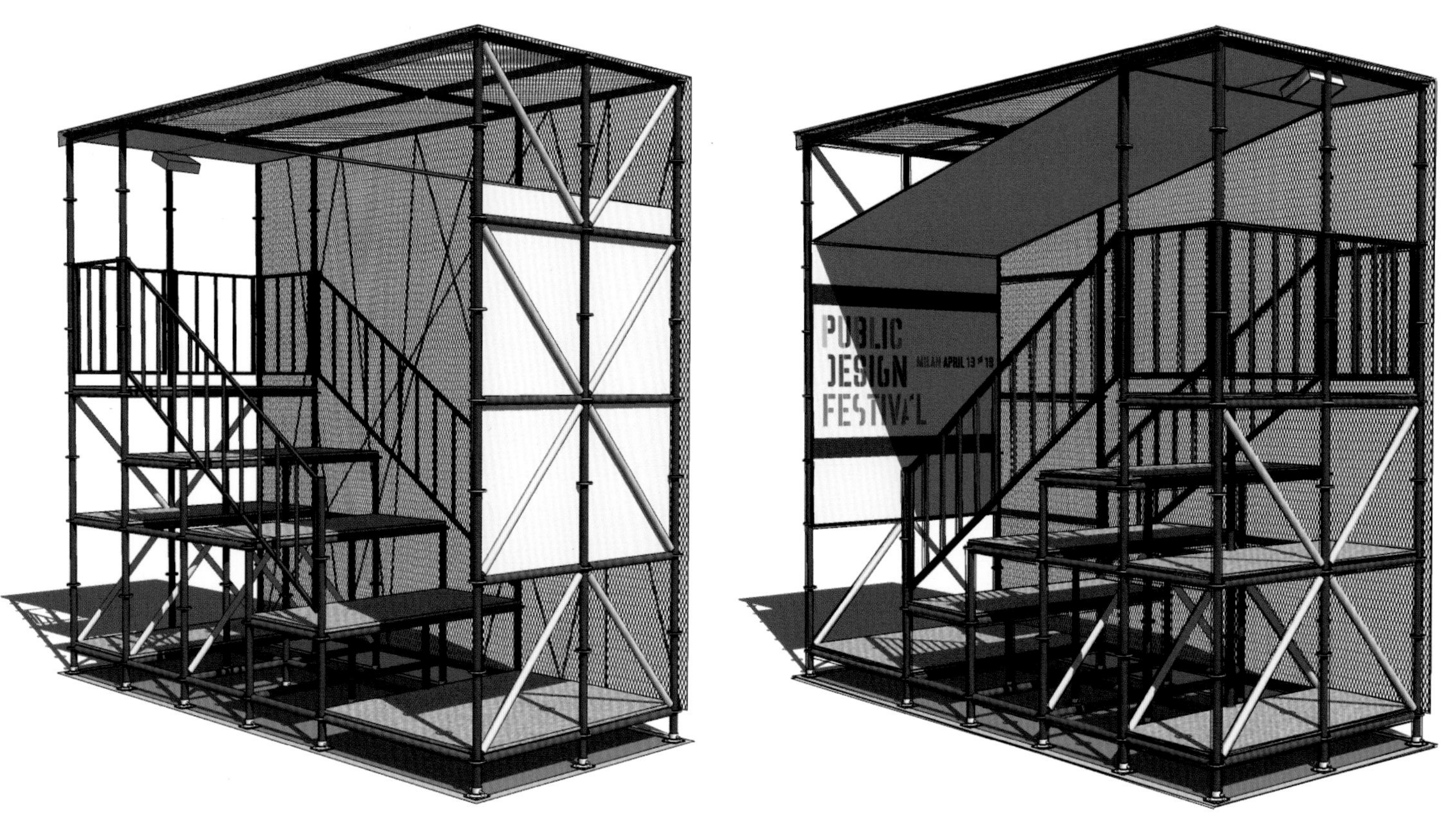

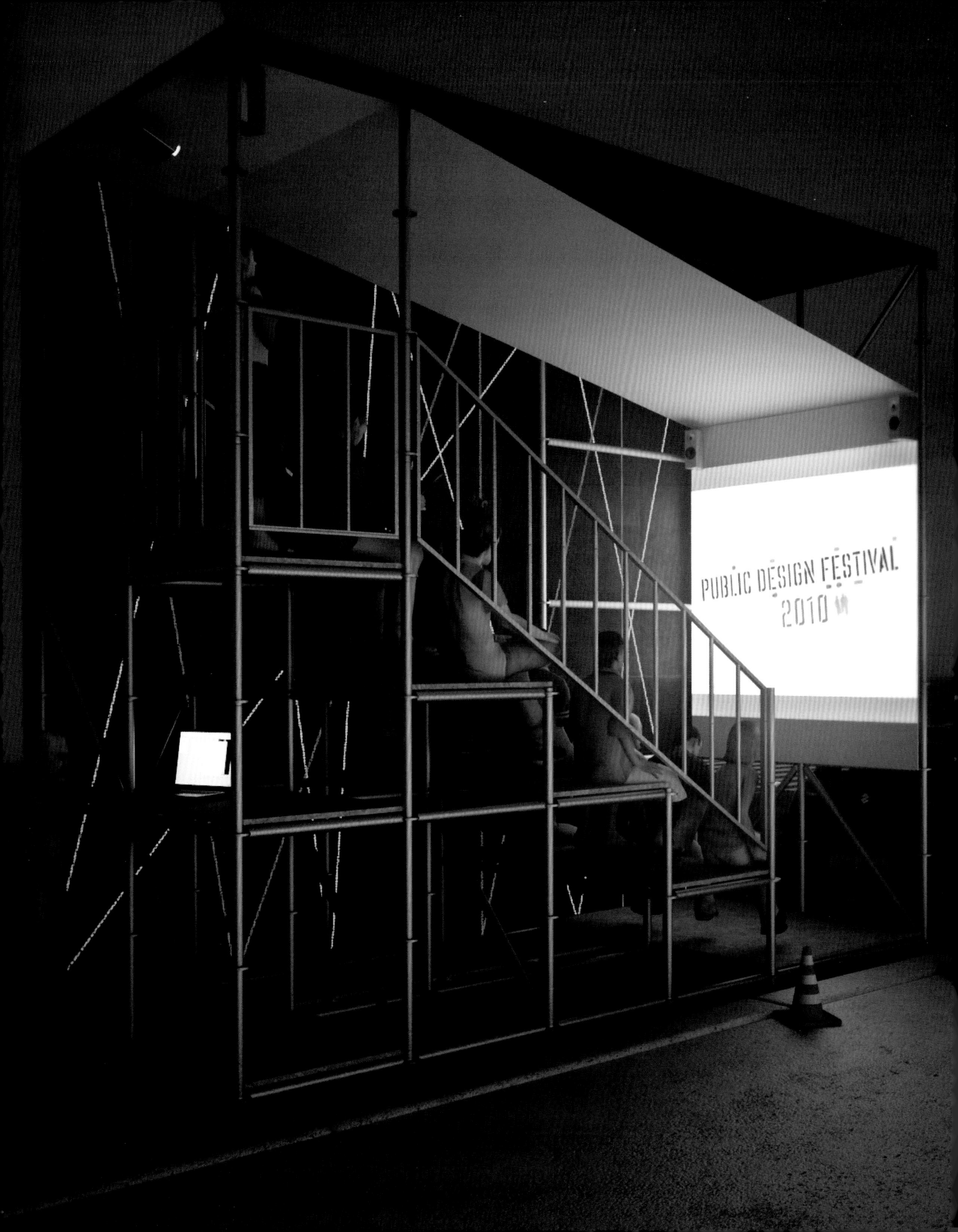
PUBLIC DESIGN FESTIVAL
2010

Hopital Lyon Sub Metro Station, France

AZC

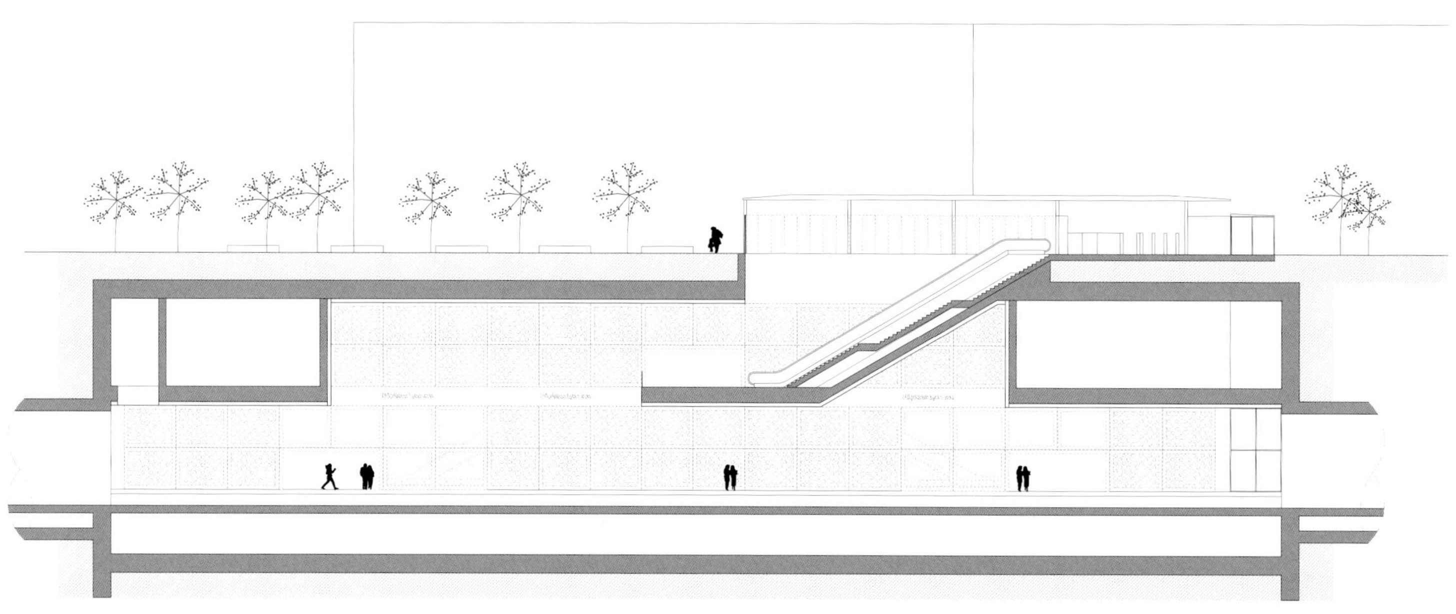

AUX LYON SUD
HÔPITAUX LYON SUD
SORTIE

INSTANT LUNG, Anywhere

2RAM

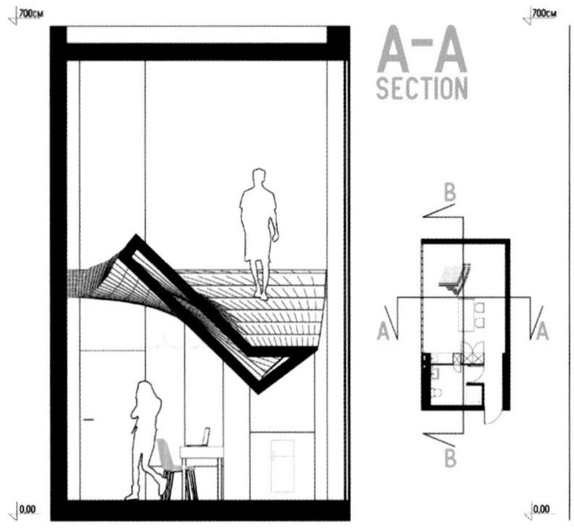

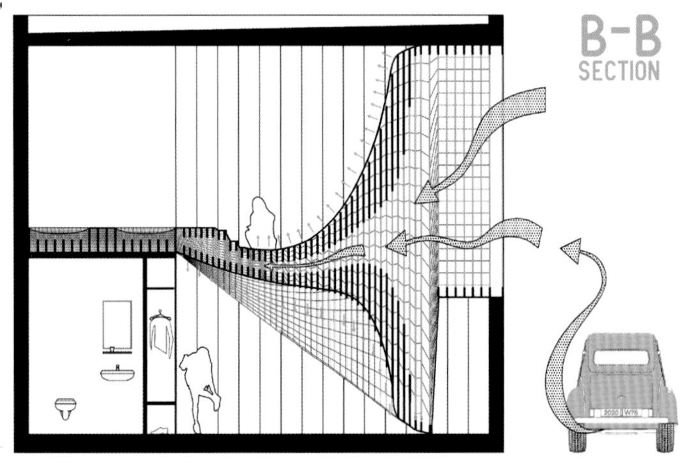

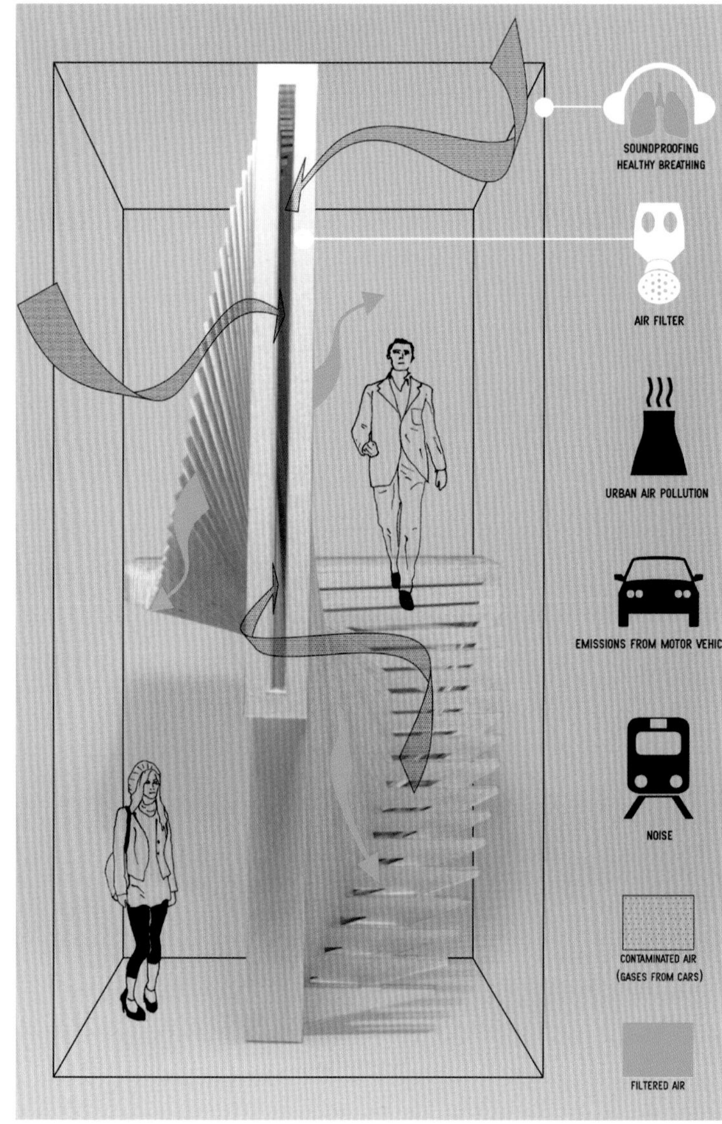

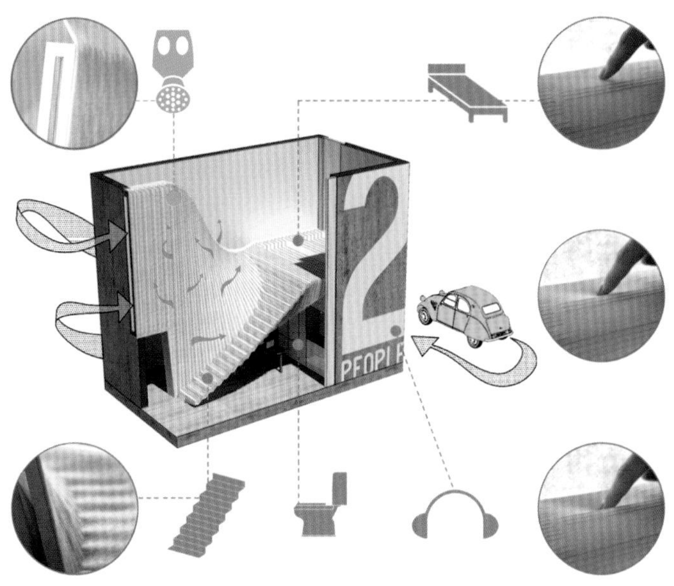

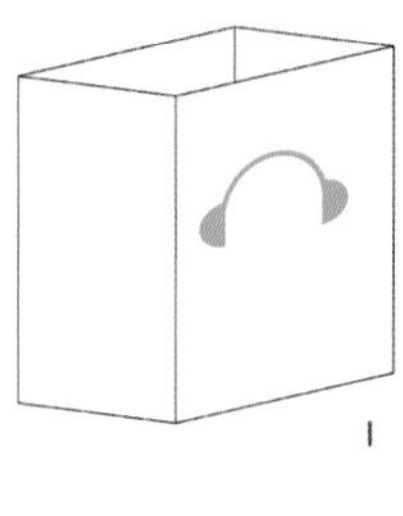

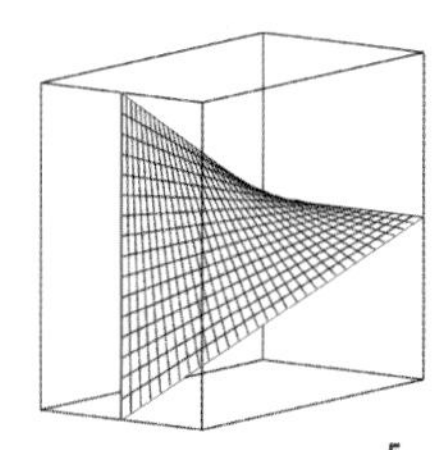

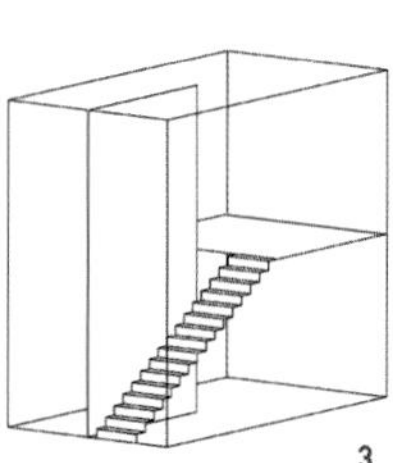

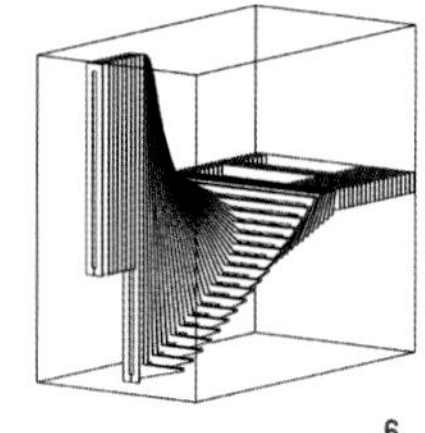

Loius Vuitton Church, Korea

Moon Hoon + Moto Architecture

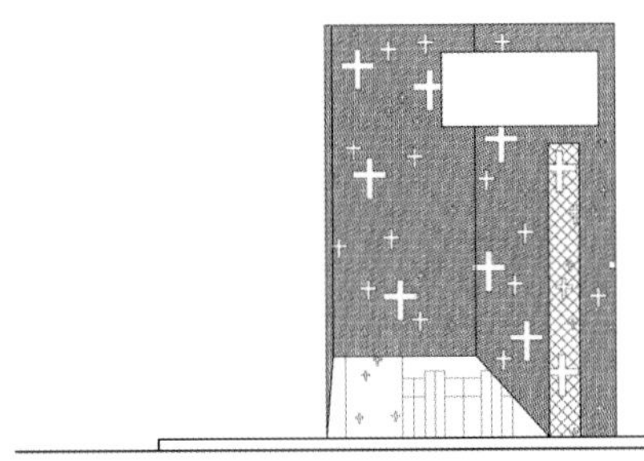

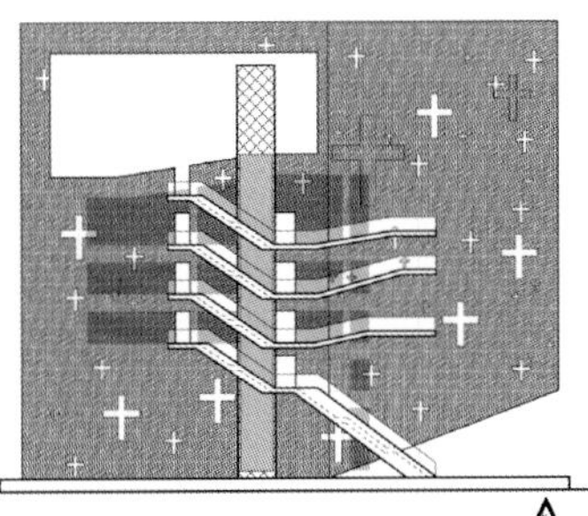

IAOIZ Nedim Uysal Technical High School, Turkey

M artı D Mimarlık

Loop-the-Loop, Netherlands

NL Architects

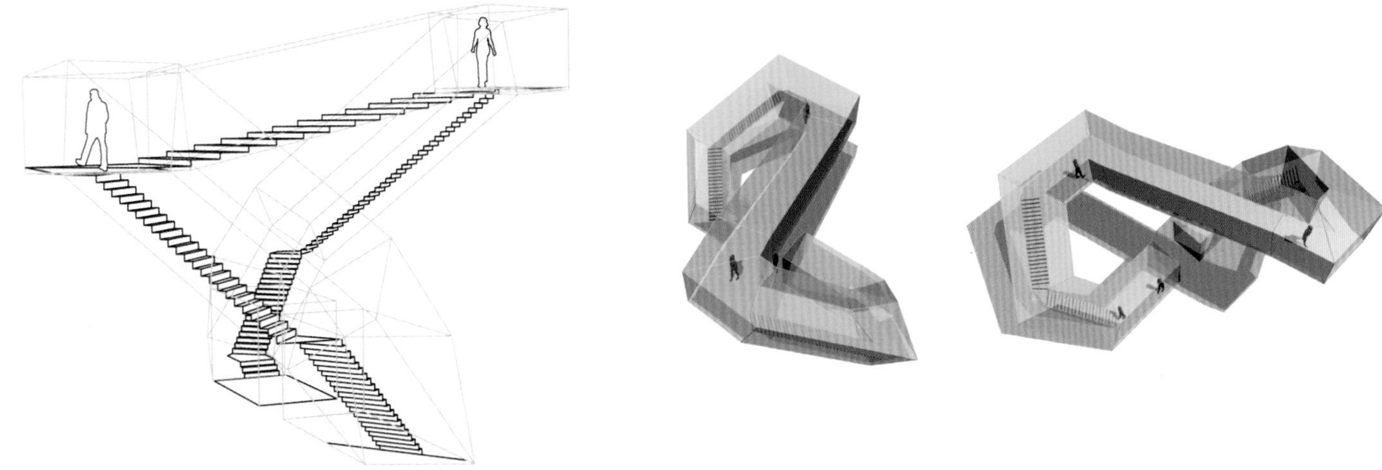

NATURE TECH BRIDGE, Korea

D.P.J.& Partners, Ltd.

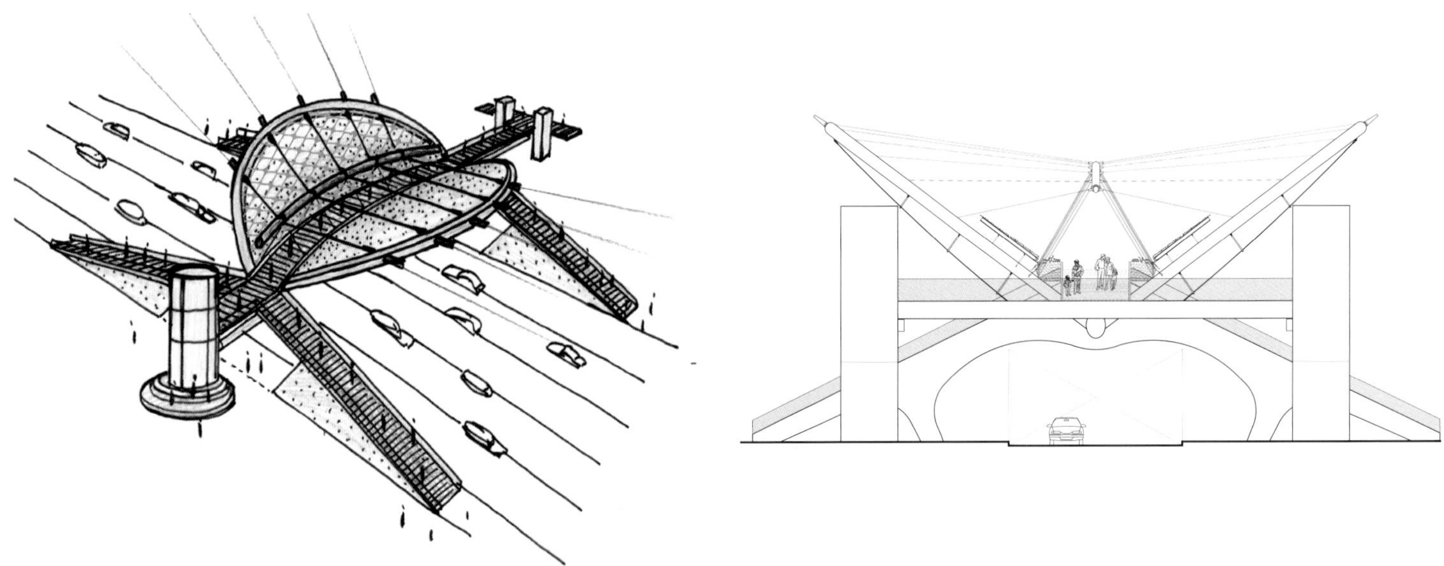

MISFIT TOWER, Korea

Bureau des Mesarchitectures

© Park Wan soon

+1495
+1265
+1150
+1035
+920
+805
+690
+575
+460
+345
+230
+115
+0

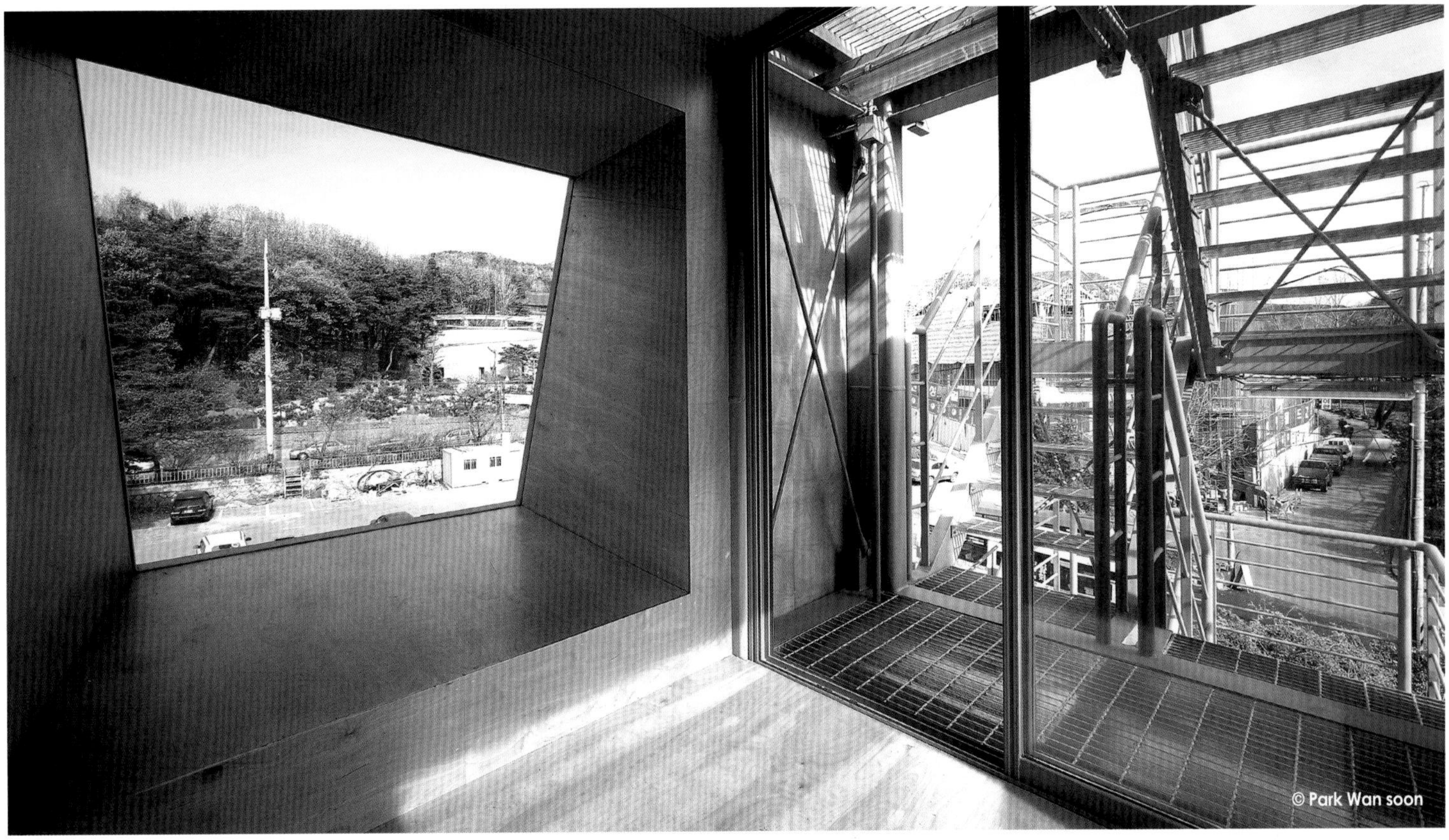

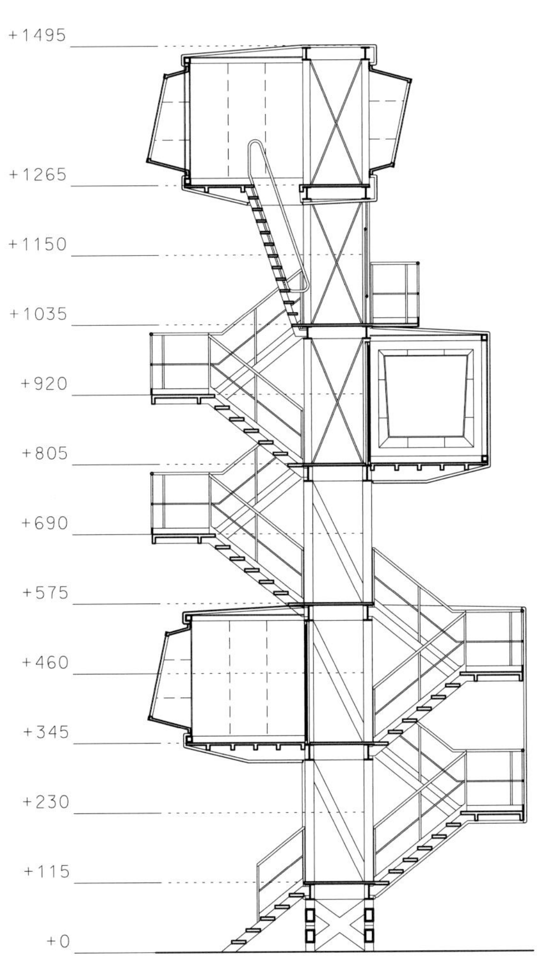

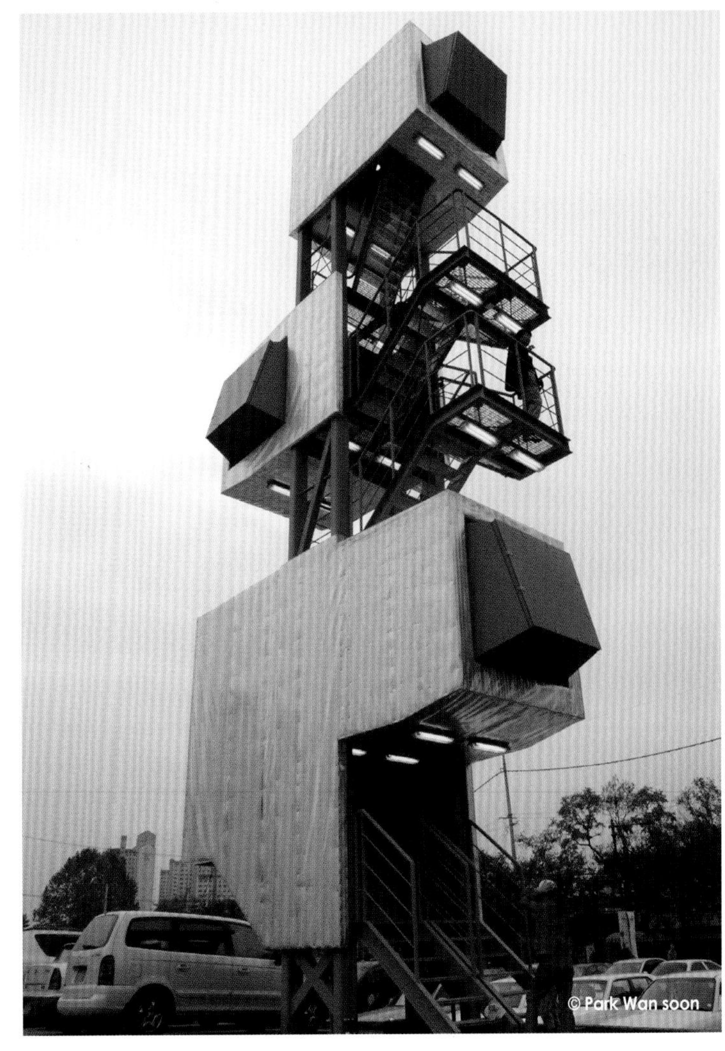

© Park Wan soon

Mongkey Paradise, Korea

Moonbalsso + DN

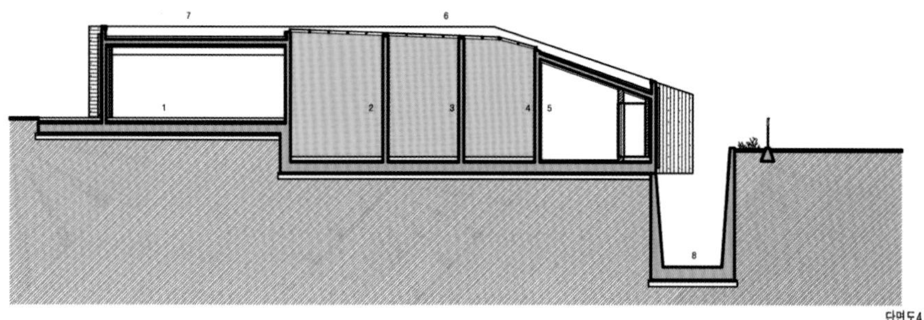

단면도4

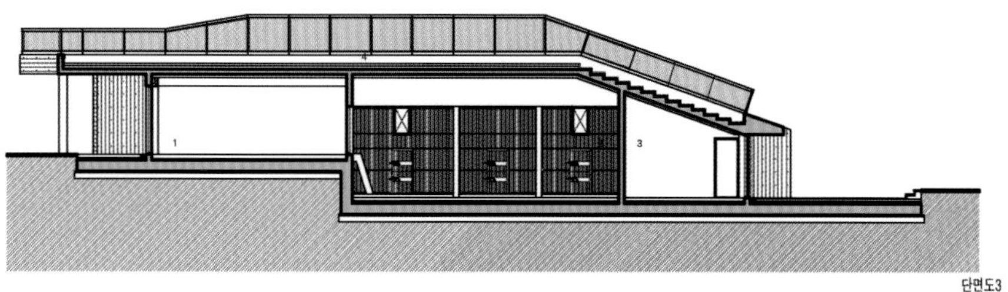

단면도3

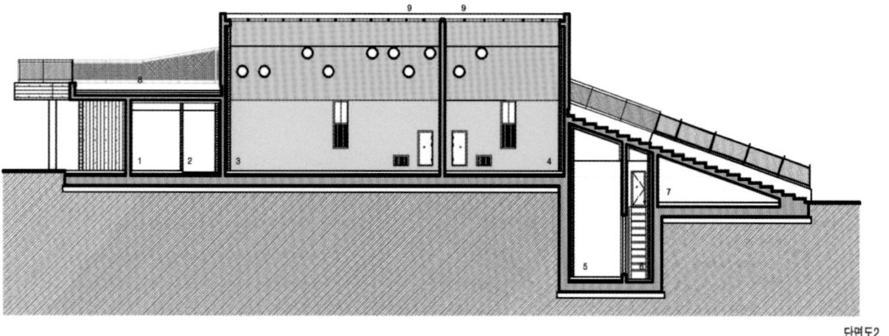

단면도2

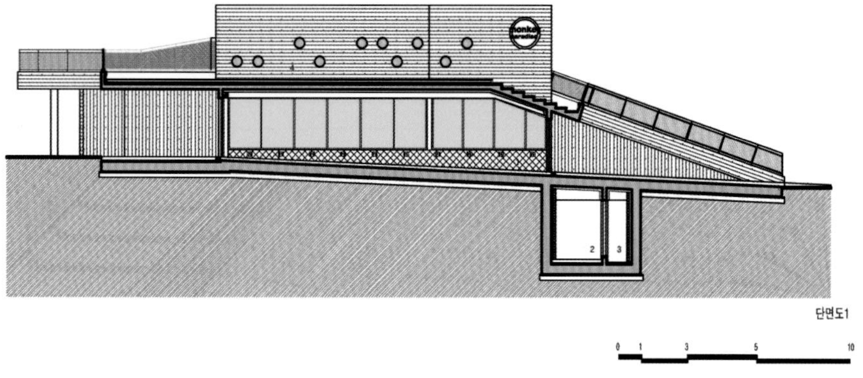

단면도1

0 1 3 5 10

Open-air Pavilion, Austria

the next ENTERprise

© Lukas Schaller

Sailing World Championship Facilities, Spain

AZPML

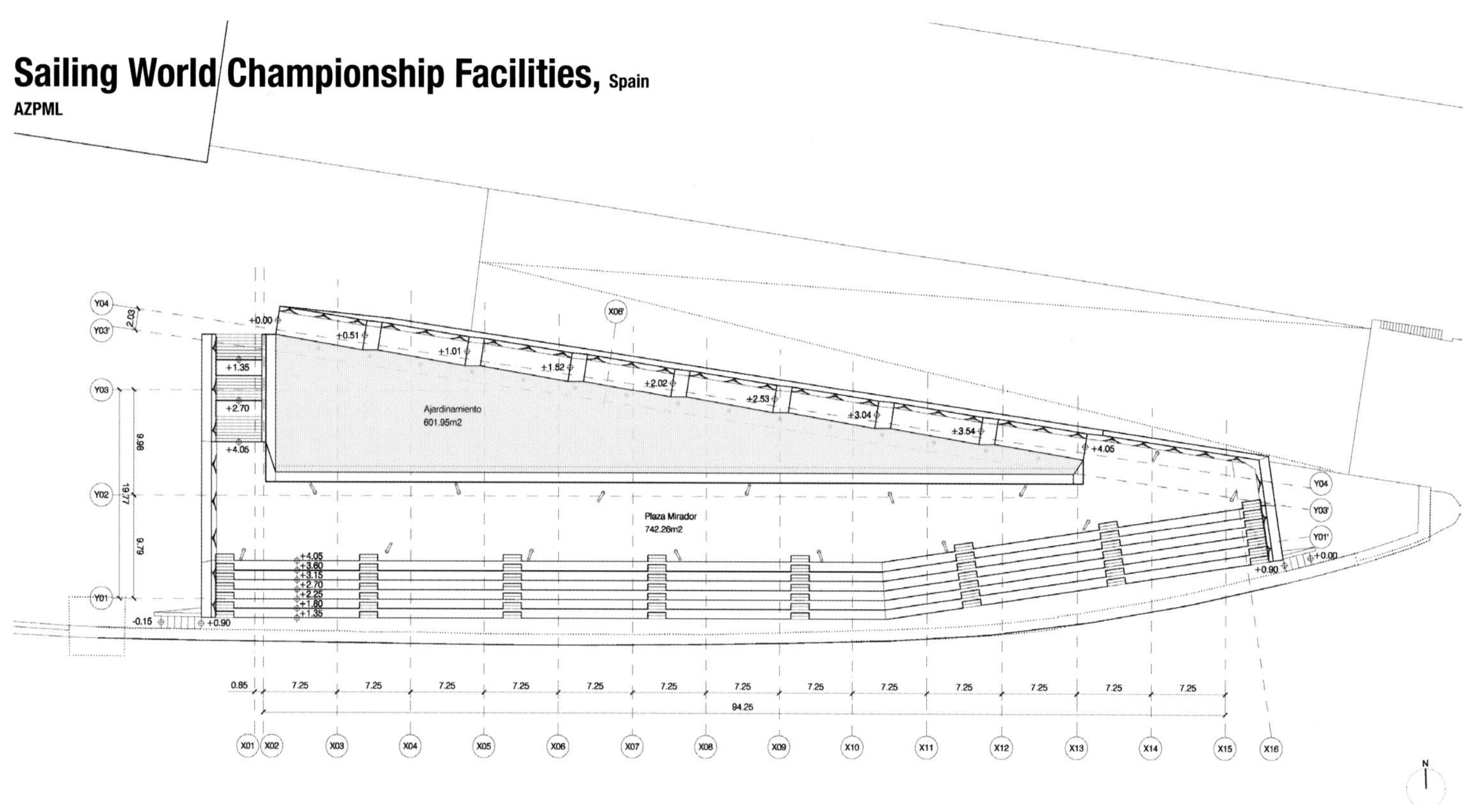

© Riancho & Herrero

© Andres Fernandez

Sanhe Three Rivers Kindergarten, China

OBRA Architects

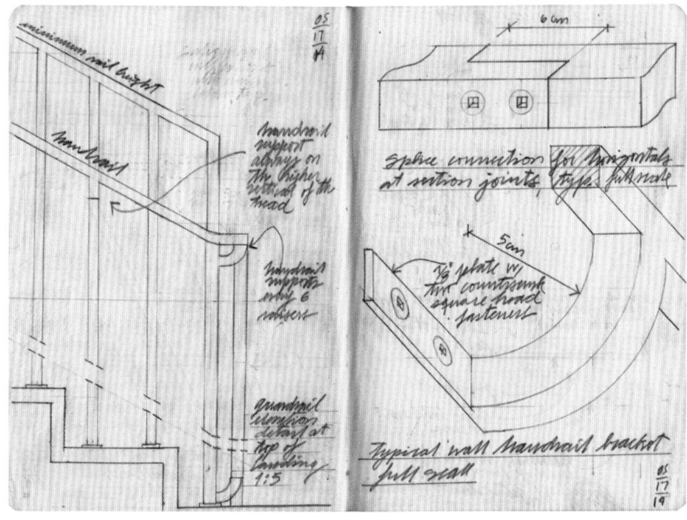
minimum rail height
handrail
6 cm
Splice connection for horizontals at section joints, typ. full scale
5 cm
Typical wall handrail bracket full scale

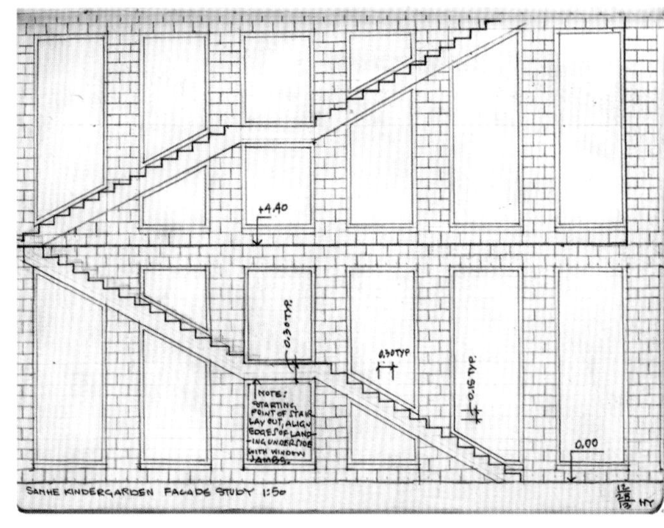
+4.40
NOTE: STARTING POINT OF STAIR LAY OUT, ALIGN EDGES OF LANDING UNDERSIDE WITH WINDOW JAMBS.
0.00
SANHE KINDERGARDEN FACADE STUDY 1:50

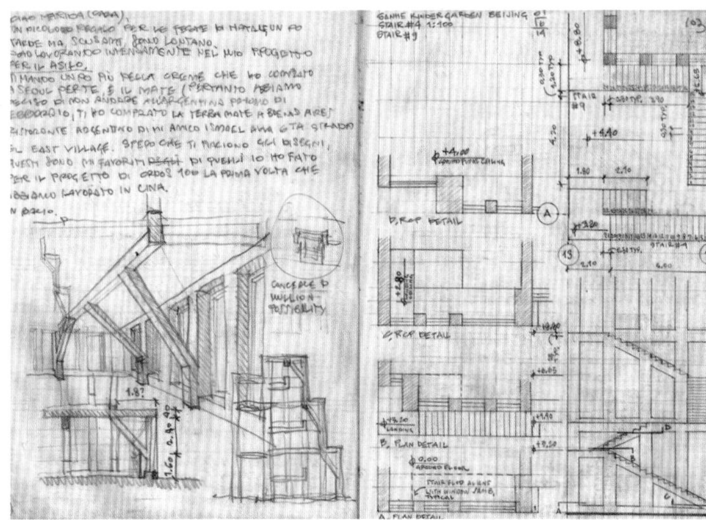
SANHE KINDERGARDEN BEIJING
+4.40

school 03, Netherlands
i29 interior architects

© Jeroen Musch

San Antonio de Padua de Chépica, Chile

cheungvogl

School at Kuchl, Norway

kadawittfeldarchitektur

School at Mittersill, Norway

kadawittfeldarchitektur

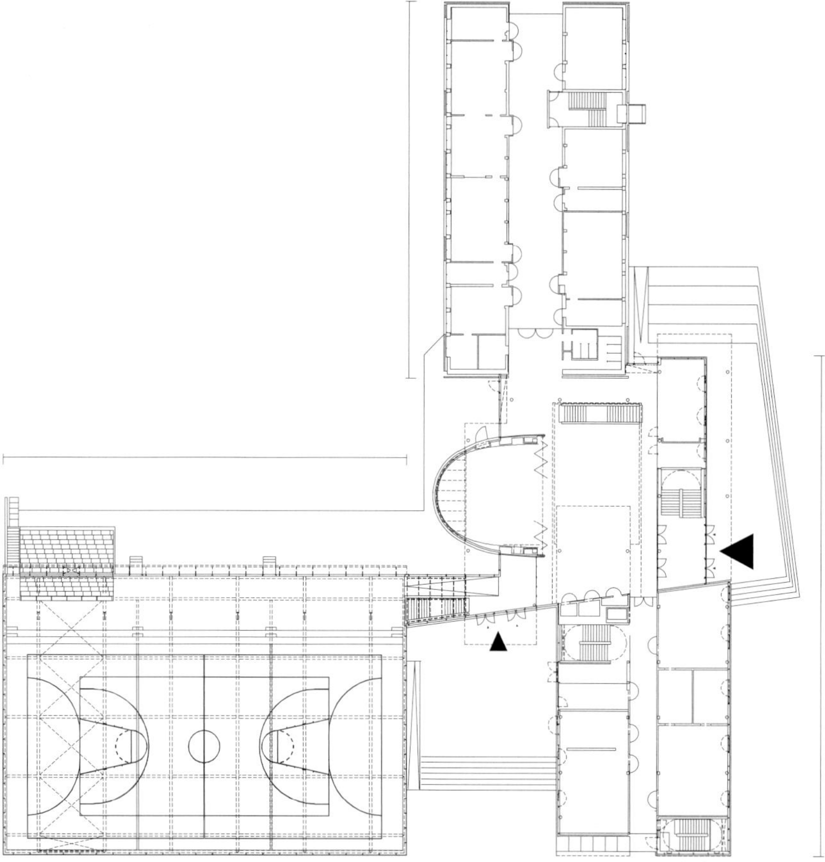

SCHOOL IN HERAT, Afghanistan

2A+P/A

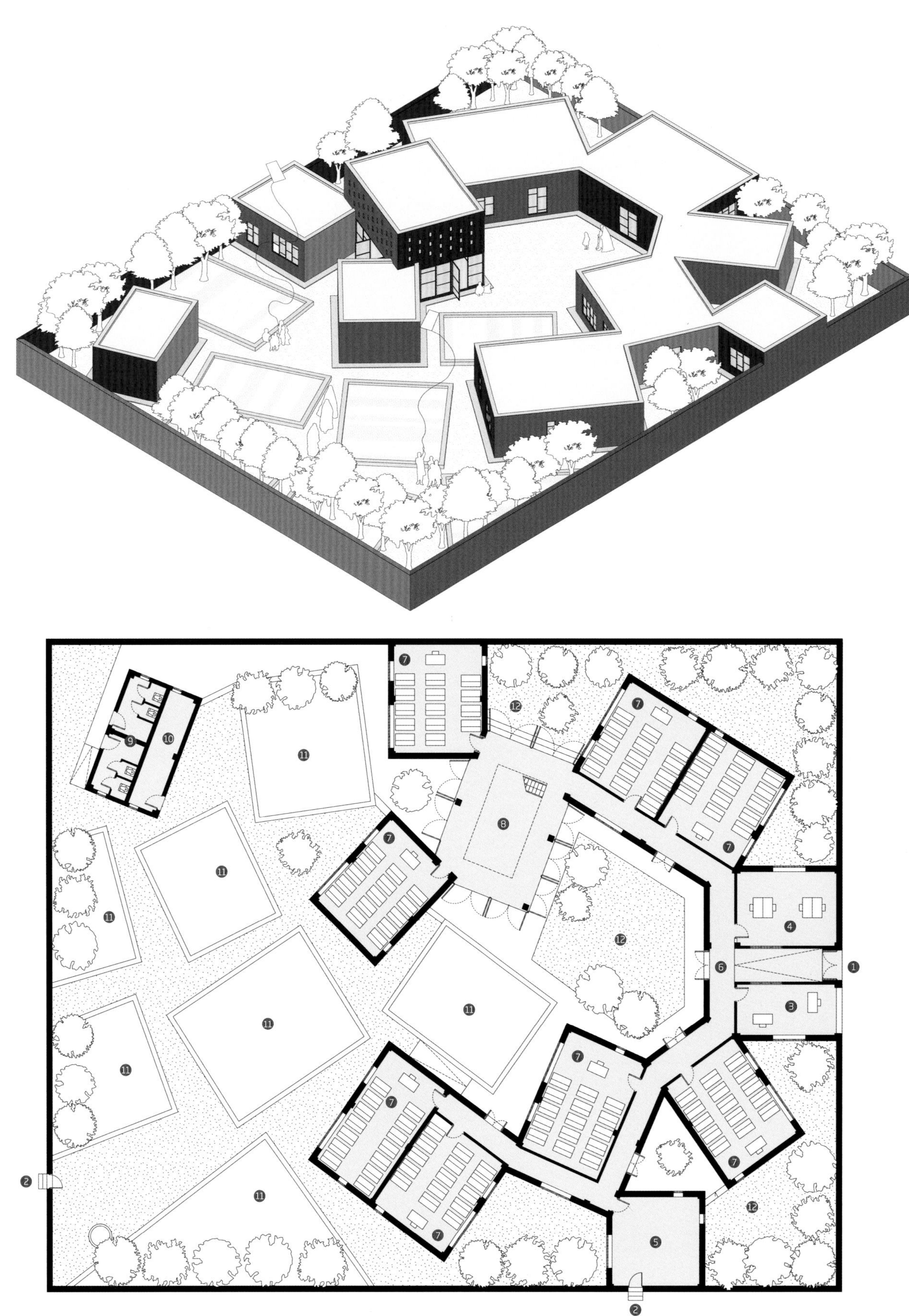

SKY IS THE LIMIt, Korea

Bureau des Mesarchitectures

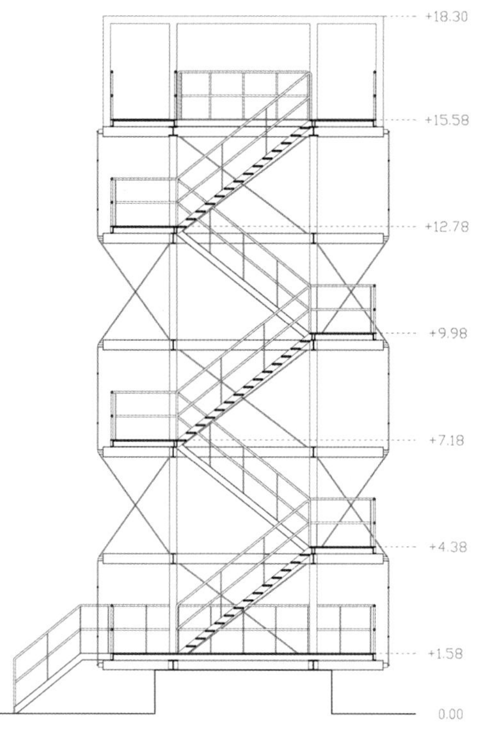

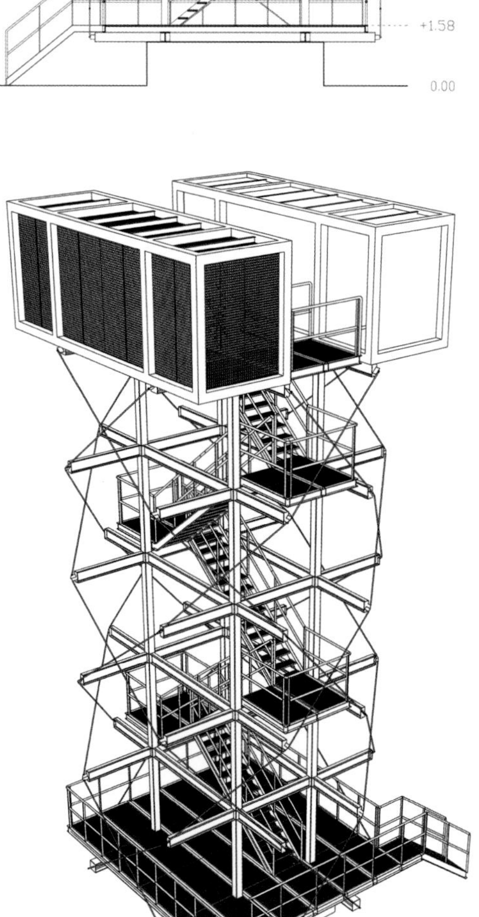

Speed Art Museum, U.S.A

WHY ARCHITECTURE

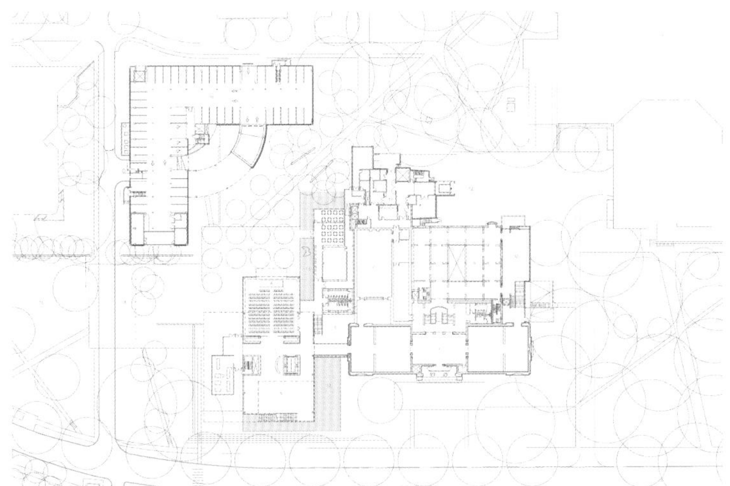

Townhall Scharnhauser Park, Germany

J. MAYER H.

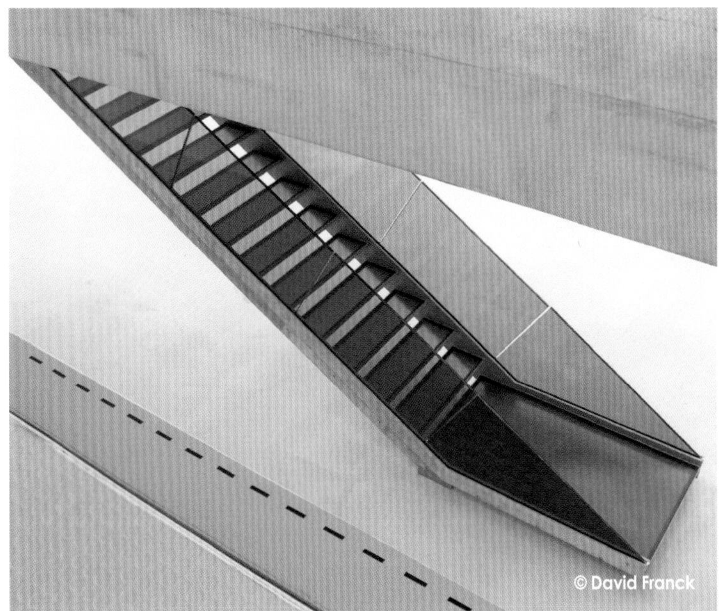

© David Franck

Turkey Embassy, Germany

J. Mayer H.

Wilson Secondary School, U.S.A

BIG

University of Southern Denmark, Denmark

Henning Larsen Architects

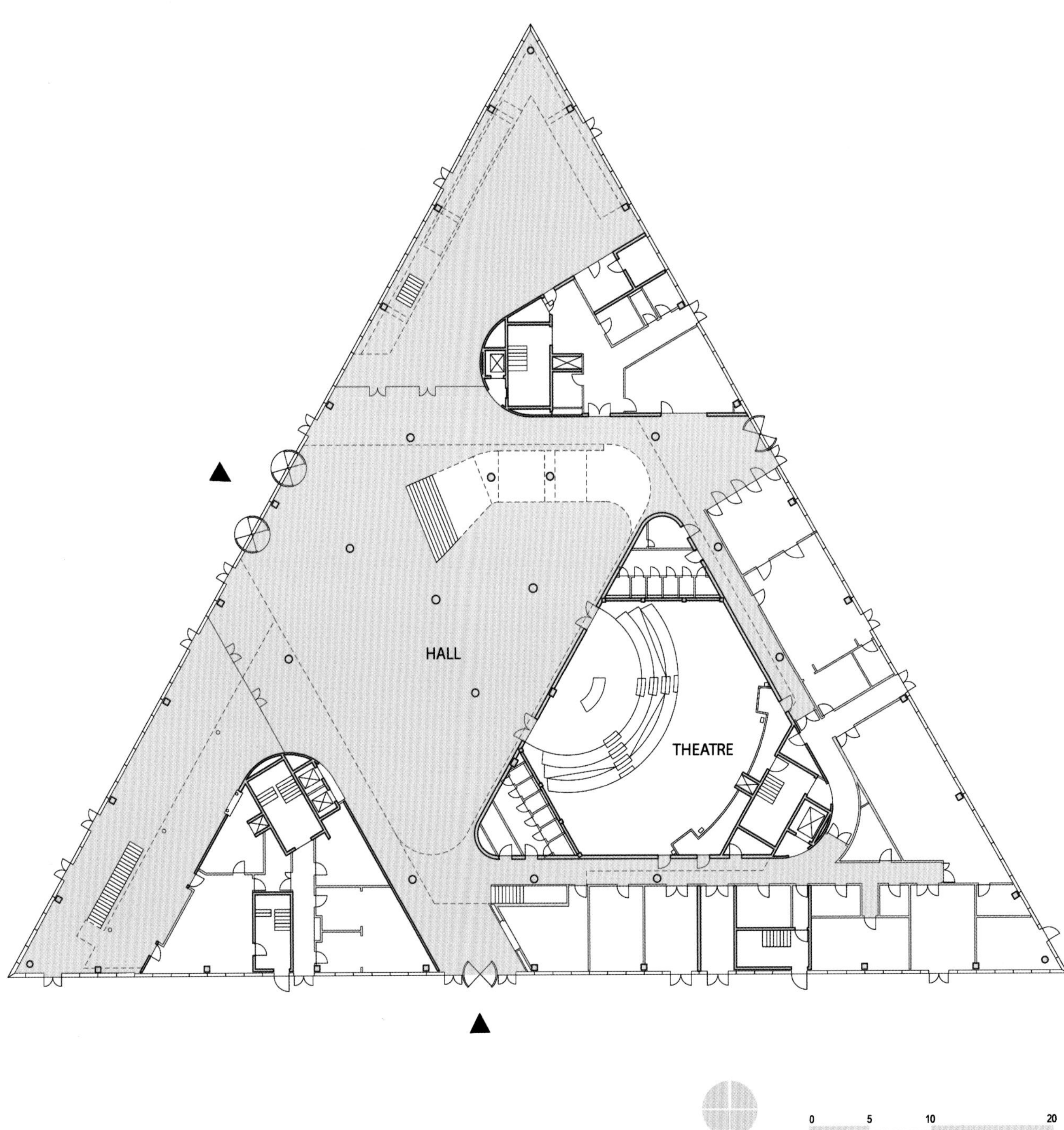

University Campus & Research Park, Norway

kadawittfeldarchitektur

A Case Study of
Classical Stairs

Gyeongbokgung-The palanquin path toward Geunjeongjeon (경복궁 근정전으로 향하는 왕도)

Gyeongbokgung-Geunjeongjeon Woldae (경복궁 근정전 월대)

2.

Gyeongbokgung-Geunjeongjeon Corridor (경복궁 근정전 회랑)

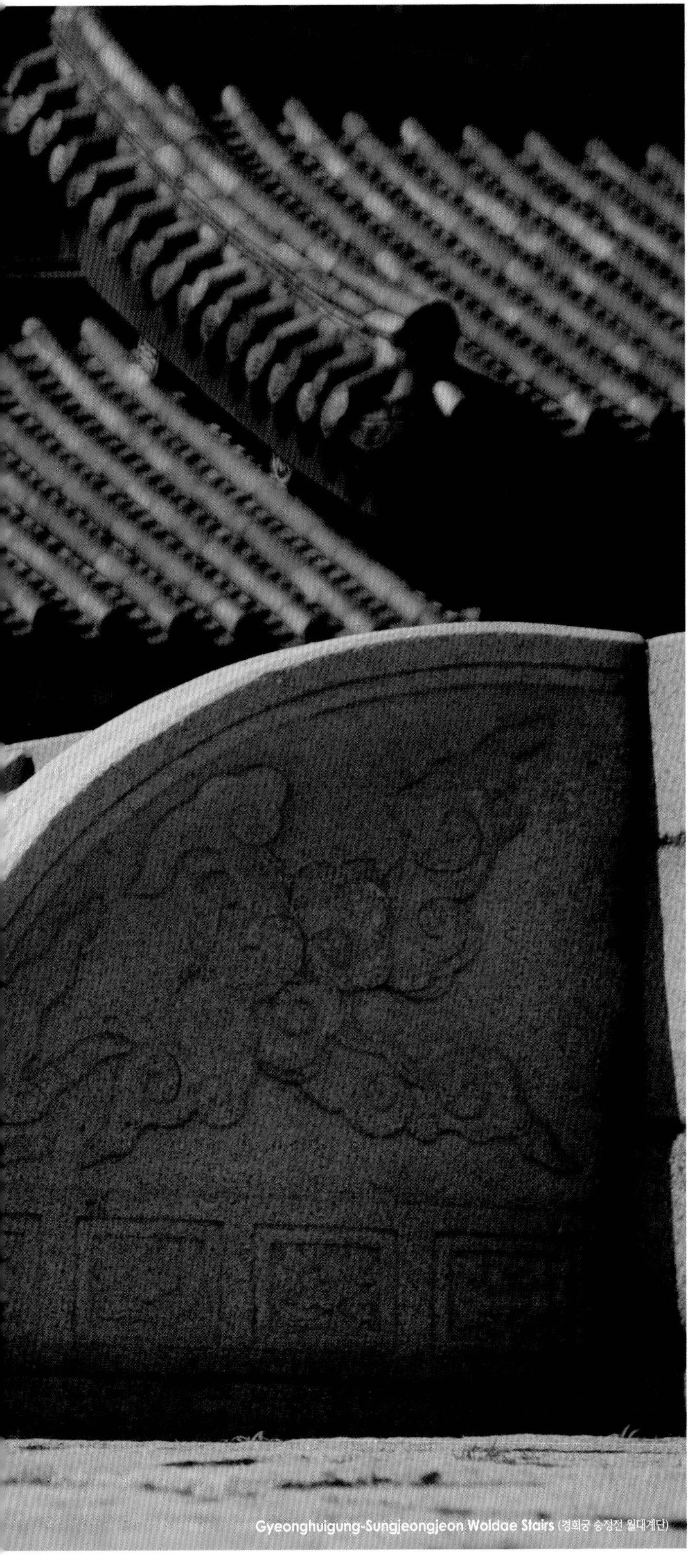

Gyeonghuigung-Sungjeongjeon Woldae Stairs (경희궁 숭정전 월대계단)

Gyeonghuigung-Sungjeongjeon Woldae Stairs (경희궁 숭정전 월대계단)

Gyeonghuigung-Jajeongmun (경희궁 자정문 계단)

Deoksugung-Hwangudan (덕수궁 환구단)

Deoksugung-Hamnyeongjeon (덕수궁 함녕전)

Deoksugung-Jeonggwanheon (덕수궁 정관헌)

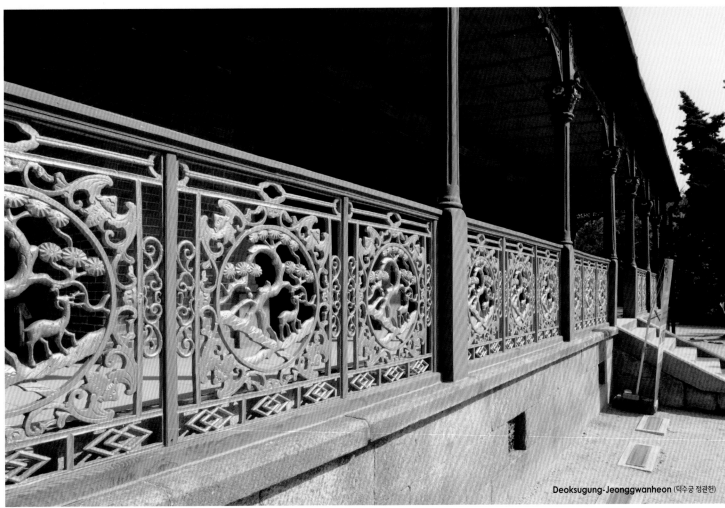

Deoksugung-Jeonggwanheon (덕수궁 정관헌)

Changgyeonggung-Myeongjeongjeon (창경궁 명정전)

Changdeokgung-Way to Nongsujeong (창덕궁 농수정 가는길)

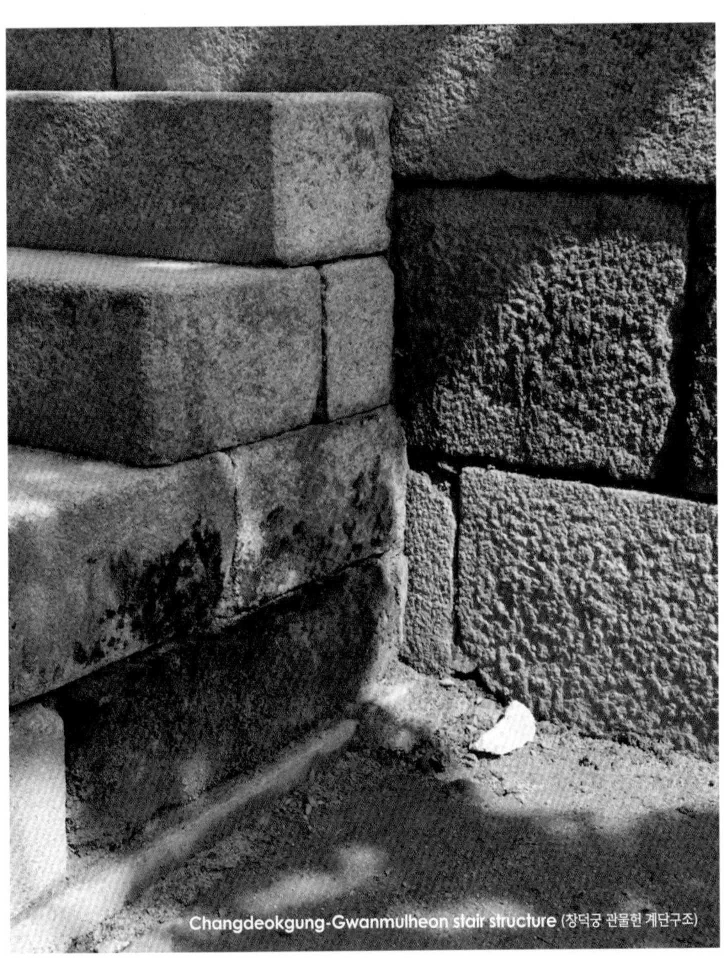

Changdeokgung-Gwanmulheon stair structure (창덕궁 관물헌 계단구조)

Changdeokgung-Daejojeon (창덕궁 대조전)

Changdeokgung-Gwallamjeong (창덕궁 관람정)

문화재 사랑
Please do not enter.
들어가지 마세요
Do Not Enter

Changdeokgung-Nakseonjae (창덕궁 낙선재)

Changdeokgung-Daejojeon (창덕궁 대조전)

Changdeokgung-Daejojeon (창덕궁 대조전)

Changdeokgung-Daejojeon (창덕궁 대조전)

Changdeokgung-Daejojeon (창덕궁 대조전)

Changdeokgung-Daejojeon (창덕궁 대조전)

Changdeokgung-Seunghwaru (창덕궁 승화루)

Changdeokgung-Seunghwaru (창덕궁 승화루)

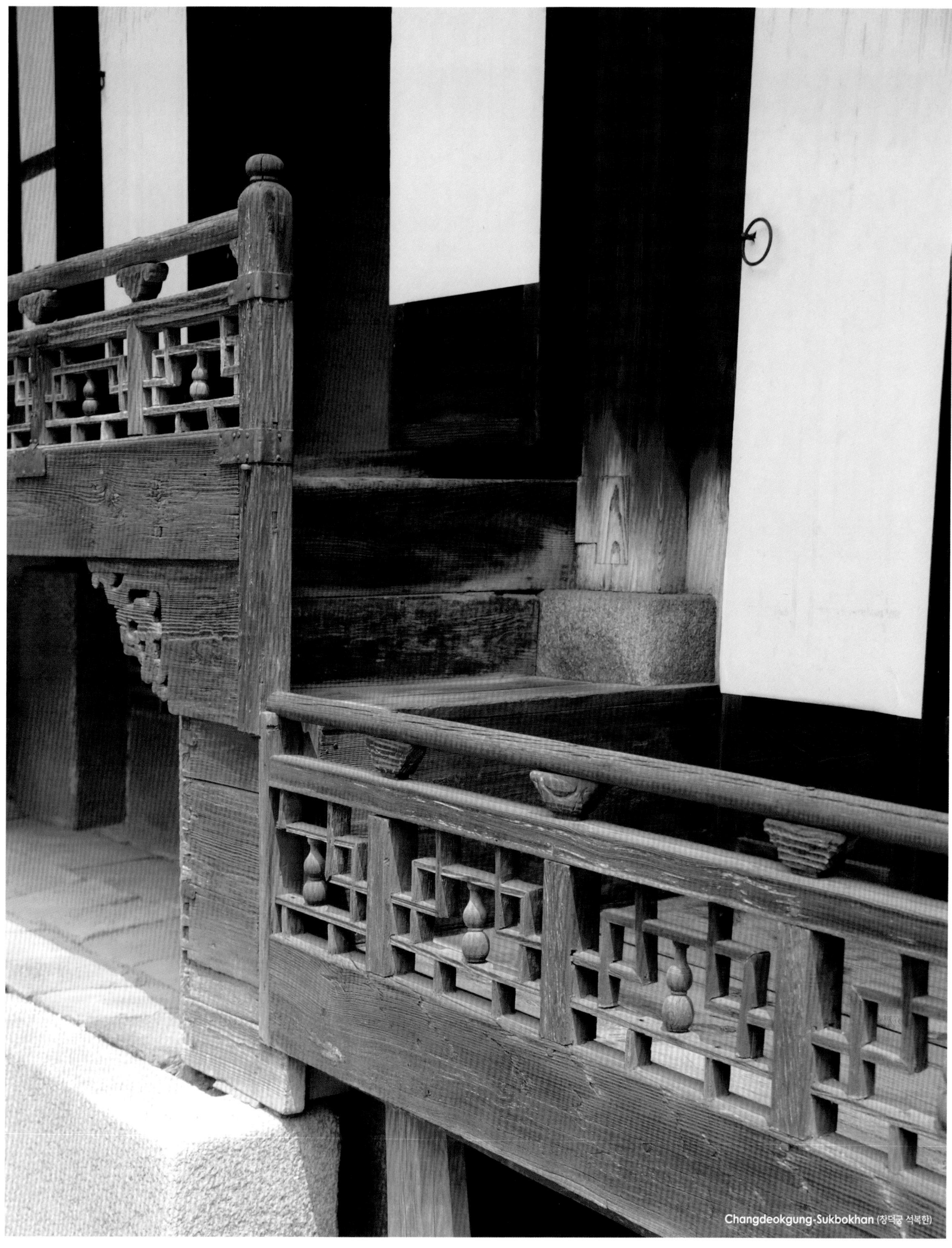
Changdeokgung-Sukbokhan (창덕궁 석복헌)

Changdeokgung-Injeongjeon (창덕궁 인정전)

Changdeokgung-Injeongjeon (창덕궁 인정전)

Changdeokgung-Injeongjeon (창덕궁 인정전)

Changdeokgung-Injeongjeon (창덕궁 인정전)

Changdeokgung-Injeongjeon (창덕궁 인정전)

Buddhist Temple

Gaesimsa-Pond (개심사 연못)

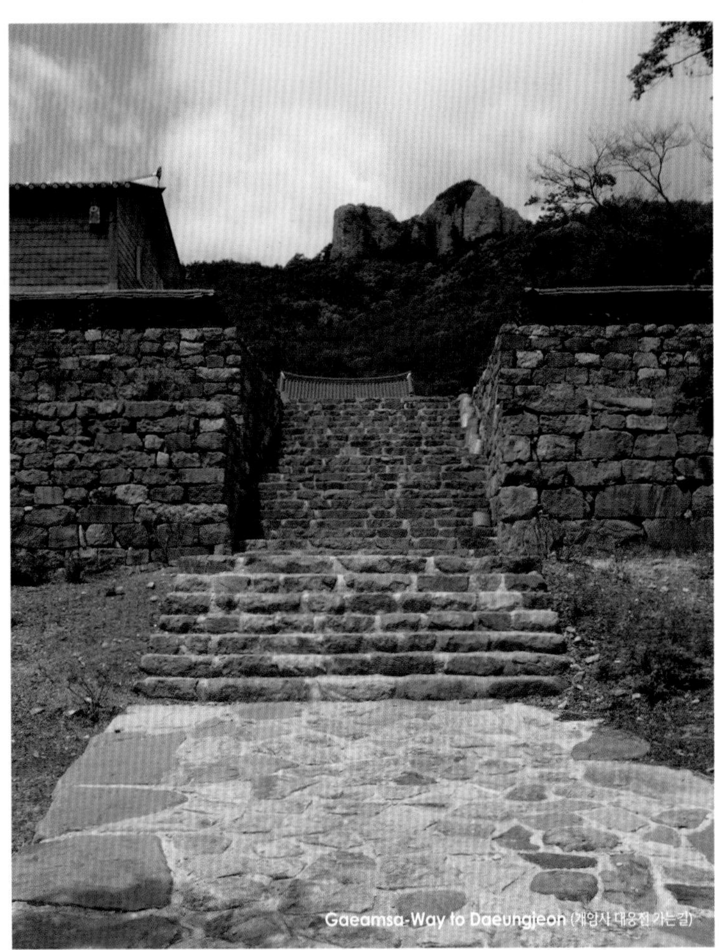

Gaeamsa-Way to Daeungjeon (개암사 대웅전 가는길)

Gaeamsa-Way to Daeungjeon (개암사 대웅전 가는길)

Gaeamsa (개암사)

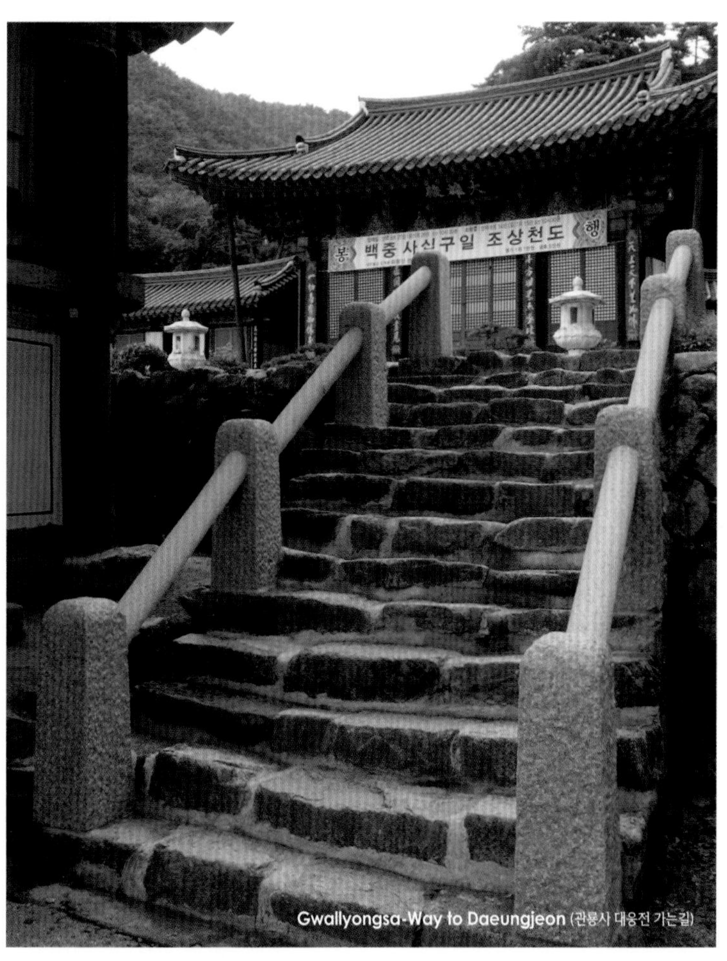

Gwallyongsa-Way to Daeungjeon (관룡사 대웅전 가는길)

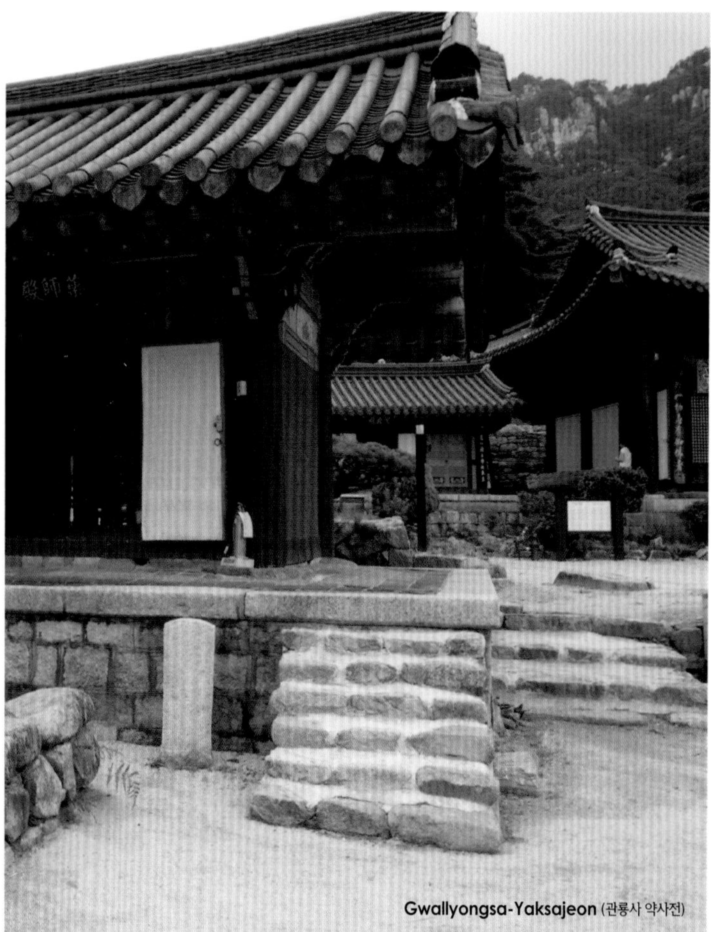

Gwallyongsa-Yaksajeon (관룡사 약사전)

Gwallyongsa-Chilseonggak, Sansingak (관룡사 칠성각, 산신각)

Gwallyongsa-Cheonwangmun (관룡사 천왕문)

Naesosa-Daeungbojeon (내소사 대웅보전)

Naesosa-Way to Bongraeru (내소사 봉래루 가는길)

Naesosa-Way to Bongraeru (내소사 봉래루 가는길)

Naesosa-Way to Daeungbojeon (내소사 대웅보전 가는길)

Baengnyeonsa (백련사)

Dasolsa-Daeyangru (다솔사 대양루)

Dasolsa-Daeyangru (다솔사 대양루)

Dasolsa-Daeyangru (다솔사 대양루)

Dasolsa-Shrine for Sakyamuni Buddha's Sarira (다솔사 적멸보궁)

Dasolsa (다솔사)

Dasolsa-Shrine for Sakyamuni Buddha's Sarira (다솔사 적멸보궁)

Dasolsa-Way to Shrine for Sakyamuni Buddha's Sarira (다솔사 적멸보궁 가는길)

Munsusa-Way to Burimun (문수사 불이문 가는길)

Beopjusa-Daeungbojeon (법주사 대웅보전)

Beopjusa-Daeungbojeon (법주사 대웅보전)

Beopjusa-Daeungbojeon (법주사 대웅보전)

Baengnyeonsa (백련사)

Geumsansa (금산사)

Baengnyeonsa-Mangyeongru (백련사 만경루)

Bongjeongsa-Eungjinjeon (봉정사 응진전)

Bongjeongsa (봉정사)

Bongjeongsa-Way to Manseru (봉정사 만세루 가는길)

Bongjeongsa-Eungjinjeon (봉정사 응진전)

Buseoksa-Anyangru (부석사 안양루)

Buseoksa-Muryangsujeon (부석사 무량수전)

Buseoksa-Muryangsujeon (부석사 무량수전)

Buseoksa (부석사)

Buseoksa-Way to Beomjonggak (부석사 범종각 가는길)

Bulguksa-Yeonhwagyo, Chilbogyo (불국사 연화, 칠보교)

Bulguksa-Cheongungyo, Baegungyo (불국사 천운, 백운교)

Bulguksa-Yeonhwagyo, Chilbogyo (불국사 연화, 칠보교)

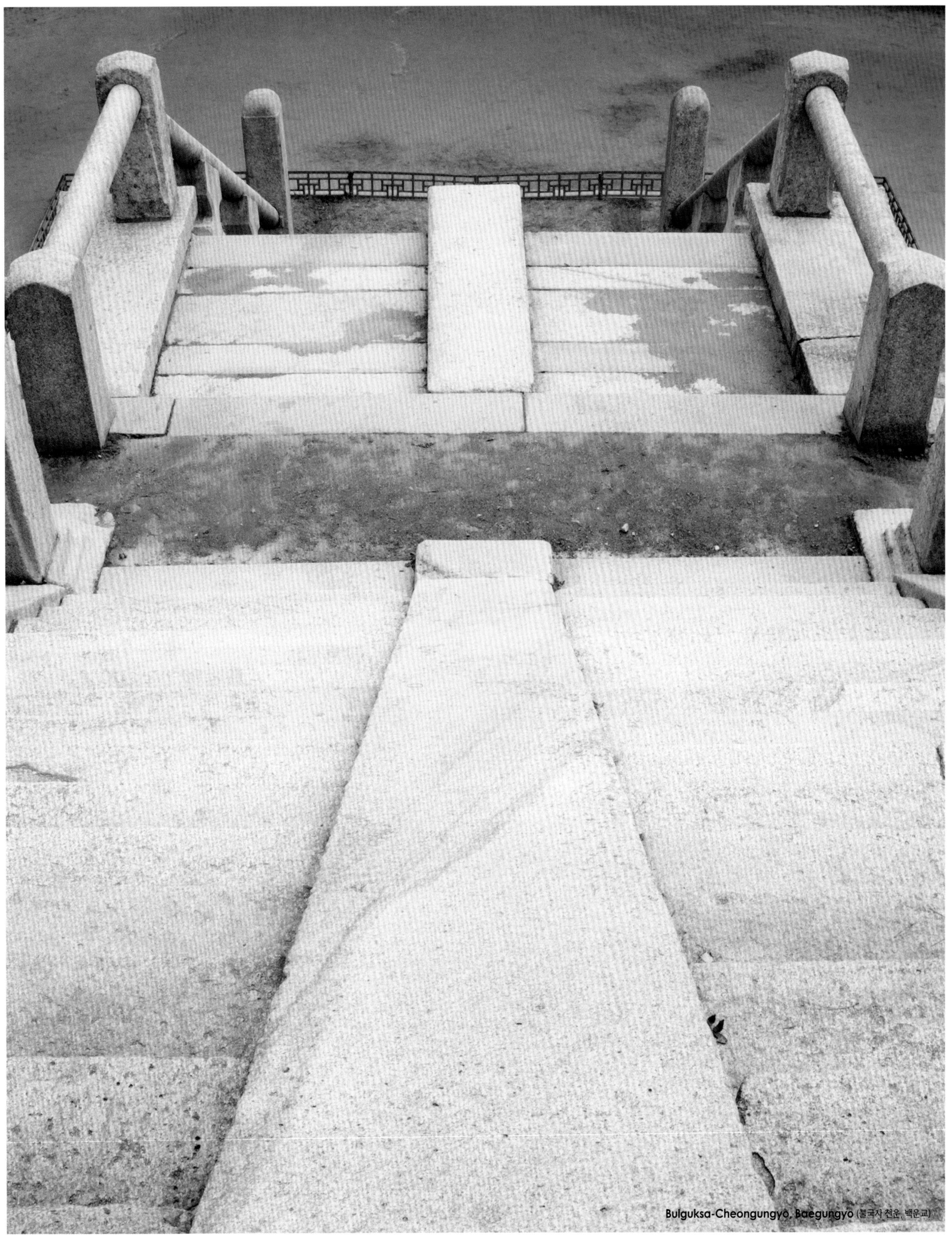

Bulguksa-Cheongungyo, Baegungyo (불국사 천운, 백운교)

Seonamsa-Eungjindang (선암사 응진당)

Seonamsa-Sansingak (선암사 산신각)

Seonamsa-Samsunggak (선암사 삼성각)

大雄殿
우란분재) 49일

Jingwansa-Hongjeru (진관사 홍제루)

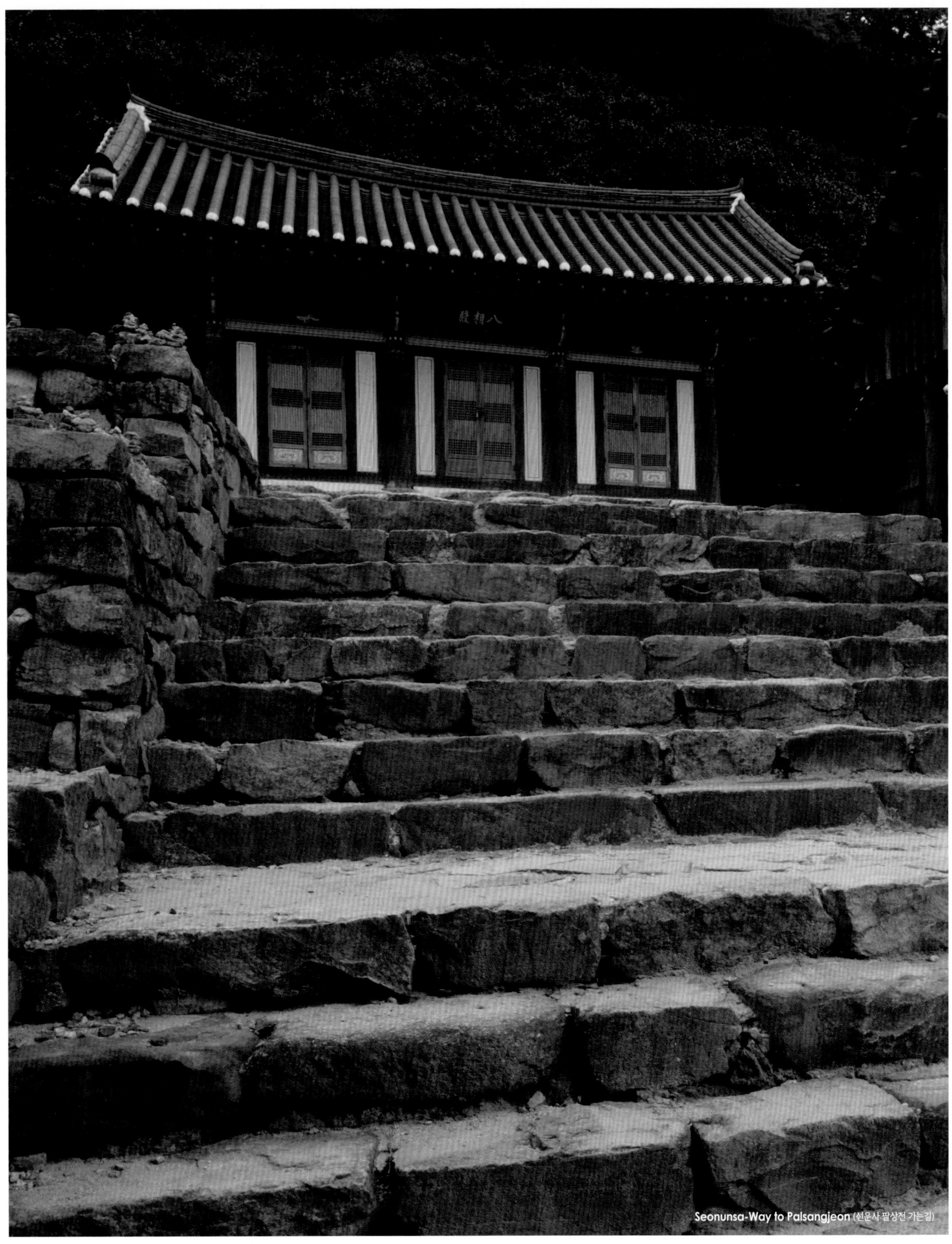
Seonunsa-Way to Palsangjeon (선운사 팔상전 가는길)

Seonunsa-Daeungbojeon (선운사 대웅보전)

Seonunsa-Yeongsanjeon (선운사 영산전)

Ssanggyesa-Daeungjeon (쌍계사 대웅전)

Songgwangsa-Jinyeomun (송광사 진여문)

Wibongsa-Bogwangmyeongjeon (위봉사 보광명전)

Wibongsa-Bogwangmyeongjeon (위봉사 보광명전)

Wibongsa-Bogwangmyeongjeon (위봉사 보광명전)

Wibongsa-Way to Cheonwangmun (위봉사 천왕문 가는길)

Wibongsa-Cheonwangmun (위봉사 천왕문)

Wibongsa-Way to Bongseoru (위봉사 봉서루 가는길)

정숙

Wibongsa-Iljumun (위봉사 일주문)

Tongdosa-Daeungjeon (통도사 대웅전)

Tongdosa-Daeungjeon (통도사 대웅전)

Tongdosa-Daeungjeon (통도사 대웅전)

海東圓宗大伽藍

Haeinsa-Haetalmun (해인사 해탈문)

Hwaeomsa-Way to Cheonwangmun (화엄사 천왕문 가는길)

Hwaeomsa Cheonwangmun (화엄사 천왕문)

Hwaeomsa-Way to Pagoda (화엄사 탑전 가는길)

Hwaeomsa-Way to Bojeru (화엄사 보제루 가는길)

Hwaeomsa-Way to Pagoda (화엄사 탑전 가는길)

Pavilion
(A pavilion garden)

Way to House of Dasan (다산초당 가는길)

House of Dasan (다산초당)

Soswaewon (소쇄원)

Between Youngnamru and Chimryugak (영남루와 침류각 사이 계단)

Between Youngnamru and Chimryugak (영남루와 침류각 사이 계단)

Way to Amseojae (암서재 가는길)

Donghojeong (동호정)

Jarakjeong (자락정)

An altar to the State deities,
Royal mausoleum, Jongmyo Shrine

Jongmyo Shrine-Jeongjeon (종묘 정전)

Jongmyo Shrine-Jeongjeon (종묘 정전)

Heereung (희릉)

Hongneung-T-shaped house (홍릉 정자각)

Hongneung (홍릉)

Lecture hall

Oksanseowon-Mubyunru (옥산서원 무변루)

Hwacheonseowon (화천서원)

Namkyeseowon-Shrine (남계서원 사당)

Namkyeseowon-Shrine (남계서원 사당)

Dosanseowon-Shrine (도산서원 사당)

Dosanseowon-Shrine (도산서원 사당)

Dosanseowon-Shrine (도산서원 사당)

Dosanseowon-Shrine (도산서원 사당)

Dosanseowon-Shrine (도산서원 사당)

Dosanseowan-Shrine (도산서원 사당)

院書

Byeongsanseowon-Ypgyodang (병산서원 입교당)

Seogyeseowon-Naesammun (서계서원 내삼문)

Seogyeseowon-Naesammun (서계서원 내삼문)

Mountain Fortress

Gohyunseong-Gyeryongru (고현성 계룡루)

Namhansanseong-East Gate (남한산성 동문)

Namhansanseong-West Gate (남한산성 서문)

Samnyeonsanseong (삼년산성)

Bukhansanseong-Daedongmun (북한산성 대동문)

Bukhansanseong-Daeseongmun (북한산성 대성문)

Ganghwa Cheomseong (강화 첨성)

Private residence

Mugwagoga-Shrine (묵와고가 사당)

Mugwagoga-Sarangchae (묵와고가 사랑채)

Way to Baekindang (백인당 가는길)

Baekindang (백인당)

Baekindang (백인당)

House of Huh Family-Sarangchea (허씨고가 사랑채)

House of Jung Yeochang-Sarangchea (정여창고택 사랑채)

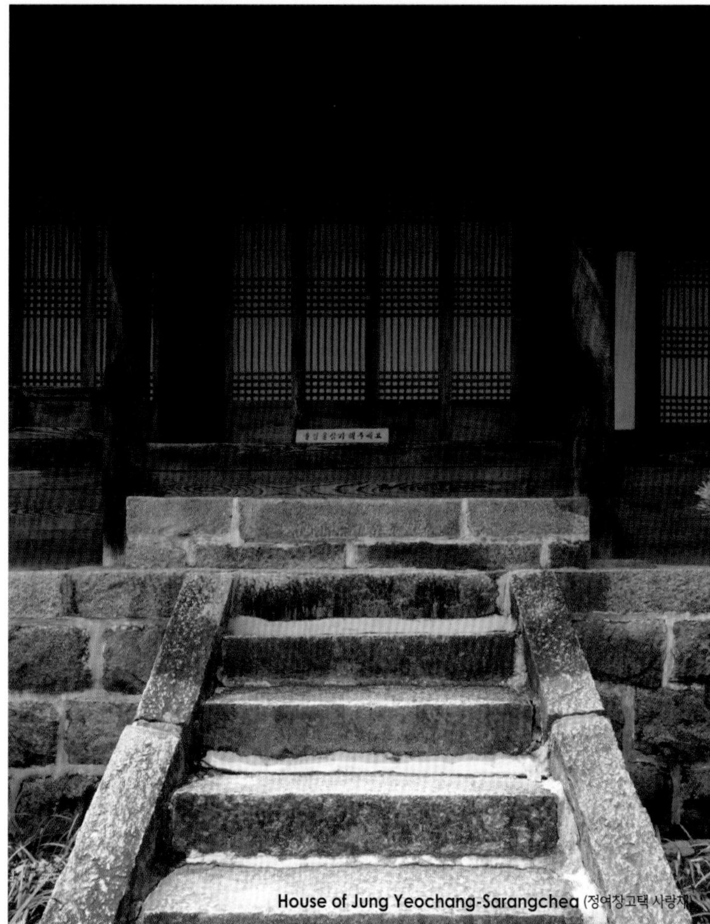

House of Jung Yeochang-Sarangchea (정여창고택 사랑채)

House of Lee Yongwook-Anchea (이용욱 가옥 안채)

House of Lee Yongwook-Anchea (이용욱 가옥 안채)

House of Lee Yongwook-Anchea (이용욱 가옥 안채)

Taejangjeasa (태장재사)

Taejangjeasa-Numaru (태장재사 누마루)

Obongseangga (오봉생가)

Obongseangga (오봉생가)

Yeolhwajeong (열화정)

Yeolhwajeong (열화정)

Yeolhwajeong (열화정)

Cheongamjeong (청암정)

Cheongamjeong (청암정)

House of Wolgok-Sarangchea (월곡댁 사랑채)

House of Wolgok-Sarangchea (월곡댁 사랑채)

House of Wolgok-Sarangchea (월곡댁 사랑채)

House of Wolgok-Sarangchea (월곡댁 사랑채)

祖雲憲陶齋

Hanjujeongsa (한주정사)

Architectural Element Series

To be Continued